Intelligence
and Cultural Differences

Intelligence
and Cultural Differences

A Study of Cultural Learning and Problem-solving

KENNETH EELLS

ALLISON DAVIS

ROBERT J. HAVIGHURST

VIRGIL E. HERRICK

RALPH W. TYLER

Under the Chairmanship of

ALLISON DAVIS

THE UNIVERSITY OF CHICAGO PRESS
CHICAGO AND LONDON

THE UNIVERSITY OF CHICAGO PRESS, CHICAGO 60637
The University of Chicago Press, Ltd., London

International Standard Book Number: 0-226-18838-8
Library of Congress Catalog Card Number: 72-178887

PREFACE

This work is the first part of an extended study of cultural learning as it bears upon the solution of problems in mental tests. The total project was originated in 1945 by Professor Allison Davis of the Department of Education and the Committee on Human Development of the University of Chicago. The research has been carried on with the advice, and under the sponsorship of an interdepartmental committee made up as follows:

Allison Davis, <u>chairman</u>

Robert J. Havighurst, Professor of Education, University of Chicago

Ralph W. Tyler, Dean of the Division of Social Sciences and University Examiner, University of Chicago

W. Lloyd Warner, Professor of Anthropology and Sociology, University of Chicago

Virgil Herrick, formerly Associate Professor of Education, University of Chicago, now Professor of Education, University of Wisconsin

Lee Cronbach, formerly Assistant Professor of Education, University of Chicago, now Associate Professor, Bureau of Research and Service, College of Education, University of Illinois

The specific research work reported in this volume was carried on as a doctoral dissertation under the supervision of a committee composed of four of the men listed above (Davis, Havighurst, Herrick, Cronbach). Dr. Havighurst and Dr. Herrick acted, at different times, as chairmen of this dissertation committee.

Various aspects of the research have been completed; others are still in process. Among the major projects completed may be mentioned the following:

1. A comparison of the responses to standard intelligence-test items by white children from different socioeconomic levels

2. A comparison of the responses to standard intelligence-test items by Negro children from different socioeconomic levels

3. An experimental study of the effect of cultural situations, symbols, reading skill, special motivation, and special practice on the responses made by children from different socioeconomic backgrounds to various types of intelligence-test items

4. An experimental study of the effect of individual administration, as compared with the effect of group administration of an intelligence test, upon the responses of children from different socioeconomic levels

5. A study of the influence of vocabulary knowledge upon the responses to different socioeconomic groups to intelligence tests

6. A study of the reasons verbalized by children of different socioeconomic groups for their choices of responses to intelligence-test items

A number of journal articles have been published, a number of addresses have been delivered before professional and lay audiences, and several Doctor's dissertations and Master's theses have been written or are now in process (<u>1</u>, <u>2</u>, <u>3</u>, <u>4</u>, <u>5</u>).[1] The present volume is, however, the first book-length report to be published. It is devoted primarily to the research carried out in connection with Project No. 1 listed above. The findings of Projects Nos. 2 and 5 are available in unpublished form (4, 5). A report on Project No. 3 is now in process of publication (<u>3a</u>). Reports on Projects Nos. 4 and 6 will be published in the near future.

The authors of the present volume are greatly indebted to a number of our colleagues who have counseled with us at various steps in the development of the investigation reported here, or whose work on other phases of the larger project has contributed substantially to the significance of the material in this volume.

On questions involving socioeconomic status and its measurement, we have been greatly helped by W. Lloyd Warner, Professor of Anthropology and Sociology, and member of the Committee on Human Development, University of Chicago, who has worked closely with us in the use of the social-class measurement techniques described in chapter xi. On statistical matters we have had the benefit of advice from Karl Holzinger, Professor of Education, University of Chicago; Dr. Frances Swineford, now with the Educational Testing Service, Princeton, New Jersey; and Dr. Lee Cronbach, now with the Bureau of Research and Service, College of Education, University of Illinois. Dr. Cronbach also read the entire manuscript of Parts II and III critically and made many helpful suggestions for its improvement.

Professor Ernest Haggard and Dr. Robert Hess, of the Committee on Human Development, University of Chicago, and Dr. Walter I. Murray, principal of the Dunbar School, Phoenix, Arizona, have been responsible for the development of research projects in areas closely related to the one reported upon here, and their assistance with the present study has been helpful.

We also owe a debt of gratitude to Mr. and Mrs. Charles Warriner (now connected with the Department of Sociology, University of Kansas), who lived in Rockford, Illinois, for a period of ten months and carried out the community study and social-class stratification referred to in chapter xi. They were also responsible for the rating of some four thousand residences according to house type and for the delineation of the city into residential areas — the basis for two of the four ratings required for the Index of Status Characteristics described in the same chapter.

Wilfrid Bailey and Theresa Neumann, at that time graduate students in the departments of Anthropology and Education, respectively, University of Chicago, were primarily responsible for rating approximately four thousand families by occupation and by education, as required for the Index of Status Characteristics. Much of the rather voluminous statistical computation required for the investigation was carried out capably by Mrs. Irene Olsen.

And, finally, very genuine appreciation is expressed for the fine — and sometimes long-suffering — co-operation extended by Mr. Selmer Berg, then superintendent of schools, Rockford, Illinois; by Miss Maud

---

1. Numbers underlined refer to the correspondingly numbered items in the Bibliography at the end of this volume.

E. Johnson, supervisor of instruction in the elementary schools, Rockford, Illinois; and by the principals and teachers of all the public and private schools participating in the testing program. The names of the principals are listed in Appendix A. Without the co-operation of these principals and teachers, the project could not even have been begun.

THE AUTHORS

Chicago, Illinois
    January 1950

ACKNOWLEDGMENTS

Three of the chapters in Part I of the present volume are revisions of material previously published in journal articles. Appreciation is expressed to the American Association for the Advancement of Science for permission to use material previously published by W. Allison Davis and Robert J. Havighurst as "The Measurement of Mental Systems" in the April, 1948, issue of the Scientific Monthly. This material appears in modified form as chapters iv and v of the present work. Appreciation is also expressed to the University of Chicago Press for permission to reproduce chapter vi, which is an abridged form of material originally published by Ralph W. Tyler as "Educability and the Schools" in the December, 1948, issue of the Elementary School Journal.

Appreciation is also due the following publishers and copyright owners for permission to make brief quotations from copyrighted materials, as indicated: Educational Test Bureau, Minneapolis, Minnesota: F. Kuhlmann, Tests of Mental Development: A Complete Scale for Individual Examination. Henry Goddard, Santa Barbara, California: Alfred Binet and Th. Simon, The Development of Intelligence in Children, Williams and Wilkins Company, Baltimore, Maryland. Graduate School of Education, Harvard University, Cambridge, Massachusetts: Frederick B. Davis, Item-Analysis Data: Their Computation, Interpretation and Use in Test Construction. Houghton Mifflin Company, Boston, Massachusetts: W. Allison Davis and Robert J. Havighurst, Father of the Man: How Your Child Gets His Personality; Lewis M. Terman and Maud E. Merrill, Measuring Intelligence; and V. A. C. Henmon and M. J. Nelson, Teacher's Manual: The Henmon-Nelson Tests of Mental Ability. National Society for the Study of Education, Chicago, Illinois: Thirty-ninth Yearbook, 1940. Odyssey Press, New York, New York: E. B. Greene, Measurements of Human Behavior. University of Chicago Press, Chicago, Illinois: Allison Davis, Burleigh B. Gardner, and Mary R. Gardner, Deep South: A Social Anthropological Study of Caste and Class; and L. L. Thurstone, Multiple-Factor Analysis. Warwick & York, Inc., Baltimore, Maryland: William Stern, The Psychological Methods of Testing Intelligence; and Lewis M. Terman et al., The Stanford Revision and Extension of the Binet-Simon Scale for Measuring Intelligence. John Wiley & Sons, Inc., New York, New York: L. Carmichael, Manual of Child Psychology. World Book Company, Yonkers-on-Hudson, New York: Arthur S. Otis, Otis Quick-scoring Mental Ability Tests: Manual of Directions for Alpha Test; and Lewis M. Terman and Quinn McNemar, Terman-McNemar Test of Mental Ability: Manual of Directions.

Particular appreciation is expressed to the publishers who courteously gave permission for the reproduction in chapters xxii and xxiii of a rather large number of items from tests which they publish, as follows: California Test Bureau, Hollywood, California, California Short-Form Test of Mental Maturity; Educational Test Bureau, Minneapolis, Minnesota, Kuhlmann-Anderson Intelligence Tests; Houghton Mifflin Company, Boston, Massachusetts, Henmon-Nelson Tests of Mental Ability; Science Research Associates, Chicago, Illinois, Chicago Tests of Primary Mental Abilities; World Book Company, Yonkers-on-Hudson, New York, Otis Quick-scoring Mental Ability Tests and Terman-McNemar Test of Mental Ability.

TABLE OF CONTENTS

PART I. THE PROBLEM AND ITS SETTING

PART II. A SUMMARY OF THE FIELD STUDY

By Kenneth Eells, Associate Professor of Psychology,
San Diego State College, San Diego, California

PART III. A REPORT OF THE FIELD STUDY

By Kenneth Eells, Associate Professor of Psychology,
San Diego State College, San Diego, California

APPENDIXES

BIBLIOGRAPHY

INDEX

PART I

THE PROBLEM AND ITS SETTING

CHAPTER I

WHAT IS THE PROBLEM?

By Kenneth Eells, Associate Professor of Psychology
San Diego State College, San Diego, California

Intelligence tests have come to play a tremendously important role in modern educational and psychological procedures. They are used in many public schools as one of the bases – sometimes practically the sole basis – for assigning pupils to class groups under some plan of homogeneous grouping. They are used as a basis for advising students with respect to selection of courses and vocations. They are used as a means of determining which students should be excluded from regular school work and sent either to special classes or to special institutions. They are used as one of the bases for admission to institutions of higher education. They are widely used in research as (a) a means of measuring ability of pupils when it is desired to hold that factor constant and (b) as the subject of research when the nature of intelligence itself is to be studied. They are used as an important tool in clinical, guidance, and diagnostic procedures. While there is great variation in the extent of their use in different places, and in the degree of scientific sophistication with which they are used, intelligence tests have certainly come to play a highly important part in an increasing number of educational and psychological situations.

Are these "intelligence" tests valid? Do they really measure what those who use them think they measure? In particular, are they satisfactory measures of the "intelligence" of children from widely varying cultural backgrounds? The question of the fairness of our present intelligence tests is one of great importance, both to the individual pupils and to society as a whole. If, as many competent educators, psychologists, and sociologists believe, the intelligence tests are really unfair to children from certain kinds of backgrounds, and do not reveal the full abilities of these children, then grave injustices are done to such children when school people base curricular, instructional, and guidance practices on the I.Q. as determined by such tests. Moreover, a serious loss to society may result through failure to identify and develop the real talents of all its members. No democratic society in today's world is in such a secure position that it can afford to waste, through nonrecognition, the leadership or other talents of any large group of its people.

What Is Already Known?

Almost since the advent of intelligence testing, educators and psychologists have debated -- and investigated – the relationship of the I.Q. to environmental factors. The fact that there is a definite and measureable relationship between the scores which pupils obtain on intelligence tests and the social status, or cultural background, of their parents has been known since the time of Binet. It has been investigated in many countries and at grade levels reaching from preschool through college.

It has been investigated for individual tests and for group tests. It has been investigated for pupils classified by father's occupation, by parental education, by family income, and by a number of special scales intended to serve as indicators of social or socioeconomic status.

All these studies are virtually unanimous in finding that children from "high" or "favorable" socioeconomic backgrounds tend to secure higher scores on the usual intelligence tests (both individual and group) than do children from lower or less favorable socioeconomic backgrounds. A number of these studies are reviewed in chapter ii.

In view of the large number of research studies which have shown the existence of sizable and statistically significant I.Q. differences between pupils from different social-status backgrounds, and in view of the almost total lack of any contrary indications from any of the research to date, it seems abundantly clear that there is no need for further research aimed merely at establishing the existence or nonexistence of such differences. The existence of these I.Q. differences must today be accepted as a demonstrated fact -- at least so far as intelligence tests now in common use are concerned.

With respect to the significance and interpretation of these differences, however, there is no such agreement. Do the higher test scores of the children from high socioeconomic backgrounds reflect genuine superiority in inherited, or genetic, equipment? Or do the high scores result from a superior environment which has brought about real superiority of the child's "intelligence"? Or do they reflect a bias in the test materials and not any important differences in the children at all? Each of these interpretations has had its supporters, and each has been defended vigorously.

The first line of argument has pointed out that if (a) the intelligence of adults is so distributed socially that the persons of higher intelligence tend to be concentrated in the "higher" social-status levels, and if (b) intelligence is genetically determined, one would expect (c) that children from the higher social-status levels would show higher I.Q.'s than those from the lower levels. This argument tends to conclude that the observed differences in I.Q.'s are due in large part to hereditary factors.

The second line of argument has pointed out that if (a) the child's intelligence is not fixed by genetic factors but is subject to modification by a stimulating or a nonstimulating environment, and if (b) the higher social-status levels provide more stimulation for mental growth than do the lower social-status levels, one would expect (c) that children from the higher social-status levels would show higher I.Q.'s than those from the lower levels. This argument tends to conclude that the observed differences in I.Q.'s, while real, are due in large part to environmental factors.

The third line of argument has pointed out that if (a) the children from different social-status levels have different kinds of experiences and have experiences with different kinds of material, and if (b) the intelligence tests contain a disproportionate amount of material drawn from the cultural experiences with which pupils from the higher social-status levels are more familiar, one would expect (c) that children from the higher social-status levels would show higher I.Q.'s than those from the lower levels. This argument tends to conclude that the observed differences in pupil I.Q.'s are artifacts dependent upon the specific content of the test items and do not reflect accurately any important underlying ability in the pupils.

The above statements represent, of course, great oversimplifications. Probably few present-day psychologists or educators would subscribe to the idea that all the observed differences are to be accounted for by any one of the three factors given. It is convenient, however, for purposes of sharpening the issue, to consider these rather different emphases as separate lines of interpretations.

It will be noticed that each one of these three lines of argument involves the statement of two assumptions or hypotheses (a and b above) and the deriving from them of an expected conclusion (c above). In each case the conclusion in the argument follows correctly from the assumptions stated. It is important to notice, however, that the conclusions are identical for all three sets of hypotheses. The truth or falsity of the hypotheses cannot, therefore, be demonstrated merely by finding that the observed data support the expected conclusion. The research studies do all agree in showing that the pupils from high social-status levels show higher I.Q.'s than do those from low social-status levels. The difficulty arises, of course, when different writers and investigators argue back from that fact to prove that their particular set of hypotheses is thereby substantiated. The fallacy in this procedure is obvious, but the research literature in the field is full of just such "reasoning."

This is far from being an academic debate of interest only to its participants. It must be obvious that important school — and social — policies which would be sound if these I.Q. differences reflect differences in innate ability might be quite unsound if the differences in the I.Q.'s are due in large part to environmental factors and might be even more seriously unsound if the differences in I.Q.'s are due primarily to cultural bias in the material included in the tests themselves.

The importance of the problem has been more sharply pointed up by the recent contributions of sociologists and anthropologists to our understanding of the great variations in types of real-life experiences which children coming from different cultural backgrounds may be expected to have. Some of the more important of these findings are summarized in chapter iii.

What More Is Needed?

It is clear that future work in this field should be directed toward trying to establish the meaning or significance which should be attached to the I.Q. differences which are known to exist whenever pupils are classified on any important social-status or socioeconomic basis. This is not an easy task — not nearly so easy as the mere demonstration of the existence of such differences.

Stern, writing in Germany in 1912, only two years after the question of social-class differences with respect to intelligence-test results had first been investigated, pointed out the difficulty of assigning causes to, or interpreting, the findings with relation to social-class differences. His statement is so cogent for the conception underlying the present study that it is reproduced here even though it is somewhat lengthy:

A question as interesting as it is difficult to answer arises when we seek the causes of these differences in performance. It would obviously be very premature to assume as already positively demonstrated that the intelligence, considered as innate mental ability,

was of lower grade in children of the lower and poorer classes. Of course, it is not impossible that this may have been operative as a causal factor. One might, perhaps, assume that the very rise into the higher and better-off classes would itself predicate a certain intellectual selection, and that thus the children of these classes would have come into the world equipped with a superior intellectual endowment.

But, on the other hand, it must be remembered that no series of tests, however skillfully selected it may be, does reach the innate intellectual endowment, stripped of all complications, but rather this endowment in conjunction with all the influences to which the examinee has been subjected up to the moment of the testing. And it is just these external influences that are different in the lower social classes. Children of higher social status are much more often in the company of adults, are stimulated in manifold ways, are busy in play and amusements with things that require thinking, acquire a totally different vocabulary and a notable command of language, and receive better school instruction; all this must bring it about that they meet the demands of the tests better than children of the uncultured classes /47, pp. 52-53/[1].

Stern goes on to point out that "the way to approach this problem is by special analysis of the data: it will be necessary to find out in which tests the superiority of the children of the cultured classes is particularly evident and which tests are passed with equal facility by children of both classes" (47, p. 53; underlining not in original). It is rather surprising that in the thirty-five years that have elapsed since Stern made this suggestion very few such item-analysis studies have been made; none has been satisfactorily comprehensive — either as to the number of items studied, the size of the pupil sample used for the study, or the methods used for determining the cultural backgrounds of the children.

What Does the Present Study Attempt To Do?

The present study analyzes the responses of pupils from high and low social-status backgrounds to more than 650 items in eight widely used group intelligence tests. Its primary purpose is to identify (a) those kinds of test problems on which children from high socioeconomic backgrounds show the greatest superiority and (b) those kinds of test problems on which children from low socioeconomic backgrounds do relatively well.

On the basis of these data, an attempt is made to assess the importance of various factors as possible explanations for the differences in I.Q.'s found for children from different kinds of cultural background. Particular attention is directed to investigating the extent to which group differences in I.Q.'s may be due to the presence of culturally biased material in the test items.

More specifically, the study is designed to answer the following questions:

1. What is the degree and nature of the relationship between I.Q.'s

---

1. The number underlined refers to the correspondingly numbered item in the Bibliography at the end of this volume.

and cultural or status level?

2. Do children from high-status homes do better than children from low-status homes on all items in the intelligence tests in about the same proportion, or is there wide variation among the different items?

3. If the items are grouped into categories on such bases as the following:

   a) Type of symbols used (verbal, pictorial, geometric design, etc.)
   b) Type of question asked (opposites, analogies, classification, etc.)
   c) Placing of the correct answers in relation to the distractors
   d) Difficulty of the item

   are there significant differences in the status difference shown by different types of items?

4. If there are certain items which show significantly greater intercultural differences than others, do these items have anything in common which might help explain their large differences? Do those items which show little or no difference have anything in common?

5. Do pupils from high-status and from low-status homes show any significant differences in the incorrect responses which they give to items? Do these suggest any explanation for the cultural differences in correct responses?

6. Are there significant differences, on any of the factors referred to in Questions 1 to 5 above, as between ethnics and nonethnics when social status is held constant?

7. Are there significant differences, with respect to any of the factors referred to in Questions 1 to 5 above, in the intercultural patterns at different age levels? That is, are the differences found for younger children the same as those found for older children, or do the differences vary in either type or degree according to age?

What Are Some of the Limitations of the Study?

There are several important limitations of the present study which should be understood clearly.

In the first place, no assumption is made in the research study that there either are or are not "genuine" differences in "real" ability among different status groups. Nor does the study provide any direct basis for determining whether such differences do or do not exist. It has as its purpose the identification and preliminary analysis of the structure, content, and other characteristics of items which show significant discrimination between different status groups. Every effort is made to suggest possible explanations for such differences, on the basis of internal evidence within the test data themselves, but no attempt is made to attack this phase of the problem experimentally.

Second, the study cannot be expected to provide final and conclusive evidence, although on many points it does provide more definite evidence than has heretofore been available. Owing to the fact that the various bases for categorizing items (difficulty of item, form of symbolism used, type of question asked, etc.) overlap and cannot be mutually exclusive, only tentative conclusions as to gross differences in discrimination among the different categories of items can be hoped for.

Third, the findings of this study with regard to the amount of status difference in the several tests, in different types of test items, and in particular individual items can have direct applicability only to the specific group of pupils upon which the present study is based. It is believed, however, that many of the more important conclusions drawn from the study can be generalized at least to other communities of the same general size and socioeconomic structure. The representativeness of the pupils studied is discussed more fully in chapter xii.

Fourth, the study is limited to the type of intelligence tests in most widespread use in the schools of the country today — that is, group paper-and-pencil tests. Neither performance tests nor individual tests of the Binet type are included.

Fifth, the study is limited to intercultural differences among groups of white pupils. The test responses of all nonwhite pupils were eliminated from the analysis. A somewhat similar study of the responses of Negro children from high and from low socioeconomic backgrounds is, however, available (4, 4a, and 4b).

How Is the Book Organized?

This volume is divided into three parts. Each is intended to serve a definite function. It may help the reader if the purposes which the authors had in mind in preparing the chapters in each of these parts are stated explicitly. At the same time the kind of material which will be found in each section will be outlined briefly.

Part I

This part, consisting of six chapters, is intended to define the problem to be investigated, to provide certain historical and sociological background against which the problem must be considered, and — most important of all — to raise a number of questions of a theoretical nature about the basic issues involved in the relation of intelligence tests to cultural differences in the background of children taking the tests.

Chapter i is introductory in nature; it defines the problem in simple, explicit terms, and introduces the reader to the rest of the material.

Chapter ii summarizes briefly the findings of previous studies dealing with the relationship of the I.Q. to cultural background. This chapter is intended to enable the reader to see the present study in its proper historical setting.

Chapter iii presents a summary of some of the more important findings of modern cultural anthropologists and sociologists as to the cultural differences which exist among different groups of children in typical American communities. The chapter establishes the bases for hypotheses as to cultural explanations for differences in test behavior reported in later chapters. In this chapter cultural differences are described which it seems reasonable to suppose may influence test behavior of children from different cultural backgrounds. The extent to which they actually do influence the test behavior is treated in later chapters.

Chapters iv, v, and vi raise a number of basic questions about possible relationships between cultural background and intelligence testing. These chapters are intended to stimulate thinking along somewhat new lines, to point out the very great importance of the issues involved, and to emphasize that the questions involved are not superficial or shallow ones but ones which are basic to much educational practice and basic to much thinking about the nature of intelligence itself.

These three chapters attempt (a) to clarify the general conceptual framework within which the research study was undertaken, planned, and carried out and (b) to aid the reader in making interpretation of the factual findings of the study. The chapters are not intended to be primarily interpretations of the data reported in later sections. In some respects they go beyond the particular data reported in this volume; in other respects they deal with facets of the problem not investigated in the present study. To put it another way, these chapters are to be read not as conclusions from the study but rather as introductions to it — as aids to the reader in gaining insight into the way in which the study was conceived and ways in which its findings may be interpreted.

Part II

This part consists of three chapters and provides a brief overview of the procedures, findings, and conclusions of the research study. Chapter vii summarizes the research procedures and the factual findings. Chapters viii and ix point out possible implications of these findings for (a) interpretation of the I.Q. from existing intelligence tests and (b) construction of new intelligence tests.

Part II is intended to be complete within itself — to be intelligible to the reader who wants to know the general nature of findings of the investigation without reading all the more detailed report in Part III. It is also intended to serve as an introductory overview for those who do wish to read all or parts of Part III. It is so organized as to facilitate selective reading of certain chapters in Part III by those who wish to pursue in more detail the evidence supporting some one particular type of conclusion stated in more general terms in Part II.

Part III

The fourteen chapters which comprise Part III present a detailed report of the actual findings of the study. They constitute the evidence underlying the generalizations and summaries contained in Part II. Part III is intended primarily for those interested in examining at first hand the evidence upon which the generalizations in Part II are based.

CHAPTER II

WHAT IS ALREADY KNOWN ABOUT THE RELATION OF THE I.Q. TO CULTURAL BACKGROUND?

By Virgil E. Herrick, Professor of Education
University of Wisconsin, Madison, Wisconsin

This chapter does not attempt to provide a comprehensive coverage of the research on the relation of environmental-cultural factors and intelligence in the sense that every study bearing on this problem is reviewed. For more general reviews of the whole problem the reader should consider the material found in: (a) the two yearbooks of the National Society for the Study of Education prepared by Terman et al. (1928, 27)[1] and by Stoddard et al. (1940, 26); (b) the six issues of the Review of Educational Research which deal with this subject (1933 to 1947, 29, 30); and (c) numerous textbook treatments.

For more specific attention to the problem of social status and intelligence, the reader is referred to the critical reviews and summaries of research by Burks (1928, 21), Schieffelin and Schwesinger (1930, 31), Sorokin et al. (1932, 33), Schwesinger (1933, 32), Lorimer and Osborn (1934, 24), Murphy et al. (1937, 25), Neff (1938, 28), Loevinger (1940, 23), Stoddard and Wellman (1940, 34), Jones (1946, 22), Murray (1947, 4), and Eells (1948, 3). The most recent of these summaries, by Eells, reviews and summarizes approximately ninety original research studies in this field.

The point of view taken here regarding the nature of cultural influences is that it is not necessary to argue at the level of whether culture does or does not influence intelligence. It seems obvious that the social environment of the individual at least supports and gives direction to his growth. It is possible and proper, however, to argue as to the relative importance of cultural status and of other factors in affecting differences in intelligence-test performance. It seems likely that the relationship of social status to intelligence constitutes not a single problem but a complex of problems, each with its own series of answers.

Two major questions will be used to organize this summary: (a) What is the relationship between the social status of individuals of school age and their I.Q.'s or intelligence-test scores? (b) What is the relationship between social-status differences and performance on subtests and individual items of commonly used intelligence tests?

Early Historical Approaches

Many workers in the field of social status and its influence on intelligence-test performance would add to their perspective and understanding of this complex problem if they would read or reread the early dis-

---

1. The first figure indicates the date of publication; the underlined figure indicates the number of the item in the Bibliography.

cussions of Binet and Stern. Binet's comments on the work of Decroly and Degand and on the five studies (35, pp. 316-29) he and his associates made on the relationship of social status and intelligence have been restated many times in the forty years since. While these studies were the first reported and do not represent good techniques in experimental design as we now know them, Binet's conclusion that differences in social status and in school experiences produced definite and substantial differences in intelligence-test results is nevertheless significant. His comments are particularly interesting if one recognizes that he was one of the first investigators writing about a problem which he was exploring for the first time. Binet's views on this subject are discussed somewhat more fully in chapter v.

William Stern, writing in 1912 (47), reported the results of administering the tests in the Binet-Simon series to children of the Volksschule (lower class) and to the children of the Vorschule (upper class). He found that the ten-year-old group in the low-status school showed exactly the same degree of proficiency on the tests as did the nine-year-old group in the high-status school. He forecast, also, the emphasis of studies forty years later by analyzing separately the easier and more difficult items from the point of view of the indicated status differences.

The first research study in this country dealing with the relation of social status to the newly developed intelligence tests was the one by Weintrob and Weintrob, published in 1912 (51). This study is interesting because it is one of the few studies which do not show a definite positive relationship between the two factors. These investigators used the Goddard Revision of the Binet-Simon tests to test children in three institutions which they thought represented quite different social backgrounds -- the Horace Mann School ("wealthy, or, at least, unburdened, families"), the Speyer School (representing a middle group), and the Hebrew Sheltering Orphan Asylum (a barrack-plan orphanage with very limited cultural advantages).

Weintrob and Weintrob summarized their findings by saying that "the three institutions showed very small and inconsistent differences. Speyer, which should have been second, was invariably last, and Horace Mann and the Asylum, whose environmental influences are diametrically opposite, were always close together, the Asylum in many instances being ahead" (51, p. 582).

In the authors' explanation of these findings they placed most emphasis on the racial composition of their groups. The Horace Mann School was partly Jewish and the Asylum entirely so. This is an early pointing-out of the importance of recognizing racial factors in studies of social status and intelligence. Although Weintrob and Weintrob used a point scale which made comparisons between groups possible, the statistical significances of these differences were not determined.

These early studies in the pioneer period of intelligence testing portray the prominence of the question of social status in interpreting intelligence-test results. Their interest, too, in following through to find the subtests and test items which reflected these differences provides a background for the most recent studies on this point.

General Nature of the Relationship

A large number of studies have been made since the Weintrob study in 1912; they have used such different definitions of social status as: judgments of teachers as to favorable and unfavorable social environments, occupational classification of the father, educational background of parents, measures of the economic status of the family (family income, tax assessments, etc.), and a number of composite social-status scales. Various revisions of the Binet-Simon test form the basis of the majority of these studies; commonly used group tests of intelligence are the Kuhlmann-Anderson, Otis Self-administering, Chicago Primary Mental Abilities, and the American Council on Education Psychological Examination.

All these studies tend to show the same results. The research is close to unanimous in showing that there are significant differences in intelligence-test performance of children and youth from different socioeconomic backgrounds, with children from the higher levels always securing the higher intelligence-test scores. When the comparisons are made in terms of differences of median or mean I.Q., typical differences between I.Q.'s of children of professional parents and those of children of unskilled laborers range from 15 to 25 I.Q. points. Where correlation techniques have been used, the correlations range from .03 to .58. Typical relationships are represented by a correlation coefficient of around .35, with half of the studies reporting coefficients ranging between .25 and .50. These findings remain substantially the same irrespective of the test used (performance tests excluded) or how the social status is defined or measured.

In the studies which used a composite index or scale to measure social status, the results on one scale varied almost as widely as the findings based on the use of different definitions of social status. For example, studies using the Chapman-Sims Scale (61) as a measure of social status reported correlations between this scale and the results of intelligence tests given to elementary-school children ranging from .21 to .56.

Four studies (4, 41, 42, 43) have used Warner's social-class concepts (18) as a measure of social status and have corroborated the findings of other investigators that there is a steady decrease in the intelligence-test performance of pupils as the social-class level increases. A variety of other socioeconomic scales have been used, with substantially similar results.

The Effect of Pupils' Age on the Relationship

The effect of age on the relationship between social status and intelligence is an interesting one, since the usual expectation would be that, if differences in social status are a factor in causing differences in intelligence-test performance, these differences should be further accentuated by the factor of age. What this accentuation might be, however, might be subject to a number of different interpretations. One might be that certain status levels provide environments more stimulating to mental growth and that, in general, children tend to acquire the intellectual status characteristic of the environment to which they are exposed; the longer the time of exposure, the greater the effect should be. Another, and equally logical, explanation might be based on the maturation of inherited characteristics. The present findings are not conclusive -- particularly as to the causal relationships.

Yerkes and his associates reported (1915, 52, 53) mean scores on their revision of the Binet Tests for ages four, five, six, seven, and eight for a "favored" (high-status) and an "unfavored" (low-status) group of pupils. The children in the "unfavored" group scored slightly higher than those in the "favored" group at age four, but the difference was reversed and increased steadily in size for each age level above four. Terman (1915, 49, 50), on the other hand, found that the degree of correlation between intelligence and social status (judged by teachers on a five-point scale) decreased steadily with advancing age: age five to eight, .43; age nine to eleven, .41; age twelve to fifteen, .29. More recent studies present no evidence to substantiate any increasing or decreasing effect of age on the relationship between social status and intelligence-test scores. The findings on this point must remain inconclusive until further studies are made.

Specific Social-Status Factors and Intelligence-Test Performance

Since the question of whether differentials in social status are accompanied by significant differences in total scores or I.Q.'s obtained from intelligence tests can now be answered conclusively, two additional questions can be examined: (a) Is it possible to identify the particular aspects of the social environment which are most significant in causing differences in intelligence-test performance? (b) Is it possible to identify the particular subtests and test items which are most influenced by social-class differences?

It is possible to argue that Loevinger's conclusion that social status must influence intelligence via "relatively narrow aspects or concomitants" (23, p. 205) may be questioned. Eells, for example, comments: "It is entirely possible that the major influence /of social status on intelligence/ may grow out of the broad constellation of cultural differences which are known to exist, and that to attempt to analyze these into detailed component parts will be artificial and will result in destruction of the very relationship it is sought to explain" (3, p. 59). It is quite likely that Eells's argument for not particularizing the relative importance of the factors in determining social status would hold equally well for not particularizing the specific intelligence tests and test items most influenced by social-status differences. The effort to particularize the test items is justified merely because it is of greater value to test-makers, not because it has any more logic on its side.

Three studies make some attempt to break the environmental factors down to determine their differential relationships to intelligence-test scores. The studies by Burks (1928, 37), Cuff (1934, 39, 40), and Osborn (1943, 45) are open to some question on the basis of procedures but are probably no worse in this respect than are many other studies in this field. Burks ranked nineteen cultural factors by the size of their correlations with I.Q. and found some interesting results. Home instruction, at ages prior to six, had no relationship with I.Q. — while private tutoring in music and dancing (for girls) was tied with parents' mental ages as the most significant factor. The fathers' and mothers' vocabularies and their mental ages were more significant than income, owning or renting a home, and grade reached by father or mother. The number of books in the home and in the child's library was midway in the list of factors.

Cuff used an intelligence test to select the top and bottom groups

(quarters) of 758 college freshmen. He than calculated the percentages of students in the high fourth and in the low fourth who "possessed" each of twenty-three items in the Chapman-Sims Socio-economic Scale. He subtracted, for each item in the scale, the percentage for the high quarter from the one for the low quarter and used the difference as a measure of the importance of the item in predicting intelligence. This procedure is open to considerable question on statistical grounds. Cuff's ranking, however, placed at the top of his list the questions: About how many books are in your home? Did your mother go to high school? Do you belong to any organization where you have to pay dues? Did your father go to high school? It is interesting to note that corresponding factors were less important in Burks's study.

Osborn studied 886 college freshmen and concluded that "those groups which were superior in test performance had a significantly different background as shown by the higher education of parents; they live in larger towns, come from smaller families, have parents with larger incomes, own more and newer modern conveniences, enjoy more literary life, and travel more extensively. In short, they had more of those features which are usually considered as constituting superior social and economic background" (45, pp. 222-24).

These studies tend to show, although not at all conclusively, what developers of social indexes have known for some time — that the level of education of the parents, their income, interests in reading and books, and nature of housing are particular elements which tend to be significantly related to differences in the intelligence-test performance of their children.

Social Status and Performance on Individual Test Items

Investigators of the problem of social status and intelligence, after finding the clear-cut difference in the intelligence-test performance of different social-status groups, were naturally curious as to the particular kinds of test items which contributed the most, and the least, to social-status differences. This kind of investigation has as long a history as that of the problem itself. Recent studies differ from the older ones mainly in the refinement of their procedures and in the racial, ethnic, or other socioeconomic group considered, rather than in their examination of new and significant aspects of the problem. Table 1 shows, for nine of these item-analysis studies, the investigator, nature of the group studied, test used, and the kinds of test items showing the greatest social-class differences in test performance.

Detailed perusal of some of these studies will reveal many inadequacies of procedure, and examination of Table 1 will disclose some apparent inconsistency of findings. Nevertheless, it appears that these studies indicate that, in general, test items which are essentially linguistic or scholastic in nature show comparatively large differences in favor of children from high socioeconomic backgrounds, while test items which are primarily perceptual or "practical" in nature show either smaller differences or differences in favor of children from the lower socioeconomic backgrounds.

TABLE 1

KINDS OF ITEMS SHOWING UNUSUALLY LARGE AND UNUSUALLY SMALL STATUS
DIFFERENCES, AS FOUND BY NINE INVESTIGATORS

Investigation*	Kinds of Items Showing Largest Differences in Favor of High-Status Pupils	Kinds of Items Showing Smallest Status Differences (or Differences in Favor of Low-Status Pupils)
Binet (1911, 35) Binet-Simon (White)	Tests judged to depend on: language, 6 tests; home training, 4 tests; attention, 3 tests	Tests judged to depend on: scholastic training, 6 tests; language, 2 tests; home training 1 test; judgment, 1 test
Stern (1912, 47) Binet-Simon (White)	Items of considerably above average difficulty	Items of only average difficulty
Weintrob and Weintrob (1912, 51) Binet-Simon (White)	Items judged to involve the ability to reason	Items judged to involve the use of language
Bridges and Coler (1917, 36) Binet-Simon (White)	Absurd statements Comprehension of questions Comparison of familiar objects Concrete definitions Counting backward from 20 to 1	Arranging weights Aesthetic judgment Copying square and diamond Comparison of lines Drawing designs from memory
Burt (1922, 38) Binet-Simon (White)	Linguistic tests — wide vocabulary Scholastic tests — literary subjects Memory tests — repetition of sentences Memory tests — items of information in cultural homes	Tests with money Perceptual and drawing tests "Practical" tests Tests of critical shrewdness
Stoke (1927, 48) Stanford-Binet (White)	Linguistic tests — original thinking	Linguistic tests — rote memory
Long (1935, 44) Kuhlmann-Anderson (Negro)	Completion Counting taps Likeness in pictures Finding of words that do not belong with others	Finding similar forms among a group of varied forms Substituting numbers for letters
Saltzman (1940, 46) Stanford-Binet (White)	Vocabulary Verbal comprehension of everyday situations Motor control	Counting and handling money Rote memory Sensory discrimination
Murray (1947, 4) Henmon-Nelson Kuhlmann-Anderson Otis Beta Chicago Tests of Primary Mental Abilities (Negro)	Items dependent on verbal ability	Items employing perception of form and space (geometric-design items)

* This column shows (a) name of investigator, (b) date of publication of the study, (c) number of reference in the Bibliography at the end of this volume, (d) test analyzed, and (e) race of pupils studied.

CHAPTER III

WHAT ARE THE CULTURAL DIFFERENCES WHICH MAY AFFECT PERFORMANCE ON INTELLIGENCE TESTS?

By Robert J. Havighurst, Professor of Education
University of Chicago, Chicago, Illinois

To be equally fair to all persons, an intelligence test should present problems which are either equally familiar or equally unfamiliar to them. To ask whether a given problem is familiar to a person is to ask whether the person has met something like this problem in his previous experience and how often he has had such experience.

The experience of the child is bounded by his culture. All American children have certain common experience because they share a common American culture. They can all recognize the American flag. Nearly all of them know the English language. Almost all of them know what apple pie is, what a basketball is, and most could give the names of the current movie stars. A test which asked ordinary questions about these things would probably be a fair test, but it would be too easy for all except the youngest pupils.

To make a test more difficult, there are two possible procedures. One is to include problems which are intrinsically more complex and therefore more difficult for all people. The other possible procedure is to include problems which are not in the experience of most people, such as to ask for a synonym for the work "cerebrate." This is not intrinsically difficult, but few people would happen on this word, and hence few would know its meaning. If this word occurs more frequently in the language of one social group than in the language of other social groups, it is unfair to use it in a test of intelligence which is supposed to be valid for a variety of social groups.

A simple inspection of the commonly used intelligence tests will convince anyone familiar with the extent of cultural differences in present-day America that the problems of these tests are not limited to the common American cultural experience which is shared by all or nearly all American boys and girls. The problems of these tests appear to be drawn very largely from the cultural experience of the middle-class group. If this is so, children of ethnic groups and of lower than middle socio-economic groups -- and these are the great majority of American children[1] -- are disadvantaged by these tests.

Test-makers have long recognized this difficulty so far as children from foreign-language backgrounds go. They have almost universally warned that their tests would not be fair to such children. Recent findings

1. The specific statements made in the rest of this chapter are not each specifically documented. They are supported in large part, however, by material from the studies by Warner and others whose works are listed in the Bibliography at the end of this volume (6-20).

of sociologists and cultural anthropologists are confirming, however, the insight of those who have believed that there are at least equally wide differences in cultural background even among children who are homogeneous with respect to such obvious cultural facts as ethnicity and race. Hence a familiarity with the latest available knowledge of cultural differences among the various social groups in the United States will be useful in the process of criticizing and improving intelligence-test items.

The Role of Social Classes in the United States in Determining the Experience of Children

There are three major types of culture in the United States:

1. The common American cultural traits and behaviors.
2. The various cultural behaviors and traits of the different socio-economic (or social-class) groups.
3. The cultural traits and behaviors of the different ethnic or nationality groups.

The system of socioeconomic or social-class groups existing in the United States has been examined in detail in New England, in the Deep South, and in the Midwest by social anthropologists. A number of these studies are listed in the Bibliography at the end of this volume (6-20). They have found a hierarchy of groups into which people fit themselves, with a considerable degree of movement existing between them. Each group consists of people who participate, or may participate, in intimate social relationships with one another, but who do not associate so freely with the groups which are socially defined as "above" or "below" them. The people within a given social group or level visit with one another, spend their spare time together, and encourage their children to marry into families of the same social level. In America, however, the social classes or levels are not closed, hard, and fast. People are always climbing up and going down the social ladder — leaving one social level behind and entering another.

In a community of a hundred thousand in the Midwest, and even in smaller communities in the East, there are six clearly marked social classes. In other types of communities there are probably more or fewer social classes, depending on the size and complexity of the community.

When the six social classes are ranked on the basis of their prestige in the thinking of the people who live in the community, they have been named, as follows:

Upper Upper
Lower Upper
Upper Middle
Lower Middle
Upper Lower
Lower Lower

The social anthropologists have found that each of these social classes has its own cultural traits and behaviors -- a social-class culture — as well as the common American culture which it shares with the other social classes. There are differences in attitudes toward education and in the amount and types of reading done in homes of different social classes. There are differences in attitudes toward property, and of course there are differences in the quality and variety of property — furniture,

size of house, tableware, pictures on the walls, books on shelves, and so on and on. There are also differences in practices of child-rearing, starting with the earliest training the child receives, in eating and toilet habits (9).

In size, but not in power and prestige, the two upper classes are almost insignificant. They make up together no more than 3 per cent of the population. Even the upper-middle class is rather small, being about 7 or 8 per cent of the total population. The two largest classes are the lower-middle and the upper-lower classes, which contain altogether about 70 per cent of the total population, distributed differently between the two classes in different types of communities. The lower-lower class consists of 15 to 25 per cent of the population.

Important Social Class Differences Which Might Affect Test Performance

In the following analysis of social-class cultures, the characteristics which appear to be relevant to intelligence-test performance will be presented. Comparison will be made of upper-middle-class culture with lower-lower-class culture. The classes between these two on the social scale, lower-middle and upper-lower, have cultures which differ from the ones above and below them primarily in degree of possession of this or that characteristic, although there are also certain specific differences in quality which may be significant for intelligence-test performance.

Cultural differences in home and family life

The houses in which upper-middle-class people live are usually larger and more elaborately furnished than the houses of lower-class people. Hence a test item which requires knowledge of any of the following may touch the experience of a middle-class child but not that of a lower-class child: fireplace, chandelier, wallpaper, salad fork, dining-room. On the other hand, the following characteristics of lower-class homes would probably favor a lower-class child if they appeared in test items: pump, rain barrel, kerosene lamp, coal stove.[2]

Middle-class children are more likely to go on trips with their families and thus to learn about other parts of the country. They are also more likely to go to summer camps and thus to get experience with plants and animals which is usually denied to urban lower-class children. Church and Sunday-school attendance is more frequent for middle-class children than for lower-class children. Hence test problems requiring familiarity with the Bible, or with church activities and church services, would probably favor middle-class children.

Books, magazines, and newspapers are more plentiful in middle-class than in lower-class homes, and consequently the middle-class children have more opportunity to become familiar with the topics dealt with in such literature. Middle-class homes usually have a greater quantity

2. It should be emphasized that these examples, and others in this chapter, are cited as examples of kinds of items which appear, on inspection, to give advantage to one or another cultural group of children. The statements made are to be considered as reasonable hypotheses. The study reported in later chapters is designed to determine more exactly the extent to which such differences do actually occur on various types of items.

and variety than lower-class homes of games involving language and literature. For example, the middle-class child may have learned to know the names of books and writers through the game of "Authors," and he may have had practice in making up words in the game of "Anagrams" which should give him an advantage in test items that involve the rearrangement of letters to make words. Map puzzles often give middle-class children a familiarity with names of states and their capital cities.

Hobbies are more frequent in middle-class homes. Such activities as amateur photography, chemistry, and stamp-collecting give middle-class children information and skills that may be useful on an intelligence test. Special lessons in music and art give middle-class children knowledge of music and art and of musical instruments and art techniques which may serve these interests.

Vocabularies of middle-class parents are usually larger and more "correct" by the usual middle-class standards than are the vocabularies of lower-class parents. Furthermore, middle-class parents are more likely to read to their children and to converse with them than are lower-class parents. Hence middle-class children get vocabulary and grammar training at home which is better by the usual intelligence-test standards of vocabulary and grammar.

Cultural differences in neighborhood and community life

Many items from current tests are drawn from experience that the child may have in the course of going about in his neighborhood and community. But middle- and lower-class children have different neighborhood and community experiences.

Middle-class children are more likely to belong to the Boy or Girl Scouts, the YMCA, the YWCA, and similar youth organizations. Lower-class youth tend to frequent settlement houses, park recreation centers, and the like.

The most common games, which can be played without expensive equipment and specially equipped playing space, are as frequent in the experience of lower-class as of middle-class youth. Marbles, jacks, hop-scotch, baseball, and many varieties of ball games fall in this group, as well as basketball and certain other games often played in schools with facilities open to all children. Only the specifically middle- and upper-class games, such as tennis, golf, and polo, are likely to be more familiar to one group than to the other.

Museums, concerts, and theaters are familiar elements in the middle-class child's experience and much less familiar in lower-class experience. Hence test items requiring familiarity with art and the history of art, music (especially classical music), drama, anthropology, archeology, and natural history are likely to favor middle-class children. Libraries are frequented more by middle-class than by lower-class children and thus contribute more to the literary information and experience of middle-class children.

Experience with movies, on the other hand, is about equally frequent in both social classes. Children of both groups go about equally often to the movies, and the pictures they see are not greatly different, though there is evidence that certain "quality" movies for children are seen more frequently by middle-class children. The radio is also a part of the life of both groups, though perhaps slightly more frequent in middle-class experience. Probably the programs listened to by children are not greatly different from one class to another.

Movement about the city, experiencing its variety and learning its characteristic pattern and structure, is more characteristic of middle-class than of lower-class youth. This finding is contradictory to the prevailing conception of lower-class youth as wanderers, free to come and go with little parental control. But a recent study by Volberding (12) of the geographical mobility of eleven-year-olds in a small city showed that middle-class children habitually traveled over a wider area of the city than did the lower-lower-class group. Furthermore, Davis and Havighurst (9) found that middle-class mothers in Chicago expected their children to go downtown alone at an earlier age than did lower-class mothers.

Cultural differences in school experience

School is an extension of home to the average middle-class child. It rewards and punishes him for the same things that the home does. It is familiar ground. On the contrary, school is often a strange place to the lower-class child, with strange expectations. It often contradicts the home in its rewards and punishments.

From school experience are drawn many of the items of current intelligence tests. Hence the child who spends the greatest amount of time in school, and who is most receptive to the school's teaching, prepares himself best for intelligence tests. Middle-class children tend to stay longer in school than lower-class children. In many cities the best-equipped schools and the best-prepared teachers are in the higher-status areas of the community, while the lower-class pupils go to run-down schools with less able teachers. Consequently, the experience of the lower-class children is less conducive to good performance on intelligence tests. There is also more retardation of lower-class pupils, which means that they are exposed to less advanced school work, with a consequent decreased experience with the material from which the more difficult test items are drawn.

There is a tendency to place and to keep middle-class children in the most academic or "bookish" curriculums in school. Test items which are drawn from these curriculums will probably favor middle-class children. For example, a test item requiring the pupil to know that geometry, algebra, and trigonometry all belong together, but that botany does not belong closely with them, would more probably be known by a pupil in the college preparatory than in the vocational or general curriculum.

The sectioning of children by "ability" tends to place the middle-class children in "high" sections and the lower-class children in "low" sections. Where exceptions are made to place children of lower "ability" in higher sections, these usually involve middle-class children who appear low on test but are thought to deserve the stimulation of being with higher groups. The higher groups get more verbal and abstract learning experience, which gives them an advantage with intelligence tests of a verbal or abstract character.

Cultural differences in motivation for test performance

The cultural differences thus far mentioned have dealt with opportunities for experiences that could be expected to make the middle-class child more familiar with the usual problems of intelligence tests. In addition, there are cultural differences which probably _motivate_ the middle-class child to try harder than the lower-class child in general school work and especially on school tests.

The characteristic middle-class attitude toward education is taught by middle-class parents to their children. School is important for future success. One must do one's very best in school. Report cards are studied by the parents carefully, and the parents give rewards for good grades, warnings and penalties for poor grades. Lower-class parents, on the other hand, seldom push the children hard in school and do not show by example or by precept that they believe education is highly important. In fact, they usually show the opposite attitude. With the exception of a minority who urgently desire mobility for their children, lower-class parents tend to place little value on high achievement in school or on school attendance beyond the minimum age.

When the middle-class child comes to a test, he has been taught to do his very best on it. Life stretches ahead of him as a long series of tests, and he must always work himself to the very limit on them. To the average lower-class child, on the other hand, a test is just another place to be punished, to have one's weaknesses shown up, to be reminded that one is at the tail end of the procession. Hence this child soon learns to accept the inevitable and to get it over with as quickly as possible. Observation of the performance of lower-class children on speed tests leads one to suspect that such children often work very rapidly through a test, making responses more or less at random. Apparently they are convinced in advance that they cannot do well on the test, and they find that by getting through the test rapidly they can shorten the period of discomfort which it produces.

Not only the rewarding and punishing behavior of the parents stimulates middle-class children in school more than lower-class children but also the example of the parents. Middle-class parents have gone further in school than lower-class parents, and they do more reading and make more use of education than do lower-class parents. Hence the middle-class child, unconsciously imitating his parents, takes on their educational roles and attitudes, while the lower-class child does the same thing with respect to his parents.

Conclusion

It is clear, then, from the current findings of sociologists and cultural anthropologists, that middle-class and lower-class children bring to the intelligence-test situation widely disparate cultural experiences by virtue of their social-class experience and that middle-class children get more out of themselves in the ordinary school test situation than do lower-class children. An intelligence test which is to get at the "real" problem-solving ability of children must draw its problems entirely from experiences which are common to all or nearly all the children to be tested; at the same time such a test must be given under conditions which motivate lower-class children to do their best and which teach them to expect that they can succeed and that they will be rewarded for doing their best.

CHAPTER IV

WHAT ARE SOME OF THE BASIC ISSUES IN THE RELATION OF INTELLIGENCE TESTS TO CULTURAL BACKGROUND?[1]

By Allison Davis, Professor of Education
University of Chicago, Chicago, Illinois

The preceding chapter describes the wide cultural differences in experiences which children from different social-class levels may be expected to have. The present chapter will examine further the implications of these differentials in experience for the construction and interpretation of intelligence tests.

The crucial problem raised by the attempt to compare scientifically the capacity of any two individuals to learn is that of finding situations with which the two individuals have had equal experience. To state this issue more exactly, two major systems of behavior are involved in problem-solving. They are (a) the individual's genetic equipment for problem-solving and (b) the individual's particular cultural experience, training, and motivation, which have developed certain areas of his mental behavior and certain skills more than others. In a test of general hereditary capacity, the second factor must be equalized for all those tested.

Consider two children with equal hereditary mental factors. The child who obtains more practice in working on mental problems of a certain type may be expected to prove superior in that particular area of mental functioning. If one of these equally endowed children is reared in a family of high socioeconomic status, and the other in a slum family, we should expect that the first child will prove superior on academic types of problems, such as nearly all those in "intelligence" tests. This seems to be the case, if one accepts the sample, obtained by Newman, Freeman, and Holzinger, of identical twins, separated early and reared in different socioeconomic strata.

But if one compares any two children not genetically identical — and this is the chief task of mental tests — the fact that one child proves superior within a certain narrow range of academic problems does not imply that he is superior likewise in dealing with all other types of problems. Mental processes are highly varied; so are the types of specific mental problems presented by our society. Problem-solving activities in man exist as a configuration of systems of activities. In one child, systems A and B may exist at a high level, but systems C and D may exist at a low level, as a result both of genetic factors and of training. A second child may have this pattern of strong and weak activities exactly reversed.

Criteria for Constructing Culture-Fair Intelligence Tests

Any scientific effort to compare the mental status of individuals

---

1. Adapted from material first published in the Scientific Monthly (2).

throughout the whole cultural range of the population of the United States, therefore, must satisfy two conditions. The two requirements for such a test may be stated thus:

1. A great range of systems of mental behavior exists. This range extends from those at the most complex level, such as (a) the systems of mental acts which direct and organize the personality or (b) the mental acts which organize experience at the creative level, to those at the extreme of scholasticism and of relative simplicity, such as (c) the recognition of the proper order of words in a sentence or of letters in a word; or the identification of verbal opposites, or verbal analogies. Since, in life, human beings engage in an incredible variety of mental activities, the test-maker must discover those systems of acts that are most representative of all mental behaviors. In practical terms of test-making, this requirement means that those types of problems which are put into tests must represent a wide range of those mental systems exhibited by normal human beings (and not merely a sampling of their academic or linguistic activities). We assume that linguistic skills are not in themselves a crucial index of mental status, because many primitive tribes learn as complex a language as do middle-class American pupils. The same assumption is made by leading anthropologists and linguists.[2]

2. In order to compare the genetic mental equipment of different individuals, the test-maker must select those problems in each mental-system area which are common to the culture and practice of all socio-economic groups in the population to be tested. In addition, the test-maker must learn how to express these problems in symbols (words, pictures, etc.) common to all the scioeconomic groups to be tested. He must likewise find problems which motivate equally all the groups to be tested.

Those problems for whose solution the training of different socio-economic groups has been unequal cannot be used as constituting in themselves a test of the general mental activity of those cultural groups. Nor may they be used to measure the genetic potential of two individuals from different subcultures. They may be used only as measures of the present skills of two individuals who almost certainly have different genetic equipment and who certainly have had different amounts of training on the skills tested.

Although Alfred Binet, who founded modern tests of intelligence, was keenly aware of the danger that his test problems were too scholastic and too closely related to home training, he did not live to face the extremely complex task of creating new tests that would be less biased in these respects. During the last twenty-five years, therefore, many research psychologists have criticized all such intelligence tests as including a strong cultural handicap for pupils of the lower socioeconomic groups.

We regard mental behavior as the interaction of many systems of mental acts. The Spearman theory considers intelligence as composed of one general (or G) "ability" and several specific "abilities." We raise the question whether the child tested will have a fair chance, however, to show how much of G he possesses unless he has had equal access, with all other testees, to the situations and symbols by which he is tested and unless he is equally motivated as all other testees. The necessity for culturally common situations, symbols, and motivation would apply to

Thurstone's tests of the so-called "primary mental abilities" also.

Our chief criterion for a measure of general mental behavior, however, is that the problems must represent a wide range of mental systems and mental problems. We do not believe that the present tests meet this criterion. Thurstone isolated his "primary abilities" by analysis of fifty-six current psychological tests, constructed by many persons, but all limited, we believe, to a few systems of mental behavior, and formulated in academic abstract problems. Thurstone quite frankly makes no claim that his tests cover a wide range of mental factors or problems. Good-enough has made the same point: "Thurstone's primary abilities are not presumed to cover the complete range of human talent. . . . They involve only the abstract abilities needed for success in the conventional type of intelligence tests and in the academic pursuits of the classroom" (64, p. 459). Thurstone himself has stated that his "primary" mental factors may vary in their definition. Some may "be defined by endocrinological effects"; others, in effects of the central or autonomic nervous systems; "still others may be defined in terms of experience and schooling" (74, p. 56).

Culture and Mental Behavior

The sociologist and social anthropologist have been convinced, through studies of a great many human societies, that cultural learning runs through nearly all the "mental" behavior of human beings. Social anthropologists therefore strongly doubt that cultural behavior can be eliminated from any intelligence-test response. We hope, however, that cultural bias in the tests, favoring any particular socioeconomic group, can be eliminated. This position requires the construction both of test problems and of total testing situations that so control all the major cultural elements in these tests that no cultural advantage is offered by the test to any socioeconomic group in the United States.

Fortunately, sociologists and social anthropologists now have developed a typology of the cultural systems within the United States. We know that Americans exhibit three major types of cultural behavior. These are:

1. The common American cultural traits and behaviors

2. The various cultural behaviors of the different socioeconomic (social-class) groups

3. The cultural patterns of the different "ethnic" or nationality groups

The culture of the United States, in which the test problems inevitably must be expressed, is therefore composed of (a) common problems and behaviors and (b) limited, "subcultural" traits or problems. Here, then, in this discrimination between common cultural problems and more limited subculture-group problems, lies the way to improve our tests of general problem-solving activities. We must try to control or equalize the cultural factors in test problems if we hope to use these problems to measure comparative ability (i.e., mental activity as developed in similar learning environments). One way to attack this problem would be to try to avoid all types of problems in which one socioeconomic group (and this means, in present test practice, the middle-class group) has had more

2. See the works of Edward Sapir and M. Swadesh, as quoted in Allison Davis, Social-Class Influences upon Learning (1, pp. 79-85).

training and experience than some other group. We might choose, therefore, problem situations which are equally general in all our socioeconomic levels of pupils. Second, we might express these problems in symbols that are equally common, and in a manner that is equally motivating, to all socioeconomic groups.

Our position with regard to the present tests may be summarized in a series of four interdependent hypotheses:

1. All responses to all items in all tests of general intelligence are inevitably influenced by the culture of the respondent.

2. In a test of general mental ability to be used in the United States, the problems should be selected from the common culture, expressed in cultural symbols common to all native inhabitants of the United States, and selected from that common culture only.

3. In all available tests of general intelligence, however, there are numerous items implying experience that is part of the culture of the higher socioeconomic groups, but not equally a part of the culture of the approximately 60 per cent of all Americans who grow up in the lower socioeconomic groups.

4. Therefore, the basic cultural flaws in all available tests of general intelligence may be overcome by including only those problems and symbols that imply experience that is part of the general American culture.

At the biochemical level the total mental system of a human being must be presumed to be an organization primarily of activities of the brain, the central nervous system, and of certain of the endocrine glands, extending only secondarily to the autonomic nervous system. Of this biochemical level, where mental behavior originates, we know very little.

At the level of gross, or molar, behavior, however, where observation of learning sequences and records of conscious thought are the pertinent phenomena, we may study mental behavior in terms both of learning theory and measurement.

At this molar level, mental or intellectual behavior is a natural system of phenomena, occurring within the individual organism. It is a system because all mental phenomena function interdependently. Furthermore, all such phenomena interact so as to maintain both processes of change (learning and unlearning) and processes of continuing organization or stability.

Mental behavior, in this molar system, is presumed to result from both genetic and developmental phenomena. The developmental aspects of mental behavior vary, as between individuals and as between cultural groups, according to the amount and intensity of the mobilization (functioning) of the genetic and other organic processes, as stimulated and guided by both the natural and the cultural environments. This mobilization of genetic mental equipment is stimulated and goal-directed principally by the cultural environment.

We assume that the following phenomena[3] enter into the system of acts that constitute a pupil's response to a test problem; they are, there-

---

3. For a slightly different formulation of these factors see pp. 57-58.

fore, responsible for the status of one pupil on a test, as compared with that of another pupil:

H Hereditary phenomena, determining certain complex organic structural relationships and functional patterns, probably organized by the brain and central nervous system. These hereditary factors are almost never the same in a child as in either of his parents, because the number of possible different combinations of the parents' genes is more than 1,000,000. There is no evidence that such hereditary factors are segregated by socioeconomic levels.

C Cultural phenomena involved in the pupil's degree of experience, obtained in his family or play group, with that particular social environment that determines both the content and the symbols of the test problem.

C_1 Training phenomena in school and home, involving more specific, repetitive, and purposeful experiences with cultural situations and symbols that are closely related to the test problem.

C_2 Cultural motivational phenomena, or "drive"; those rewards and punishments that exist at a level sufficient to impel the pupil to use his full pattern of activities to solve the test problem.

E Emotional phenomena, such as the type and degree of the pupil's anxiety in the test situation.

S The phenomena of "speed," which are complex functions of the hereditary factors, the physical condition and stamina of the testee at the particular time, his cultural habits of work, his familiarity with the cultural form and content of the problem, and his previous experience or training with this specific type of problem.

The relative success of two persons in solving a given test problem, therefore, depends not simply upon their hereditary equipment but also upon their relative familiarity with the cultural situations and symbols in the problem, their relative degree of training with similar problems, and the relative strength of their motivation. The factor of time may or may not be involved, depending upon the nature of the test.

The lifelong process by which culture helps to guide, develop, limit, and evaluate all mental problem-solving has not received sufficiently serious attention from either test-makers or educators. They continually make the error of regarding middle-class culture, and even more narrowly, middle-class school culture, as the "true" culture, or the "best" culture. More than 95 per cent of our teachers and professors are middle-class in their socioeconomic status. Like all other cultural groups, teachers and professors regard that particular version of culture (those mores, emotional patterns, and social values) which they have learned from their own families, friends, and teachers, as the "best" and only "true" culture. This attitude is powerfully reflected in school curriculums, in intelligence tests, and in teachers' judgments of their pupils. It is an attitude which is fatal to the development of the full mental capacity of either the teacher or the pupil. The belief, for instance, that the skills of reading, or of writing compositions, or of learning the usual academic materials are the primary essentials of "education" destroys the real aim of education, which is to learn how to think so as to solve life-problems. Most schools do not teach pupils how to explore even the simplest real-life problems, how to define their crucial issues, and how to proceed to solve them. The public schools, especially, seek to teach pupils only how to read, how to carry out memorized, routine arithmetical operations, and how to paraphrase textbooks. Furthermore, intelligence tests seek to predict this kind of behavior; therefore, they include chiefly those problems that are closely related to the culture of the schools.

In acquiring this middle-class academic culture, children of low socioeconomic groups do not perform well, on the average, either on scholastic tasks or on the intelligence tests that are designed to measure types of learning closely related to scholastic problems. These low socioeconomic groups fail because their parents themselves have not been trained to read; nor do they regard reading or school curriculums as important. Moreover, neither the parent nor the child's social group urges the child to practice reading or school exercises or sets him an example for attainment in this field. The parents and friends of the average child in the high socioeconomic groups, on the other hand, do offer him a powerful example of their skill in reading and in the school type of culture. Furthermore, this latter group of parents consciously and unconsciously reveals an interest in the child's learning this behavior; they likewise afford him practice in such problem-solving. For this very reason, Binet and Simon continually stated specifically that reading and other school-type activities were suspect as devices for measuring the intelligence of such children.

This example of reading skill should focus our attention upon the primary role of culture both in identifying those problems which a specific human group regards as important and in training members of this group to think about such problems. "Culture" includes all behavior and thought learned in conformity with a social group. Pupils coming from the top and bottom social strata live in cultures which, though alike in certain fundamental American activities, are yet different in many other cultural habits and motives. At a great many points, therefore, their cultures differ with respect to the types of problems they teach each group to recognize and to solve.

The Genetic Ability of Different Cultural Groups

It is not known whether the middle class is genetically superior, mentally, to the lower class. This view, however, does not seem likely, because it appears that mental behavior, at the physiological level, must involve not one or two genetic factors but many genetic factors, and in a complex relationship. If "intelligence" is influenced by several genetic factors, the chances are very low that a child would have the same superior or inferior factors as his parents. Furthermore, if there were group differences in genetic mental factors, we assume that the greatest genetic group differences in mentality would exist as between "races." Yet we now know that northern urban Negroes have higher I.Q.'s than southern Negroes, that the difference increases with length of residence in the North, and that northern Negroes have higher I.Q.'s than some southern white groups (67, pp. 36-46). We assume that this is clear evidence of the great influence of school training and other cultural acts upon prob-

lem-solving. We assume, therefore, that hereditary mental factors are numerous and so related that there is no significant tendency for a random group of middle-class families to segregate genetically more superior mentalities than does a random group of lower-class families.

It may well be that upward-mobile lower-class parents are above average for their social class, but only in those areas of mental behavior which are adaptive for middle-class culture. Development of other types of mental ability may be hindered by the middle-class culture.

Hypotheses as to Cultural Factors in Present Intelligence Tests

Assuming that the range of systems of mental acts is as wide as indicated above, it follows by inspection of present tests that they are tests not of general mental activity but only of a few types of activity.

It is possible to hypothesize that the present test problems lie entirely within those areas in which middle-class experience is greater. If, however, it is granted that the genetic potential is equal between classes, it follows that there should be some major problem areas in which the more pertinent lower-class cultural experience would render the lower class superior.

The middle class may be expected to prove superior on the present tests, because this group has had more training on the specific test problems or on closely related problems. Their motivation is also more adaptive, as a result of their cultural training.

It is possible that the middle class will also prove superior on all, or nearly all, types of possible test problems, because they have a cultural advantage in habits of work and in test motivation. That is, since training is an essential part of all problem-solving, it may be that the superiority of middle-class culture in establishing habits of school work will generalize to all kinds of mental problems, including also those in which the cultural content and symbols are common to all social classes.

We do not know, however, that the work habits of the middle class will remain superior on those problems with which they have not had more experience than the lower class. In fact, we know that training in one mental area and type of problem frequently does not generalize to other quite different areas and problems.

CHAPTER V

HOW DOES CULTURAL BIAS IN INTELLIGENCE TESTS ARISE?[1]

By Allison Davis, Professor of Education
University of Chicago, Chicago, Illinois

In chapter iv we have tried to state the general cultural issues involved in any effort to measure the comparative level of problem-solving activities in different individuals. It may clarify our grasp of the issues further if we examine, from the point of view of its effect on cultural bias, the course actually followed by test-makers in the construction and standardization of their tests.

Binet and Cultural Influences

Alfred Binet excelled most of his successors both in the realism of his test problems and in his desire to control the cultural aspects of these tests.

Binet constantly exhibited a keen awareness of the cultural situations in which children learn their behavior. Time and again, with regard to testing, he pointed out that the child's vocabulary and much of his other knowledge, along with the more subtle manifestations of motivation and work habits, are strongly influenced by the home training and the school training of the child (35, pp. 42, 237, 258-59, 275, 281, 294). Binet was aware, furthermore, of the different social strata in French communities, for he repeatedly stated that he tested only children in the lower economic ("working-class") neighborhoods. He first standardized his tests with reference only to "working-class" children.

Binet made it perfectly clear that he had been greatly concerned over the danger that large sections of his test measured chiefly the effects of cultural training rather than of "mental capacity." He had eliminated certain tests, he wrote, because their solutions could be greatly facilitated by the home or school training of the child:

There are tests which require a knowledge outside the intelligence of the child. To know his age, count his fingers, recite the days of the week indicate that he has learned these little facts from his parents or friends; we have thought well to suppress these three tests.

There are tests too exclusively scholastic, as that of reading and retaining a given number of memories of what has been read, or copying a written model, or writing from dictation. We suppress these / 35, p. 275 /.

In seeking to avoid problems whose solution could be influenced either by home or by school training, Binet went so far as to eliminate questions

1. Adapted from material first published in the Scientific Monthly (2).

requiring a child of six years to tell his age, or a child of seven years to copy a sentence, or a child of nine years to "read and retain six facts." Those tests eliminated by him because they had scholastic and other cultural bias included:

Tests of 6 years: Tell the age
                    Distinguish evening and morning

Tests of 7 years: The fingers of the hand
                    Copy a written sentence
                    Name four pieces of money

Tests of 8 years: Read and remember two facts
                    Write from dictation

Tests of 9 years: Days of the week
                    Read and retain six facts / 35, p. 294 /

Binet then considered the research of Decroly and Degand, which indicated that forty-seven children tested in Brussels, of "a social class in easy circumstances," showed an average advance in test level of one and one-half years over Binet's "working-class" children. Binet could not face the implications of this fact, when considered in the light of his own views that home and school training influenced the responses to most of his test problems. First, he himself conducted a better and more conclusive research, in which he had M. Morlé test one group of children of high socioeconomic status and another of low socioeconomic status. This research likewise revealed that the children of low socioeconomic groups did less well on Binet's tests and that they also did less well in scholastic work. At the same time Binet pointed out that nearly all the problems in his tests were "correlated" with cultural "aptitudes," which he called "home training," "attention" (motivation), "language," "habit of looking at pictures," and "scholastic exercise."

At this point, Binet appears to have stopped reasoning. He simply ignored the facts in making a final estimate of his tests. He could not, or would not, follow through to the obvious conclusion that other kinds of problems were needed. Although he said that these types of training were more highly developed in the schools and homes of children of high socioeconomic status, and although he knew, from his own research, that children of high socioeconomic status had a much easier time with his type of tests, he did not face the clear inference that his tests were not a fair basis for comparing the mental capacity of children of different socioeconomic levels.

Had Binet failed? In seeking the answer to this question, we must first ask another question: What had Binet tried to do? Unlike most of his successors, Binet was forthright about the aim of his tests. With the publication of their first series of tests in 1905, Binet and Simon boldly stated that their purpose was "to measure the intellectual capacity of a child who is brought to us in order to know whether he is normal or retarded -- we shall limit ourselves to the measuring of their general intelligence. We shall determine their intellectual level, and, in order the better to appreciate this level, we shall compare it with that of normal children of the same age or of an analogous level" (35, pp. 37-39; underlining not in original). Broadening the aim of their test by 1908, they emphasized that it was a scale for all children. "We set for ourselves the following program: first to determine the law of the intellectual development of children and to devise a method of measuring their intelligence; and, second, to study the diversity of their intellectual aptitudes" (35, p. 182).

Binet started out to measure "intellectual capacity," therefore. Moreover, he wished to make a test of intellectual capacity as a whole -- not of just one or two narrow areas of "intelligence" but of a wide range of ("general") intellectual areas. He wanted a scale which would measure the child's status in areas which would be <u>representative</u> of all his mental areas.

By 1908 Binet had revised his earlier belief that his tests measured "intellectual capacity":

> It is something far more complex that we measure. The result depends: first, on the intelligence pure and simple; second, on extra-scholastic acquisition capable of being gained precociously; third, on scholastic acquisitions made at a fixed date; fourth, on acquisitions relative to language and vocabulary, which are at once scholastic and extra-scholastic, depending <u>partly</u> on the school and partly on the family circumstances /35, p. 259/.

After thus specifying the cultural influences in test performance, Binet and Simon immediately claimed that their tests actually did justice to children of all socioeconomic levels. Three years later they had evidence which raised doubts on the point. These doubts continue to exist in our day.

Social science was unable to point out clearly the basic fallacy in Binet's effort to validate his scale, until social anthropologists, sociologists, and social psychologists had studied intensively the deep and varied ramifications of social status, and of social-class cultural learning, into modern social life. For Binet's fallacy in his efforts to validate his tests was one which neither he nor any other test-maker could have been expected to see. It was, so to speak, a sociological fallacy.

Out of all the problems invented by his predecessors, Binet chose relatively few. He based his selection of these few upon his testing of children from "working-class" neighborhoods. He included in his scale only those problems which were answered correctly more often by "good pupils" than by "poor pupils" in these "working-class" neighborhoods. A "good pupil" was one who received high marks in school or was not retarded in grade placement. Thus the "validity" of a test item was determined by its positive relation to school achievement.

All Binet's pupils lived in "working-class" neighborhoods, however. Therefore, Binet thought the differences in school achievement, within this group, resulted chiefly from differences in capacity and not from differences in social training and motivation. <u>He assumed that all children from these neighborhoods had roughly the same cultural background and social motivation</u>.

We now know that this assumption is incorrect for cities in the United States; European sociologists also have pointed out that social strata with differential social motivation exist <u>within the European urban "working class."</u> In terms of recognizable family types, one must distinguish (<u>a</u>) the very bottom, "demoralized" group within the "working class" and (<u>b</u>) the "clean, hard-working, respectable," skilled group in the "working class."

There is still another kind of social difference within the lower class,

as students of modern society have recently emphasized. There are the "ambitious" families, who train their children "to get up in the world," that is, to seek the skills necessary to gain a higher social level than that of the parents; this group constitutes an important minority in most lower-class neighborhoods. In many of these "ambitious" lower-class families there is one parent — usually the mother — who was born into a middle-class family but married a lower-class spouse. This parent, as life-histories almost invariably show, tries to teach the children good study habits and strong motivation for reading and all academic skills.

Sociologists use the term "social mobility" to designate this process by which individuals improve or worsen their social status. Those families or individuals who are "ambitious," in the sense given above, are attempting "upward social mobility." They are said to be "upward mobile, socially." That type of family, in any social class, which makes little change in its culture or social status is said to be "nonmobile socially," or "stable" with regard to social class. Individuals or families who lose their "respectability" (their original social-class status) are described as "downward mobile, socially."

Middle-class children, as research summarized in chapter iii has shown, usually learn from their familial culture both the kind of skills and the kind of motivation necessary for school achievement. <u>Similarly the "ambitious" or upward-mobile children in the lower class, responding to stimulation in their family, learn to seek academic goals</u>. They soon attain more skill in school work, on the average, than do the majority of lower-class children who meet no such parental urging.

How does this sociological finding bear upon Binet's method of "validation"? When Binet faced the problem of discovering those items which were "valid" as tests of "intelligence" from among all the items he had collected, he first divided his pupils, all of whom were from "working-class" neighborhoods, into two groups. These were (<u>a</u>) the group who received "good marks" in school and (<u>b</u>) those who received "poor marks" in school. A valid item, he claimed, was one on which the group of pupils having good marks proved superior to the group having poor marks. Sociologists now would have no doubt that the "good marks" group was chiefly a cultural group, composed overwhelmingly of (<u>a</u>) the upward-mobile "working-class" children, plus (<u>b</u>) those middle-class children who lived in the "working-class" neighborhoods (for some such are to be found in nearly all "working-class" neighborhoods).

Thus Binet used as his criterion for a "valid" item the same <u>kind</u> of measure which Terman and Otis later used: a measure of <u>cultural</u> difference, related to social-class status. His "good marks" group were chiefly the pupils aspiring for academic skills and goals, within the working class. That even his "best group" had significantly less of this <u>academic kind</u> of problem-solving facility than did upper-middle-class children of the same age was soon revealed by Decroly and Degand. In essence, these authors showed simply that a "good" mark in a school in a "prosperous" neighborhood did not mean the same thing as a "good" mark in a school in a poor neighborhood. Binet had not foreseen this cultural fact. Thus Binet's "validation" and his standardization for age were both unsound.

Terman and Cultural Influences

To obtain problems on which all socioeconomic groups have had equal training, Terman's procedures were no more objective than Binet's. In choosing problems for the first Stanford-Binet scale, Terman used school marks and school progress, together with age increment, as his objective criteria of "intelligence." Before making the second form of the Stanford-Binet, Terman says he realized the circularity of this effort to validate his problems. His subsequent choice of new criteria, however, showed that he did not solve his problem:

> Validity . . . was judged by two criteria: (1) increase in the percents passing from one age (or mental age) to the next, and (2) a weight based on the ratio of the difference to the standard error of the difference between the mean age (or mental age) of subjects passing the test and of subjects failing in it. . . . Increase in percents passing by mental age is better /than chronological age/, but exclusive reliance upon this technique predetermines that the scale based upon this criterion will measure approximately the same functions as that used in selecting the mental age groups. In the present case this was not objectionable, since the purpose of the revision was to provide scales closely comparable to the old with respect to the mental abilities tested / 73, pp. 9-10/.

The fallacy here seems obvious; Terman's failure to perceive it reveals the complete unawareness, in even a good test-maker, of the fact that the basic problem in validation is a cultural one, which cannot be met by changing a simple quantitative index for a more complex one. The fallacy is, of course, that mental age, as taken from the first Stanford-Binet standardization, was a direct function of the kind of problems selected by Terman for the first scale. He had selected only those problems which showed age increments and which proved easier for the "good marks" group of pupils. Therefore, when he used "mental age" as determined by the first scale to "validate" his choice of problems for the second Stanford-Binet, he chose only problems which were highly related to the problems on the first scale.

Cultural Influences in Group Tests

The recent makers of group tests have erred in selecting problems; as a rule, just as did Binet and Terman. For his "Alpha" nonverbal test, Otis selected only those problems which discriminate against "retarded" pupils. He explains:

> Pupils were divided into two groups -- a "good group" and a "poor group" -- according to whether the pupils were advanced or retarded for their ages. The value of each item was then investigated as follows: The per cent of the "good group" which passed each item was found and the per cent of the "poor group" which passed each item was found. Only those items were retained which showed a distinct difference between those two per cents / 70, p. 13/.

But we know that those groups of children in elementary schools who are retarded in grade placement are overwhelmingly from the lower socioeconomic groups.[2] Therefore, Otis' method, like Binet's and Terman's, rules out all problems on which the lower socioeconomic groups are

2. See, e.g., the evidence presented on pp. 111-14 of the present volume.

equal or superior to the top socioeconomic groups.

Otis likewise says that he preferred geometric items for the same reason, that is, they discriminate more clearly against the "retarded" pupil:

> Since the first investigation showed a tendency for "geometric" items to be more valid /i.e., to be relatively harder for low socioeconomic groups/ than purely pictorial items, more "geometric" items were added / 70, p. 13/.

To validate the second and third experimental editions of the test, Otis used a "good group," which ranked highest on a composite score; this composite score was based upon a pupil's scores in earlier forms of Otis' tests and upon the pupil's grade-age position. Both these criteria for selecting problems, of course, also penalize the low socioeconomic groups, for (a) such groups are more often retarded and (b) the previous forms of the test had been made so as to give them lower average scores.

Otis used the same method to select items for his "Alpha" verbal test. Unlike most other test-makers, however, Otis states specifically that there is a heavy cultural influence in verbal tests (70, p. 14). But he does not recommend that his verbal test should, therefore, not be used to measure the "mental ability" of the lower socioeconomic groups in the United States.

Otis likewise chose only those problems for his "Beta" test (Grades IV-IX) which were easier for those pupils "who were making rapid progress through school" and much more difficult for those pupils "who were making slow progress through school." The same error exists, therefore, in the validation of this test.

Henmon and Nelson used the same kind of circular reasoning in selecting their problems. They explain: "Only such items as proved to differentiate between pupils of known superior and known inferior mental ability were retained" (66, p. 1). In other words, no independent measure of validity was found.

Edward B. Greene, author of a standard text on measurement, illustrates in a chapter on the construction and evaluation of test items the "best method" for selecting items. This method divides the group of pupils (on whom "validation" is being based) into thirds, judged by their total scores on the experimental form of the test. An item is considered a "valid" item if a higher percentage of the top third of pupils (judged by total scores) passes it than of the lowest third. Any item, on which the performance of the lowest third is as good as, or superior to, that of the highest third, is to be thrown out! (65, pp. 121-23).

Thus it is impossible to get a range of types of problems in the test. Since the author always starts with academic types of problems, and since the "top third" of the pupils on these academic-like problems will be chiefly the middle-class pupils, the test inevitably will include more and more such academic problems. The "lowest third" of pupils, who will be chiefly in the lowest socioeconomic groups, will not be allowed to show, in the final test, any of the activities at which they are superior or equal!

Terman and McNemar selected for their group test only those items which showed "successive increments from Grades 7 to 9 to 11, in the percentages /of pupils/ giving correct responses. . . . The average per cent passing an item for the three grades was used as the final measure of item difficulty" (72, p. 1). Although they did not use pupils' ratings and grade placement as criteria for selecting items, they got the same result as those test-makers who did. Actually, their group test has a higher proportion of items which discriminate between high and low socioeconomic groups, at ages thirteen and fourteen, than either the Otis or the California Mental Maturity tests.

The reason for this high socioeconomic discrimination is that Terman and McNemar chose a very narrow range of academic problems, all of which were verbal. As we have pointed out, middle-class pupils really are "older" mentally on such problems. Therefore, if one restricts his test to academic-like areas, he will get very high discrimination between socioeconomic groups, even if he overtly selects problems merely because they show age differentiation. He has already discriminated effectively against the low socioeconomic groups by deciding to use only verbal analogies, verbal opposites, syllogisms, etc. He gets significant increases in the percentage of pupils passing such items between Grades VII and IX, and IX and XI, because the pace of verbal learning and training increases in middle class, as compared with lower class, at these ages. Furthermore, since he chooses those items which show the largest increment from age to age, in percentage passing, he selects exactly those items which are relatively easiest for the children of the higher socioeconomic status, for we have found that it is the middle-class pupils who are responsible for the big age jumps in percentage passing this kind of item. Their progress in verbal school training is accelerating at these ages (eleven to sixteen years), whereas the rate of the low socioeconomic groups is decreasing.

The difficulty in solving the problem of test validity has led Terman into some novel arguments. Thus he and McNemar say with regard to their group test:

> In the early days of the development of group tests of mental ability an attempt was made to validate them by correlating the scores with teachers' marks. As has been pointed out many times in the intervening years this procedure is unsatisfactory because of the serious shortcomings in teachers' judgments of mental ability. The best evidence of the validity of the Terman test is to be found in its successful use over the period of years since the test was first issued. Many instances may be cited where the Terman test has been used with great success in guidance and administration. In some situations where the use of the Terman test with entering high school students has been made a standard practice, it has been found that year after year those students who were graduated with honors were those who made scores in the highest range of the test. The correlation of the revised test with the original test is .91, which indicates that the new test can be considered to be measuring essentially the same basic abilities covered by the original forms / 72, pp. 3-4 /.

Exactly what is it, however, that pupils who ranked high on this test have also accomplished? They have received high ratings from their teachers! Another criterion used by Terman and McNemar for selecting problems was

> the tetrachoric correlation of each item with the total score based on all three test forms / computed for Grades VII, IX, and XI separately 7. . . . No item was retained which yielded an average tetra-

choric correlation / for the three grades 7 of less than .30 and only 10 per cent of the final items have validities of less than .40. The average coefficient for all retained items was .53 / 72, pp. 1-2 /.

This is still a circular "validation." The fact that successes on an item correlated significantly with successes on the whole test simply indicates that this individual item requires use of the same, or closely related, aspects of problem-solving as the whole test. But it does not indicate that the whole test is a representative sample of mental problems, nor does it set up any independent measure of mental ability. It simply says that the test is of one piece.[3] But that is exactly why the test does not measure general mental ability; it is restricted to verbal systems of academic problems. Kuhlmann and others likewise have used this criterion, of significant correlation between an item and the total score, as a basis for selecting each item.

The authors of the California Test of Mental Maturity have stated that they have found "no purely objective criteria" to use in validation (71, p. 2). Instead they have relied upon significant correlations with other tests of "mental ability" and upon "samplings" of "factors." From our point of view, a high correlation with other tests may merely indicate that the test is characterized by the same kind of bias as the other tests.

The effort to validate the test by means of factor sampling follows Thurstone's method. Thurstone himself, however, has depended upon conventional academic types of problems. To select problems so as to obtain "factorial saturations" does not of itself meet the basic requirements for a fair test. First, one must sample a wide range of "factors." One must also, and above everything else, see that the "factors" are expressed in common cultural symbols. Verbal comprehension, for instance, must be tested in the language of the respondent. The lower socioeconomic groups, however, talk in their own language, which is, from the middle-class point of view, a "dialect."

By far the best theoretical analysis of the unsound basis of "validation" used by test-makers has been that of Kuhlmann and Anderson. These authors see clearly the errors in present tests, and by common sense they have done a little to improve them, but nothing to validate adequately their choice of items. They have simply selected those items for which the percentage of correct answers increases most rapidly with age of pupils (69, pp. 6-9). We have already shown that this method, when applied to academic types of problems, inevitably leads to the selection of those specific verbal, pictorial, or geometric problems in which middle-class pupils are most superior.

Kuhlmann recognizes the bias which may exist in the selection both

---

3. Yerkes, analyzing the correlations of the separate subtests in the Army verbal tests (1917) with the total weighted scores, found that any subtest which correlated highly with total score likewise correlated significantly with the other subtests. Greene, summarizing this work, concludes that "it is impossible to secure subtests which will correlate highly with a criterion, and nearly zero with each other" (65, p. 307). The Army tests were "validated" also by the circular process of showing that they were significantly related to other measures of a similar kind, namely: school accomplishment, Stanford-Binet scores, and ratings by officers.

of mental areas and of specific problems:

In selecting tests, the utmost care should be exercised in finding what is universal and common to all in both school and home.
The final answer to how near any test comes to meeting this requirement can be reached only through extensive research, of which relatively little has yet been done. . . . The present selection of our
tests as regards this factor was done, of course, by inspection. The
research necessary to determine this question experimentally would
have been far more extensive than all the rest taken together $\underline{/\,68,}$
p. 5 $\underline{/}$.

Conclusion

In spite of the vast amount of research done with regard to other
aspects of the present tests, there has been no adequate research carried
out to effect (a) the discovery of problems and symbols that are equally
familiar and motivating to all socioeconomic groups or (b) the discovery
of the proportion of items that favor rural as compared to urban groups.
Since test-makers have been largely unaware of the cultural influences
upon both school and test behavior, they have not understood that their
chief method of so-called "validation" is circular. To prove that a given
problem, or test, measures problem-solving behavior, one must find a
significant positive relationship between that test and some independent
measure of problem-solving activity. But teachers' ratings of pupils are
not independent of the activity measured by the standard tests. The tests
include chiefly verbal or picture problems, based upon highly abstract
academic concepts — so does the school curriculum. Therefore, a teacher's rating of a pupil is an estimate of the pupil's performance on the
same kind of problems as those in the standard tests. Grade placement,
likewise, is a measure of a pupil's success on this same kind of academic
problem. Neither the teachers' ratings nor grade placement, therefore,
may be used as an independent measure against which a test of general
problem-solving behavior can be validated.

Furthermore, as Binet himself pointed out, school achievement depends largely upon traits of character rather than upon mental capacity
-- upon attention, drive, desire for success in the middle-class culture.
Lack of this drive causes the children of low socioeconomic groups to
do poor school work. Thus, teachers' ratings are partly an index of work
habits and motivation as well as of mental capacity.

To justify their choice of types of problems, the test-makers have
claimed that their verbal, abstract, and academic types measure the so-
called "basic mental processes," the same processes which would be involved in more lifelike problems. This claim is based upon the concept
that intelligence is not a system of behaviors but is a substance, an entity,
which pervades all its manifestations; or the claim that it is a number of
such entities. This theory is hopeless as a guide to research; it has led,
on the one hand, to literally hundreds of "definitions" of intelligence; on
the other hand, to the setting-up of a few academic "categories" of intel-
lectuality, which are supposed to be the "basic" manifestations of human
intelligence. When one examines them in a comparative framework, however, they are seen to be only the most basic mental activities in school
work, in academic problem-solving.

To escape from the real problem, which is to get some measure of

a subject's general mental potential for problem-solving — the problem
which Binet at first set himself -- the later test-makers have gradually
shifted to the ground that the primary aim of a test of mental ability
should be to predict school achievement! So long, however, as "intelligence tests" are designed only to predict achievement in terms of the
present curriculums of the schools, so long will their items be too limited in mental range, in cultural content, and in intrinsic motivation, to
be capable of measuring the general problem-solving activities of human
beings. Good tests of problem-solving activities, like good curriculums,
must deal with a wider range of mental problems (logical, organizational,
inventive) than those now touched upon by the usual curriculums. They
must discover and tap a great many areas of mental talent and of problem-solving skills which simply are not included within the present
academic view of the human intellect.

CHAPTER VI

CAN INTELLIGENCE TESTS BE USED TO PREDICT EDUCABILITY?[1]

By Ralph W. Tyler, Dean, Division of the Social Sciences and
University Examiner, University of Chicago, Chicago, Illinois

Any discussion of educability is likely to bog down in confusion. Much of this confusion is caused by failure to distinguish the theoretical from the operational definitions of educability. The term "educability" implies a potentiality for education existing in an individual or in a group of individuals, whether or not these individuals actually become educated, but the existence of educability can be demonstrated only by their actual response to educational opportunities. Hence, although we can theoretically postulate certain characteristics which, if possessed by persons, provide the essential potential of their education, nevertheless, any objective test of such postulates requires the demonstration that persons with these characteristics actually respond to educational opportunities while those without them do not. Therefore, any tested concept of educability is dependent on the kind of educational opportunities that are available.

It is possible to conceive of persons who are educable but for whom we have not yet devised appropriate educational programs. We cannot demonstrate this concept, however, until we devise these programs. This limitation is serious since, as almost everyone will admit, our present educational opportunities are not ideal and are restricted both in terms of the concept of ends to be attained by education and in terms of the adequacy of the means for education. Hence, a more comprehensive understanding of educability is dependent partly on the development of more adequate educational opportunities and on experimentation with more varied means of education.

In relation to the schools, educability is particularly involved in this confusion growing out of our failure to recognize that its operational definition depends on the objectives of, and the available opportunities for, education, whereas its theoretical definition is not so limited. From the standpoint of the practical work of the schools, the problem of educability can take one of two forms. The first form can be stated in the following terms: Given our present American schools, with the ends which they accept and the means which they provide, what measurable characteristics of persons can be used to predict the extent to which these persons will do successful work in the schools? The second form can be stated as follows: What measurable characteristics of persons can be identified that reveal abilities which can be developed into socially or personally valuable behavior if school programs are planned and administered to capitalize on these abilities?

1. Adapted from material first published in the Elementary School
Journal (75).

The first formulation of the problem accepts American schools as they are with reference both to ends and to means. Expressed in operational terms, the problem becomes one of finding in individuals measurable characteristics which are correlated with success in these schools.

The second problem, on the other hand, does not accept American schools as they now are; it does not consider the present ends and means as fixed. In operational terms, the second problem is one of identifying and measuring characteristics that, on hypothetical grounds, are basic to various types of learning and then of experimenting with persons possessing these characteristics to discover whether they have potential talents that can, through learning, become personally or socially significant. In a sense, the second problem can never be answered once and for all, but it becomes a matter for continuing long-term research. The failure to distinguish between these two problems causes much of the current controversy over educability as a concept guiding school practices.

The First Formulation

The research conducted over the past fifty years has been particularly significant in dealing with the first formulation of the problem. The pioneer work of Binet in developing intelligence tests was quickly seized on by research workers in this country. Many American scientists constructed psychological tests and validated them largely in terms of their correlation with the success of pupils in our present American schools. Thousands of studies have been made of the results of these tests. From these investigations we know that, of all the characteristics measured, facility in the use of words is most highly correlated with success in American schools. This is to say that so-called "verbal intelligence" is a major aspect of educability when educability is defined as ability to succeed in typical American schools.

From the researches of Allison Davis (2) and others we also know that it is not verbal facility in terms of the vocabulary characteristic of the individual's own social group that is highly correlated with success in American schools but rather his facility in the use of middle-class vocabulary. Lower-class children use a great many words, and a number of them use these words with a high degree of precision, but facility with words commonly used by the lower classes is not correlated with success in school. In general, our present American schools are most successful with children who have a large middle-class vocabulary and who use these middle-class words with a fair degree of precision.

Research of the last fifty years has also demonstrated that the ability to handle number relations, sometimes referred to as the "quantitative factor" in intelligence, has some relation to success in contemporary American schools although the correlation is considerably lower than that between verbal facility and success. This quantitative factor is of most significance in mathematics and engineering. Even in these fields, however, the verbal factor shows a somewhat higher correlation with students' marks than does the quantitative factor. Although many other so-called "factors of intelligence," such as spatial factors, reasoning factors, and the like, have been measured, none of them has a high relationship with success in most courses in the present American schools. Hence, so far as the factors now measured by intelligence tests are concerned, it is possible to appraise educability for the majority of school courses primarily in terms of verbal facility and secondarily in terms of quantitative factors. Furthermore, it is possible to indicate, at least roughly, the mental age required on specified intelligence tests for success in particular school systems.

Recent research has made further contributions to the solution of the problem of educability as first formulated. Certain other components of educability have been identified in addition to those measured by intelligence tests. Of these, motivation to learn school tasks, or, in general, to do good work in school, has a significant correlation with school success. With intelligence-test scores held constant, the correlation between measures of interest in school work and average marks in school is usually positive, averaging about .30. This compares with a mean of about .50 for the correlation between intelligence-test scores and success as measured by average school marks. Furthermore, motivation is particularly significant in predicting the number of years of schooling which a person will get. The primary differentials between those students who graduate from high school and go on to college and those who drop out after graduating from high school are income of the parents and interest in school work.

In recognizing the importance of motivation as a factor in educability, it is necessary also to realize that motivation is not an inherent characteristic deeply based in the biological mechanism of a human being. Much of individual motivation is acquired from a variety of sources; even school experiences themselves may sharply modify the motivation of an individual. Studies in child development at a number of centers indicate that the parents' attitude toward the school greatly affects the child's motivation. If the parents look on the school as a means by which their children can attain greater opportunities than they themselves have had and if they place great emphasis on their children's success in school, the probabilities are more than two to one that the children will show interest in succeeding in school. On the other hand — and this is particularly characteristic of many lower-class parents — if the school is viewed as a "sissy institution," a place in which children must remain until the compulsory attendance law permits them to do useful work, then it is likely that the children's attitude toward school will be negative and their corresponding motivation low.

The child's experience in school also affects his motivation. If he is encouraged by the teacher, is reasonably successful, and is happy in his relations with other children in school, it is again likely that motivation will be positive. On the other hand, when the teacher views the child as a "dirty little brat" who never seems to learn and who usually makes trouble for him, it is likely that motivation will be low and will decrease as the child moves through school. Hence, although motivation is an important factor in educability, it is neither an inherent factor in the individual nor a constant one. It is affected by home environment, cultural contacts, attitudes of the child's peer group, and school experiences.

In contemporary American schools it is possible to measure motivation with a fair degree of accuracy by the time the child has reached Grade IV or V and, from these measurements, to make predictions about his later success. Interestingly enough, motivation so measured at this stage in the pupil's development rarely changes markedly from this time until the end of high school. However, it is likely that this relatively fixed index of motivation is not attributable to the principle that motivation

is inevitably fixed by the age of ten or eleven but is more probably due to the fact that the home, community, and school environment are so consistent in the kinds of things they emphasize over the years that there is no compensating condition affecting the children to modify the type of motivation developed in the first few grades of school. Thus, with American schools as they now are, it is possible to measure and predict motivation with a fair degree of precision by the middle of the elementary school.

With the findings of scientific studies and the instruments of measurement which have been developed, it is possible to appraise educability, in terms of the first formulation of the problem, with a fair degree of precision. As long as American schools and colleges remain as they are, it is possible to predict the success of individuals in these institutions at the elementary-school level, at the high-school level, and at the college level. It is possible to identify children and youth who will drop out. It is possible to find the so-called "superior" students at a fairly early age and to provide for their continued education. It is possible to administer a system of state or national scholarships to provide for the advanced education of those students who are educable in this sense. On the whole, the sciences of psychology, sociology, education, and statistics have made contributions to this field which have not only theoretical, but immense practical, value.

The Second Formulation

Our past success in dealing with the first formulation of the problem of educability, however, should not blind us to the fact that this is not a satisfactory formulation for a long-term program. The identification of persons who are educable in our present schools and colleges and the definition of the characteristics associated with success in school are inadequate because our schools and colleges as they are now conducted are not ideal and do not accomplish all that an enlightened citizenship would expect of a comprehensive system of elementary, secondary, and higher education. There are several respects in which the present practices in American schools and colleges are inadequate to deal with educability in the sense of the second formulation of the problem, namely, to provide opportunity for the development of all talents which persons possess that can be trained for desirable personal and social ends.

The aims of the schools

The schools are inadequate, in the first place, with reference to their real aims. By and large, although there are many noteworthy exceptions, American schools and colleges place primary exphasis on memorization of textbook content and on the development of certain limited subject skills, like computation in arithmetic, grammatical usage in English, and reading at the plain sense level of interpretation. The development of an intelligent person — one who is able to analyze problems, to think them through clearly, and to bring to bear on them a wide variety of information, who understands and cherishes significant and desirable social and personal values, who can formulate and carry out a plan of action in the light of his knowledge and values — is not the goal toward which schools and colleges are aiming in practice. Yet it is an end which is essential to the adequate education of a competent citizenry.

Furthermore, in a world as complex as ours, a wide variety of special abilities and talents can be utilized. The tendency of the schools to capitalize solely on verbal abilities does not take into account what could be gained by more adequately educating persons who have other talents which are needed but which are often unidentified and usually untrained. If broader objectives were aimed at by the schools and colleges, it is quite conceivable that the characteristics of persons who are educable in this sense are more varied than is indicated by previous studies in which the objectives of the schools and colleges are so narrow and the requirements of school and college education are so largely those of a verbal sort. If we seek to educate those persons whose thought, feeling, and action are unified and guided by a high sense of social values and a broad understanding of the situations with which they deal, it is probable that the factors important in educability for such purposes are more extensive than those which have been identified in previous studies.

At this point the question may be raised: Why do the so-called "general intelligence tests" fail to give us an indication of a variety of abilities that could be developed if the aims of schools were broader? By and large, the general intelligence tests used in America have been validated by checking each item in terms of the relative school success of those persons answering the item correctly and persons failing the item. This procedure has resulted in the elimination of items that do not show this kind of differentiation in terms of school success. An item on which students who get poor marks in the present school do just as well as students who get good marks will not be retained. As might be expected, this practice increases the validity of the test as a means of predicting success in contemporary American schools, but it has caused the elimination of a number of items which are nonverbal in character and has heavily weighted intelligence tests with verbal items, and particularly with items that involve academic and middle-class vocabulary.

Eells[2] and Murray (4) have shown that more than three-fourths of all items in the most widely used intelligence tests of today sharply differentiate middle-class from lower-class children. They have also shown that lower-class children are frequently familiar with the object or the phenomenon named in the vocabulary item but that they do not have the same terms for referring to it. Furthermore, so far as problem-solving exercises are concerned, the typical intelligence tests lean heavily on academic, school-type problems, whereas lower-class children frequently have had more experience than have middle-class children in dealing with the kinds of practical problems encountered on the street and in the playground. That is to say, it seems clear from such researches that youngsters who do not show up well on intelligence tests do possess abilities that indicate some skill in solving practical problems and that suggest potentialities for further education if the schools had broad enough goals to utilize talents of these kinds.

The means used by the schools

Not only do our present schools and colleges fail to aim at a broad set of ends, but they also are inadequate with respect to means. For example, the medium of communication and of expression in the schools is largely a verbal one. Although most educators recognize the existence

2. See Part III of the present volume.

43

of a wide range of mediums of communication, including pictures, diagrams, motion pictures, radio, and other auditory materials, as well as concrete experiences in laboratories, shops, and in the community, the typical American school makes little use of these nonverbal means of communication. A child who has not already developed a middle-class vocabulary and who comes from a home in which the words used by teachers and textbooks are not common finds it difficult to benefit from school work because of the failure of the school to provide a wide range of mediums of communication to draw to any great extent on the child's experience as a basis for learning. It seems probable that, if the schools used a wider range of mediums of communication, we should find many persons more educable than now seems true because we should have more avenues for communicating with them and more avenues of expression by which they could demonstrate their learning and continue practice until their learning became more adequate. The broadening of the mediums of communication and expression used in schools and colleges should make it possible to identify wider ranges of talent with which the school could work effectively. This extension would then broaden our concept of educability.

Inadequate use of motivation

A second inadequacy in the means of education used in American schools to capitalize on all the existing learning potential is the employment of motivation, including rewards and punishments, that has primary significance only for the middle class. Warner, Havighurst, and Loeb, in their little volume, Who Shall Be Educated?, have spelled out the implications of recent research on the social-class structure of American society for the motivation of school learning (14). Middle-class children are typically encouraged by their parents to do good school work. The ideals held by teachers, such as cleanliness, "good language," neatness, avoiding fights, and the like, are the ideals emphasized in middle-class homes — ideals which middle-class children generally accept and approve. On the other hand, these ideals have not been emphasized for lower-class children nor made a part of their value system. School work is not highly regarded in most lower-class homes. Cleanliness is difficult for them to attain and is not usually emphasized by lower-class parents. Fighting is viewed as desirable, not something to avoid. In most cases, to refuse to fight would mean that the child would be injured and would lose status with his playmates. Hence, in our present American schools, teachers expect lower-class children to follow a value system which, in many instances, is in opposition to the one which they follow outside the school. Furthermore, most middle-class teachers are unable to mask their disgust at the language, the filth, the odor, and the rough behavior of lower-class children. As a result, many lower-class children receive little encouragement at school and almost no rewards and symbols of success.

Thus, when these children bring any talents to school, their talents are not likely to be developed in the classroom; for the methods used for motivation by the teachers are likely to inhibit, rather than to develop, learning among these children. As long as the problem of educability is viewed only in the first sense, as that of identifying those pupils who can get along in schools as they are now constituted, it is clear that our present tests and devices serve rather satisfactorily. If, on the other hand, our concern is to identify characteristics indicating abilities that could

44

be educated under appropriate learning conditions, it is evident that the present methods used in schools may fail to capitalize on some of these abilities. It is, therefore, necessary for us to find out what abilities exist that have learning potentials and to experiment with ways of modifying the schools so as to make the most of the talents the children bring with them.

Limitation of experience

A third respect in which the practices of our present schools are inadequate to capitalize on potential educability is the narrow limitation in the areas of experience with which schools commonly deal. The fact that writers of textbooks and teachers have come from a fairly restricted middle-class environment may account to a great extent for the limiting of the content of elementary-school reading materials and of the books used in other subjects to those aspects of life which are largely middle-class in character. Elementary school books do not deal with homes as they are known by a large percentage of American children. The books in use treat of business, industry, politics, and the professions, usually in terms of the white-collar participant, rather than in terms that would be most understandable to a large fraction of the children. In so far as background experience is essential or helpful in providing for school learning, the work of the schools has not adequately capitalized on the wide range of background experience which a majority of their children possess.

Lack of practice

A fourth respect in which American schools do not capitalize on all the potential educable characteristics of their pupils is the way in which practice or repetition is employed. Research in learning has clearly demonstrated the importance that practice or repetition has for effective learning. Things to be learned must be practiced again and again under favorable conditions of motivation. Many of the things taught in school, such as reading and writing and arithmetic, require continuous practice over long periods of time for any sort of full development.

The researches of sociologists and social anthropologists indicate that middle-class children carry on a great deal of this practice outside the school, in the home, and under the supervision of the home. On the other hand, in a large majority of cases, children from lower-class homes do not have the opportunity or the stimulus for practice of school work. Consequently, an important aspect required for effective learning is inadequately provided for many pupils. If the schools were to become conscious of this lack, it seems probably that some means could be devised for extending opportunities for practice of school learning under conditions that would be appropriate and possible for lower-class children, and thus this essential for effective learning would not so often be neglected.

Social Effects of the First Formulation

From the standpoint of its social effects, perhaps the most serious result of attacking the problem of educability in terms simply of predicting the success of children in our present schools has been the way in which this practice has tended to deny more adequate educational opportunity to those students who need it most. In his studies of acculturation in the Southwest, Davis (62) has shown that it is common to test children of Negro background, Mexican background, and lower-class children in general with the existing verbal intelligence tests. Their test results are low and are often interpreted by the school administration as indicating very limited potentiality for education. This interpretation serves, on the one hand, to justify teachers in expending little effort in teaching these children, on the grounds that there is not much chance of their learning anyway; and it also serves to justify providing inadequate buildings, poorer teachers, and heavier pupil-teacher ratios for the areas in which these children live. Teachers and principals are not encouraged to devise ways of capitalizing on the talents the children possess when the results of such measurement indicate little or no talent available for education.

Suggestions for Improvement

Although the majority of studies of educability to date have been concerned with predicting the success of children in our present schools and colleges, there have been some other lines of experimentation that suggest promising leads for the future. Special work with superior children, schools for backward children, work with emotionally disturbed children, experimentation with juvenile delinquents and with various types of mental deficiency -- all indicate clearly that the potentialities for some kind of learning of children and youth at all levels, from the most superior to the least, are greater than are commonly realized.

Our present schools and colleges do not achieve anything like the results that are suggested by the potentialities indicated by these experiments. Typical schools -- although there are many noteworthy exceptions -- are doing a rather unimaginative job in providing learning opportunities for those pupils already motivated by the home, children whose homes provide practice that accounts for further development of learning. There should be a narrowing of this great gap between the level of present school practice and the potentialities for learning which is indicated by many experimental studies.

What is needed is an attack on two fronts: (a) on the identification and measurement of abilities which indicate talents that can be developed by educational means and (b) on experimentation with learning, so that we may know how to capitalize on the talents that are thus identified. The first type of investigation will require a rethinking of the whole intelligence-tests problem. In place of seeking validation in terms of school marks, we shall need to look for successful problem-solving in all aspects of life, not only for middle-class children, but also for lower-class pupils. We shall need to study the kinds of problems these children attack; the ways in which they attack these problems; the respects in which their solutions are more or less appropriate; the ways in which the problems are symbolized by different children -- whether in words or in other forms; and, eventually, to devise ways of testing for a wide range of problem-solving abilities, so that we can identify in children a more complete range of potentialities for meeting new situations, that is, abilities to learn.

No doubt this investigation will call for the use of a variety of tests, in addition to paper-and-pencil intelligence tests. It will certainly mean the use of nonverbal as well as verbal materials. However, if we can really identify, in children in all walks of life, a wide range of abilities to learn, we shall have made an important contribution to the concept of educability.

Hand in hand with this development of ways of measuring potential educability must go a wider attack on learning in school and in other controlled experimental conditions. Even as the measurement of potential educability can be guided somewhat by indications of what children are learning outside the school, so studies of children outside the school — studies of the kinds of abilities now utilized by children in informal situations, the mediums of communication they use, the kinds of symbols they employ, the motives they have, and other matters related to learning — should enable us to see more clearly the ways in which we can use learning theory to capitalize on a wide range of abilities not now utilized by typical American schools. The construction of these measures of more varied potentialities for learning and the development of more adequate ends and means of learning will make an intellectual and social contribution of great magnitude.

Making children more effective and happy in their lives and creating for society benefits which result from the training and development of a much larger range of talents are important reasons for emphasizing concentration of study on these two phases of an important American problem. We have learned a great deal about educability for our present school programs, but we have only scratched the surface when it comes to understanding educability in the broadest possible framework of what American schools could be. May the next fifty years bring as marked a contribution to this problem as the last fifty years have done to the first problem.

PART   II

A   SUMMARY   OF   THE   FIELD   STUDY

By Kenneth Eells, Associate Professor of Psychology
San Diego State College, San Diego, California

CHAPTER VII

WHAT WERE THE MAJOR PROCEDURES
AND FINDINGS OF THE STUDY?

Previous chapters have explored various aspects of the general problem of the relationship between children's performance on intelligence tests and the cultural, or social-status, backgrounds of the children. This is the setting against which to consider a rather extensive research investigation, the more detailed account of which constitutes Part III of the present monograph.

Since the complete report of the research study is somewhat lengthy, and in some parts moderately technical, the general nature of the procedures and of the more important findings of the study will be reported in the present chapter. The material included here should be sufficient for intelligent reading of the two chapters which follow, which suggest interpretations and conclusions to be drawn from the findings of the study. The reader is urged, however, to refer to the more detailed account of procedures and findings, contained in Part III, on any points which are not clear in this briefer summary, or on any points of particular interest to him. Frequent cross-references are included in this chapter to facilitate use of the material in Part III.

Statement of the Problem

The study analyzes the behavior of pupils from high and low social-status backgrounds on more than 650 items in several widely used group intelligence tests. Its principal purpose is to provide a basis for tentative inferences, and for further research, dealing with the extent to which group differences in I.Q.'s, as between cultural status groups, may be due to the presence in the tests of materials drawn more largely from the cultural characteristic of high-status pupils than from that with which low-status pupils are familiar. More specifically, the study was designed to answer the seven questions stated in chapter i.[1]

Summary of Procedures

There were four steps in the procedures used: (a) collection of the test data, (b) securing of a socioeconomic or social-status classification of the pupils, (c) analysis of the relation between social status and I.Q.'s secured from the tests, and (d) analysis of individual item responses in terms of several subgroups of pupils.

The first step was the collection of basic test data. A battery of standard intelligence tests was given in January, 1946, to nearly five thousand white pupils of ages nine, ten, thirteen, and fourteen. The pupils tested constituted practically all the white pupils at these age levels in a midwestern industrial community of approximately 100,000 population. One set of four tests was given to the nine- and ten-year-old pupils; another set of five tests was given to the thirteen- and fourteen-year-olds. The basis for selecting the community, the age levels, and the tests are described in chapter x, which also describes how the tests were administered and scored.

For the families of most of these children an index of socioeconomic status was computed. This index was based upon ratings of the occupation of parents, education of parents, house type, and dwelling area. It is a modification of an index developed and tested by Warner and his associates in another community. Field data were available, from a study of the community in which the testing was done, for validating this index in terms of social-class participation and status. On the basis of the index, three groups of children were selected, one high-status group and two low-status groups, the latter divided on the basis of ethnicity. The various aspects of this procedure are described in detail in chapter xi. In chapters xii and xiii the three special status groups — and the total group of pupils — are described in terms of representativeness, chronological age, school attended, grade placement, intelligence quotients, socioeconomic status, ethnicity, and social class. This is done both by means of statistical data and through brief case descriptions of typical individuals from the different status groups.

The relationship of social status to I.Q.'s (or to percentile ranks on certain tests) was analyzed both by correlation procedures involving the total group of pupils at each age level and by comparing the mean I.Q.'s and the distributions of I.Q.'s for the three special status groups. Special attention was given to determining whether the relationship between I.Q. and cultural status is more or less uniform along the entire status scale, or whether there are critical points at which the nature of the relationship changes (chaps. xiv and xv).

The relationship of social status to the responses on more than 650 individual items was analyzed by computing the percentage passing each item for each of the three special status groups separately. The inter-group differences for all items were tested for statistical significance. In order to make the unit of status difference equivalent at all points on the scale, all percentages (except for the ethnic pupils) were then converted into a normalized index and status differences determined in terms of this index (chaps. xvi and xvii).

The relationship between size of status difference and various objective factors was then analyzed by comparing mean status differences for groups of items categorized according to (a) test, (b) position of the correct response among the distractors, (c) form of symbolism in which the item was expressed, (d) type of question asked by the item, and (e) difficulty of the item. In the latter case, correlation procedures were also used (chaps. xvii-xx).

The possible relation of status differences to age of the pupils was studied by (a) contrasting the status differences on items given to the nine- and ten-year-old pupils with those on items given to the thirteen- and fourteen-year-old pupils and (b) contrasting the status differences for nine-year-olds with those for ten-year-olds, and the status differences for thirteen-year-olds with those for fourteen-year-olds, on identical test items (chap. xxi).

---

1. See pp. 6-7.

A large number of individual items showing atypical status differences either with respect to the pattern of wrong responses or with respect to the proportion of right responses were then examined on a subjective basis, and a number of tentative hypotheses suggested as possible explanations for the unusual status differences found (chaps. xxii and xxiii).

Summary of Major Findings

The seven questions with which the investigation began will here be answered briefly, without extended discussion and without presentation of the detailed evidence underlying each answer, since this is reported in detail in Part III. Chapter references are provided so that the reader who may wish to refer to the original evidence on any point may do so easily.

1. What is the degree and nature of the relationship between I.Q.'s and cultural or status level?

Correlations between I.Q.'s (or percentile ranks on certain tests) and the Index of Status Characteristics vary with the test used and the age level tested. They are moderate in size (.20 to .43) and are all definitely significant in the statistical sense. The correlation is linear for the thirteen- and fourteen-year-old pupils but is not linear for the nine- and ten-year-olds. In the latter case the relationship is linear for social-status ranges below the lower limit of the upper-middle class; within the upper-middle and upper classes, however, there is no observable relationship between social status and I.Q. (chap. xiv).

When the special high- and low-status groups are contrasted, the mean I.Q.'s of the high-status pupils are from 8 to 23 I.Q. points higher than those for the low-status pupils, with the amount varying from test to test and from age level to age level (chap. xv).

Despite the average superiority of high-status pupils on each of the tests, there is a large amount of overlapping at all social-status levels, with many high-status pupils receiving low scores and many low-status pupils securing high scores (chaps. xiv and xv).

2. Do children from high-status homes do better than children from low-status homes on all items in the intelligence test in about the same proportion, or is there wide variation among the different items?

About half of the items in the tests for nine- and ten-year-old pupils and about 85 per cent of the items in the tests for the thirteen- and fourteen-year-old pupils show differences between high- and low-status groups large enough to be significant at the 1 per cent level. On the other hand, more than a third of the items from the tests for the younger pupils, and about a tenth of those from the tests for the older pupils, show status differences too small to be significant even at the 5 per cent level. For a number of items these insignificant differences may be due to the item being either extremely easy or extremely difficult for both status groups. There are twenty-seven items, however, which show insignificant differences even though the items are at neither extreme of difficulty (chap. xvii).

Further evidence that status differences vary from item to item is found in the fact that, when the items are grouped according to test, form of symbolism used, type of question asked, and level of difficulty, signif-

icant variations in mean status difference appear (chaps. xvii, xix, and xx).

3. If the items are grouped into categories on such bases as type of symbols used, type of question asked, placing of the correct answer in relation to the distractors, and difficulty of the item, are there significant differences in the status differences shown by different types of items?

Mean status differences are largest for verbal and smallest for picture, geometric-design, and stylized-drawing items. The dispersion of status differences is greater for verbal and for picture items than it is for geometric-design, stylized-drawing, number-combination, or letter-combination items (chap. xix).

Mean status differences for different types of test questions (opposites, analogies, etc.) vary from category to category, but no consistent trends appear, and no meaningful generalization appears to be possible regarding the types of questions showing large or small differences, provided the form of symbolism is held constant (chap. xix).

For no type of item do mean status differences vary significantly with the position of the correct response in relation to the distractors (chap. xviii).

Status differences for verbal items are fairly closely related (r = .46 to .62) to the difficulty of the items as determined for high-status pupils, with the easier items showing the larger status differences. The relationship of status difference to difficulty is stronger when difficulty is determined for high-status pupils than when determined for low-status pupils, and it is stronger for the nine- and ten-year-old pupils than for the thirteen- and fourteen-year-olds. Status differences for nonverbal items are not so markedly related to difficulty of the item. For the nine- and ten-year-old pupils there is some tendency for the relationship for nonverbal items to be a negative one, with the easier items showing the smaller status differences, and also a tendency for the status differences to be related to the degree of difficulty for the low-status pupils rather than that for high-status pupils (chap. xx).

4. If there are certain items which show significantly greater intercultural differences than others, do these items have anything in common which might help to explain their larger differences? Do those items which show little or no difference have anything in common?

Practically all the items showing unusually large status differences are verbal in symbolism. A substantial number of them involve what appears to be a relatively academic or bookish vocabulary. A number of them involve words, objects, or concepts with which high-status pupils probably have more opportunity for familiarity through home and other nonschool experiences. A number of such items also appear to involve definite school learning. There are a substantial number of items, however, which show unusually large status differences for which no particular explanation is apparent, and through which runs no common factor (other than their verbal symbolism) that is apparent to the present writer (chaps. xxii and xxiii).

Items which show small differences are almost without exception either nonverbal in symbolism or involve simple everyday words which do not appear to be intended as testers of vocabulary knowledge. The subject matter of such items is usually either relatively "noncultural" or drawn from materials quite common to the experience of children at all status levels (chap. xxiii).

5. Do pupils from high-status and from low-status homes show any significant differences in the incorrect responses which they give to items? Do these suggest any explanation for the cultural differences in correct responses?

There is some tendency for pupils in both status groups to check one of the first two distractors of a five-choice question more frequently than any of the last three, but no significant status difference is found with respect to this tendency. The low-status pupils omit the items more often than do high-status pupils, but only to the same extent that they also mark the answer incorrectly more frequently. The proportion of errors accounted for by omissions is not significantly different for the two status groups (chap. xviii).

Out of the 315 items for which the distribution of wrong answers was compared for the two status groups, more than two-fifths show substantially similar patterns of wrong responses for the two groups, even though the number of wrong responses is usually much larger for the low-status pupils. Nearly a quarter of the items, however, show differences in the pattern of errors which are significant at the 1 per cent level (chap. xxii).

When the 75 items showing significantly different patterns of errors for the two status groups are examined on a subjective basis, it is found that a number of the differences can be accounted for in terms of status differences in opportunity for familiarity with certain objects, words, or processes. On a large number of additional items the high-status errors are found to be concentrated on a near-correct or next-best answer, an answer with associational or alliterative value, or a distractor apparently selected for some other definite reason — while the errors of the low-status pupils tend to be spread out more nearly uniformly over all available distractors. From this it is concluded that the low-status pupils probably indulge in more random guessing than do the high-status pupils. On about a sixth of the items showing significant status differences in distribution of the errors, no explanation for the variation in pattern of response is apparent to the writer (chap. xxii).

6. Are there significant differences, on any of the factors referred to in Questions 1 to 5 above, as between ethnics and nonethnics when social status is held constant?

Differences between the mean I.Q.'s and mean percentile ranks of low-status ethnics and of low-status nonethnics are small (never more than 3 I.Q. points or 5 percentile-rank points) and are in most cases not significant. In no case do they even approach the magnitude of the differences found between high-status and low-status pupils (chap. xv).

The relationship between I.Q. and Index of Status Characteristics, when expressed in correlation form, is about the same for Old Americans, for Scandinavians, and for ethnics, when allowance is made for differences in the range of social status involved (chap. xiv).

On only 12 out of 647 items are the status differences between the performance of low-status Old Americans and of low-status ethnics significant at the 1 per cent level. For none of these 12 items is there any apparent reason for the difference. Because of the small number of items showing significant differences between ethnics and nonethnics when status is held constant, the responses of ethnic pupils were not analyzed in terms of the other factors involved in the study (chaps. xvii and xxiii).

7. Are there significant differences, with respect to any of the factors referred to in Questions 1 to 5 above, in the intercultural patterns at different age levels?

Status differences in I.Q. terms appear to be, on the basis of all the tests used in this study, larger for the thirteen- and fourteen-year-old pupils than for the nine- and ten-year-old pupils, but the age comparison depends upon the tests used. Tests can be selected at each age level so that the younger pupils show larger status differences in I.Q. than the older pupils. The relationship between I.Q. and Index of Status Characteristics, expressed in correlation form, is linear for the thirteen- and fourteen-year-old pupils but is not linear for the nine- and ten-year-old pupils (chaps. xiv and xv).

The proportion of items showing statistically significant status differences is larger in the tests for thirteen- and fourteen-year-old pupils than it is in the tests for nine- and ten-year-old pupils; conversely, the proportion of items showing differences which are not significant is larger in the tests for the younger pupils. When status differences are expressed in index form, the mean status difference for items from the tests for the older pupils is significantly larger than for items from the tests for the younger pupils (chaps. xvii and xxi).

This age differential is, however, due in part to the presence of a larger proportion of verbal items in the tests for the older pupils and a larger proportion of picture, geometric-design, and stylized-drawing items in the tests for the younger pupils. The age differential is reduced if symbolism is held constant, and it disappears entirely if the age comparison is made on the basis of responses, to identical items, of pupils separated by one year of age (chap. xxi).

CHAPTER VIII

WHAT ARE THE IMPLICATIONS OF THE STUDY

FOR THE INTERPRETATION OF THE I.Q.?

The proper meaning to be attached to differences in mean I.Q. between different cultural groups, or to differences in I.Q. between two individuals from different cultural backgrounds, depends on the kinds of factors which are assumed to operate to produce the differences.

Factors Which May Contribute to Status Differences
in Intelligence-Test Performance

At least five possible kinds of factors may be mentioned: (a) genetic ability, (b) developmental factors, (c) cultural bias in test items, (d) test motivation, and (e) test-work habits or test skills.

By genetic ability is meant those aspects of intelligence which may be presumed to be directly inherited through the genetic structure of the individual. It may be pointed out in passing that even those who deny that group I.Q. differences are due primarily to differences in genetic ability do not necessarily deny the existence of genetic factors in the determination of the I.Q. of any individual person.

It can be argued that upward mobility within the social-status scale is related to intelligence, so that the people at the top of the scale tend to be selected with respect to intelligence and that this superior parental intelligence is then inherited by their children. On the other hand, it can be argued that this "intelligence" which helps to determine upward mobility is a "middle-class" intelligence, related only to the ability to solve problems valued by the middle class, and that the person remaining well down the scale may be just as "capable" if judged in terms of his ability to solve the problems presented by his own cultural environment.

By developmental factors is meant those elements of the environment of the child which contribute to his mental growth and development. Even those who argue most strongly for the inherited basis of intelligence are usually willing to agree that some part is played by the stimulating or nonstimulating nature of the environment in which the genetically determined intelligence develops. Whether a given environment is stimulating or nonstimulating depends in part upon the opportunities which are available for mental activity and in part upon the motivation provided to direct the mental activity of the child.

In terms of developmental factors, it can be argued that the high-status pupil is brought up in an environment that is more stimulating and more motivating for mental growth than is the low-status environment, so that after the passage of time the high-status pupil will be genuinely superior to the low-status pupil, even though both might have started with identical genetic structures. It can also be argued, however, that the evaluation of the middle-class environment as "more stimulating and more motivating for mental growth" is a middle-class evaluation and that, if an impartial measuring stick were available, it might be that lower-class environment is just as stimulating, or possibly even more stimulating, for the kind of mental growth which is important for problem-solving in that environment.

By cultural bias in test items is meant differences in the extent to which the child being tested has had the opportunity to know and become familiar with the specific subject matter or specific process required by the test item. If a test item requires, for example, familiarity with symphony instruments, those children who have opportunity to attend symphony concerts frequently will presumably be able to answer the question more readily than can those children who have never seen a symphony orchestra. To the extent that intelligence-test items are drawn from cultural materials of this sort, with which high-status pupils have more opportunity for familiarity, status differences in I.Q.'s will be expected.

By test motivation is meant the factors which make a particular test, or a particular test item, draw out the best effort of a child, so that his fullest mental power, or capacity, is revealed. Status differences in test motivation may result from either (a) the more favorable attitude of high-status parents toward the importance of the child doing well in all school work, including tests, or (b) a higher proportion of material in the test which is of intrinsic interest or which presents more challenge to high-status pupils than to low-status pupils.

By test work habits or test skills is meant such factors as speed of test work, response sets, and training in or familiarity with specific test procedures. To the extent that high-status pupils may, because of their background, have more favorable test work habits or test skills, group differences in I.Q.'s would result.

The last three types of factors are distinguished from the first two in an important respect. Both genetic and developmental factors are presumed to determine the actual intelligence of the child as it might be evidenced in thinking clearly and in solving appropriate problems in real-life situations. The last three factors -- cultural bias in test items, test motivation, and test work habits or test skills — on the other hand, are oriented toward the test situation as such and are assumed to affect the pupil's ability to score well on the test but not to affect materially his ability to think clearly and to solve appropriate problems in real-life situations.

This classification of possible factors entering into intelligence-test scores is somewhat parallel to the one given by Davis in chapter iv[1] and also to one developed by Cattell and his associates (60, pp. 81-83). It is obvious that any scheme of classifying possible factors in intelligence-test scores is oversimplified and that the various categories cannot be separated by hard and fast lines. In actual practice genetic and developmental factors cannot be entirely separated, since differences in genetic ability may result in a child taking more or less advantage of a stimulating environment. Developmental factors and test-motivation factors cannot be entirely separated because there is no clear line between motivation that is directed toward genuine mental growth and that which is directed merely toward superior test performance. Developmental factors cannot be entirely separated from cultural bias in the test items, because

---

1. See p. 26.

it is not possible to draw a sharp line between a rich cultural environment which contributes to genuine mental growth through greater stimulation and opportunities and a cultural environment which merely contributes specific familiarity with particular material needed for answering certain test items correctly. Nor can genetic and developmental factors be entirely separated from test-work-habit or test-skill factors. To the extent, for example, that test work habits reflect general work habits, they should be regarded as indicators of genetic or developmental factors rather than merely as a test factor.

While the divisions between these five factors are not — and cannot be — hard and fast lines, the emphases are nevertheless quite different. It will be useful for purposes of analysis in the paragraphs which follow to consider them somewhat separately.

The Relative Importance of These Factors

Some of the findings of the present study appear to throw additional light on the probable weight to be attached to each of the factors defined in the preceding section, although in no case can any definitive conclusions be drawn. It is believed, however, that a consideration of some of the possible implications will serve at least to sharpen the issues for further consideration. They are presented with the caution that the discussion is to be regarded as suggestive only, since the study was not designed to provide definitive answers to the question of causal relationships.

The procedure in the paragraphs which follow will be (a) to state the research finding briefly, with a reference to the chapter in which the data are reported more fully, and (b) to consider for each of the four factors (excluding test work habits and test skills) what assumptions would be necessary in order to account for the findings in terms of that particular factor. At the close of the chapter the writer will give a personal evaluation of the kinds of explanations which seem to him most reasonable in view of the findings of this study.

Test work habits and test skills are excluded from consideration in this section, since most of the findings discussed here seem to have little bearing on this question. Findings which do bear on certain aspects of test work habits — those related to possible status differences in speed of working, tendency to omit items, and tendency to guess — have already been summarized in the preceding chapter. The findings discussed in the rest of this chapter are all ones already summarized in chapter vii, but the arrangement is in some cases different, and here important implications of each finding are suggested.

Existence of overlapping of I.Q.'s

Despite the average superiority of high-status pupils on each of the tests, there is a large amount of overlapping, with many high-status pupils securing low scores and many low-status pupils securing high scores (chaps. xiv and xv).

This finding can easily be explained in terms of the genetic hypothesis, by assuming that the process of social mobility involves only imperfect selection with regard to intelligence, that is, that other factors than intelligence serve also to determine mobility, so that high-status parents tend to be of higher intelligence than low-status parents but without that being true for every individual in each group. It can also be explained by postulating a genetic factor as determining part of the I.Q. but allowing for other nongenetic factors as well.

The existence of this same overlap can be explained in terms of developmental factors, test motivation, and cultural bias in items by assuming that, while these factors are in part determined by environmental forces which are differentiated by social-status levels, they are also affected by environmental forces which vary widely among individuals within both status levels. It would be necessary to assume, for example, that a number of low-status homes provide environments more stimulating to growth and development (even "middle-class" growth and development) than those provided by a number of high-status homes.

A third explanation may be suggested by assuming that the differences in group averages, as between the status groups, are determined by status differences in developmental, test-motivation, or specific cultural-bias factors, but that wide variations of genetic ability among individual pupils within each group produce the overlap. In terms of this explanation, the low-status pupils who secure high I.Q.'s would be those pupils whose genetic constitution makes them definitely superior, so that they are able to overcome many of the handicaps imposed by their poor environment, while the high-status pupils with low I.Q.'s would be those pupils whose inferior genetic constitution makes them unable to profit by the advantages of their environment.

Lack of linearity in the relationship

The relationship between social status and I.Q.'s is not linear for nine- and ten-year-old pupils but involves a fairly sharp break at the dividing line between lower-middle and upper-middle classes, above which additional increments of social status are not accompanied by increased I.Q.'s. The relationship for thirteen- and fourteen-year-old pupils is, however, linear throughout the range of the social-status scale (chap. xiv).

Various explanations of this lack of linearity are possible. From a genetic point of view one may argue that the process of social selection operates in the lower and middle ranges of social status but that from upper-middle class upward it is not important. This would fit in with the idea that upward mobility in the lower and middle ranges is related to hard work and "making a success" of one's business, and the like, but that rising within the upper-middle class and particularly from the upper-middle class to the upper classes is more closely related to matters of behavior, family connections, and other factors having little to do with intelligence. From this point of view it could be argued that upper-class parents are not likely to be more intelligent than upper-middle-class parents, although upper-middle-class parents are likely to be more intelligent than lower-middle-class parents, etc.

From the point of view of developmental factors, an analogous argument may be made. It may be that upper-middle-class life provides a more stimulating environment for mental growth than does lower-middle class and lower-class life but that upper-class life does not enjoy any such advantage, from the child's point of view, over upper-middle-class life. This would be in conformity with what is known about the characteristics of typical living patterns at various class levels. Upper-class, or even upper-middle-class, family life is not so likely to be child-centered as is lower-middle-class life.

From the point of view of test motivation, it can likewise be argued that lower-middle-class families, who tend to stress the importance of schooling as a means of upward mobility, will encourage their children to do their best on all school work (including the taking of intelligence tests) but that above the upper-middle-class level the drive for upward mobility is, for many people, less strong, and is in any case more likely to be channeled into means other than the school work of the children. The children in these upper groups are more likely to be encouraged to have the required social graces, to cultivate the "right" people, etc., than to work hard for superior school grades.

From the point of view of cultural bias in test items, two explanations may be offered. First, it may be that in the lower and middle status ranges each advance up the status scale carries with it a richer (in terms of what is required by the test) cultural environment and therefore more opportunities for becoming acquainted with certain words, objects, and processes important for doing well on intelligence-test items — but that a maximum of such opportunities is reached at about the bottom of the upper-middle class and that above that point additional status is not accompanied by increased cultural opportunities.

The second explanation in terms of cultural bias in the test items assumes that most of the status differences are due to differences in cultural opportunities and that the tests for the younger pupils are pitched at a cultural level equal to that of the lower limit of the upper-middle class. Pupils below that limit are penalized through not having the same opportunities as those above them in the social-status scale, but pupils above that limit do not receive any additional benefit, since the tests give them no opportunity to exhibit their superior opportunities.

Each of the explanations given above is adequate to account for the break in the nature of the relationship between social status and intelligence at the point on the status scale that corresponds to the lower limit of the upper-middle class. Only the last one, however, seems to offer any promise for accounting for the fact that this break occurs on all tests for the nine- and ten-year-old pupils but that it does not appear to occur at all for the thirteen- and fourteen-year-old pupils. In terms of the argument in the preceding paragraph, it is only necessary to postulate that the cultural level of the tests for the older pupils is pitched higher than that of the tests for the younger pupils, so that the older pupils with the very highest opportunities do have an opportunity on the test to use the superior cultural advantages which they enjoy. This explanation seems to the writer a reasonable one — and the only one that will account for the change in nature of the relationship at the different age levels.

Insignificance of ethnic differences

The differences between the test performance of Old Americans and ethnics when status is held constant (by considering both within the low-status group only) are small and statistically insignificant. This is true for comparisons in terms of I.Q.'s and also for comparisons based upon analysis of individual items (chaps. xv and xvii).

In order to explain the lack of status difference in this case on the basis of the genetic argument, it is necessary to assume that the parents of the low-status ethnic group are at the same intelligence level as the parents of the Old American low-status group. If social mobility is selective with respect to parental intelligence — and that is a necessary assumption for the genetic argument — it seems probable that the ethnics are depressed in the status scale, by the very fact of their ethnicity, to a point lower than their inherent genetic intelligence would "entitle" them. Warner and Srole have shown, for instance, that each successive generation of ethnics raises itself in the social-status scale (19, pp. 67-102). This suggests that the present status level of any given group of ethnics is depressed below its "normal" position, with its corollary that at any given status level the ethnic parents are likely to have a higher real level of intelligence than that of the Old Americans at the same status level. According to the genetic argument, then, the ethnic children should show higher I.Q.'s than the Old Americans, which is not what is found in this study.

From the point of view of developmental factors or of test motivation, it would likewise seem reasonable to expect higher I.Q.'s for the ethnic children. It has generally been found that ethnic low-status groups are more upward mobile than Old American groups at the same status level and that they usually place a great deal of value on the importance of formal schooling for their children. This would lead one to expect possibly a more stimulating home environment and certainly an emphasis on good performance in school work and on tests.

These three types of factors — genetic, developmental, and motivational — would all lead to an expectation of higher I.Q.'s for the ethnic group, whereas actually no significant differences appear. It should be pointed out, however, that it is possible that some or all of these forces do operate in this way but that the superiority they should produce is offset by a language handicap growing out of the kind and quantity of English which they hear at home and among their friends.

The finding of no differences between ethnics and Old Americans of the same status level is entirely in harmony with the hypothesis of cultural bias in the items. While the cultural background of the low-status ethnic children is undoubtedly somewhat different from that of the low-status Old Americans, there seems no particular reason to believe that it is either richer or poorer in its opportunities for learning the kinds of specific things required by the test items. No evidence has been found in the present study of the presence in the tests of any items involving material which might be more familiar to the ethnic or to the nonethnic low-status pupils.

Variation of mean status difference with symbolism used in item

Mean status differences are largest for verbal and smallest for picture, geometric-design, and stylized-drawing items (chap. xix).

These variations in status difference according to the symbolism in which the item is expressed may be explained in a variety of ways. They may be explained in genetic terms by assuming that verbal items are better measures of general intelligence than are the other types of items and that therefore they reflect more clearly the true genetic differences assumed to exist between the status differences. The validity of this assumption seems doubtful.

Probably a better explanation in genetic terms would be to assume that intelligence is not a unitary trait but that there are different kinds of intelligence, perhaps all genetically determined, but with the "verbal" intelligence distributed in parents in a manner more closely related to social status than is true of "picture" or "geometric-design" intelligence. The reasonableness of this assumption, at least as applied to verbal intelligence, could be defended in terms of the premium which American culture and social-status mobility place on verbal competency -- or at least on competency with the kinds of words and the kinds of syntax that are used in the tests.

The differences could also be explained in terms of a test-motivation hypothesis, by assuming that picture items present more inherent interest or motivation than do verbal items. This seems reasonable, but it is difficult to account for the small differences shown by geometric-design items on this basis, since they appear to be almost completely lacking in any inherent motivation.

In terms of the hypothesis of cultural bias in the items, it is reasonable to find large status differences for verbal items and small status differences for geometric-design items. Verbal items, because of their cultural content, deal with the kind of material which may be subject to differences of opportunity for familiarity, while the content of the geometric-design items is comparatively noncultural. It is difficult on this basis, however, to explain the small status differences for picture items.

The large differences on verbal items and the small differences on picture and geometric-design items can also be accounted for, in terms of the hypothesis of developmental factors, by assuming that the different kinds of items represent different kinds of intelligence and that the high-status environment is such that it is most stimulating in the development of verbal intelligence and least stimulating in the development of picture and geometric-design intelligence.

It seems likely that the true explanation in this case may be a somewhat complicated one. It may be, for example, that the picture items show small status differences because of relatively better motivation for the low-status pupils (and despite the cultural content of these items); that the geometric-design items show small differences because of their relative freedom from cultural content (and despite motivational factors); and that the large differences on verbal items are due to the interplay of several or all of the postulated factors.

Variation of standard deviations of status differences with symbolism used in item

The variation of status differences from item to item is greater for verbal and picture items than it is for other types (chap. xix).

It is difficult to see how this finding can be interpreted in terms of genetic, developmental, or motivational factors, although it is, of course, possible that some argument along these lines might be developed. In terms of cultural bias in the items, however, the finding is just what would be expected. The verbal and picture items are the two categories of items which involve cultural content and which therefore are likely to have variation in the extent to which the required cultural information may be familiar. The "noncultural" items — geometric-design, letter-combination, and number-combination — would be expected to show less variation from item to item, which is exactly what they do show.

Variation of status differences among individual items, and presence of zero differences

Status differences vary in size among individual items in all item categories and are sometimes zero (chaps. xvii to xx and xxiii).

This individual variation can be accounted for in terms of either genetic or developmental factors only by assuming that individual items vary in their power to measure intelligence and that the items which are the most potent measures of intelligence show the largest status differences. Items with zero status differences can be accounted for by this line of reasoning only by assuming that they are items which are worthless as measurers of intelligence — which casts considerable doubt on the adequacy of the genetic or developmental explanations for this particular finding.

In order to account for these variations in terms of test motivation, it would be necessary to postulate a fluctuation of motivation from item to item. Differences of motivation for different kinds of items, particularly when grouped together in subtests, would seem reasonable, but it is difficult to believe that any very significant fluctuation of motivation occurs from one to another of a more or less homogeneous verbal test like the Henmon-Nelson; yet wide variations of status difference occur within such a test.

In terms of cultural bias in the items, variation from item to item would obviously be expected, since the degree of status difference would depend upon the particular degree of difference in opportunity for familiarity with the particular cultural fact needed for each item. The validity of this hypothesis is strengthened by the fact that, for a number of individual items showing large status differences, reasonable cultural explanations can be suggested. It is weakened, however, by the fact that for a number of other items showing large status differences, no such specific explanation is evident. This hypothesis will not, moreover, explain fluctuations in status differences from item to item in the letter-combination, number-combination, and geometric-design categories. It should be remembered, however, that these kinds of items showed less inter-item variation in status differences than the verbal and pictorial items.

Relation of status difference to difficulty of the item

For verbal items the status differences are largest for the easiest items and smallest for the most difficult items. The relationship is stronger when item difficulty is determined for the high-status pupils than when item difficulty is determined for the low-status pupils. For nonverbal items the relationship is less marked, and the directions of the relationship show conflicting tendencies at the two age levels and with the two measures of difficulty (chap. xx).

The hypothesis that status differences in I.Q.'s are due largely to genetic differences can be used to explain these particular findings by assuming that the easier verbal items are better measures of genetic intelligence than are the more difficult ones. This seems reasonable enough if the more difficult items depend for their difficulty upon the relative unfamiliarity or strangeness of their vocabulary, while the easier ones are better measures of actual mental processes, relatively free from the influence of vocabulary knowledge. This explanation would also account for the lack of the same kind of relationship for nonverbal items. It would however, hardly account for the fact that the relationship for verbal items is stronger when difficulty is determined for the high-status pupils than when difficulty is determined for the low-status pupils.

A genetic explanation may also be given on the basis that the easier items are those which are more subject to home and school training, while the difficult items are those which even such training does not affect materially. It could be argued that the superior genetic endowment of the high-status pupils enables them to take more advantage of such training. The lack of a similar relationship for nonverbal items could be explained on the basis that most of the nonverbal items are probably not so subject to home or school training as are the verbal items. Furthermore, the fact that the relationship, for verbal items, is stronger when item difficulty is determined for high-status pupils than when it is determined for low-status pupils is consistent with this interpretation. It is probably true that the order of difficulty of the items for high-status pupils is more closely correlated with degree of school and home training than is the order of difficulty for low-status pupils. It is precisely those items which are subject to such training which are thereby made the easier items for the high-status pupils, while the order of difficulty for low-status pupils has less to do with the degree of their trainability. The fact that nonverbal items do not show as marked a relationship may well indicate that such items are probably less subject to either home or school training than are the verbal items.

The above argument regarding school and home training has been in favor of a supposed superior genetic ability on the part of high-status pupils. To the extent, however, that the superior performance of the high-status pupils on the easier, more trainable, items is due not to superior genetic ability but to superior opportunities for such training, both at home and in school, precisely the same line of arguments leads to the conclusion that the difference could be due to developmental rather than to genetic differences.

Explanation of the main findings in terms of test-motivational differences is also possible. The easier items may be presumed to be those where motivation can operate to a greater extent than on the more difficult items. When a pupil can answer an item, the question of his motivation for trying to do so becomes important, and those with superior motivation will make superior records. When the pupil cannot answer the question because it is too hard for him, the influence of variations in motivation is unimportant. It is difficult, however, to see how this interpretation could account for the fact that the relationship is stronger when item difficulty is determined for the high-status pupils than when it is determined for the low-status pupils. Furthermore, this interpretation would lead one to expect the same kind of relationship for nonverbal items than for verbal items, which is contrary to what is found.

The hypothesis of cultural bias in the items is the only one of those being considered in this chapter which seems completely inadequate to explain the findings. The easier items may be presumed to be those which involve words and objects which are most likely to be familiar to all status groups, while the more difficult items are probably those which involve words and objects more likely to be familiar to high-status pupils alone. In terms of this hypothesis, therefore, one would expect results exactly the opposite of those found.

Lack of change in status differences with advancing age

When allowance is made for variations in the proportion of verbal and nonverbal items in the tests given to pupils of different ages, no significant changes in the size of status differences appear with advancing age (chap. xxi).

This finding is entirely in harmony with the genetic conception, since the genetic structure is determined at birth and since intelligence dependent entirely upon it should not change with advancing years.

In the case of either the developmental factors or the cultural bias in the items, it is possible to argue either (a) that the status differences should become larger or (b) that they should become smaller with the passage of time. In one case the continued impact of increasingly divergent cultures is stressed. In the other case the leveling effect of a common school environment is assigned more weight; it is possible that the cultural backgrounds of high- and low-status groups are more divergent at younger age levels than they are at older age levels. Possibly both of these forces are at work, with different aspects of the environment, and the net effect is to cancel each other.

The finding is likewise consistent with the test-motivation hypothesis. There seems to be no reason to suppose that the relative motivation of the two groups should change with advancing years.

Relation of status differences to type of vocabulary

Many items showing large status differences appear, on purely subjective analysis, to involve academic or bookish vocabulary, while items which show small status differences are either nonverbal or in simple language (chaps. xxii and xxiii).

In order to explain this finding on the basis of genetic factors, it would be necessary to assume that items which obviously test word knowledge or word meaning are better measures of genetic intelligence than those which apparently test primarily a mental process. Or, alternatively, it would be necessary to postulate two kinds of verbal intelligence, the one involving more academic or bookish words being more closely related to social status in the parents. Of these two assumptions, the second seems the more reasonable.

These differences might be explained in terms of the motivation factor, by assuming that low-status pupils shy away from the academic language and do not answer these items even if they can do so.

The explanation of these differences in terms of different opportunities for familiarity with words of this type is an obvious one, depending only upon the reasonable assumption that high-status pupils have more opportunity for hearing, seeing, and using more formal middle-class vocabulary than do low-status pupils. Whether this is to be regarded as a developmental factor or as cultural bias in the items depends upon whether it is assumed that opportunity for learning vocabulary of this kind is part of a stimulating environment and that the resultant vocabulary is a legitimate part of what is to be termed "intelligence" or whether it is assumed that these opportunities result in a test superiority which reflects no real-life superiority. This will vary with the purpose for which the test is to be used. This point will be discussed somewhat more fully in the next chapter.[2]

---
2. See pp. 71-73.

No attempt was made to classify all items according to whether they did or did not involve school learning. It was noted, however, that a number of the items showing unusually large status differences appeared to involve school learning (chaps. xxii and xxiii).

This finding can be explained in several different ways. It is consistent with the genetic hypothesis, since one would expect those children with the greatest inherited ability to take fullest advantage of the school work and to learn most easily; they would therefore excel particularly on those items where school learning is helpful. The same argument could be applied to developmental factors, with the additional advantage accruing to the high-status pupils because of good home backing for making the most of school opportunities and good home co-operation with the school.

In motivational terms, it may be that low-status pupils, both because of repeated frustrations in school work and because of negative parental attitudes toward the school, may take little interest in attempting to solve a problem that looks like just more typical school work and that they may, therefore, not exhibit their full power on such items.

In terms of cultural bias in the items, it is only necessary to point out that (a) a larger proportion of low-status children will be retarded in school and therefore not have had certain opportunities available to the high-status children and that (b), where classes are sectioned or curriculum differentiated, low-status pupils are likely to be found in the less academic sections.

Conclusion

Probably the most reasonable over-all conclusion to be suggested from the discussion in the previous paragraphs — certainly the most conservative one — is that there is no conclusive proof in these data that any one or any particular combination of factors is chiefly responsible for status differences. Certain findings point in one direction; others point in other directions. Frequently data which seem at first glance to indicate one type of causal factor are seen upon closer examination to be equally interpretable in other ways. Many of the findings can be explained in terms of any one of the hypothecated factors by making certain special assumptions in each case. Only more extended research, directed to the specific assumptions involved, can determine to what extent these assumptions may be valid.

While the validity of the explanations just presented cannot be determined objectively from the data available in this study, certain subjective conclusions are possible.

With respect to the explanation of status differences in terms of the genetic factor, it is clear that most of the findings can be explained fairly well on the basis of differences in genetic ability as between high- and low-status pupils, provided one is willing to make certain assumptions. In some cases, however, the validity of the necessary assumptions seems to the writer questionable and the lines of argument sometimes seem rather tortuous. Furthermore, the genetic argument sometimes accounts for part of the finding but leaves certain facts unexplained.

Developmental and motivational factors may be considered together, since they are closely related and since the expected effect of each on

test performance is frequently the same. Most of the major findings of the study can be explained, or partially explained, in terms of developmental or motivational factors, although some of the explanations in these terms seem to the writer to be somewhat strained.

Variations in opportunity for familiarity with specific cultural words, objects, or processes required for answering the test items seem to the writer to appear in the preceding paragraphs as the most adequate general explanation for most of the findings. It is the only explanation offered for the finding with regard to dispersion of status differences among items of different symbolism forms. It seems to the writer to be the most convincing and reasonable explanation offered in the case of findings with respect to lack of linearity in the intelligence-status relationship, the lack of difference between ethnics and nonethnics, and the variation of status differences among individual items. With regard to the relation between status differences and item difficulty, however, no reasonable explanation in terms of this hypothesis appears possible.

It seems likely that status differences in response to intelligence-test items are not due solely to any single simple cause but are the result of various types of factors, quite possibly including both genetic or developmental differences in real ability, on the one hand, and motivational and culture-bias factors in the tests, on the other. Interpretation of I.Q. differences between pupils of differing cultural backgrounds should, therefore, be made with extreme caution. Their true significance cannot be stated with any degree of certainty on the basis of present research knowledge.

CHAPTER IX

WHAT ARE THE IMPLICATIONS OF THE STUDY FOR THE CONSTRUCTION OF NEW INTELLIGENCE TESTS?

The question of what is or is not a valid intelligence-test item cannot be answered, of course, except in terms of the use to which the test is to be put — or in terms of some agreed-upon definition, or criterion, of intelligence. Such agreement is difficult, if not impossible, to secure. There are those who seek to avoid the problem of definition by declaring that intelligence is that which is measured by intelligence tests. This is a justifiable procedure for certain practical purposes, but as the basis for theoretical discussion it merely results in defining intelligence in terms of whatever is used as the criterion for the construction and standardization of the test — frequently some form of school marks or scores on some other intelligence test similarly standardized.

Intelligence has been defined by many authors and in many ways. It has been defined in terms of abstract thinking, capacity for learning, adaptability to new situations, inhibition of instinctive behavior, effectiveness of behavior, problem-solving activities, a capacity for the perceiving of complex relations, and in a host of other phrases. Binet wrote, as early as 1908, of "this problem of fearful complexity, the definition of intelligence" (35, p. 253). Part of this multiplicity of definitions is no doubt due to semantic difficulties, but part of it also reflects the fact that "intelligence" is looked at differently by different people and in different situations. The problem of determining whether a given "intelligence" test is a good one or not is an insuperable problem except in terms of some initial decision as to what the user of the test means by "intelligence" in the particular situation in which he is using it.

Furthermore — and perhaps even more important — whether a given kind of item is a good or a bad test item will vary not only with the particular definition of intelligence adopted but also according to the time of the pupil's life for which it is desired to estimate his ability. It is extremely important to know whether what is wanted is (a) a measure of the pupil's ability to solve problems (or adapt to new situations, or to think abstractly) as it was present in the child at birth; (b) a measure of what his ability is at the present moment; or (c) a measure of what his ability might become in the future. In terms of a low-status pupil who has been subject to a variety of environmental handicaps, the problem becomes one of (a) measuring what the pupil's ability to solve problems (or whatever else is taken as indicating intelligent activity) would have been if he had been placed in a better environment from birth; (b) measuring the pupil's actual ability to solve problems at the present time, regardless of its source; or (c) predicting what his ability would be if he were now put into a better environment.

Any one of these concepts may be appropriate in its own kind of problem, but only confusion results from not keeping the distinctions clearly in mind. Many fallacious conclusions have been drawn, for example, by

taking "intelligence" tests designed by their authors primarily to measure a pupil's present ability to perform academic school work and using the results from them as an indication of inherent and unchangeable racial or cultural differences.

Three Conceptions of Intelligence

It is the belief of the present writer that the meaning of intelligence-test results would be clarified by making more clear-cut distinctions between three types of intelligence which may be termed (a) genetic intelligence, (b) developmental intelligence, and (c) test intelligence. While only the third of these can be measured directly, the chief theoretical importance is attached to the first two.

By genetic intelligence is meant those biological and physiological structures (neural system, etc.) which may be determined at conception by the genetic structure of the individual. It is, by definition, an inherited trait (or traits). Little is known about the nature or extent of any such genetic intelligence on a sound scientific basis, although its existence may be inferred from some of the foster-home and twin studies. It may be merely mentioned in passing that to assume the existence of genetic factors in the determination of the I.Q. of an individual child is not at all to assume that there are real differences in genetic ability among different racial, status, or cultural groups. That is a much more complicated question about which even less is known than about individual inheritance of intelligence.

By developmental intelligence is meant the mental abilities or capacities of a child at any given time after birth, when environment has had opportunity to have some impact on the development of the child. Just what kinds of "abilities" or "capacities" are to be considered as part of the developmental intelligence will be examined in the next section of this chapter.

At one time controversy raged as to whether intelligence is due to nature or nurture; that is, is it the product of hereditary factors or of environmental factors? The question is less often posed today on this simply either-or basis. It is probable that most students of the problem of intelligence would now agree that mental ability as it exists in any given individual after birth is due to both hereditary and environmental forces or — more exactly — to the dynamic interaction of the two. This would be true whether intelligence is defined specifically as problem-solving ability, as ability to think abstractly, or in some other way. Differences would occur only at the point of determining the relative importance of the two factors in the interaction.

Developmental intelligence may be manifested in either of two ways. Children who grow up in a stimulating environment may be expected to develop nearly to the limits imposed by their genetic inheritance, while children who grow up in a nonstimulating environment may be expected to develop problem-solving abilities (or other manifestations of intelligence) considerably below their inherited capacities. It is also probable that two children, with identical genetic structures, placed in equally stimulating but culturally quite different environments, would develop differently — and that after the passage of a few years' time the present abilities, or intelligence, of the two children might be qualitatively different. Thus the environment may be thought of as limiting the extent of the development of the child or as affecting the direction of the growth of the child.

The developmental factors in the environment include such things as opportunities and motivations for home and school learning — in so far as the home or school learning results in genuine development (or retardation of development) of the child's ability to think clearly, to engage in problem-solving activities, or to do whatever else is regarded as intelligent activity. These factors are a legitimate part of the intelligence of a child if what is wanted from the testing is his present level of intelligence, no matter what its source (developmental intelligence) and not a measure of his original or potential ability (genetic intelligence).

By test intelligence is meant that which is measured by any given intelligence test. It will ordinarily vary from test to test. Scores on intelligence tests are sometimes interpreted as estimates of either genetic or developmental intelligence, although the test scores always include some extraneous factors such as test motivation, cultural bias in the items, and test skills. Test intelligence can, however, be conveniently considered also as a concept in its own right. It derives its significance chiefly on an empirical basis. If the test items are chosen and standardized in such a manner that the test gives a good prediction of ability to perform school work, or in terms of any other selected criterion, that criterion becomes the definition of intelligence, and the question of whether the items are valid or not fails to arise. No item that correlates positively with the outside criterion can be ruled out as extraneous or invalid by saying that what it measures is not "intelligence" — if at the outset the criterion (e.g., ability to perform school work) has been accepted as a working definition of intelligence.

To the extent, however, that intelligence tests developed on an empirical basis are used as a means of estimating supposed genetic or developmental intelligence — or as a means of estimating intelligence defined in any way whatever other than by the standardizing criterion — the question of appropriateness of the materials is a vital one. In actual practice, of course, genetic intelligence and developmental intelligence as here defined are theoretical conceptions only and can be only approximately measured by means of available tests — while test intelligence may, by definition, be measured exactly. The question of the appropriateness of items in modern intelligence tests for the purpose of estimating genetic or developmental intelligence is, therefore, an important one.

Intelligence in What Kinds of Situations?

While the distinctions just drawn between genetic, developmental, and test intelligence seem to the writer to be important ones, they are not sufficient for clear interpretation of intelligence-test results. The problem of actually defining intelligence remains, except for the case of test intelligence. Test intelligence is defined empirically, and no theoretical definition is necessary. But genetic and developmental intelligence have so far been defined in terms of "abilities" or "capacities" — the distinction between genetic and developmental being only in terms of the time of measurement and the source of the abilities or capacities. The necessity for a more explicit definition of "abilities" or "capacities" cannot, however, be avoided if test interpretation is to be made on a sound basis.

Is intelligence to be thought of as the ability to think clearly, the ability to think abstractly, the ability to solve problems, the ability to learn from experience, the ability to adapt to new situations — or in some other way? Until some substantial measure of agreement is reached, no single basis of interpreting I.Q.'s can be developed. This agreement might be one involving the selection of some one of the concepts mentioned in the first sentence of this paragraph as defining what is to be meant by intelligence. Alternatively, agreement might be reached involving a clearer delineation of several different conceptions of intelligence, with tests designed to measure each. There is also, of course, the possibility — perhaps the probability — that the multiplicity of phrases used by different authors differ more in their verbal expression than in the underlying reality and that there is more real agreement as to what intelligence means — at this level of thinking — than the variety of phrases used would indicate.

But even agreement on some one of these phrases, or discovery that the distinctions between them are not great, would still leave untouched a crucial question. To think about what? To solve what kinds of problems? To learn from what kinds of experiences? To adapt to what kinds of new situations? If one could assume that there is some abstract "problem-solving ability" which operates equally well in all situations and with all kinds of problems, the question of measuring intelligence would be greatly simplified. This might be a reasonable assumption with regard to genetic intelligence; it does not seem a reasonable one with regard to developmental intelligence. This may be illustrated with an extreme example.

Suppose two children, with equal genetic ability, are brought up in two entirely different cultures — one in an Alaskan fishing village and one in a slum area in New York City. Do they have equal developmental intelligence; that is, equal present ability to solve problems? If both children are presented with the normal everyday problems involved in living in the Alaskan culture and climate, is there any doubt as to which child will be better able to solve the most important problems? Or, if both children are set down in a teeming metropolitan slum, is there any doubt as to which will be better able to solve the important problems? The relative ranking in developmental intelligence of these two children will differ markedly, then, according to the kinds of problems in terms of which it is considered.

Furthermore, the kinds of problems in terms of which developmental intelligence should be considered will vary according to the situation in which the intelligence test is being used. In certain kinds of situations the measurement that will be wanted will be a measurement of the ability of the child to solve problems of the kind important to him in his own culture. In other situations it may be appropriate to specify certain uniform types of problems for all children and to measure the ability of all pupils to solve them. This latter approach might, for example, be appropriate for a scholastic aptitude test, if it is appropriate to assume that the school program is fixed and that only pupils capable of profiting from it are to be admitted.

Unfortunately, the problem is even more complicated than indicated thus far. Even if attention is confined, for the moment, to a single fairly homogeneous cultural group, there are still important difficulties. Developmental intelligence has been tentatively defined as present-day problem-solving ability. But even within the comparatively homogeneous group of high-status Old Americans there would be important differentiations. Ability to solve the problem of making the proper social contacts for maintaining and improving one's social status? Ability to solve the problems of making a success in a highly competitive business world? Ability to solve the problem of making satisfying friendships with one's peers? Ability to solve the problem of finding enjoyable recreational pursuits? Ability to solve the problem of becoming a responsible citizen in the community? Ability to solve the problems of home and family living? Ability to derive information and enjoyment from reading? All these, and many more, could be thought of as important kinds of problems faced by children and adults even in a comparatively homogeneous cultural group. Unless one is willing to assume that a person's present ability to solve problems (i.e., developmental intelligence) is a generalized factor which operates equally in all directions, the problem of defining intelligence satisfactorily is thus further complicated!

In short, an adequate definition of intelligence must include at least three elements: (a) a statement as to the source from which "intelligence" is to be considered as coming — genetic or genetic plus environmental; (b) a statement as to the kinds of mental activity to be considered as reflecting intelligence — problem-solving, abstract thinking, etc.; and (c) a statement as to the kinds of specific problems and situations in terms of which intelligence is to be considered.

It is not the purpose of this section to arrive at a brief and specific definition of intelligence. The purpose is rather to raise a number of issues, to indicate the importance of the definition adopted, and to suggest that the "proper" definition of intelligence may vary from one situation to another. Nothing is gained by oversimplifying the problem — in fact, much confusion may result (and has resulted) from just such oversimplification.

The Construction of New Intelligence Tests

Most of the implications of the study for the construction of new tests are clearly implicit in the discussion of the preceding sections. The present study provides information as to the kinds of items which will yield relatively large status differences and the kinds of items which will yield relatively small status differences. Whether any particular kind of item is, on this basis, to be judged to be a "good" intelligence-test item or to be a "bad" one will depend upon (a) the test constructor's judgment as to the most likely explanation for the difference found and upon (b) his conception of intelligence, or of what he wants his test to measure. The first of these factors is open to further research investigation; the present study provides, it is hoped, a better basis for making such a judgment than has heretofore been available. The second is, of course, a question of values and definitions and cannot be settled on a research basis.

If the test constructor is one who believes that intelligence (of the kind that he wishes his test to measure) is so distributed in the population that it is not concentrated in the higher social-status levels, then this study indicates that he should make up his test primarily of picture, geometric-design, and stylized-drawing items — and that he should avoid questions affected materially by school or home learning. If, on the other hand, he believes that the process of social mobility is such as to bring

about a selection with regard to parental intelligence and that intelligence is inherited, then these matters may not concern him particularly. He may, in fact, decide that the kinds of items shown in this study to be characterized by small status differences are for that very reason poor items.

Some of the confusion in the minds of many test users might be reduced if test authors, in the construction of new intelligence tests, would differentiate clearly three different kinds of intelligence tests: (a) tests purporting to measure genetic ability, (b) tests purporting to measure developmental intelligence, and (c) tests purporting to measure scholastic and other special aptitudes.

Tests of genetic ability

It may be that it is unwise even to attempt to estimate genetic ability, since it is probably impossible to do so at all accurately at any time after birth, if one assumes that the genetic and developmental factors interact in a dynamic manner. At any rate, any test which claims to approach an estimate of genetic intelligence would have to be planned for that specific purpose and should be clearly so labeled. Such labeling might aid in guarding against the present naïve tendency of some test users to interpret as measures of genetic ability tests which in many cases not even their authors would claim should be so regarded.

Tests of developmental intelligence

For a great many purposes, however, what is needed is not a measure of genetic ability but a measure of developmental intelligence. What is wanted is knowledge of the ability which a child has now for meeting and solving life-problems, for making adaptations, for thinking abstractly, or for doing whatever else is regarded as intelligent behavior — regardless of whether the ability may have resulted from genetic inheritance or from the stimulative character of the environment. A test of developmental intelligence should exclude items showing status differences due to the cultural-bias factor and types of items especially subject to cultural differences in test motivation. It should not, however, exclude those cultural or status influences which are reflected in true differences of present ability.

It has been pointed out earlier that the distinction between an item reflecting genuine developmental intelligence and one reflecting mere cultural bias is not an easy one to make. To some extent the distinction is an arbitrary one. It can be argued that any advantage that high-status pupils have on any item, for whatever reason, must be of some aid to them in problem-solving on some kind of problems. Even an item showing large status differences in knowledge of symphony instruments could be defended as a legitimate test item if the kind of problem-solving ability to be estimated by the test was closely related to the field of music. When the kind of problem-solving that is to be predicted has been clearly defined, the distinction suggested here is an important one.

This may be illustrated by another example. The presence of a large proportion of academic vocabulary items in an intelligence test may be perfectly legitimate in a test designed to measure ability to solve problems important to middle-class culture, since success within that culture is probably highly related to verbal facility of the kind represented by such items. The same type of items would probably be entirely out of place in a test designed to measure ability to solve problems important to low-status culture.

This raises again the question of how an intelligence test can possibly make valid comparisons of the problem-solving abilities of pupils from different cultural backgrounds if many of the most important problems faced by the children and adults in those cultures are not common to both cultures. What is meant by a comparison of the developmental intelligence of a child in an Alaskan fishing village and one in the slums of New York City? How is it possible to say that one is more intelligent, or less intelligent, than the other — or that they show equal intelligence? What does "equal" mean in such a connotation? There seem to the writer to be just two possible meanings to be attached to a comparison of the "intelligence" of children raised in backgrounds such that the kinds of problems normally met by them are different. Each of these meanings would require its own approach to the testing of developmental intelligence.

Common-culture approach. — One possibility is to confine the comparison to problem-solving as it is reflected in only those particular problems or types of problems which are equally common and prominent in both cultures. There would be two difficulties with such an approach.

In the first place, it might be difficult to find a sufficient number of suitable problems to use as a basis for the comparison. The more extreme the cultural differences, the more difficult would be the task of identifying common problems — particularly if it is recognized that a problem which may appear on superficial examination to be identical in two cultures may, through differences in motivation, attitude, and the like, actually be two quite different problems in the two cultures when seen from the point of view of the people involved.

Furthermore, by limiting the problems on which comparison is to be based to those common to both cultures, it may be that some of the most important kinds of problems — when judged in terms of their importance within the culture — may have to be eliminated entirely. The result would be an estimate of intelligence which, while unbiased so far as the cultural comparison is concerned, might be quite unrepresentative of various kinds of abilities — some of which might be much more important for the well-being of the child, and of his society, than those selected on the basis of their cultural communality.

Own-culture approach. — The only other meaning which it seems possible to attach to a comparison of intelligence of children coming from different cultures is to judge each child's intelligence in terms of the kinds of problems and experiences which are important in his own culture and which seem important to him (so as to equalize motivation so far as possible). This would involve the definition of intelligence in terms of different sets of problems for each cultural group. Two major difficulties would arise with such an approach: (a) making adequate comparisons across cultural lines, since the problems upon which the judgment of intelligence was based would not be the same for the two groups, and (b) deciding what is to be regarded as a "cultural group" for this purpose.

The first difficulty might be taken care of fairly well by expressing the scores on problem-solving in terms of standard scores, ratios, or some other comparable unit. If ratios were used, the conventional I.Q. could be utilized. The comparison of one I.Q. with another would be similar to such a comparison with the present I.Q.'s from different tests, except that in the proposed case the differences in the I.Q.'s due to

differences in the content of the tests would be planned for rather than accidental. In terms of standard scores, one might determine that a given Alaskan child could solve problems typical of his culture to a degree represented by one sigma above the average of all Alaskan fishing-village children of his age, while a given New York City child might be able to solve problems typical of his environment to a degree represented by one and a half sigmas above the average New York City slum children of his age. The New York City child would thus be judged to be more "intelligent."

The second difficulty would be harder to overcome. What is a "cultural group" for which a separate set of problems would be selected? Would there be one set of problems for rural children and one for urban children? Would there be one set of problems for New York children from a high-status neighborhood and another set for New York children from a low-status neighborhood? Would there be one set of problems for Italian New York children in a low-status neighborhood and another set for Polish New York children in a low-status neighborhood? There are cultural differences in all these groups — and the example could easily be multiplied many, many times. How far would the process of setting up separate standards go? Before this question could be answered satisfactorily, it would be necessary to have much more research into the kinds of problems important to pupils of all possible different groups than is now available. On the basis of such information it would be possible to set up, for intelligence-testing purposes, those cultural groups found to have significantly different patterns of important problems.

It should be noted that this approach, involving the selection of problems appropriate to each cultural group, would make possible the comparison of individuals within any one group, and the comparison of individuals from one group to another in terms of their relative positions within their own groups; but it would not permit the comparison of one group average with another. It would not allow, for example, any conclusion as to the relative intelligence of Italian children as compared to Polish children, or of rural children as compared with urban children, or of high-status children as compared with low-status children. There are probably, however, comparatively few situations where this comparison of group averages is a vital question.

Which approach is preferable? — It seems obvious to the writer that the first of these alternatives, the construction of a common-culture test, is a simpler and more satisfactory solution to the measurement of developmental intelligence, provided that two essential conditions can be met. The first is that a sufficient number and variety of problems can be identified which are essentially common to all status levels and all important subcultural groups, even after allowing for differences due to motivation, attitudes, and the like. The second is that it can be shown either (a) that these common-culture problems include all of the types of problems which are most important in each culture and that the problems unique to particular cultural levels are relatively unimportant or (b) that ability in the common-culture problems is so closely related to ability in the unique-culture problems that describing a pupil's ability in terms of common-culture problems is a sufficiently accurate description of his ability to solve all his most important problems.

Whether these two essential conditions can be met is a problem for which insufficient research information is now available, although far more is known in this area now than was known when intelligence tests, and their interpretation, were in their infancy. Intelligence tests of the past have usually been built upon the assumption that the cultural background of all American children (with the possible exception of children of foreign-born parents) was, while not uniform, at least sufficiently similar that differences could be disregarded.

Thus Terman could write, in 1917:

It would hardly be reasonable . . . to expect that a little incidental experience and instruction in the home, amounting perhaps in most cases to not more than a few minutes per day, would weigh very heavily against . . . native differences. Even in good homes, children are likely to learn less from their parents than from their play fellows and nurses /49, p. 95/.

Even as late as 1940, Loevinger criticized the authors of research studies dealing with social status and I.Q.'s for not recognizing that " 'socio-economic status' influences intelligence via some relatively narrow aspects or concomitants" (23, p. 205). Community studies of the kind being made currently by Warner and his associates emphasize, however, that the differences between different social-class groups in experiences, motivations, values — and choice of playfellows, incidentally — are much greater than was earlier recognized. As more such scientific community and social-status studies become available, there will be a better basis for judging the extent to which differences in child upbringing at different status levels are not mere matters of "a little incidental experience and instruction in the home" or "narrow aspects or concomitants" but instead involve pervasive and far-reaching differences in outlook as well as in the kinds of specific experiences with which the child is likely to come in contact.

It seems possible, on the basis of present knowledge in this field, that to confine an intelligence test to those areas which are common to the experiences of pupils from high-status and from low-status homes (to say nothing of pupils from rural and urban backgrounds or from different ethnic or other cultural subgroups) might necessitate limiting the test to such a narrow range of experiences that it could not possibly be representative of the most important kinds of problem-solving ability in either high-status or low-status culture. If further research in this field should confirm the truth of this possibility, some form of separate own-culture tests would seem to be necessary.

It might be that what is needed is a battery of tests, each measuring problem-solving ability in some one cultural or status area, with the pupil's score reported in a profile form. A given pupil's profile might, for example, show that he had high ability in meeting problems important in low-status culture but only mediocre ability in meeting middle-class problems. Another child might be found to possess high middle-class intelligence but low ability to solve low-status problems. The battery of tests could, of course, be made more detailed, so that it would give scores not only on high-status problems and low-status problems but also on different kinds of problems within each group. The extent to which such specificity would be useful could be established by means of factor-analysis methods, provided the types of material subjected to such an analysis were varied enough to represent a wide range of types of problem-solving abilities at all status levels.

Tests of special aptitudes

So far, three different kinds of tests have been suggested: (a) a test of genetic ability, (b) a test of developmental intelligence based on common-culture problems, and (c) a test of developmental intelligence based on own-culture problems. One further possibility remains. For certain purposes what is wanted is a measure of the pupil's ability to do certain specified kinds of mental activity — regardless of whether the source of the ability is genetic or environmental and regardless of whether the kinds of problem-solving are important or typical of the pupil's own culture. Such tests may most appropriately be called "aptitude tests." They may, of course, represent as wide a variety of aptitudes as there are types of problems.

If, for example, what is wanted is a test of a person's ability to do scholastic work of a highly verbal and academic kind, the tests will appropriately consist of that kind of material. While low-status pupils will doubtless score low on such a test, that low score will represent, not a bias in the test, but a genuine deficiency in those pupils — a deficiency of the particular kind of ability being measured. Such tests should, however, be clearly labeled as tests of specific aptitudes, and they should not be confused with general intelligence tests.

PART III

A REPORT OF THE FIELD STUDY

By Kenneth Eells, Associate Professor of Psychology
San Diego State College, San Diego, California

CHAPTER X

SELECTION OF SUBJECTS AND SECURING OF TEST DATA

The purpose, general procedures, and major findings of the present investigation have already been presented. In the chapters which comprise Part III a more detailed report of the procedures and findings will be presented. Chapters x and xi deal with the general methods used in the investigation. They are followed by two chapters which present a description of the pupils upon whom the study is based. Chapters xiv and xv present those parts of the findings which deal with the I.Q., or total score, from the test. Chapter xvi discusses certain aspects of the procedures used in making the item analysis which forms the main contribution of the present study. The results of this item analysis are reported in chapters xvii - xxiii.

In the present chapter the manner in which the basic data for this study were secured will be discussed under four headings: (a) selection of the community, (b) selection of the age levels to be studied, (c) selection of the tests, and (d) administration and scoring of the tests.

Selection of the Community

In choosing a community in which to carry on the research activities of this investigation, several conditions were imposed by the requirements of the research.

Since the study was to be concerned with factors relating to social-class status, it was necessary to have a fairly well-settled, stable community so that the class stratification would have "solidified" into more or less stable patterns. If the community were a relatively new one, or one characterized by substantial recent growth, the social participation patterns might be too unorganized and unsettled to lend themselves to the kind of analysis which was required. This was particularly important, since it was realized in advance that the social-status position of most of the subjects of the research would have to be determined from certain "indicators" which could be obtained readily for large numbers of people. Such indexes of social status are probably more reliable and valid when applied to old, well-established communities than when used in communities where change and flux are the predominant characteristic of the social structure.

The study was to concern itself primarily with the contrasting test behavior of a high-status and two low-status groups; it was important, therefore, that the community should be one characterized by considerable extremes in social status. No attempt was made to select an extremely atypical community in this respect, but care was taken to avoid choosing a community which would be seriously deficient in either of the extremes of social status.

Because the study was to include a comparison of the test responses of ethnic pupils with those of nonethnic pupils, it was important that the community should include a substantial number of families of sufficiently recent foreign origin so that they would have preserved their ethnic character and identity — and from countries such that their subculture might be expected to be substantially different from that of families with a longer history in the United States.

An attempt was made to select a city sufficiently typical of other cities that the findings of the study might be presumed to have general applicability to a number of other American communities. For this reason communities which were in any sense suburban to a large metropolitan center were avoided, as well as cities dominated by large colleges, hospitals, or other similar institutions which might affect importantly the social-status structure of the community.

The size of the community to be studied was governed by two considerations. It was necessary to have a community of sufficient size that the pupil groups to be studied would be large enough to yield results that would be statistically significant. On the other hand, the larger the community, the more difficult and complicated would be the job of understanding and analyzing the social-class structure within the limits of time and resources available.

Two other considerations of a practical nature were present. First, the study of the community social structure and the carrying-out of the testing would involve close co-operation of many persons within the school system and the community. It was important, therefore, that the community be one in which the school authorities were interested in the project and willing to provide the very substantial amount of co-operation required. Second, the project would necessarily involve considerable traveling between the community and the University of Chicago. It was necessary, therefore, that the community be easily accessible.

The general considerations described above were formulated into the following specific criteria for selection of a community for the study:

Size and stability of the population

1. The city should have a population of at least 40,000, and preferably 80,000 or more — but should not have more than 200,000.

2. The city should have not more than doubled in population between 1910 and 1940 and should not have increased more than 10 per cent between 1930 and 1940.

Socioeconomic structure

3. There should be a strong well-defined upper-middle class. The industry of the community should be primarily home-owned rather than absentee-owned.

4. There should be substantial low-wage heavy industry, with an accompanying large group of low-status workers.

5. There should be a large ethnic group, representing primarily immigration since 1900, and preferably including substantial numbers from southern or eastern European countries.

6. The community should not be within forty miles of any large metropolitan center.

7. The community should not be primarily a college town or be dominated in any important way by a college, hospital, or other similar institution.

8. The community should be within 150 miles of Chicago and be provided with satisfactory transportation facilities.

9. All the schools in the community, both public and private, must be willing to participate in the testing program, to provide access to school records, and to sponsor the necessary home interviews and questionnaires to parents.

A preliminary examination of possible cities indicated that there were seven cities which met the purely objective criteria listed as Nos. 1, 2, 6, and 8 above. These seven cities were then examined on the basis of all available data dealing with the other criteria listed above. Rockford, Illinois, was finally selected as the city conforming most nearly to all the desired criteria.

Rockford had, in 1940, a population of nearly 85,000, with slightly more than 105,000 if the surrounding metropolitan area is included. The population increased 86 per cent from 1910 to 1940, despite a slight decline after 1930; it increased again during the wartime boom years. Foreign-born whites constituted 16 per cent of the population in 1940, the proportion having declined slightly from a high point in 1930. In 1940 more than half of the foreign-born white population were of Swedish origin, while nearly a fifth were from Italy; no other country contributed as much as 10 per cent of the total foreign-born white population. Negroes constituted less than 2 per cent of the population in 1940.

Rockford is primarily a manufacturing city, with major importance attaching to the production of machine tools. The distribution of its employed workers by occupation and by industry is indicated in Figure 1. The top diagram in Figure 1 indicates that 17 per cent of the employed workers in Rockford are in the professional, semiprofessional, and managerial groups, 68 per cent in clerical, skilled, and semiskilled positions, and 15 per cent in mostly unskilled occupations. The bottom diagram indicates that half of the employed workers are engaged in manufacturing industries, with iron and steel products and machinery accounting for nearly a third of the workers.

The data reported in Figure 1 relate to the actual city of Rockford. There is, in addition, a considerable suburban population in areas just outside the city limits. These areas are closely related to the city itself, both economically and sociologically. Some of these suburban areas include substantial numbers of relatively low-status families. Since it was desired to have as large groups as possible at the low-status end of the scale, it was decided that several of these surrounding areas should be included in the study. The districts served by three county schools were added in this way.

The public school system of Rockford consists of eighteen six-year elementary schools, three junior high schools, and two senior high schools. In addition, there are seven parochial eight-year elementary schools, two Catholic four-year high schools, and an independent private elementary school. In areas adjoining the city which were included in the present study there are four eight-grade elementary schools — three public and one parochial.

The responsible officials in charge of these thirty-seven schools were asked whether they would be willing to participate in a study of the general type outlined to them and, in the case of the public schools, were

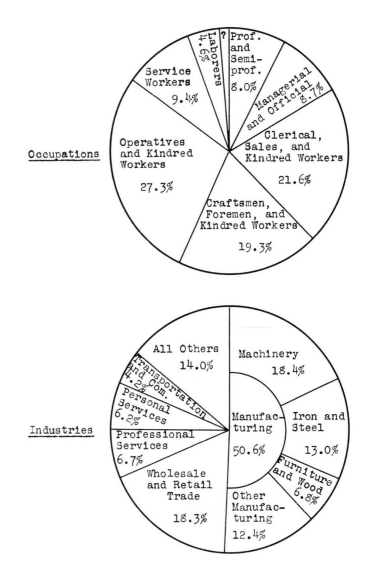

Fig. 1. – Distribution of 35,083 employed workers in Rockford, Illinois, in 1940, by occupation and industry. (Source: U. S. Census, 1940.)

asked to secure the approval of their respective boards of education. Favorable replies were received from all the schools. A list of the schools, and their principals at the time of the testing, appears in Appendix A.

Selection of the Age Levels To Be Studied

There were several considerations which governed the selection of the age levels to be studied. It was thought desirable to study at least two age levels, as widely separated as possible, so that any change in status differentials with increase in chronological age might be discovered. This seemed particularly important because of the direct relationship between advancing chronological age and degree of exposure to cultural influences in the environment.

Purely technical limitations placed the upper and lower limits to the age groups that could be studied. The lower limit was set by the age for which a sufficient number of appropriate intelligence tests could be found. There are some group tests which purport to measure intelligence in the first and second grades; as will be shown later, three of these tests were given to the younger group of pupils in this study. It was desired, however, to include at least one primarily verbal test for this younger group. This led to the decision not to test pupils who would normally be found below the third grade, since the verbal test which was used was not recommended for use in the first two grades. The upper limit was set by the desire to test substantially all the children of any selected age so that a representative group might be assured. This would not be possible at any age where a large number of children might be expected to have left school. On this basis it was decided not to test any children over the age of fourteen.

In order to be sure of securing a sufficiently large number of cases at each age level studied, a two-year age range was included. The final selection of ages in terms of the above considerations resulted in the study of two groups of pupils, defined as follows:

Nine- and ten-year-olds . . . . Pupils born any time in the calendar years 1935 or 1936

Thirteen- and fourteen-year-olds . . . Pupils born any time in the calendar years 1931 or 1932

Since the testing was done early in January, 1946, except for a few absentees who were tested two months later, the characterization of these two groups as "nine- and ten-year-olds" and as "thirteen- and fourteen-year-olds" is substantially correct. They will be referred to in this manner throughout this report.

Selection of the Tests

In choosing the particular tests to be analyzed, consideration was given to the following factors:

1. The tests should be ones that are in wide use today.
2. The battery of tests had to be such that it could be administered in five one-hour periods -- one each day for a week.
3. Each test had to be available in a form suitable either for nine- and ten-year-olds or for thirteen- and fourteen-year-olds, and in some one form suitable for a considerable range of grade levels.

The tests chosen as best meeting these criteria were the following:

Nine- and ten-year-old pupils

Otis Quick-scoring Mental Ability Tests, Alpha Test: Form A, for Grades I-IV, World Book Company, Yonkers, New York, 1936.

The Henmon-Nelson Tests of Mental Ability — Form A, Elementary School Examination — Grades III-VIII, Houghton Mifflin Company, Boston, Massachusetts, 1931.

Kuhlmann-Anderson Intelligence Tests, Fifth Edition, Grade III and Grade VI, Educational Test Bureau, Minneapolis, Minnesota, 1942.

Thirteen- and fourteen-year-old pupils

Terman-McNemar Test of Mental Ability, Form C, World Book Company, Yonkers, New York, 1941.

Otis Quick-scoring Mental Ability Tests, Beta Test: Form Cm, for Grades IV-IX, World Book Company, Yonkers, New York, 1937.

California Short-Form Test of Mental Maturity, Intermediate S-Form, Grades VII-X, California Test Bureau, Los Angeles, California, 1942.

The Chicago Tests of Primary Mental Abilities for Ages 11 to 17, American Council on Education, Washington, D.C., 1941. Spatial and Reasoning factors only.

The Otis Alpha test may be given in two different ways, either as a "verbal" or as a "nonverbal" test. In the present study the test was given both ways, on separate days; throughout the analysis the results from the two different administrations are treated as two separate tests. The Kuhlmann-Anderson test booklets for Grades III and VI include all the material recommended by the authors for use in Grades III, IV, V, and VI. The Chicago Tests of Primary Mental Abilities have been published in several forms. The form used in this study was the one in which each factor is tested by means of two subtests. The Spatial and Reasoning factors were treated as separate tests throughout this study.

In the case of the tests for the older pupils, machine-scoring forms of the tests were used; for the younger pupils, only hand-scoring forms were used.

Administering and Scoring the Tests

The tests were administered by a group of twenty specially trained administrators, using detailed instructions to insure uniformity of procedure. The test schedule was arranged in such a way that not more than one test was given in a single day to any one pupil, that no test occupied more than one class period (45-60 minutes) at a time, and that all tests were given within a five-day period and in the same sequence to all pupils. The schedule for the testing was as follows:

	9- and 10-Year- Old Pupils	13- and 14-Year- Old Pupils
First day	Otis Alpha Nonverbal	Thurstone Spatial[1]
Second day . . .	Otis Alpha Verbal	Thurstone Reasoning[1]
Third day	Henmon-Nelson	Otis Beta
Fourth day . . .	Kuhlmann-Anderson III	Terman-McNemar
Fifth day	Kuhlmann-Anderson VI	California Mental Maturity

The Kuhlmann-Anderson test was given on two days, the Grade III booklet on one day and the Grade VI booklet on another. The California Mental Maturity test was too long for satisfactory administration in the time available; subtests 2 and 6 were omitted in order to allow pupils to have the recommended time for the other subtests. The testing was carried out during a two-week period in January, 1946, with half of the schools being tested during the first week and half during the second week.

In March, 1946, some retesting was done in an effort to secure tests from as many as possible of those who had been absent in January. Whenever there were as many as ten absentees for any one test in any school in the January testing, a retest was given in March. This later testing involved 165 nine- and ten-year-old pupils and 246 thirteen- and fourteen-year-old pupils. It was thought that the two-month lapse in time between the two testings would not introduce any serious discrepancy in pupil responses. In any case, the number of tests obtained from the later testing was a very minor portion of the total number of tests, as will be shown later.

In the case of the Otis Alpha Nonverbal, Henmon-Nelson, Thurstone Spatial, Thurstone Reasoning, and Otis Beta tests, additional time was allowed, after the completion of the standard time, so that as many pupils as possible might finish all the items in the test. In these cases the pupils were given the test under standard conditions, with no mention of the fact that they were later to be given extra time. After time had been called in accordance with the test author's instructions, the students were given colored pencils and told that they might take additional time to finish the test items. In all other respects the tests were given in accordance with the directions provided by the authors of the tests.

More than three-fourths of the younger pupils were tested in classroom groups of from 25 to 35; in no case did the groups include less than 10 or more than 45. The testing of the older pupils was, of necessity, carried out under a wider variety of conditions. Approximately three-fourths of the older pupils were, however, tested in high-school auditoriums in groups of from 75 to 175. Whenever the groups were larger than 35, proctors assisted the administrator, so that there was one proctor for each 30 to 35 pupils. While there were a number of small test groups for older pupils in the elementary schools, they did not involve a very significant proportion of the total students tested; less than 8 per cent of the older pupils were tested in groups of less than 30 each. When the pupils to be tested in any one school were less than 5 in number (at either age level), they were eliminated from the testing program. This resulted in the elimination of 19 of the older pupils in nine different elementary schools.

---

1. These are the Chicago Tests of Primary Mental Abilities referred to on p. 86. Since they are probably better known by their author's name, they are hereafter referred to in this fashion.

In converting the scores on these tests to I.Q.'s or other derived scores, somewhat different procedures were used for the different tests. With one exception (No. 5 below) the procedure used was that recommended by the author of each test.

In all, five different types of derived scores were secured, as follows:[2]

1. Henmon-Nelson test . . . . . . { Intelligence quotients, based on mental ages secured from age norms for the total score

2. Kuhlmann-Anderson test . . . { Intelligence quotients, based on medians of mental ages obtained from subtests

3. Otis Alpha Nonverbal test }
 Otis Alpha Verbal test }
 Otis Beta test } . . { So-called "deviation I.Q.'s" obtained from a special procedure recommended by the authors of these four tests
 Terman-McNemar test }

4. Thurstone Spatial test }
 Thurstone Reasoning test } . . { Percentile ranks based upon norms provided by the authors for six-month age groups

5. California Mental Maturity test . . . . { Percentile ranks based upon local Rockford norms for six-month age groups

For the Kuhlmann-Anderson test, special procedures were worked out, in accordance with the test authors' suggestions, for making adjustments in the case of pupils for whom several of the early subtests showed perfect scores or for whom several of the later subtests showed zero scores. Tests requiring these adjustments were somewhat more frequent than would usually be the case because of the wide range of Kuhlmann-Anderson test material (Grades III through VI) presented to each pupil.

For the California Mental Maturity test, a modification had to be made because of the necessity, already mentioned, of omitting two of the subtests due to lack of time. Since no authors' norms were available for this abbreviated form of the test, percentile tables were constructed (for six-month age groups) from the scores of the pupils in the present study, and each pupil assigned a percentile rank on the basis of them. These percentile-rank scores show the relation of each pupil's score to those of other children of the same chronological age in Rockford.

In the case of those tests for which extra time was allowed, the I.Q.'s or percentile ranks were computed on the basis of the responses made during the standard prescribed time.

Summary

Rockford, Illinois, was selected as the locale for the study because it fitted certain stated criteria which made it suitable for the purpose of this study. The co-operation of all the schools in the community, both public and private, was secured. Two age groups were selected for study -- nine- and ten-year-olds because they represented as young a group as it was possible to obtain a number of suitable intelligence tests for, and

---

2. For reference to a more detailed account of the exact procedures used in the computation of these scores see Note 1 in Appendix D.

thirteen- and fourteen-year-olds because they represented as old a group as it was possible to secure without the likelihood of introducing serious socioeconomic bias into the sample through students dropping out of school to work. Nine widely used group intelligence tests were selected for analysis; four of them were given to all of the nine- and ten-year-old pupils, while five were given to all the thirteen- and fourteen-year-old pupils.

The tests were administered, scored, and I.Q.'s or percentile ranks computed in accordance with the standard procedures established by the authors of the tests, except in the case of the California Mental Maturity test, for which certain modifications had to be made to meet time limitations. On certain of the tests, additional time was allowed after the expiration of the standard time, so that more pupils would be enabled to finish a larger number of the items. In such cases the I.Q.'s or percentile ranks were computed on the basis of the items marked in the standard time, but the item analysis was carried out on the basis of all pupil responses, regardless of when they were made.

CHAPTER XI

THE MEASUREMENT OF SOCIAL STATUS

In order to study the relation of cultural factors to responses of pupils on test items, it is necessary to have some definite measure of cultural factors, or some means of classifying pupils into cultural groups. There are, of course, a number of such measurement or classification schemes which might have been used. The method actually used in this study is one involving what is here called "social status" and which is shown to be closely related to "social class" as that term is used by sociologists.

As indicated in chapter iii, modern sociologists and cultural anthropologists place a great deal of importance upon the location of an individual in the social-class structure of his community as a basic determiner of many of the cultural and environmental experiences which a child may be expected to have. Since it is these differences in cultural experience which may affect the responses of pupils to intelligence-test items, an analysis of test responses in terms of these larger social-status or social-class concepts seems to be indicated.

To make a complete community study as a basis for accurate social-class placement of the nearly five thousand pupils included in the present study would, however, have been a task far beyond the resources available. Fortunately, Warner and his associates have found (18), on the basis of experience in studying several communities in different parts of the country, that social-class placement of an individual is quite closely related to socioeconomic status as measured by a comparatively simple index. He calls the latter an Index of Status Characteristics; for the sake of brevity it will frequently be referred to hereafter as "I.S.C."

The Index of Status Characteristics

In a study of the I.S.C. in a midwestern community, Warner found that there was a very close relationship between the Index of Status Characteristics and social-class placement as determined from interview and other primary sources relating to actual social participation and social reputation in the community. He found a correlation of .97 between the I.S.C. and social-class placement, based on 209 families (18, p. 183). This correlation was obtained from the same cases on which the I.S.C. was standardized; it would not be so high for another group. Nevertheless, the relationship is undoubtedly sufficiently close to make possible the prediction with a considerable degree of accuracy of the social-class position of an individual on the basis of his I.S.C. score.

Modification of Warner's I.S.C.

The method of measuring social status used in the present study is a modification of this I.S.C. developed by Warner. Warner's index is based upon ratings, on seven-point scales, of four different "status characteristics" — occupation, source of income, type of house lived in, and dwelling area in the community. These four ratings are combined into a single index by means of a weighting scheme which weights occupation most heavily and dwelling area least heavily. These weights were derived by means of a regression equation based upon social-class placement as a criterion (18, p. 181).

Because of the relatively large number of Rockford families for whom information was desired, it was apparent that the necessary information would have to be secured by questionnaire rather than by personal interview. For this reason, it was decided to modify the Warner index by substituting education of the parents for source of income, since it seemed unlikely that reliable information as to income source could be secured by questionnaire. Warner suggests the desirability of making such modifications and substitutions in his index when special conditions seem to warrant it and presents data (18, pp. 173-74) to show that the correlation of the index with social-class placement is not seriously impaired if different combinations of certain status characteristics are used. The index as modified is based on ratings on the occupation of parents, education of the parents, type of house lived in, and dwelling area in the community.

The Warner index provides for varying weights for the different status characteristics. These same weights could not be used in the present instance, however, since the list of traits included in the index was modified as described above. Since no basis existed for assigning weights to the elements of the modified index, the four traits were tentatively weighted equally. It was originally planned to refine this modified index by assigning weights to the various factors on the basis of the social-class stratification which will be described briefly below, but this was found to be unnecessary, since the unweighted index proved to be satisfactory for the present purpose.

That these modifications of the Warner I.S.C. did not change its basic nature very substantially was demonstrated by comparing the two indexes on a carefully selected sample of one hundred pupils. This group was selected on a random basis except that it was stratified by age groups and by I.S.C. levels (using the modified Rockford index), so that it contained pupils at the various I.S.C. levels in exactly the same proportion in each age group as did the total group of Rockford pupils. For each of these one hundred pupils two index values were computed, one the original Warner index, including source-of-income ratings, excluding education ratings, and with all ratings weighted — the other the modified Rockford index just described. For this group of pupils the correlation between the two indexes was .93, indicating that the two indexes give very similar results. If the original index had been used instead of the revised one, a few changes in status-group assignment would doubtless have been made, especially in border-line cases, but the general composition of the status groups would have been much the same.

Source of data for the status ratings

The basic data needed with regard to each pupil for making ratings on the four factors underlying the I.S.C. were relatively simple. They consisted of a brief statement of the occupation of the father, and of the mother, if also employed; a statement of the highest grade in school completed by each of the parents; and the address of the family's residence.

For the great majority of the pupils this information was secured from a one-page questionnaire taken home by the pupil to be filled out by the parent. The questionnaire is reproduced in Appendix B. In addition, each pupil was asked, at the time of the testing, to fill out a card giving the father's occupation and the pupil's residence address; no attempt was made to secure information as to the parent's education from the pupil. The pupil cards were used as a basis for making the I.S.C. ratings only when no usable parent questionnaire was returned, and only when the pupil's information was sufficiently precise for proper classification of the occupation. In cases where neither of these sources of information was available in usable form, an attempt was made to secure the necessary data by direct interview with the parent in the home. A small number of pupils had to be eliminated from the analysis because it proved impossible to secure from any source satisfactory information as a basis for computing an I.S.C. for them.

The source of I.S.C. information is indicated in Table 2.

TABLE 2

SOURCE OF INFORMATION FOR THE INDEX OF

STATUS CHARACTERISTICS

Source of Information	Number of Pupils		Per Cent of Total Pupils	
	Age 9-10	Age 13-14	Age 9-10	Age 13-14
Questionnaire returned by parent in usable form*	2,175	2,274	94.8%	90.6%
Card filled out by pupil	71	136	3.1	5.4
Personal interview with parent	49	100	2.1	4.0
Total pupils in the study ..	2,295	2,510	100.0%	100.0%

* Includes a few cases in which the original questionnaires returned by the parents were not complete but which were supplemented by personal interview with the parents.

It is clear from this table that the great majority of the pupils were included in the study on the basis of I.S.C.'s computed from data supplied from the parent questionnaire, although small numbers of pupils were added from the other sources. A very small proportion of the total number of pupils were eliminated because of the lack of necessary data for determining socioeconomic status. These include 42 pupils for whom insufficient usable information could be obtained from any source, 13 pupils living in an orphanage, and 61 pupils giving rural addresses. The children from the orphanage were eliminated, since no ratings could be made on either the occupation or the education of the parents, and the I.S.C. cannot be satisfactorily based on only two of the four status characteristics. Most pupils giving rural addresses were included in the study with no special difficulty. Those who were eliminated on this basis were either pupils whose addresses were too vague to permit the field worker to locate the house, or pupils who lived in near-by small villages or towns not contiguous with Rockford. In both such cases no comparable house-type or area ratings could be made.

Even though it may be suspected that the pupils living at rural addresses and those whose parents failed to return the questionnaires may be predominantly low-status children, the effect on the representativeness of the total group must be negligible.

Rating of the four status characteristics

The ratings on each of the four status characteristics were made in accordance with the scales and procedures described by Warner (18, pp. 121-59); for this reason only a brief outline of the procedures will be given here.

Occupation. — Warner provides two alternate methods of rating occupations for I.S.C. purposes. The method used in the present study was the one Warner designates as the revised scale. This is a modification of the occupation classification developed by Edwards for the Bureau of the Census (63). Warner's rating plan makes allowance for the fact that most of the census occupational groups include occupations with a considerable range of "social prestige" value. Thus the census classification includes auditors, salesmen, office clerks, and service-station attendants under a single heading, "clerks and kindred workers." The Warner rating plan attempts to equate those occupations, from whatever census group, which enjoy approximately equal "social prestige" in the community.

The Warner rating plan for occupations is illustrated for some sample occupations in Figure 2. Figure 2 indicates that there is considerable range, on the rating scale, for most of the census classifications. Thus persons classified by the census as "professional" may be rated 1, 2, or 3, while persons classified as "proprietors, managers, and officials" may be rated 1, 2, 3, 4, 5, or 6, depending primarily upon the size of their businesses.

The seven points of the rating scale may be described somewhat roughly as follows:

Rating	Occupation
1	Professional, managerial (very large businesses)
2	Semiprofessional, managerial (large businesses), high-status white-collar workers
3	Managerial (medium-size businesses), medium-status white-collar workers
4	Managerial (small businesses), low-status white-collar workers, skilled workers
5	Managerial (very small businesses), apprentices
6	Semiskilled workers
7	Unskilled workers

All the occupation ratings were made by one person in order to secure as much uniformity in interpretation as possible.

Education. — The ratings on education were made according to the following scale:

Rating	Schooling Completed
1	Professional school or graduate work
2	College (1-4 years)
3	High-school graduate
4	High-school nongraduate (1-3 years)
5	Grammar-school graduate (8th grade)
6	Grammar-school nongraduate (4-7 years)
7	Grammar-school nongraduate (0-3 years)

Several difficulties were encountered in applying this scale. The first arose from two unfortunate ambiguities in the questionnaire. The question asked of parents was: "What grade, or year of high school, had the pupil's father /or mother/ finished when he stopped school?" In some cases the parent responded with "third" in such a way that it was not clear whether third grade or third year of high school was meant. In some cases the parent reported high-school graduation when it was evident from the occupation that the parent must have had college training. This was doubtless due to the fact that the question as asked did not make it clear that all education, including that above high school, was to be included. In most cases it was possible to determine fairly accurately what the parent's real education was; in cases where it was impossible to do so the education rating was omitted.

The second difficulty arose in connection with a few foreign-born parents whose education had been in foreign schools; in most such cases the parent reported his education in terms of number of years completed, and the above scale was applied. Where it was impossible to translate a foreign schooling into the terms required by the rating scale, no rating was made.

A third difficulty arose in connection with cases where the father's and the mother's education were sufficiently different as to receive different ratings on the above scale. In such cases the mid-point between the two ratings was used, except that when this would result in a fractional value, a whole number was used, giving preference to the one closest to the father's rating. The greater weight was given to the father's rating because various community studies have shown that the social status of the family is more directly affected by the education of the father than of the mother.

In order that all interpretations of questionable cases in the ratings might be made in as uniform a manner as possible, one person made all of the 4,500-odd education ratings.

House type. — The ratings on house type were made according to the second, or revised, scale provided by Warner for this purpose. As a matter of fact, the revised house-type scale presented by Warner was first developed in connection with the present study. This scale is as follows:

Rating	Interpretation
1	Excellent houses
2	Very good houses
3	Good houses
4	Average houses
5	Fair houses
6	Poor houses
7	Very poor houses

Specific descriptions of the kinds of houses to be included in each of these ratings were developed. The house-type ratings were made by four individ-

Fig. 2.—Some sample occupations, illustrating rating plan for occupations

Rating of Occupations	Professional Persons	Proprietors, Managers, and Officials (except Farmers)	Clerks and Kindred Workers	Skilled Workers and Foremen	Semiskilled Workers	Servant Workers	Other Laborers (except Farm)
1	Doctor Dentist Lawyer Minister Engineer	Prop. or Mgr. of very large business ($75,000 and over) State bank examiner					
2	High-school teacher Artist Editor Nurse	Prop. or Mgr. of large business ($20,000-$75,000) Stock broker Army colonel	Auditor Insurance agent Real estate agent				
3	Grade-school teacher Draftsman and tool designer	Prop. or Mgr. of medium-size business ($5,000-$20,000) Contractor City official	Wholesale salesman Secretary Laboratory technician		Craftsman's apprentice		
4		Prop. or Mgr. of small business ($2,000-$5,000)	Retail salesman Store clerk Bookkeeper Stenographer Office clerk	Craftsman and any skilled worker (carpenter, mason, plumber, etc.) Foreman Policeman			
5		Prop. or Mgr. of very small business ($500-$2,000)	Telephone operator				
6		Prop. or Mgr. of business under $500	Service-station attendant Freight checker		Semiskilled worker (taxi-driver, knitter, grinder, machine operator, etc.)	Waitress Elevator operator Janitor	
7						Domestic servant Window washer	Unskilled worker (ash collector, excavator, factory laborer, etc.)

uals, operating in two teams of two each. Each house was rated jointly by two individuals, on the basis of an external inspection. In a number of cases the same houses were rated by both pairs of raters. The existence of very few discrepancies in such duplicate ratings indicated that those making the ratings were able to make them on the basis of the more or less objective descriptions agreed upon in advance.[1]

Dwelling area. — For the rating on dwelling area it was necessary to divide the community geographically into sections and to assign ratings to these various sections on the basis of the community evaluation placed upon them as desirable or undesirable places of residence. The general types of areas to be assigned different ratings are described by Warner as follows:

Rating	Description of Dwelling Area
1	Very high; Gold Coast, North Shore, etc.
2	High; the better suburbs and apartment-house areas, houses with spacious yards, etc.
3	Above average; areas all residential, larger than average space around houses; apartment areas in good condition, etc.
4	Average; residential neighborhoods, no deterioration in the area.
5	Below average; area not quite holding its own, beginning to deteriorate, business entering, etc.
6	Low; considerably deteriorated, run-down and semi-slum.
7	Very low; slum.

The method of applying these descriptions to the Rockford community involved two steps. The first was the determination, from interviews with parents of children in the testing program and with leaders and other key people in different parts of the community, of the general community evaluation placed upon different areas of the city as desirable or undesirable places of residence. The second involved inspection of the general appearance of different neighborhoods. The second method was a supplementary one, used for assigning ratings to areas not specifically delineated in the interview material. Detailed descriptions were prepared of typical neighborhoods at the different points on the rating scale — descriptions in terms of social reputation and evaluation as well as in terms of appearance of housing, appearance and size of yard, condition of streets, appearance of children at play, and density of population. The entire city and surrounding areas were divided into subareas and assigned ratings corresponding to the general descriptions in the Warner rating plan.

When these geographical areas were defined and ratings determined for them, each pupil was assigned a dwelling-area rating corresponding to that of the section of the city in which he lived.[2]

---

1. For a reference to more detailed description of the characteristics of these seven categories of houses, and of the procedures by which they were applied in Rockford, prepared by Charles Warriner, who was in charge of this phase of the project, see Note 1 in Appendix D.
2. For a reference to a more detailed description of the procedures used in this dwelling-area analysis, prepared by Marian Warriner, who worked on this phase of the project, see Note 1 in Appendix D.

Computation of the I.S.C.

Once the four ratings just described were completed for all the pupils in the study, it was a simple matter to compute the I.S.C. summarizing them into a single figure. In most cases this was done by simply adding the four ratings together; the sum is the Index of Status Characteristics.

When data were lacking for one of the ratings, the other three were totaled and the sum multiplied by 1 $1/3$ to make the totals comparable to those based on four ratings. This is the procedure recommended by Warner in such cases. It has the effect of assigning to the missing characteristic a rating equal to the average of the three which were available. When data were lacking for two of the four ratings, no index was computed and the case was eliminated. The great majority of the I.S.C.'s for the pupils included in the study were based upon the four traits which comprise the full index. In about 10 per cent of the cases, however, the I.S.C.'s were based upon three of the four traits, with occupation being the most frequently missing trait for the younger pupils, and education being the most frequently missing trait for the older pupils.

Validation of the I.S.C. in Social-Class Terms

In the form just described, the Index of Status Characteristics is a numerical index of socioeconomic characteristics and can be used as such without any reference to social-class equivalence. Warner has shown, however, that an index of this type bears a close relationship to social-class participation; he found, in one community study, that it can be used for estimating social-class participation within remarkably narrow limits (18, pp. 163-216). His procedure was to demonstrate a positive linear relationship between the I.S.C. and social-class participation, then to determine empirically the critical points on the I.S.C. scale which separate one social-class level from another.

The specific prediction formulas developed by Warner could not be used in the present instance, however, both because of the modifications in the form of the index, as described above, and because there was no assurance that the exact relationships found to hold in one community would necessarily be true for another community of quite a different type. "Jonesville," the community from the study of which Warner developed the I.S.C., is a town of less than 10,000 population, with only one important factory and serving as a marketing and trade center for a surrounding agricultural area. Rockford, on the other hand, is a community of nearly 100,000 population, with a wide variety of industrial and commercial establishments.

Some procedure for validating the modified index, as used in this study, against social-class participation in the community upon which this study was to be based was obviously needed. To provide the basis for this validation of the I.S.C. in Rockford, a partial social-class stratification of the Rockford community was carried out by Charles Warriner, at that time a graduate student in the Department of Sociology, the University of Chicago, and now instructor in the Department of Sociology, University of Kansas. His study involved an analysis of the social structure of the community from a social-class point of view and the placement of a number of individuals in the social-class scale by means of information as to their actual participation and the evaluations placed upon them by other members of the community.

Warriner was able to assign fairly definite social-class placements to 133 families, with more families being placed at the upper and lower ends of the social-class scale than in the middle range. The relationship between the social-class placement for these families and the I.S.C. for the same families was found to be fairly close, with a correlation of .86 between the two factors. While the dividing lines between different social-class groups could not be expressed exactly in terms of the index scale, fairly close approximations were made.[3]

The findings of the present study do not depend upon the acceptance of any social-class interpretation of the Index of Status Characteristics; the index may be taken merely as an indication of the socioeconomic background of the family. However, the available evidence indicates that it is probably closely related to social-class participation; this increases the significance of the test findings reported later for those who believe that social class is an important factor in determining the cultural content of a pupil's environment.

Selection of Three Special Status Groups

Since the main analysis of the relationship between social status and test performance was to be carried out by means of contrasting extreme status groups rather than by studying the entire group of pupils, it was necessary to set up some criteria for the selection of such groups. Three criteria were established:

1. The groups should consist of a sufficient number of individuals, at each age level, so that the necessary statistical procedures could be carried out without serious difficulties resulting from too small samples.

2. Each of the groups should be as homogeneous as possible with respect to socioeconomic status and cultural background.

3. The contrast between the socioeconomic status or cultural background of the extreme groups should be as great as possible.

The basic statistical measure to be used in the later analysis was the difference between two percentages (the percentage of high-status pupils answering a given item correctly and the percentage of low-status pupils answering the same item correctly). Attention was, therefore, given to the size of difference which could be considered statistically significant with groups of various sizes. The size of the difference between two percentages which can be considered significant decreases as the percentages involved approach 0 or 100 and increases as they approach 50. It was determined that groups of approximately 150 to 200 pupils should be secured at each age level and in each status classification, so that differences of 15 percentage points or more would be statistically significant at the 1 per cent level no matter at what point along the percentage scale they might occur.

The entire range of the Index of Status Characteristics (4 to 28) was

---

3. For a reference to a further account of the procedures used by Warriner for determining social-class placements in the community, and of the analysis of the relationship between social-class placements and the Index of Status Characteristics, see Note 1 in Appendix D.

then divided into three areas, a high-status area (I.S.C. 4 to 12), a middle-status area (I.S.C. 13 to 20), and a low-status area (I.S.C. 21 to 28). The particular dividing points for these groupings were decided upon after careful examination of the available data with regard to the social-class equivalence of different index values, so that the high- and low-status ranges would be as nearly equivalent as possible to upper-middle-class and lower-lower-class groups. Attention was also given to selecting the dividing points so as to secure the desired number of pupils in the two extreme groups. The dividing points were determined primarily on the basis of the Rockford data, but comparisons were also made with the location of similar class dividing points obtained in a study of another community.[4]

The pupils were then classified on the basis of ethnicity into three groups: Old Americans, Scandinavians, and ethnics. "Old American" is the term used to identify pupils who, on the basis of the best information available, appear to participate in the total community culture and are neither ethnic nor Scandinavian within the meanings assigned to those terms in this study. "Scandinavian" designates pupils one or both of whose parents were born in one of the Scandinavian countries. "Ethnic" refers to pupils belonging to a foreign-culture group — other than Scandinavian — of sufficient size and cultural cohesiveness as to constitute a separate subculture in the community, recognized as such both by the ethnic group in question and by the community at large.

Several different sources of information were used for making this classification, but the great majority of pupils classified as either Scandinavian or ethnic were classified as such on the basis of the birthplace of one or both of their parents as obtained from the parents' questionnaire. Not all pupils of foreign-born parents were classified as ethnic, however, and some pupils were classified as ethnic even though both parents were born in the United States. The latter cases occurred when there was evidence available to indicate that they were probably part of an ethnic subculture in the community and were probably so regarded by other members of the community. This evidence was sometimes in the form of interviews with the family involved but was more often dependent upon the reputation of the neighborhood in which the family lived and the ethnic appearance of the pupil's name.[5]

The relationship of these two sets of categories — one based on the I.S.C. and the other based on ethnicity — is indicated in Table 3. From the right-hand "total" column of this table it can be seen that about 10 per cent of the total group of pupils are classified as high status, 22 per cent as low status, and the remaining 68 per cent as medium status. For comparative purposes it may be noted that Warner, in his Yankee City study, found 13 per cent of the population were upper-middle class or higher and that 25 per cent were in the lower-lower class (16, p. 203).

The total line at the bottom of Table 3 indicates that 81 per cent of the pupils are classified as Old American, 7 per cent as Scandinavian,

---

4. For a reference to a description of the exact process by which these dividing lines were determined see Note 1 in Appendix D.

5. For reference to a more detailed description of the process of classification according to ethnicity, see Note 1 in Appendix D. The countries which were considered as "ethnic" and those considered as "non-ethnic" are shown in Table 16, on p. 129 of the present volume.

TABLE 3

DISTRIBUTION OF PUPILS BY STATUS LEVELS
AND ETHNICITY CLASSIFICATIONS

Status Level	Ethnicity Classifications			Total
	Old American	Scandinavian	Ethnic	
High status (I.S.C. 4-12)	230-237*	9-18	4-3	243-258
	9.7%*	0.6%	0.1%	10.4%
Medium status (I.S.C. 13-20)	1,326-1,397	114-181	113-127	1,553-1,705
	56.7%	6.1%	5.0%	67.8%
Low status (I.S.C. 21-27)	332-374	19-16	148-157	499-547
	14.7%	0.7%	6.3%	21.8%
Total	1,888-2,008	142-215	265-287	2,295-2,510
	81.1%	7.4%	11.5%	100.0%

* The first two figures in each "cell" represent the number of pupils — the first figure being the number of nine- and ten-year-old pupils and the second being the number of thirteen- and fourteen-year-old pupils. The third figure in each cell, which is underlined, gives the number of pupils (both age groups combined) as a percentage of the total number of pupils.

and 12 per cent as ethnic. This greatly underestimates the size and importance of the Scandinavian group in the community studied, since with a very few exceptions only pupils whose parents were born in one of the Scandinavian countries are so classified in this study. Most of the children who are regarded by the community as Scandinavians are third- and fourth-generation Scandinavians and appear in this study as Old Americans under the definitions explained in the preceding paragraphs.

Table 3 indicates clearly that there is quite a different distribution of I.S.C.'s for the three groups classified on the basis of ethnicity. The

Old American group is distributed in substantial numbers over the entire social-status scale, although heavily predominating in the middle I.S.C. range. The few Scandinavians are even more heavily concentrated in the middle range, with only a few scattered individuals appearing in either the high-status or the low-status ranges. The ethnics are found in both the middle-status and the low-status ranges, with the heaviest predominance in the low-status area; practically no ethnics are found in the high-status groups.

Table 3 shows the total group of pupils divided into nine "cells," each characterized by a certain type of social status and a certain category of ethnicity. Certain of these cells are of much more interest for the analysis to be described in this report than others. Since the main comparisons are to be made between high- and low-status groups, the three medium-status cells are relatively unimportant. The high- and low-status Scandinavian groups, and the high-status ethnic group, can be eliminated from consideration, since there are insufficient cases in any of them to make valid comparisons possible. This leaves the three cells which are shaded in Table 3. They are the three groups in terms of which most of the analysis which follows is made. It will be seen that the number of pupils available for study in these three cells varies from 148 to 374.

Summary

An Index of Status Characteristics, modified from one employed in another community study, was used to estimate the socioeconomic status of the families from which all the children in the study came. This index is based upon ratings of the parents' occupation, parents' education, type of house, and dwelling area in the community.

A sociological field worker made a partial social-class stratification of the community, based upon interviews and other sources of primary data, and made tentative social-class placements of several hundred families. These were used as a basis for checking the validity of using the Index of Status Characteristics for estimating social-class placement.

By means of the Index of Status Characteristics, a high-status group and a low-status group of pupils were selected for special study. These two groups were then subdivided, on the basis of ethnicity, into Old American, Scandinavian, and "ethnic" groups. Of the six groups thus secured, only three included sufficient numbers of pupils to make detailed item analysis practical. The three groups so established were high-status Old American, low-status Old American, and low-status ethnic. These groups were established separately at each of the two age levels.

CHAPTER XII

DESCRIPTION OF PUPILS IN THE STUDY:
GENERAL CHARACTERISTICS

This study is based on a particular group of children. It is important, therefore, to have some basis for judging the extent to which conclusions drawn from this analysis may be applied to other groups of children, and the extent to which the application of the conclusions may be limited by special characteristics of the particular group of children studied here.

In this chapter the pupils will be described in terms of number, representativeness, age, school attended, grade placement, and intelligence-test scores. In the following chapter they will be described in terms of their socioeconomic characteristics.

Number and Representativeness of Pupils

The question of how representative the pupils in the present study are in relation to some larger group may be resolved into two questions:

1. How typical and representative is Rockford in relation to other communities?

2. How representative of the Rockford population are the pupils included in the study?

No claim is made that Rockford is just like any other community or that conclusions drawn on the basis of a study of one community can be applied indiscriminately to all types of communities. Data for judging the extent to which Rockford is typical of other communities and other parts of the country are reported in Tables 4 and 5, which show census data for Rockford, for the total United States, and for the total urban population of the United States, on sex, age, nativity, race, education of adults, school attendance of children, and occupation.

The last two columns of these tables indicate that in most of these aspects the composition of the Rockford population is remarkably similar to that of the total United States and also to that of the total urban population of the United States. The fact that the Rockford population contains a somewhat larger proportion of foreign-born whites and a smaller proportion of Negroes than is true for the national population is a reflection of the criteria used for selecting Rockford, as described in chapter x. The variations of the Rockford occupational distribution from the national data reflect (a) the relatively high incidence of skilled and semiskilled workers in the machine-tool industry which predominates in Rockford and (b) the almost total lack of farmers and farm laborers in an urban community.

There are five items in these two tables for which the percentages for the total United States and those for the total urban population differ by 5 or more percentage points.[1] On three of these five, the Rockford popula-

---

1. "Urban population" is used here, as defined in the census, to include all persons living in cities or towns of 2,500 or more.

TABLE 4

COMPARATIVE STATUS OF ROCKFORD POPULATION WITH
RESPECT TO SEX, AGE, NATIVITY, RACE, AND EDUCATION*

	Percentage Composition			Rockford Deviation (if More than 5%)	
	Rockford	U.S. Total	U.S. Urban Total	Rockford--U.S. Total	Rockford--U.S. Urban Total
Sex:					
Males	49.5%	50.2%	48.9%	. . .	. . .
Females	50.5	49.8	51.1	. . .	. . .
	100.0%	100.0%	100.0%	. . .	. . .
Age:					
0-14	19.3%	25.0%	21.4%	-5.7%	. . .
15-29	26.2	26.6	26.8	. . .	. . .
30-44	23.9	21.7	23.7	. . .	. . .
45-59	19.2	16.2	17.5	. . .	. . .
60 and over	11.4	10.4	10.6	. . .	. . .
	100.0%	100.0%	100.0%	. . .	. . .
Nativity and race:					
Native-born white	82.4%	81.1%	79.1%	. . .	. . .
Foreign-born white . . .	16.2	8.7	12.3	7.5%	. . .
Negro	1.4	9.8	8.4	- 8.4	-7.0%
Other races	. . . .	0.4	0.3	. . .	. . .
	100.0%	100.0%	100.0%	. . .	. . .
Number of years of school completed by adults:					
None	2.4%	3.7%	3.6%	. . .	. . .
Grade school {1-4	4.9	9.8	7.7	. . .	. . .
{5-6	8.5	11.4	9.9	. . .	. . .
{7-8	39.0	34.6	33.3	. . .	5.7%
High school {1-3	17.2	15.0	15.9	. . .	. . .
{4	17.4	14.1	16.6	. . .	. . .
College {1-3	5.4	5.4	6.0	. . .	. . .
{4	4.4	4.6	5.7	. . .	. . .
Not reported	0.8	1.4	1.3	. . .	. . .
	100.0%	100.0%	100.0%	. . .	. . .
Proportion of children of school age actually in school:					
Age 5-6	42.4%	43.0%	53.6%	. . .	-11.2%
Age 7-13	97.5	95.0	97.1	. . .	. . .
Age 14-15	96.0	90.0	94.7	6.0%	. . .
Age 16-17	72.9	68.7	75.6	. . .	. . .
Age 18-20	21.6	28.9	26.1	-7.3	. . .
Age 21-24	4.1	5.1	6.1	. . .	. . .

* Data from U.S. Census, 1940.

TABLE 5

COMPARATIVE STATUS OF ROCKFORD POPULATION
WITH RESPECT TO OCCUPATION*

Occupation	Rockford	U.S. Total	U.S. Urban Total	Rockford Deviation (if More than 5%)	
				Rockford--U.S. Total	Rockford--U.S. Urban Total
Professional and managerial:					
Professional	6.2%	6.4%	7.6%	. . .	. . .
Semiprofessional	1.8	1.0	1.4	. . .	. . .
Farmers and farm managers	0.1	11.4	0.3	-11.3%	. . .
Proprietors, managers, and officials	8.6	8.3	9.9	. . .	. . .
Clerks, salesmen, and kindred workers	21.6	16.6	22.9	5.0	. . .
Skilled and semiskilled:					
Craftsmen, foremen, and kindred workers	19.3	11.2	13.3	8.1	6.0%
Operatives and kindred workers	27.3	18.3	21.4	9.0	5.9
Largely unskilled:					
Domestic service	2.3	4.7	5.3	. . .	. . .
Service workers, except domestic	7.1	7.7	9.9	. . .	. . .
Farm laborers	0.1	6.9	0.5	-6.8	. . .
Laborers, except farm	4.5	6.8	6.7	. . .	. . .
Not reported	1.1	0.8	0.8	. . .	. . .
Total	100.0%	100.0%	100.0%	. . .	. . .

* Data from U.S. Census, 1940.

tion is, not unexpectedly, more nearly like the total urban population than it is like the total United States population. It is clear that in almost all respects for which census data are available Rockford is remarkably typical of the total urban population of the United States and that it is fairly representative even of the total population. It seems reasonable to suppose, therefore, that interpretations drawn from the data presented in this report can, with a reasonable amount of caution, be applied in many other similar communities.

Whether the interpretations could be carried over into an entirely different kind of community — one that is primarily agricultural, for instance — would be open to more serious doubt. It is probable that in such cases the general findings of the study (e.g., that variations in cultural background of children may have an important influence on their response to certain kinds of intelligence-test items) would be applicable even though the specific instances of that cultural influence might be somewhat different from those exhibited for this particular urban community.

The question as to whether the pupils included in this study are representative of the Rockford population itself is capable of more precise determination. The group studied was drawn from the nine-, ten-, thirteen-, and fourteen-year-old age ranges and, with certain exceptions to be explained below, includes all the children in these age ranges living in Rockford or in certain of its adjacent suburban areas. So far as is known, the only children in these age ranges living within the geographical area covered by the study but not included in the reported analysis are the following:

1. Children not enrolled in any public or private school in the area

2. Negro, Oriental, and Indian pupils

3. Pupils for whom it was impossible, because of absence or other special reasons (deafness, poor eyesight, etc.), to secure satisfactory test data

4. Pupils for whom it was impossible to secure the necessary information as a basis for determining socioeconomic status

It does not seem likely that the first classification includes any significant number of individuals, even though a polio epidemic in the fall of the year in which the testing was done did result in the long-term hospitalization and complete withdrawal from school of some children. There were also probably a few children whose homes were in Rockford but who were in boarding schools elsewhere. It is possible that some pupils had dropped out of school to go to work, but the distribution of ages reported later in this chapter, as well as the data reported in Table 4, on page 103, lend support to the belief that there were not many who had done so.

Nonwhite children were intentionally excluded from the study, since there were not a sufficient number of them (144 at both age levels) to make possible a separate analysis and since it seemed possible, even likely, that the cultural relationships between status factors and performance on intelligence tests might be different in nature, or degree, from those exhibited for white children.

The principal of each of the thirty-seven public, private, and parochial schools in the area being studied was asked in the fall of 1945 to compile a list of all the pupils in his school, in whatever grade, whose birthdays fell in the years 1931, 1932, 1935, or 1936. The testing took place in Jan-

uary, 1946. By this time certain of the pupils on the lists had moved out of the city, and presumably others had moved into Rockford. At the time of the testing the principals were asked to include in the test groups any pupils born in the designated years who had entered their schools since the original lists had been made out; the extent to which this was done systematically was not known. However, 113 pupils who had not been on the original lists were tested in this way — compared with 36 pupils who had been on the original lists but who had left the schools between the time of compiling the lists and the time of administering the tests.

The extent to which lack of usable test data or of usable social status data limited the number of pupils included in the study is indicated in Table 6. This table indicates that the group of pupils who were supposed to be included in the present study (after eliminating nonwhites and those who had left the city) included 2,363 nine- and ten-year-olds and 2,645 thirteen- and fourteen-year-olds. This constitutes the basic group which should have been included in the present study if 100 per cent representation had been obtained; it is the group in terms of which representativeness should be judged.

TABLE 6

NUMBER OF PUPILS AVAILABLE FOR STUDY

IN TOTAL GROUP OF PUPILS

	Number of Pupils		Per Cent of Pupils Who Should Have Been Included	
	Age 9-10	Age 13-14	Age 9-10	Age 13-14
Pupils properly in group to be tested	2,363	2,645	100.0%	100.0%
Pupils eliminated because no usable tests available	34	53	1.4	2.0
Pupils eliminated because no I.S.C. available	34	82	1.4	3.1
Pupils included in the study	2,295	2,510	97.1	94.9
Pupils included in the study, for any one test	2,215-2,273	2,443-2,463	93.7-96.2	92.4-93.1

Of these two age groups, 2,295 and 2,510 pupils, respectively, were actually included in the study. These pupils comprise 97 per cent of the nine- and ten-year-old pupils and 95 per cent of the thirteen- and fourteen-year-old pupils who should have been included. This does not mean that 2,295 copies of each test were available for every nine- and ten-year-old pupil in the study, since some pupils were absent for some of the days of testing but not for the entire week. That the additional loss of data in this way was not substantial is indicated by the last line of Table 6. In no case do the tests available represent less than 92 per cent of the total number of pupils who would have been included if perfect coverage had been obtained. This includes those tests given, two months after the main testing, to pupils absent at the time of the first testing. For no test do these later tests constitute as much as 5 per cent of the total.

There can be little question but that the group studied was substantially representative of the total group. Even if there should be some bias present in the absentees or in the cases of missing status data, the error introduced could hardly be a large one, since the number of pupils eliminated for all causes was only 3 to 5 per cent of the total number of cases which should have been included to secure 100 per cent coverage. As a matter of fact, examination of partial social-status data available for 109 of the 116 pupils eliminated for lack of the necessary I.S.C. indicated that these eliminated pupils were not significantly lower in social status than the pupils included in the study.[2]

The data given in Table 6 indicate the total number of pupils and tests available for analysis. The main research procedures used in this study, however, were based on the comparison and contrast of the performance of certain special groups of pupils; this, of course, involved much smaller numbers than the total pupils indicated in Table 6. The number of pupils, and number of tests, in the three status groups used as a basis for most of the analysis reported in later chapters are shown in Table 7. The differences in Table 7 between the total number of pupils available and the number available for any one test represent pupils who were absent for from one to four days of the test week. It will be noticed that the incidence of this absence is somewhat heavier in the low-status Old American group than in either of the other two.

Chronological Age

The pupils in the testing program include all those whose birthdays fell in the years 1935, 1936, 1931, and 1932, with the exception of the few who were eliminated because of absence, lack of socioeconomic data, or race, as explained earlier. It seems reasonable to suppose that those pupils who are included in the special high- and low-status groups would constitute a cross-section of this entire population with respect to age and that there would therefore be no significant differences among the ages of the different status groups. Since, however, I.Q.'s for these groups are to be compared in the next chapter, it seems wise to establish definitely that there are no important age differences between the status groups. The data for judging this are presented in Table 8.

There are small differences in age as between some of the different status groups. The largest difference occurs with the younger pupils, where the low-status ethnics average slightly more than a month older than the high-status pupils, with low-status Old Americans falling almost midway between the other two. Even this largest difference is, however, only one and a half times its standard error. For the older pupils the differences are smaller and do not follow the same pattern as those for the younger pupils. In no case is the difference larger than its standard error.

---

2. For a brief summary of the evidence upon which this statement is based see Note 2 in Appendix D.

107

TABLE 7

NUMBER OF PUPILS AVAILABLE FOR STUDY IN
THREE SPECIAL STATUS GROUPS

	Number of Pupils		
	High-Status Old American	Low-Status Old American	Low-Status Ethnic
Nine- and ten-year-old pupils:			
Total pupils available	230	332	148
Pupils available for any one test*	223-228	316-329	141-146
Thirteen- and fourteen-year-old pupils:			
Total pupils available	237	374	157
Pupils available for any one test*	232-236	352-364	150-155

* Figures show smallest, and largest, number of pupils available for any one of the five tests given at each age level.

The standard deviations of the ages are similar for all six status groups. In no case is the difference between any two standard deviations even as large as its standard error.

Table 8 provides some evidence that no serious bias was introduced into the older group of pupils by including some pupils who could legally leave school to go to work. If any very large number of pupils had dropped out of school for this reason, the mean age for the older pupils would probably have dropped below fourteen. Furthermore, if there had been many such drop-outs, they would probably have come in disproportionately large numbers from the low-status group. This would result in lowering the average age for these two groups as compared to that of the high-status group. This may explain the somewhat lower age of the low-status Old American pupils, but it is apparent that any discrepancy introduced in this way is not a serious one. The argument of this paragraph depends, of course, upon assuming that the birth rate was fairly stable for 1931 as compared with 1932 for all three status groups. It has already been pointed out that the data in Table 4, on page 103, indicate that there is no large amount of dropping out of school in Rockford until the age of fifteen.

School Attended

The schools in which these children are enrolled are of various types.

TABLE 8

AGES OF PUPILS IN THREE STATUS GROUPS

Status Group	Nine- and Ten-Year-Old Pupils			Thirteen- and Fourteen-Year-Old Pupils		
	Number of Pupils	Mean Age (Years and Months)	Standard Deviation (Months)	Number of Pupils	Mean Age (Years and Months)	Standard Deviation (Months)
High-status Old American .	230	10 + 0.1	7.0	237	14 + 0.7	6.8
Low-status Old American .	332	10 + 0.6	7.0	374	14 + 0.1	6.9
Low-status ethnic	148	10 + 1.2	6.8	157	14 + 0.6	7.1

Nearly two-thirds of the younger pupils are found in the eighteen six-grade public elementary schools in the city school system. The rest are divided almost equally between three eight-grade county schools and six eight-grade Catholic elementary schools. Less than 1 per cent are in the one private school included in the study. The older pupils are somewhat more heavily concentrated in the Rockford public schools, since the suburban school districts do not maintain schools beyond the eighth grade but send their older children in to the city school system. Three-fourths of the older pupils are found in the Rockford public schools, with the rest divided nearly equally between the county public schools and the Catholic schools. Of those who are enrolled in the Rockford public schools, the overwhelming majority are found in three junior high schools, although 8 per cent of the total pupils at the older age level are in the two senior high schools, and 4 per cent are still in the six-year elementary schools.

It will be of interest, and of some importance, to determine the extent to which the three status groups are highly concentrated in a few individual schools and the extent to which they are spread out over a larger number of schools in the community. Table 9 indicates the individual schools which contribute more than 10 per cent of the total number of pupils in any status group. Because of the well-known fact that many residential areas in any community tend to be relatively homogeneous with regard to the status level of people living in them, it is not surprising to find that the high-status, or low-status, pupils of the community tend to be concentrated in certain schools which serve particular residential areas.

Table 9 indicates, for instance, that, for nine- and ten-year-old pupils at any one of the three status levels, one school contributes from a fifth to a fourth of the total pupils; three schools in each group contribute approximately half of the total. On the other hand, it may be seen that from a third to a half of the pupils of this age group, for each of the status groups, come from a wide scattering of schools no one of which contributes more than 10 per cent of the total of the status group. No one school contributes any substantial number of pupils to two different status levels. Even the two

109

TABLE 9

SCHOOLS ATTENDED BY PUPILS IN THREE STATUS GROUPS

Nine- and Ten-Year-Old Pupils

Status Group	School	Number of Pupils	Per Cent of Total Pupils	Cumulative Percentage
High-status Old American	School A	56	24.3%	24.3%
	School B	46	20.0	44.3
	School C	26	11.3	55.7
	School D	26	11.3	67.0
	13 schools* . . .	76	33.0	100.0
	Total	230	100.0%	. . . .
Low-status Old American	School E	78	23.5%	23.5%
	School F	48	14.5	38.0
	School G	38	11.4	49.4
	20 schools* . . .	168	50.6	100.0
	Total	332	100.0%	. . . .
Low-status ethnic	School H	30	20.3%	20.3%
	School I	29	19.6	39.9
	School J	18	12.2	52.0
	School K	18	12.2	64.2
	13 schools* . . .	53	35.8	100.0
	Total	148	100.0%	. . . .

Thirteen- and Fourteen-Year-Old Pupils

Status Group	School	Number of Pupils	Per Cent of Total Pupils	Cumulative Percentage
High-status Old American	School L	101	42.6%	42.6%
	School M	80	33.8	76.4
	School N	25	10.5	86.9
	6 schools* . . .	31	13.1	100.0
	Total	237	100.0%	. . . .
Low-status Old American	School L	83	22.2%	22.2%
	School M	72	19.3	41.4
	School E	67	17.9	59.4
	21 schools* . . .	152	40.6	100.0
	Total	374	100.0%	. . . .
Low-status ethnic	School N	57	36.3%	36.3%
	School K	19	12.1	48.4
	15 schools* . . .	81	51.6	100.0
	Total	157	100.0%	. . . .

* These are schools each of which contributes less than 10 per cent of the total status group with which it is listed.

low-status groups are largely segregated from each other in different schools.

Table 9 indicates a greater concentration of the older pupils in a few schools and more overlapping of status groups within certain schools. This is, of course, to be expected, since most of the thirteen- and fourteen-year-old pupils are in junior and senior high schools, which serve larger areas of the community than do the elementary schools. Eighty-seven per cent of the high-status children are found in three schools. On the other hand, from 40 to 50 per cent of the low-status children are found scattered among a relatively large number of schools.

Grade Placement

Information as to the grade in which the pupils were enrolled was not secured systematically from all schools. In a great many cases, however, the grades were given by the schools at the time the original lists of pupils were submitted. This was true for practically all the pupils in the public schools and for some of those in the Catholic schools. The distribution of grade placements for the younger group of pupils is shown in Table 10.

There is a considerable range of grades represented by this two-year age group. Nine- and ten-year-old pupils are found all the way from the second grade to the sixth, although most of them are, of course, in the fourth and fifth grades. There is a considerable difference between the average grade placement of the high-status and the low-status pupils; the high-status pupils are, on the average, one-half grade higher than the low-status pupils. This difference is statistically significant (critical ratios of 7.6 for the comparison with low-status Old Americans and 4.3 for the comparison with low-status ethnics).

The three lines of percentages at the bottom of Table 10 indicate that even in the elementary school there are distinct differences in the promotion rates for pupils from the different social-status groups. By the time these children have reached the age of nine and ten, 30 per cent of the low-status children are retarded behind their normal school grade, while only 4 per cent of the high-status pupils are retarded. Very few low-status children are found in accelerated grades, although high-status pupils have been accelerated somewhat more often than they have been retarded.

Similar grade-placement data for the older pupils are shown in Table 11. The thirteen- and fourteen-year-old pupils are scattered all the way from the third to the tenth grades, with most of them in the eighth and ninth grades, as would be expected. There is a difference between the mean grade placement for the high- and low-status groups amounting to four-fifths of a year for the Old Americans and three-fifths of a year for the low-status ethnics. The differences between the high- and low-status means are definitely significant (critical ratios of 11.0 for the Old Americans and 4.8 for the ethnics), and the difference between the means for the two low-status groups is probably significant (critical ratio of 2.0). Thus the half-year lag found for both low-status groups at the nine- and ten-year-old age level has apparently increased by the time the pupils reach the junior high school level. The low-status Old Americans seem to lose ground relative to the high-status pupils at a greater rate than do the low-status ethnics.

Not only is there an increasing lag in mean grade placement for the

TABLE 10

GRADE PLACEMENT OF NINE- AND TEN-YEAR-OLD PUPILS

Grade	All Pupils	High-Status Old American	Low-Status Old American	Low-Status Ethnic
	Number of Pupils			
II	44	1	13	7
III	270	8	69	21
III and IV	35	. . .	15	1
IV	972	117	123	36
V	696	74	72	24
VI	53	12	2	3
Ungraded and unknown	225	18	38	56
Total	2,295	230	332	148
Mean grade	4.2	4.4	3.9	3.9
Standard deviation	0.8	0.7	0.8	1.0
	Percentage of Retardation and Acceleration			
Per cent retarded (Grades II-III)* . .	16.0%	4.2%	30.3%	30.4%
Per cent normal (Grades IV-V)* . .	81.4	90.1	69.0	66.3
Per cent accelerated (Grade VI)	2.6	5.7	0.7	3.3

* For the purposes of these percentages the 35 pupils reported in the table as being in a combined third and fourth grade are divided equally between the "retarded" and the "normal" classifications.

TABLE 11

GRADE PLACEMENT OF THIRTEEN- AND FOURTEEN-
YEAR-OLD PUPILS

Grade	All Pupils	High-Status Old American	Low-Status Old American	Low-Status Ethnic
	Number of Pupils			
III and IV	1	. . .	1	. . .
V	12	. . .	3	3
V and VI	7	. . .	3	. . .
VI	99	. . .	34	10
VII	332	7	84	24
VIII	839	91	114	33
IX	874	105	95	38
X	219	32	13	14
Ungraded and unknown	127	2	27	35
Total	2,510	237	374	157
Mean grade	8.3	8.7	7.9	8.1
Standard deviation	1.1	0.7	1.1	1.2
	Percentage of Retardation and Acceleration			
Per cent retarded (Grades III-VII) . . .	18.9%	3.0%	36.0%	30.3%
Per cent normal (Grades VIII-IX) . .	71.9	83.4	60.2	58.2
Per cent accelerated (Grade X)	9.2	13.6	3.7	11.5

low-status pupils, but there is an increase in the extent to which the low-status pupils tend to spread out over a wide range of grades. This is indicated both in the frequency distributions at the top of Tables 10 and 11 and by the standard deviations. The standard deviations indicate that for both low-status groups the older pupils are more spread out in grade placement than are the younger pupils, while for the high-status pupils the degree of dispersion is identical at both age levels.

The relationships indicated by the retardation and acceleration percentages shown at the bottom of Table 11 are not markedly different from those shown for the younger pupils in Table 10. The proportion of pupils retarded increases somewhat in the low-status Old American group, but the general relationships are similar. At the older age level the proportion of pupils accelerated increases at all status levels over what it was for the younger pupils. For neither low-status group, however, does the proportion of pupils accelerated equal even half of the proportion retarded, while for the high-status group the proportion accelerated is more than four times the proportion retarded.

These facts regarding status differences in grade placement and rates of promotion will be important for understanding the status differences found for certain kinds of items in the analysis reported in later chapters.

These same grade-placement data are shown graphically in Figure 3. This chart shows the relationships already pointed out in connection with Tables 10 and 11. It may be seen clearly here that the low-status groups occupy a wider range of grades and that the low-status groups have a lower average grade placement. It is interesting to notice that at Grade VI there are found some low-status pupils from both age levels; there is no such overlapping for high-status pupils.

Intelligence Quotients and Percentile Ranks

While it is one of the basic hypotheses of this study that present-day intelligence tests do not necessarily measure "intelligence" in the sense of any innate ability, yet scores on these tests do reveal some pertinent information about the pupils. Since so much of this study is to deal with the responses of these pupils to items on intelligence tests, it seems worth while to examine briefly the extent to which these pupils are "typical" with respect to their intelligence-test performance.

The distribution of the I.Q.'s of the nine- and ten-year-old pupils on four different tests is indicated in Table 12. This table indicates that the I.Q.'s of more than two thousand nine- and ten-year-old children differ considerably according to what test is used to measure them. The Kuhlmann-Anderson and the two Otis Alpha tests show substantially similar results — the three tests give a distribution of I.Q.'s ranging from a few cases in the 130's to a few in the 60's, with a mean I.Q. for the entire group of close to 100 and a standard deviation of 10 to 11. Even the small differences among the mean I.Q.'s from these three tests are, however, statistically significant — none of them being less than four times its standard error. The distribution of I.Q.'s produced by the Henmon-Nelson test is, however, quite different. The lower limit of the I.Q. range is about the same as for the other three tests, but the Henmon-Nelson test yields several hundred I.Q.'s of 130 or over, with some reaching up into the 150's. As a concomitant of this greater reaching up into the higher I.Q.'s the mean I.Q. is 4 to 7 points higher than that obtained from the other

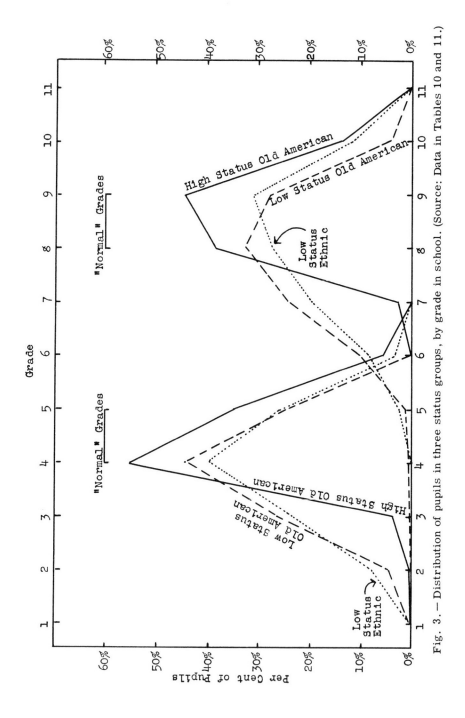

Fig. 3. – Distribution of pupils in three status groups, by grade in school. (Source: Data in Tables 10 and 11.)

TABLE 12

I.Q.'S OF NINE- AND TEN-YEAR-OLD PUPILS

Intelligence Quotients	Henmon-Nelson	Kuhlmann-Anderson	Otis Alpha Verbal	Otis Alpha Nonverbal
150 and over . . .	19	1	. . .	. . .
140-49	74	. . .	. . .	. . .
130-39	133	6	. . .	1
120-29	298	130	72	63
110-19	452	505	511	381
100-09	496	787	718	745
90-99	419	579	591	623
80-89	228	212	296	334
70-79	107	35	42	60
60-69	12	17	5	8
Below 60	. . .	1	. . .	. . .
Total	2,238	2,273	2,235	2,215
Mean I.Q.	107.2	102.9	101.3	99.9
Standard deviation	17.2	11.3	10.8	10.8

tests, and the standard deviation is 6 points larger.

These intertest differences doubtless reflect, at least in part, differences in the "intelligence" of the standardizing groups of pupils from which the age norms were obtained by the test authors. If one test is standardized upon a group of pupils selected in such a manner that they are above the average in intelligence, the age norms will be unduly inflated, and subsequent computation of I.Q.'s for other pupils will yield lower I.Q.'s than if the original standardizing group had been more representative.

The differences shown in Table 12 are also doubtless due, in part, to differences in the "ceilings" of the tests. The Henmon-Nelson test, devised for pupils in Grades III to VIII, includes a wider range of material, and more material at the higher difficulty level, than do the Otis Alpha tests, devised primarily for pupils in Grades I to IV. Table 12 indicates that several hundred of these pupils have Henmon-Nelson I.Q.'s of more than 130. For pupils aged 10-0 (approximately the median for this group), a "perfect" score on all ninety items of the Otis Alpha Verbal test would yield an I.Q. of only 128. Even a pupil aged 9-0 (the youngest in this group) can secure from the Otis Alpha Verbal an I.Q. no higher than 136. The ceiling of the Otis Alpha Nonverbal test for pupils of this age is slightly higher than that for the Otis Alpha Verbal but still well below that of the Henmon-Nelson test. The Kuhlmann-Anderson test, as given to these pupils, seems to have a ceiling only slightly below that of the Henmon-Nelson test, but, because of the nature of the method of computing the I.Q. for the Kuhlmann-Anderson test, exact comparison is difficult.

Table 13 reports similar data regarding intelligence quotients and other derived scores for the tests given to the thirteen- and fourteen-year-old pupils. In this case not so many intertest comparisons are possible, since two of the test scores are in terms of I.Q.'s, two in terms of percentile ranks based on norms supplied by the test authors, and one in terms of percentile ranks based on local Rockford norms. An examination of the means reported in this table indicates that on all the tests this group of pupils scores near the expected averages (I.Q. 100 or percentile rank 50). A comparison of the distribution of Terman-McNemar and Otis Beta I.Q.'s shows that the Terman-McNemar yields a few scores at a higher level than any given by the Otis Beta, although the average of the Terman-McNemar is slightly lower. The difference between the mean I.Q.'s on these two tests is definitely a significant one, however — being 3.7 times its standard error. The standard deviation of the Terman-McNemar I.Q.'s is somewhat larger than that for the Otis Beta test.

Since the scores for the two Thurstone tests are in percentile-rank form, a distribution of these scores would normally include an equal number of individuals in each of the ten intervals in which the data are grouped. An examination of Table 13 indicates some tendency for a larger than normal number of students to "pile up" at the bottom end of the Thurstone Spatial distribution and at the top end of the Thurstone Reasoning distribution — a tendency which results in a clearly significant difference between the means of the two distributions (critical ratio, 17.6). It is difficult to account for this difference, since the two Thurstone tests were standardized upon the same group of pupils. At least one study (41, p. 243) has shown that the Thurstone Spatial test is very sensitive to the manner of presentation by the test administrator. It may be that some unknown variations in manner of administration affected the results on this test in the present study.

The extent to which the intertest differences observed in Tables 12 and 13 are uniform for the various socioeconomic levels will be examined later. It is sufficient here to note that on most of the tests the Rockford group as a whole scores very close to the expected norm of an unselected group. On two tests the Rockford pupils score somewhat above this expected norm, however, and on one they score noticeably below it.

Summary

Those portions of the analysis which include the total group of pupils are based on from 2,215 to 2,463 pupils, the exact number varying according to the particular test and age level. Those portions of the analysis which involve only the three special status groups are based on from 141 to 364 pupils in each group, the exact number varying according to the test, age level, and status group. Evidence is presented to show that the pupils on whom the study is based are satisfactorily representative of the total groups in Rockford from which they were selected and that, in a number of respects, Rockford is reasonably typical of the total population — particularly of the total urban population — of the United States.

The nine- and ten-year-old pupils are found entirely in the elementary schools, about two-thirds of them in public six-grade elementary schools. The status groups are largely concentrated in separate schools, so that there is comparatively little overlapping of high-status and low-status pupils (or even of low-status Old Americans and low-status ethnics) in any one school.

TABLE 13

I.Q.'S AND PERCENTILE RANKS OF THIRTEEN- AND FOURTEEN-YEAR-OLD PUPILS

Intelligence Quotients	Number of Pupils	
	Terman-McNemar	Otis Beta
150 and over	1	....
140-49	16	....
130-39	86	32
120-29	244	207
110-19	478	627
100-09	590	718
90-99	469	496
80-89	310	266
70-79	175	102
60-69	62	16
Below 60	23	2
Total	2,454	2,463
Mean I.Q.	101.8	103.4
Standard deviation	16.8	13.3

Percentile Ranks	Number of Pupils		
	Thurstone Spatial*	Thurstone Reasoning*	California Mental Maturity+
90-99	192	457	273
80-89	184	323	256
70-79	194	255	261
60-69	191	219	235
50-59	197	186	227
40-49	216	158	244
30-39	245	273	275
20-29	257	193	222
10-19	321	243	239
0-9	452	150	210
Total	2,445	2,456	2,443
Mean percentile rank	41.5	56.6	51.0
Standard deviation	30.0	29.9	28.6

* Percentile ranks based on norms published by authors of test.
+ Percentile ranks based on scores of pupils in this study. The frequencies in the distribution of the California Mental Maturity percentile ranks are not all equal, as would be expected. For explanation see Note 3 in Appendix D.

The thirteen- and fourteen-year-old pupils are found predominantly in three public junior high schools, although some are still in elementary schools -- particularly in eight-grade schools -- and some are in senior high schools. For the older pupils there is more overlapping of the status groups in individual schools, because the junior and senior high schools are larger and serve wider geographical areas of the community than do the elementary schools.

The different status groups do not differ significantly in chronological age, but they do differ in grade placement. The high-status pupils tend to be either at their "normal" grade in school or accelerated ahead of it, with the proportion of accelerated pupils being greater for the thirteen- and fourteen-year-old pupils than for the nine- and ten-year-olds. The low-status pupils, whether in the Old American or ethnic groups, tend to be retarded in school from a half-year to a year behind the high-status pupils of the same age. The proportion of pupils retarded behind their normal grade is seven to twelve times as great for low-status pupils as for high-status pupils.

The average I.Q. of the pupils at both age levels is between 100 and 103, except on the Henmon-Nelson test, which shows an average I.Q. of 107 for the younger pupils. The standard deviations of the I.Q.'s range from a low of 11 points on the Otis Alpha Verbal test to a high of 17 points on the Henmon-Nelson test. The older pupils score somewhat higher than average, as judged by the published norms, on the Thurstone Reasoning test, and even more markedly below the average on the Thurstone Spatial test.

CHAPTER XIII

DESCRIPTION OF PUPILS IN THE STUDY:
SOCIOECONOMIC CHARACTERISTICS

In the preceding chapter the pupils on which the study is based were described in terms of a number of general characteristics. In this chapter the description will be extended to cover certain socioeconomic characteristics of the pupils. This will be done, first, through statistical summaries and, second, by brief case descriptions of a number of individual pupils.

Index of Status Characteristics

The distribution of the indexes of status characteristics for individual pupils at both age levels is reported in Table 14. The data indicate that there are no substantial differences between the I.S.C.'s at the two age levels, either for the total group or for any status group considered separately. In no case is the difference even as large as its standard error. The small differences which do exist are consistent, however, for all status groups, with the older pupils having a slightly lower status than the younger pupils. The two low-status groups show approximately the same distribution of I.S.C.'s, although the ethnic group has a significantly lower mean status than the Old American group (critical ratios of 2.4 and 3.1 at the two age levels). Since the three status groups were selected largely on the basis of the I.S.C., they present, of course, a substantial amount of contrast on this factor, as will be seen clearly in Table 14.

The standard deviations of the distributions for the three status groups indicate that the greatest dispersion on the I.S.C. scale is found in the high-status group and the least dispersion in the low-status group. This should be interpreted cautiously, however, since there is no assurance that the I.S.C. represents equal units of status at the opposite ends of the scale.

The similarity of the distribution of I.S.C.'s for the two age levels may be seen clearly in Figure 4, which shows the two distributions in graphic form. It will be seen that the two distributions are closely similar at either end of the I.S.C. scale, from I.S.C. 4 through 15 and from I.S.C. 20 through 27. This includes the areas which have already been defined as the high-status and low-status groups in terms of which the major part of the study is based. The unaccountable variation in the I.S.C. distribution in the middle of the range does not affect the range of social status which is of particular importance in this study. It is interesting to note, however, that the larger number of thirteen- and fourteen-year-old pupils (2,510) as compared with the number of nine- and ten-year-olds (2,295) is almost entirely composed of pupils of middle social status, between I.S.C. 15 and 20. That this discrepancy in the two distributions is not to be regarded as particularly significant, however, is indicated by the chi-square test for these two distributions. A deviation between the two distributions as large as this would be expected to occur in some 30

TABLE 14

DISTRIBUTION OF PUPILS BY INDEX OF STATUS CHARACTERISTICS

Index of Status Characteristics*	Number of Pupils							
	All Pupils		High-Status Old American		Low-Status Old American		Low-Status Ethnic	
	Age 9-10	Age 13-14	Age 9-10	Age 13-14	Age 9-10	Age 13-14	Age 9-10	Age 13-14
4.........	...	2	...	2				
5.........	6	6	6	6				
6.........	11	5	11	5				
7.........	10	8	10	8				
8.........	28	29	27	27				
9.........	27	23	26	23				
10........	35	51	33	49				
11........	55	53	49	47				
12........	71	81	68	70				
13........	117	110						
14........	120	118						
15........	182	180						
16........	202	275						
17........	258	274						
18........	240	244						
19........	208	271						
20........	226	233						
21........	180	171	...	...	122	124	46	42
22........	132	162	...	...	95	114	33	41
23........	105	121	...	...	67	81	36	36
24........	50	54	...	...	30	36	20	18
25........	22	28	...	...	12	13	9	15
26........	6	6	...	...	4	3	2	3
27........	4	5	...	...	2	3	2	2
Total.....	2,295	2,510	230	237	332	374	148	157
Mean I.S.C.	17.4	17.5	10.0	10.1	22.2	22.2	22.5	22.6
Standard deviation.	3.8	3.8	2.0	1.9	1.1	1.2	1.4	1.4

* Small index numbers indicate high status; large numbers indicate low status.

per cent of the samples drawn even if there were no variation whatever between the two groups from which these are samples.

The distributions of I.S.C.'s illustrated in Figure 4 are of a general bell-shaped form, with a bunching of cases in the middle portion of the range and a tapering-off in number of cases toward each extreme. Application of the chi-square test to a combined distribution for these two age levels indicates, however, that the distribution of I.S.C.'s is not, strictly speaking, a "normal" one ($\chi^2 = 230$; $\bar{n} = 21$; $\bar{P} < .01$).[1]

There is a marked variation in status level of pupils from school to school. In order to illustrate this variation, the distribution of I.S.C.'s for nine- and ten-year-old pupils in seventeen six-grade schools is shown in Figure 5. While there is a considerable amount of overlapping between any two adjacent schools on this chart, the contrasts between the extremes are marked. It is clear that School A and School Q, for example, represent entirely different social-status situations. The very highest I.S.C. found in School Q just equals the very lowest I.S.C. found in School A. There are five schools (M, N, O, P, Q) in which three-fourths of the pupils are of lower status than the very lowest pupil in School A. Conversely, there are four schools (A, B, D, E) in which three-fourths of the pupils are of higher status than the very highest pupil in School Q. On the other hand, there are four schools (F, H, N, O) which include pupils ranging all the way from those higher than the average pupil in School A to those lower than the average pupil in School Q.

This comparative isolation of the pupils in certain status groups in certain schools is important for an understanding of the differences found for certain kinds of items as reported in a later chapter.

Separate Status Characteristics[2]

The majority of the high-status children come from homes in which the father's occupation is professional, managerial, or semiprofessional and in which the parents have had at least some college education. They live in houses rated as "good" or "average," or better; virtually none live in houses rated as below average. Practically none of them live in areas of the community rated as below average, and a majority live in areas rated as distinctly above average.

The majority of the low-status children, on the other hand, come from homes where the father's occupation is in the semiskilled or unskilled class. A few come from families where the father is a skilled laborer, but none comes from the ranks of professional or large-managerial occupations. Most of the parents of low-status Old American pupils have completed grammar school but have had no high-school work; some of them have had some high-school education, but few have graduated, and virtually none has had any college work. The typical parent of a low-status ethnic pupil has even less education, usually having had from four to seven years of schooling. A few of the low-status children live in houses rated "average," but the majority live in houses rated as "poor" or "very poor." Most of them live in areas of the community rated as "low-semi-slum" A very few are found in the "average" areas; none is in better than average neighborhoods.

---

1. For a reference to a graph showing this combined distribution and the normal curve fitted to it see Note 1 in Appendix D.
2. For a reference to the detailed statistical data underlying this section see Note 1 in Appendix D.

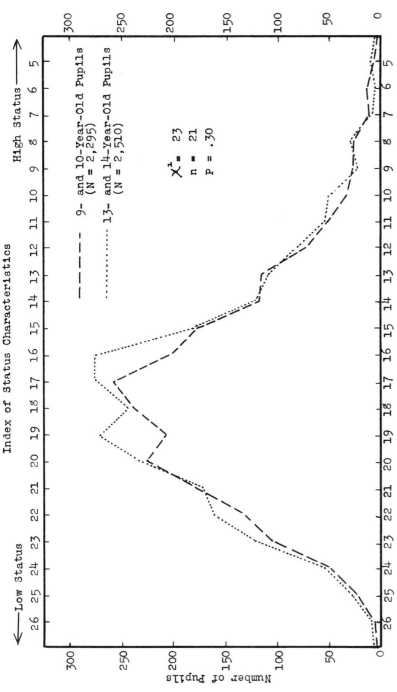

Fig. 4. – Distribution of all pupils in testing program, by Index of Status Characteristics. (Source: Data in Table 14.)

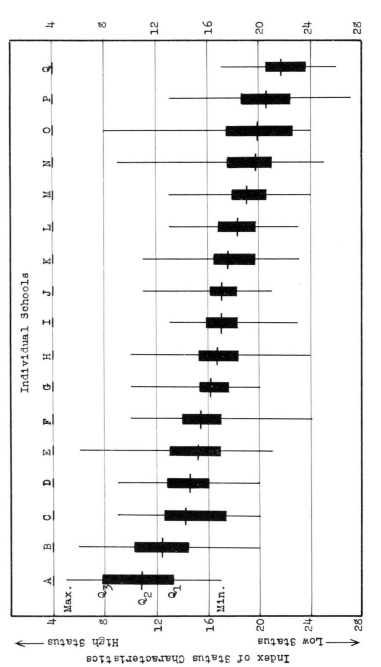

Fig. 5. – Distributions of nine- and ten-year-old pupils according to Index of Status Characteristics, for seventeen public elementary schools.

On all four status characteristics, as well as on the I.S.C. as a whole, the differences between the Old American and the ethnic low-status groups are very small in comparison to the size of the differences between the high- and low-status groups. The low-status Old American pupils receive significantly higher ratings than the ethnics on education and on dwelling area, but the low-status ethnics receive equally significantly higher ratings on house type.

Most of the differences between the two age levels are small and usually not statistically significant. The nine- and ten-year-old pupils of high status receive higher occupation and education ratings than do the thirteen- and fourteen-year-old pupils, but on the dwelling-area ratings this relationship is reversed.

Social-Class Equivalence

It would be desirable to be able to characterize the three status groups more or less exactly in terms of their social-class equivalence. It is not possible to do this precisely on the basis of the data available. Some estimate is possible, however, and an attempt was made to make the estimate as accurate as possible.

This was done by (a) estimating a probable social-class distribution of the total population of Rockford on the basis of available data for two other communities and by (b) estimating the probable allocation of families from different social-class levels to the different status groups defined for this study, on the basis of data from the field study of Rockford referred to earlier. The procedure was an unsatisfactory one, but it provides the best estimate which is available. Subject to this qualification, it can be said that the group of pupils defined for this study as "high status" probably consists entirely of pupils from middle-class and upper-class families, with from three-fifths to two-thirds of the group coming from families that are upper-middle class or higher. The pupils defined for this study as "low status" probably come entirely from lower-class families, with from two-thirds to three-fourths of them being from lower-lower-class families.[3]

Ethnicity

Ethnicity was defined as including certain foreign-origin groups and not others. Whether a given foreign-origin group was considered ethnic or not depended upon (a) whether there were sufficient numbers of the group in Rockford so that they could form a more or less self-contained group and (b) whether they were regarded by the rest of the community as constituting a group "different" and somewhat apart from the main community social structure. After this classification had been established, individual pupils were classified as Old American, ethnic, or Scandinavian. Three-fourths of the pupils classified as ethnic were so classified on the basis of one or both of their parents having been born in one of the countries previously determined to be an "ethnic" country; an additional 6 per cent were classified as ethnic on the basis of personal interview data. The remainder were judged to be ethnic on the basis of the ethnic character of their name, the residential area in which they lived, or a combination

3. For a reference to a description of the basis of this estimate see Note 1 in Appendix D.

of these two factors. In the case of the Scandinavians, only pupils one or both of whose parents were born in one of the Scandinavian countries were considered as being Scandinavian for this study (with the exception of eleven individuals so classified on the basis of interview data).[4]

An analysis of the individuals comprising each of the three status groups in terms of the nativity of their parents is reported in Table 15 and shown graphically in Figure 6. The "All Pupils" columns of Table 15 indicate that three-fourths of the younger pupils and two-thirds of the older pupils are of native-born parentage. Actually the percentages of native-born may be somewhat larger than indicated in Table 15, since it seems likely that a substantial proportion of the pupils for whom no information is available are of native-born parents. Of the remaining pupils, those with mixed parentage (one parent foreign-born and one native-born) outnumber those both of whose parents are foreign-born. There is no marked contrast between the age groups in this distribution, although the proportion of pupils of native-born parents is somewhat larger for the younger group of children than for the older.

Table 15 and Figure 6 make it clear that the Old American groups -- both high-status and low-status -- are composed largely (80 to 95 per cent) of pupils whose parents were born in the United States. The number of pupils whose parents were born in foreign countries which are classified for the purpose of this study as nonethnic is comparatively small; such pupils do not constitute a substantial proportion of any of the Old American groups. The low-status ethnic groups, on the other hand, are made up of three groups of approximately equal size, pupils of foreign-born parents, those of native-born parents, and those of mixed parentage. The children of foreign-born parents predominate somewhat in the older age group, while children of native parentage are somewhat more predominant in the younger age group. It will be noticed in Table 15 that most of the children from mixed parentages are the children of native-born mothers and foreign-born fathers; the reverse situation occurs only occasionally.

The distribution of these pupils by individual countries in which their parents were born is given in Table 16. It is clear from this table that, for the group as a whole, the pupils of foreign-born parents may be divided into three groups of roughly similar size: those whose parents were born in Sweden, those whose parents were born in Italy, and those whose parents were born in all other foreign countries combined.

Table 16 indicates that the low-status ethnic population in this study is predominantly an Italian one, with almost half of the younger age group and nearly two-thirds of the older age group having one or both parents born in Italy. There is a small group of Mexicans and even smaller groups of Poles, Lithuanians, and Belgians; none of these groups even approaches, however, the size of the Italian group. Were this not the case, one might raise the question as to whether it was wise to lump together, under the heading "ethnic," pupils from various different foreign backgrounds. It could be argued that there may be important psychological and cultural differences among the different foreign-born groups. This difficulty is not a serious one in the present study, however, since the "ethnic" group

4. For a reference to a more detailed account of the method of making these classifications on the basis of ethnicity see Note 1 in Appendix D. The process is not described in detail here, since the ethnic classification turned out to be comparatively unimportant and was dropped from most of the analysis reported in the later chapters.

TABLE 15

PERCENTAGE DISTRIBUTION OF PUPILS BY NATIVITY OF PARENTS

Nativity of Parents	All Pupils Age 9-10 (N=2,295)	All Pupils Age 13-14 (N=2,510)	High-Status Old American Age 9-10 (N=230)	High-Status Old American Age 13-14 (N=237)	Low-Status Old American Age 9-10 (N=332)	Low-Status Old American Age 13-14 (N=374)	Low-Status Ethnic Age 9-10 (N=148)	Low-Status Ethnic Age 13-14 (N=157)
Both parents native-born *	77.9%	69.2%	94.8%	91.1%	87.3%	80.7%	34.5%	21.7%
Both parents foreign-born *	6.0	8.0	0.4	0.8	0.6	0.5	27.7	42.7
Mixed parentage:								
Father native-born, mother foreign-born	2.0	3.2	1.3	1.7	0.3	1.3	2.0	5.1
Mother native-born, father foreign-born	8.5	9.8	.....	1.7	0.6	1.3	31.1	24.8
Nativity of both parents unknown	5.8	9.8	3.5	4.6	11.1	16.0	4.7	5.7
Total	100.0%	100.0%	100.0%	100.0%	100.0%	100.0%	100.0%	100.0%

* Includes a few pupils (in no case amounting to as much as 2 per cent of the total group) classified on the basis of the birthplace of one parent alone when only that information was available. In such cases the other parent was usually dead, divorced, or separated.

127

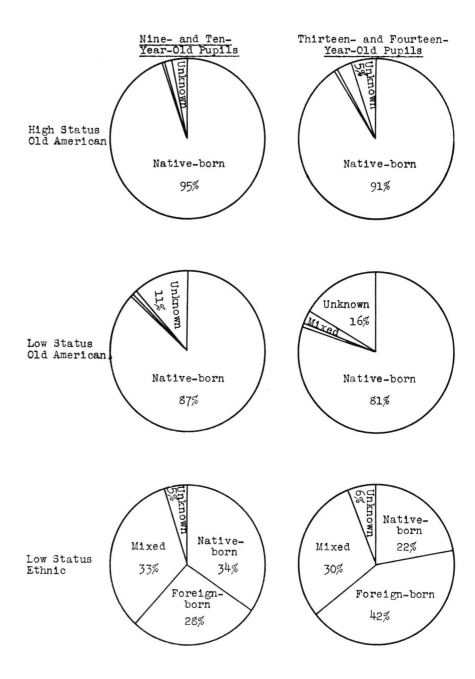

Fig. 6. — Distributions of pupils in three status groups, by nativity of parents. (Source: Data in Table 15.)

128

TABLE 16

DISTRIBUTION OF PUPILS BY COUNTRY OF BIRTH OF PARENTS

Country of Birth of Either or Both Parents	Number of Pupils							
	All Pupils		High-Status Old Americans		Low-Status Old Americans		Low-Status Ethnics	
	Age 9-10	Age 13-14	Age 9-10	Age 13-14	Age 9-10	Age 13-14	Age 9-10	Age 13-14
United States*	1,787	1,736	218	216	290	302	51	34
Countries considered as Scandinavian:								
Sweden	127	176	...	...	...	...	...	...
Norway	7	20	...	...	...	...	...	...
Countries considered as ethnic:								
Italy	114	157	...	...	...	...	66	90
Poland	13	15	...	...	...	...	4	7
Lithuania	11	15	...	...	...	...	3	5
Mexico	13	12	...	...	...	...	10	7
Belgium	9	4	...	...	...	...	2	1
Russia	6	6	...	...	...	...	...	1
Greece	4	7	...	...	...	...	1	1
Countries considered as nonethnic:								
England	10	25	2	4	...	5	...	...
Germany	14	21	...	...	3	1	...	...
Scotland	7	13	...	...	...	3	...	...
Canada	6	7	2	3	...	...	...	...
Ireland	6	6	...	1	1	1	...	...
Other Countries+	19	29	...	2	1	2	1	1
Combinations of above countries, except U.S.,‡	10	16	...	...	...	...	3	1
Birthplace of both parents unknown	132	245	8	11	37	60	7	9
Total	2,295	2,510	230	237	332	374	148	157

* Pupils are classified under United States in this table only if both parents were born in the United States or if one was born in the United States and the birthplace of the other is unknown. If one parent was born in a foreign country, the pupil is classified under the foreign country, even if the other parent was born in the United States.

+ Includes Australia, Austria, Czechoslovakia, Cuba, Denmark, Finland, France, Holland, Hungary, Yugoslavia, Latvia, Portugal, Switzerland and Syria (less than ten pupils per country).

‡ Less than five pupils in any one combination.

is so predominantly an Italian one. Actually, the Italian culture is even more predominant in the ethnic group than is indicated in Table 16, since most of the ethnic children of native-born parents are of Italian extraction.

Typical Individuals from Different Status Groups

Preceding sections of this chapter have presented data which describe, in statistical terms, some of the socioeconomic characteristics of the pupils comprising the three main status groups which constitute the subjects for most of the present investigation. In this final section a few individual pupils will be described very briefly. They have been selected to illustrate and make more concrete the kinds of pupils whose test responses are to be analyzed and compared in later chapters. The names and descriptions have been changed sufficiently to prevent the identification of any individuals, but the essential nature of the information presented is accurate.[5]

Extremely high-status pupils (I.S.C. 4 and 5)

The four individuals described briefly below are selected — two from each age level — from those pupils receiving the very highest I.S.C. rating in their respective age groups.

Ruth Collins is nine and a half years old and in the fourth grade. Her I.Q. is indicated as between 110 and 120. She is an only child. The Collins family is an old well-established upper-crust family in Rockford, having been leaders in the community for several generations. Ruth's father attended a private preparatory school, then went east to school, graduated from Harvard, and holds a Master's degree from Princeton. He is an executive in one of the larger manufacturing plants in Rockford. He has been a member of the board of directors of the Rockford Country Club and is a member of the University Club.

Ruth's mother completed high school and did secretarial work for a time but has not worked since her marriage into the Collins family. She is an active leader in social and civic affairs, particularly in the Rockford Woman's Club. They have lived for seven years in a house which was rated as "very good," in the highest-ranking section of the city. Typical comment from an interview with a high-status informant: "One of the outstanding families in the city of Rockford."

Betty Baker is ten and a half years old and in the fifth grade. Her I.Q. on the different tests ranges from 105 to 115. She is an only child. The Baker family is a prominent one in the community. Mr. Baker is a member of the Rockford Country Club. He is vice-president of a large commercial concern and has also operated an insurance business. Betty's mother has never been employed. Both parents are native-born, and both are college graduates. The family, at least on the father's side, has been in the community for several generations. They have lived for the last four years in a house rated as "excellent," in the highest-ranking part of the city.

Donald is nearly fifteen years old and is in the Sophomore year of senior high school. His I.Q. is in the low 120's. On the tests scored

5. For a reference to more detailed descriptions of four "composite" families typical of different social-status levels in Rockford, prepared by Charles Warriner, who carried out the community study, see Note 1 in Appendix D.

in percentile terms his rank ranges from 70 to 100. He is an only child. His father is not a member of an old Rockford family, but the mother's family has been well known in the community for a long time. Donald's father is an attorney in private practice; his mother is not now employed but has done substitute teaching at times in the past. The education of both parents is unknown, but in view of their occupations it presumably includes completion of college, at least. Both parents are native-born, though one of the grandparents was born in Denmark. They live in a house rated as "excellent," in the highest-ranking part of the city.

Frances is thirteen and a half years old and is in the eighth grade of a parochial school. Her I.Q. is in the low 120's. Her percentile rank on three tests is never lower than 90. Her father is an architect; her mother has done secretarial work but is not now employed outside her home. Frances' father is a college graduate; her mother finished high school. Both are native-born. They have lived for the last five years in a house rated as "excellent," in the highest-ranking part of the city.

Typical high-status pupils (I.S.C. 10)

The pupils described just above are extreme ones. In this section, four more nearly typical high-status pupils are described. They are selected from the entire group of high-status pupils on the basis that they are most nearly typical of the entire group in such respects as occupation of parents, education of parents, house type, dwelling area, birthplace of parents, grade in school, and intelligence quotients. They are not all exactly at the mean or median on all these factors, but they do not diverge markedly from the typical high-status pupil in any of these respects.

Edgar is nine years old and in the fourth grade of a public school. His I.Q. varies between 100 and 105 on three of the tests but jumps up to 120 on the Henmon-Nelson test. His father is an engineer; his mother is now a housewife but has taught school in the past. Both are college graduates and both were born in the United States. They have lived for four years in a house which was rated as "good," in a section of the community which was rated as "above average."

Ben is almost eleven years old and is in the fifth grade in a public school serving a high-status neighborhood. He has an older brother now out of school. His I.Q. is around 110 on three of the tests, and 125 according to the Henmon-Nelson test. His father is a schoolteacher; his mother is now a housewife and was formerly a part-time librarian. The father is a graduate of an eastern college; the mother completed high school. Both parents were born in the United States. The family has lived for five years in a house rated as "average," in a neighborhood described as "above average."

Thelma is thirteen years old and in the eighth grade in junior high school. Her I.Q. is approximately 110 to 115. On the Thurstone Reasoning and California Mental Maturity tests she ranked well above the average, but her percentile rank on the Thurstone Spatial test was less than 30. Her father is a stockbroker; he has also been a traveling salesman. Her mother is now a housewife and has taught school in the

past. Both parents have high-school diplomas; both were born in the United States. They have lived for six years in a house which was rated as "good," in an area of the community rated as "high."

Mary is fourteen years old and in the ninth grade in junior high school. She is an only child. Her I.Q. is in the low 120's and she scores at the 70th percentile or higher on the tests scored in percentile form. Her father is district sales manager for a national concern. Her mother is now a housewife and has in the past done office clerical work. The father is a college graduate; the mother finished the Junior year in high school. Both parents are native-born. They live in a house which was rated as "good," in a neighborhood called "above average."

Extremely low-status pupils (I.S.C. 27)

The four pupils described below — two from each age level — are chosen from those receiving the very lowest I.S.C. ratings in their respective age groups. The contrast of these children, and the kind of home backgrounds from which they come, with those described in the preceding section is obvious.

Ruby is ten and a half years old and in the third grade — approximately two years retarded for her age. Her I.Q. is in the high 70's or low 80's. She is one of a family of nine children. Her father lists himself as a window-washer; he reports a fourth-grade education. Her mother lists herself as housewife and reports a sixth-grade education. Information from other sources indicates that the father actually is unemployed and on relief.

The father has a twenty-year record for desertion, cruelty to family, neglect, and drunkenness. The mother also has a record for drunkenness. Several of the boys have been in the penitentiary, and one of the girls has been arrested for shoplifting. There is a history of epilepsy in parents and children — and a suspicion of venereal disease. Typical comments about this family: "very, very poor," "filthy," "poor white trash," "they are a social and economic problem to the community."

They live in a house rated as "very poor," in a neighborhood described as "very low; slum." The interviewer found the bathtub used for storing sprinkling cans, auto parts, etc.

Tom is ten and a half years old but is still in the second grade. His I.Q. is in the high 70's or low 80's. He is one of five children. Tom's father is dead; the family of five children is apparently supported on a widow's pension plus the wages of an older brother who works as a laborer for the street department of the city. The mother was born in Poland. As for education of the parents, the questionnaire reports that they "dided go to school" — which other information indicates is to be translated as "didn't. . ." There have been children born to the mother since the father died.

They live in a house described by the interviewer as "poor and not pleasing, but not filthy," in a section of the city rated as "very low; slum." Typical comment: "very poor Polish family."

Geraldine is nearly fourteen years old and is in the eighth grade. Her I.Q. is in the high 90's or low 100's. On the percentile-scoring tests her rank ranges from 10 to 50. Both her father and mother work in a restaurant. The father completed the fifth grade in school, the mother the eighth grade. Both parents are native-born. Geraldine spent the first seven years of her life on a farm. They have lived for the last five months in a house which is rated as "very poor," in an area described as "very low; slum."

Susan is nearly fourteen years old and is in the eighth grade. Her I.Q. is in the high 90's according to one test and between 115 and 120 on another. Her percentile rankings vary all the way from 10 to 85. Her father reports that he "works on a machine" in a factory. No information is available as to the parents' education or birthplace. They have lived for the last six months in a trailer in a temporary trailer camp located in a dirt field which turns into a quagmire of mud whenever it rains.

Typical low-status Old American pupils (I.S.C. 22-23)

The following individuals were selected from the group of low-status Old American pupils so as to represent most fairly this group on such factors as those listed earlier in connection with high-status pupils.

Bill is nine years old and in the third grade — one year retarded for his age. He has one younger brother. His I.Q. is probably somewhere in the 80's, although one test shows it somewhat higher. His father runs a separator in a laundry and has also been a grinder in a factory. Bill's mother was once a waitress but has not worked since marriage. The father has had eight years of schooling; the mother had one year of high school. Both parents are native-born. They do not belong to any clubs or associations except the Lutheran church. They have lived for one year in a five-room flat over a store, in an area of the community rated as "low — semislum."

Anne is nearly eleven years old and in the fourth grade -- two years retarded. Her I.Q. is shown by all four tests to be somewhere in the low 90's. Her father is a construction laborer and farm helper. Her mother is an inspector of machine parts in a local factory. Anne's father completed eight years of school, while the mother completed high school. Both parents are native-born. For the first five years of Anne's life her family lived on a farm. For the last five years she has lived in a house rated as "fair," in an area described as "low -- semi-slum."

Evelyn is thirteen years old — nearly fourteen — and in the seventh grade in a school which serves a predominantly low-status area. She is two years retarded for her age. Her I.Q. is somewhere in the 80's. Her percentile rank on the tests scored in that manner is never above 50, and on two of them it is below 20. Evelyn's father has done farm work in the past, though Evelyn has never lived on a farm. The father is now a galvanizer; his wife has been an assembler in a factory but is not now working outside her home. Both of the parents have had eight years of schooling, and both are native-born. Their house is rated as "fair," in a neighborhood rated as "low -- semislum."

Comment by someone who knows the family: "All the children have done wonderfully well. There is not a lot there financially, but lots of love and security." Comment by Evelyn's mother: "We came to Rockford without a penny. We bought our own home and had five children. We think that's pretty good. There was some pretty hard times

in between there — you sit down and laugh at what you went through then. It wasn't so funny when it happened but you forget about it right after it happened."

Helen is fourteen years old and is in the seventh grade in a junior high school — two years retarded. Her I.Q. is in the 70's or 80's. Her percentile scores on two tests are close to 50, but on one is above the 80th percentile. Helen's father is a truck-driver. Her mother is now a housewife and has been a teacher, a lathe operator, and has done domestic-service work. The father finished two years of high school; the mother finished only the sixth grade. From age three to ten, Helen lived on a farm; for the last two years the family has lived in a "fair" house, in a neighborhood rated as "low — semislum."

Typical low-status ethnic pupils (I.S.C. 23)

The following individuals were selected from the group of low-status ethnic pupils so as to represent that group most fairly.

Dorothy lacks a few months of being eleven years old and is in the fourth grade -- approximately two years retarded. Her I.Q. is probably somewhere in the 80's, although one test puts it close to 100. She has two older brothers. Her father is a grinder in one of the machine-tool plants; he has also been a molder. The mother is now a housewife and in the past has done molding and also has done sewing in a factory. Dorothy's father was born in Italy and completed the third grade of school; the mother was born in Georgia and completed the second grade. For eight years the family has lived in a house rated as "fair," in a "low — semislum" neighborhood.

Jackie is nearly ten and is in the fourth grade. Her I.Q. is probably around 100; one test shows it as low as 90 and another as high as 110. Her father is a truck-driver for a local hauling concern; he has never done any other kind of work. Her mother has never been employed. The father was born in Italy and completed the fourth grade in school. The mother is American-born and completed the second grade. They have lived for the last two years in a "fair" house, in a "low -- semislum" area.

Marie is thirteen years old and in the seventh grade — one year retarded. Her I.Q. is in the high 80's. Her percentile scores range from 27 to 52. Her father is a janitor in a machine-tool plant; he has also worked in a shoe-repair shop. The mother is now a housewife; she has in the past worked in a knitting factory. Both parents were born in Italy; they both completed the fifth grade in school. For the last seven years they have lived in a "fair" house, in a "low — semislum" area.

Catherine is nearly fifteen years old and is in the eighth grade. Her I.Q. on two tests is in the mid-90's. On the three tests scored in percentiles, however, her percentile rank is never above 10. Her father is a core-maker in one of the foundries. Her mother is a housewife and has also done sewing in a factory, probably before she was married. Both parents were born in Italy. The father went through the third grade in school, and the mother through the sixth. They have lived for six years in a house rated as "fair," in a "low — semislum" area.

Summary

Various aspects of the socioeconomic status of the pupils in the study are analyzed and described, by means of statistical summaries and by brief descriptions of a number of individual pupils.

The socioeconomic status of the pupils at the two age levels is substantially similar. It is, however, shown that the typical social status of pupils varies substantially from one elementary school to another. The high- and low-status pupils show marked contrasts with respect to occupation, education, house type, and dwelling area. Differences on these four status characteristics between low-status Old American pupils and low-status ethnic pupils are, on the other hand, much smaller and usually not statistically significant.

In social-class terms the high-status group probably consists of pupils entirely from middle-class and upper-class families, with from three-fifths to two-thirds coming from families that are upper-middle class or higher. The low-status groups probably consist of pupils entirely from lower-class families, with from two-thirds to three-fourths of them from lower-lower-class families.

All four Old American status groups are made up of individuals the great majority of whom have both parents born in the United States. The two ethnic groups, however, are divided into three roughly equal groups, one third from native-born parents, one third from foreign-born parents, and one third from mixed parentages. The proportion of foreign-born parents is larger in the older group of pupils. The ethnic groups are predominantly Italian in origin, with no other single national origin group having any sizable representation.

CHAPTER XIV

THE RELATION OF I.Q.'S TO SOCIAL STATUS:
CORRELATION ANALYSIS

The relationship of intelligence quotients to various factors involving socioeconomic status has been repeatedly examined under a variety of situations, as reported in chapter ii. It was not the primary purpose of the present study merely to add further research data to this field of inquiry but rather to analyze possible status differentials in responses to individual items. In the course of the study, however, detailed I.Q. data were necessarily obtained; it seemed wise to analyze the I.Q.'s in terms of socioeconomic status even though such analyses have been made many times before. This chapter, and the one which follows it, will be devoted to a report of this analysis of intelligence quotients in their relation to social status.[1]

General Relationship between I.Q. and I.S.C.

Since the I.S.C. scale used in this study is in numerical form, with a range of 24 points, it may be used as a basis for correlation analysis. When correlations were computed between each of the nine sets of I.Q.'s and the I.S.C., the results were as indicated in Table 17. The correlations show a moderate, but far from striking, degree of relationship between social status, as measured by the I.S.C., and I.Q.'s obtained from the different tests. The correlations reported here are in line with similar correlations reported by other investigators.[2]

While these coefficients are not large, there can be no question but that they represent a real relationship between the I.S.C. and I.Q.'s. In samples of this size (2,215 to 2,463) the standard error of the correlation coefficient, if the true correlation were zero, is .02. All the obtained correlations are at least ten times this standard error, so that the possibility of these coefficients representing sampling errors only is so remote as to be virtually nonexistent.

In order to be able to test the significance of intertest differences in the size of these correlation coefficients, equivalent z values, using Fisher's formula, were computed. The critical ratios of the z differences are given in the last column of Table 17. For the tests given to the younger pupils, the Henmon-Nelson, Otis Alpha Verbal, and Kuhlmann-Anderson tests yield closely similar correlations with social status, while the Otis

1. As explained earlier, the scores on the Thurstone Spatial, Thurstone Reasoning, and California Mental Maturity tests were expressed in the form of age percentile ranks rather than intelligence quotients. Throughout this chapter, for the sake of simplicity, the term "intelligence quotients" will frequently be used to refer in a general way to both types of measures. In tables reporting statistical data, the two types of units will, of course, be reported separately.

2. See pp. 11-12.

TABLE 17

RELATIONSHIP BETWEEN I.Q.'S AND INDEX
OF STATUS CHARACTERISTICS

Test (and Form of Score)	Number of Pupils	Correlation Coefficient*	z Test of Significance of Difference between Adjacent Coefficients+
Tests for Nine- and Ten-Year-Old Pupils			
Henmon-Nelson (I.Q.) . . .	2,238	.35	
Otis Alpha Verbal (I.Q.)	2,235	.34	0.4
Kuhlmann-Anderson (I.Q.)	2,273	.33	0.6
Otis Alpha Nonverbal (I.Q.)	2,215	.28	1.8
Tests for Thirteen- and Fourteen-Year-Old Pupils			
Terman-McNemar (I.Q.) .	2,454	.43	1.0
Otis Beta (I.Q.)	2,463	.40	
California Mental Maturity (percentile rank)‡	2,443	.30	4.3
Thurstone Reasoning (percentile rank)‡	2,456	.26	1.2
Thurstone Spatial (percentile rank)‡	2,445	.20	2.5

* In this table, and in all correlations in this chapter, the signs of the coefficients have been reversed, so that a positive coefficient means that high social status is associated with high I.Q.'s. This reversal of signs is necessary for convenience of interpretation, since the I.S.C. scale is itself reversed in the sense that a small numerical index denotes high social status.

+ The figure reported is the ratio of the difference between the z values corresponding to the indicated correlation coefficients and the standard error of that difference.

‡ Attention is called to the fact that the correlations of the three tests whose scores are in percentile-rank form involve one variable whose distribution is approximately rectangular rather than normal. For a brief discussion of the legitimacy of computing correlations for these data see Note 4 in Appendix D.

Alpha Nonverbal test shows a somewhat lower degree of relationship. The difference in the correlation shown by the Otis Alpha Nonverbal test and that for the Kuhlmann-Anderson test is not quite large enough to be significant at the 5 per cent level. The difference between the Henmon-Nelson and the Otis Alpha Nonverbal correlations is, however, significant at the 1 per cent level.

The tests given to the older pupils show a larger amount of variation in the degree of their relationship to social status. It will be seen that the five tests can be grouped into three sets. The Terman-McNemar and Otis Beta tests show the highest degree of relationship to status; the difference between the relationships shown by these two tests is not significant. The California Mental Maturity and the Thurstone Reasoning tests show a degree of relationship significantly lower than that shown by the Terman-McNemar and Otis Beta tests. Finally, the Thurstone Spatial test shows a degree of relationship significantly (at the 5 per cent level) lower than even the Thurstone Reasoning test.

Attention is called to the fact that the Henmon-Nelson and the Terman-McNemar tests, which show the highest correlation with social status at each age level, consist almost entirely of verbal items, while the Otis Alpha Nonverbal and Thurstone Spatial tests, which show the lowest correlations at each age level, have no verbal material in them at all, except in the introductory instructions. This suggests the possible influence which differences in kind of test material may have on the degree of relationship to social status. This subject will be explored further in chapter xix.

The variations in the size of these correlations might be due in part to differences in the reliabilities of the tests. So far as usable reliability coefficients are reported by the authors of the tests, variations in the size of the reliability coefficients parallel variations in the size of the I.S.C. − I.Q. correlations reported in Table 17. Thus reliabilities for three of the tests for younger pupils are: Henmon-Nelson, .89; Otis Alpha Verbal, .71; Otis Alpha Nonverbal, .68. For two of the tests for older pupils the coefficients are: Terman-McNemar, .96; Otis Beta, .71.[3]

Correlations similar to those reported in Table 17 were computed on two tests for Old Americans, ethnics, and Scandinavians separately. These correlations are reported in Table 18. Examination of the correlation coefficients reported in the second column of this table indicates that there is some variation in the degree of relationship between I.Q.'s and social status for the different ethnic groups. In making comparisons among the coefficients, however, allowance must be made for the fact that the ethnic and Scandinavian pupils tend to occupy a more restricted portion of the total status range than is true for the Old American pupils. The importance of this factor is indicated by the standard deviations of the I.S.C.'s for the various groups, as reported in the fourth column of the table. The standard deviation for the Scandinavian younger pupils, for example, is only three-fourths that of the Old American group.

This difficulty may be taken care of by thinking of the ethnic, Scandinavian, and Old American subgroups as samples "selected" from a larger population of such individuals whose dispersion of I.S.C.'s is equal to that

3. For more detailed description of these reliability coefficients, and the reasons for not reporting those for the four other tests, see Note 5 in Appendix D.

TABLE 18

RELATIONSHIP BETWEEN I.Q.'S AND INDEX OF STATUS CHARACTERISTICS FOR DIFFERENT ETHNIC GROUPS

Ethnic Group	Number of Pupils	Correlation Coefficient	Standard Error of Zero Correlation Coefficient	Adjustment of Coefficient to Common Range of Difficulty		z Test of Significance of Difference between Adjacent Coefficients[+]
				Standard Deviation of I.S.C.	Adjusted Coefficient*	
			Henmon-Nelson Test (Nine- and Ten-Year-Old Pupils)			
Ethnic	256	.38	.06	3.0	.47 ⎫	. . . . .
Old American	1,845	.33	.02	3.9	.34 ⎬	2.4
Scandinavian	137	.23	.09	2.9	.31 ⎭	0.4
All pupils	2,238	.35	.02	3.9	.35	. . . . .
			Terman-McNemar Test (Thirteen- and Fourteen-Year-Old Pupils)			
Old American	1,970	.43	.02	3.8	.43 ⎫	. . . . .
Ethnic	274	.31	.06	3.1	.38 ⎬	0.8
Scandinavian	210	.27	.07	2.8	.36 ⎭	0.2
All pupils	2,454	.43	.02	3.8	.43	. . . . .

* Coefficients adjusted to what they would be if the standard deviation of the I.S.C.'s of each subgroup equaled that of the total age group, using the formula developed by Pearson (57, p. 225).

+ This z test is based on the assumption that it is legitimate to use Fisher's z transformation for the adjusted correlation coefficients. For a brief discussion of this point see Note 6 in Appendix D.

of the total group of pupils. If this is done, the obtained coefficients may be adjusted to indicate what they would probably be if they had been computed from the larger population with dispersion of I.S.C.'s equal to that of the total group of pupils. The adjusted correlations are reported in the next to the last column of Table 18. It should be understood that these adjusted correlations do not indicate the degree of relationship between I.S.C. and I.Q.'s which actually obtain for the subgroups of pupils studied; that degree of relationship is indicated by the raw or unadjusted coefficients. The adjusted figures indicate what degree of relationship would be expected if the larger theoretical population described above had been measured; their only advantage is that comparisons from one group to another may be made more legitimately in terms of these adjusted coefficients.

The adjusted correlations indicate that for the younger pupils the highest degree of I.Q.-I.S.C. relationship is found for ethnic pupils, and the lowest for Scandinavians. For the older pupils the order is different, with the highest relationship found for Old Americans and the lowest for Scandinavians. The last column in Table 18 reports the critical ratios of the z differences between adjacent correlations. These ratios indicate that in only one case is the difference between any two adjacent correlations large enough to be at all significant. Even this difference — the greater degree of I.Q.-I.S.C. relationship found for ethnics as compared with Old Americans for the younger pupils — is significant only at the 5 per cent level. The probable significance of this difference is further reduced by the fact that its direction is reversed at the older age level.

It seems safest to conclude from the data in Table 18 that there is no clear evidence of any significant variation in the degree of I.Q.-status relationship as among Old American, ethnic, and Scandinavian pupils.

It should be stressed that the statistical relationships pointed out thus far, and all those to be demonstrated later in this chapter, refer to the relation between social status as measured by the I.S.C. and I.Q.'s as determined from the tests used. No claim is made that these relationships likewise would hold true for the underlying "intelligence" of pupils if there were any way of determining it. The basic hypothesis underlying the present study is that what the tests measure is not "intelligence" — at least in any sense of innate ability — but a composite of that plus a measurement of the cultural advantages accruing to certain individuals and groups of individuals. This hypothesis makes it impossible to assume that the I.Q.'s obtained from the tests are measures of real intelligence. The relationship between social status and I.Q.'s obtained from widely used tests — whatever their meaning — is in itself, however, an important matter. It is to this question that this chapter is directed.

Further insight into the nature of the relationship between intelligence quotients and social status may be gained by examining Figure 7, which presents the scatter diagram for the Henmon-Nelson test. This test was selected for special study because it showed the highest degree of relationship with social status for the younger children. The line of column means in Figure 7 makes it clear that children whose I.S.C. is in the high-status range get, on the average, higher I.Q. scores than do those children whose I.S.C. is in the low-status range. But there is marked overlapping. A considerable number of low-status children secure I.Q.'s higher than the average of the high-status children, and a number of high-status children secure I.Q.'s lower than the average of the low-status

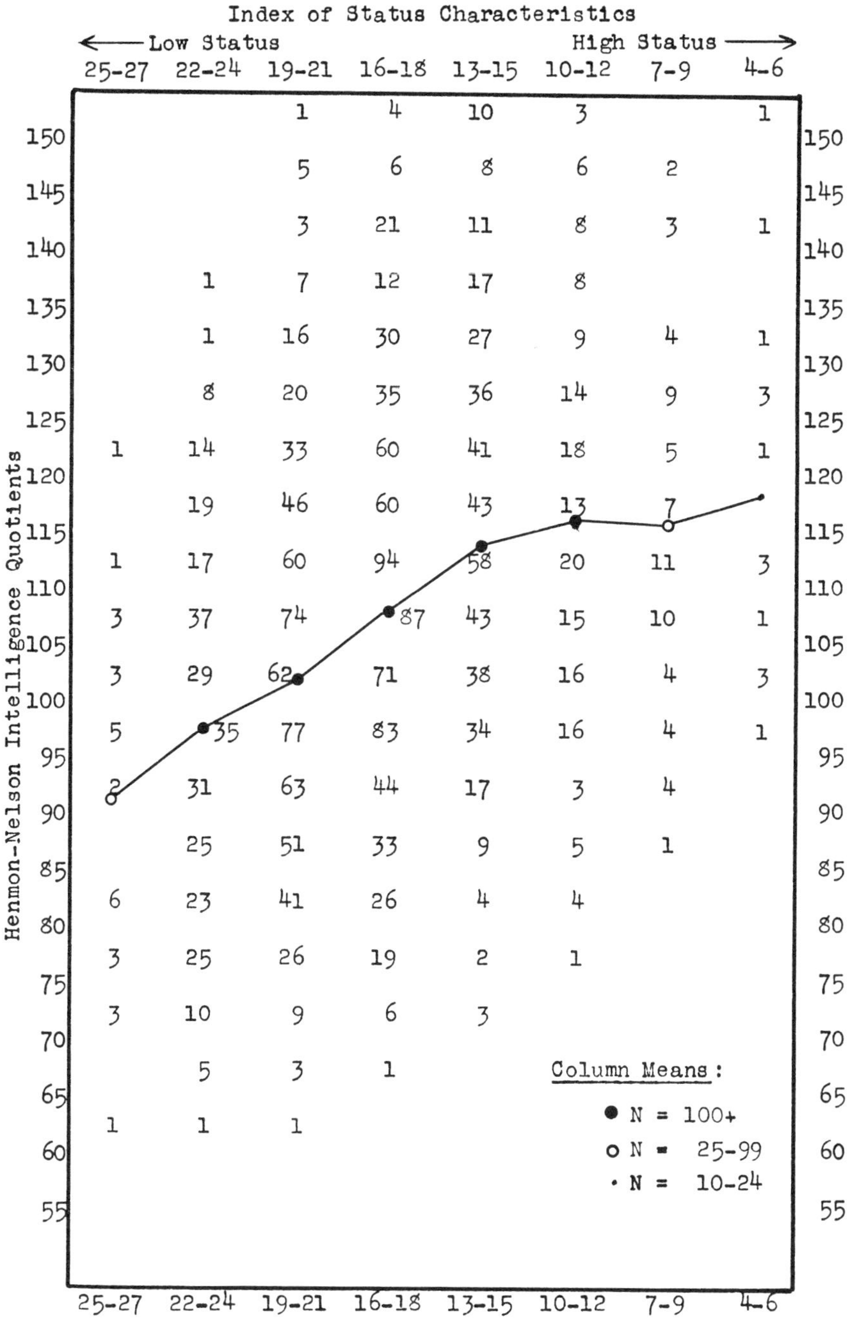

Index of Status Characteristics

Fig. 7. — Scatter diagram showing relationship between Henmon-Nelson I.Q.'s and social status for nine- and ten-year-old pupils

Henmon-Nelson Intelligence Quotients

I.Q.	25-27	22-24	19-21	16-18	13-15	10-12	7-9	4-6
150			1	4	10	3		1
145			5	6	8	6	2	
140			3	21	11	8	3	1
135		1	7	12	17	8		
130		1	16	30	27	9	4	1
125		8	20	35	36	14	9	3
120	1	14	33	60	41	18	5	1
115		19	46	60	43	13	7	
110	1	17	60	94	58	20	11	3
105	3	37	74	87	43	15	10	1
100	3	29	62	71	38	16	4	3
95	5	35	77	83	34	16	4	1
90	2	31	63	44	17	3	4	
85		25	51	33	9	5	1	
80	6	23	41	26	4	4		
75	3	25	26	19	2	1		
70	3	10	9	6	3			
65		5	3	1				
60	1	1	1					

Column Means:

● N = 100+
○ N = 25-99
· N = 10-24

Fig. 7. — Scatter diagram showing relationship between Henmon-Nelson I.Q.'s and social status for nine- and ten-year-old pupils (N = 2,238; r = .35).

---

children. It is true that a low-status pupil is more _likely_ to receive a low I.Q. rating from these tests than is a high-status pupil; it is by no means true that all the high scores go to high-status pupils and all the low scores go to low-status pupils. Possible implications of this overlapping for gaining insight into the nature of status differences in I.Q.'s are discussed in chapter viii.[4]

The relationship between I.S.C. and I.Q. is very far from being close enough to make any even reasonably accurate predictions of what a given individual's I.Q. might be expected to be on the basis of his I.S.C. This is shown clearly by the standard error of estimate for the I.Q.'s based upon a prediction from the I.S.C. The standard error of estimate is 16.1. This may be interpreted as indicating that if a large number of I.Q.'s are predicted on the basis of the pupils' I.S.C.'s, the predicted I.Q. will not be in error by more than 16.1 points in about 68 per cent of the cases.[5] The complete inadequacy of this as a prediction of I.Q.'s is obvious and is made even clearer by a comparison with the standard deviation of the original I.Q.'s, which is 17.2. If the I.S.C. is disregarded entirely and a large number of I.Q.'s predicted by simply assuming that all of them will be at the mean (107.0), 68 per cent of the predictions will not be in error by more than 17.2 points. The improvement in accuracy of prediction of individual I.Q.'s by basing the prediction upon the known degree of relationship with the I.S.C. is for all practical purposes unimportant.

The preceding paragraph refers to the prediction of the I.Q. of any given _individual_ on the basis of his I.S.C. The fact that knowing an individual pupil's I.S.C. does not help materially in predicting his I.Q. does not mean that there may not be substantial differences in the average I.Q.'s for _groups_ of high-status pupils as contrasted with _groups_ of low-status pupils. It is clear from Figure 7 that there are substantial differences in the average, or typical, I.Q.'s of low-status pupils as compared with those of high-status pupils. The size of this group difference will be examined in the next chapter.

Nonlinearity of the Relationship between I.Q. and I.S.C.

Perhaps more interesting than the degree of relationship between I.S.C. and I.Q., however, is the fact, clearly illustrated in Figure 7, that the relationship is not a linear one. From the lowest I.S.C. level (25-27) up to and including the 13-15 level, the relationship appears to be linear, and with each successive increase in the I.S.C. a regular increase in average I.Q. occurs (approximately two I.Q. points for every one I.S.C. point). This same relationship does not hold true in any significant way for children whose I.S.C. is in the 13-15 range or higher. It has already been shown that the I.S.C. range from 4 to 12, when expressed in social-class terms, is roughly equivalent to upper- and upper-middle class.[6]

It is clear from the data in Figure 7 that, whereas children in this upper- and upper-middle-class group exhibit significantly higher I.Q.'s, on the average, than do those beneath them on the social-class scale, variations of status within this upper group are not associated with similar variations in I.Q. For the lower groups, however, there is a definite

---

4. See pp. 59-60.
5. The regression equation is: I.Q. = -1.56 (I.S.C.) + 133.07.
6. See p. 125.

tendency for the I.Q. to vary with social status, not only as between major social-class levels, but more or less continuously along the I.S.C. scale. A supplementary analysis of this same relationship was made by keeping the I.S.C. scale in single-point units instead of using three-point class intervals, in order to determine whether the change in relationship at about I.S.C. 13-15 was somewhat gradual. This analysis indicates that, for this test at least, the break is a sharp one. The average I.Q. rises steadily with each advancing I.S.C. unit up to and including I.S.C. 13. There is even some indication that the average I.Q.'s may decline somewhat from I.S.C. 13 to I.S.C. 8, although the number of cases involved in this range makes mean I.Q.'s for individual I.S.C. points not so stable as those in the lower- and middle-status ranges.[7]

Since the relationship between Henmon-Nelson I.Q.'s and social status is clearly not a linear one, a somewhat higher degree of relationship should be indicated by computing the correlation ratio, instead of the correlation coefficient. The increase in the size of the measured relationship is, however, very slight:

	Number of Cases	Correlation
r	2,238	.354
ϵ_{yx}*	2,238	.365
ϵ_{yx} (corrected)	2,238	.376

The slightness of the increase is doubtless accounted for by the fact that a comparatively small proportion of the total number of pupils is found in the range where the lack of linearity is a factor. The departure from linearity is, however, statistically significant at the 1 per cent level.

In order to measure in another way the difference in nature of the relationship between I.S.C. and I.Q. for pupils above and below the critical point, correlation coefficients were computed for the two parts of the scatter diagram separately, breaking the distribution between I.S.C. 12 and 13. The coefficients are reported in Table 19. These coefficients make it clear that there is no significant relationship between the two variables in the upper end of the I.S.C. scale. Even when the coefficient is adjusted to allow for the restricted range from which it was computed, it is smaller than the standard error of a zero correlation. The correlation in that portion of the range below I.S.C. 12, on the other hand, is seen to be fairly substantial.

Figure 8 presents data for the Terman-McNemar test similar to that just reported for the Henmon-Nelson test. The Terman-McNemar test was selected for special study because it indicated the highest degree of correlation between I.S.C. and I.Q. of any one of the five tests used with the older pupils.

The general pattern of the Terman-McNemar I.Q.'s in relation to the I.S.C. is in many ways similar to that already shown for the Henmon-Nelson

---

7. For a reference to a more detailed report of these findings see Note 1 in Appendix D.
   * The coefficient ratio used here is epsilon, developed by Kelley, rather than the more familiar eta, which is unsatisfactory because its size varies with the number of categories into which the independent variable is divided. The "corrected" epsilon has been corrected for broad grouping (58, pp. 319-30).

TABLE 19

RELATIONSHIP BETWEEN I.Q.'S AND INDEX
OF STATUS CHARACTERISTICS
IN DIFFERENT PORTIONS OF SOCIAL-STATUS SCALE*

Status Level	Number of Pupils	Correlation Coefficient	Standard Error of Zero Correlation Coefficient	Adjustment of Coefficient to Common Range of Difficulty	
				Standard Deviation of I.S.C.	Adjusted Coefficient[+]
Pupils with I.S.C. 4-12	238	.02	.06	1.8	.04
Pupils with I.S.C. 13-27	2,000	.35	.02	3.0	.43
All pupils	2,238	.35	.02	3.9	.35

* Based on I.Q.'s for nine- and ten-year-old pupils obtained from Henmon-Nelson test.
+ Coefficients adjusted to what they would be if the standard deviation of the I.S.C.'s of each of the subgroups equaled 3.9, the standard deviation of the total group. The formula used is the same one referred to in the first note to Table 18.

I.Q.'s. In both tests there is an obvious and definite relationship between I.Q. and I.S.C.; in both tests there is great overlapping, with many low-status children receiving higher I.Q.'s than many high-status children. The pattern shown by the line of column means for the two tests is, however, somewhat different. In the case of the Henmon-Nelson test there is a distinct break in the linearity of the relationship, occurring at I.S.C. 13. This is not noticeably true for the Terman-McNemar test. In the latter test, unlike the Henmon-Nelson, pupils with I.S.C.'s of 10 to 12 receive higher scores than do pupils of the next lower social status, and pupils with I.S.C.'s of 7 to 9 receive still higher I.Q.'s. The sharp downward break of the Terman-McNemar line in the I.S.C. 4-6 group is not particularly significant, since that mean is based on only twelve pupils. This may just possibly represent a leveling-off of the regression line similar to that observed for the Henmon-Nelson but at a higher level on the social-status scale. There is insufficient evidence to justify anything more than a tentative guess as to the possibility.

The complete scatter diagrams for the other tests will not be presented here. The lines of means, however, comparable to those just analyzed for the Henmon-Nelson and Terman-McNemar tests, are shown, for the two age levels, in Figures 9 and 10.

In Figure 9 it may be seen that the other tests given to the nine- and ten-year-old pupils bear out the conclusion already drawn from the Henmon-Nelson data. In the case of each of the four tests, there is a steady increase in I.Q. with advancing steps up the I.S.C. scale, until a point somewhere in the I.S.C. 13-15 range is reached, after which there is an almost complete leveling-off, so that advancing social status brings with it no increase in the I.Q.'s — except possibly at the extreme upper end of

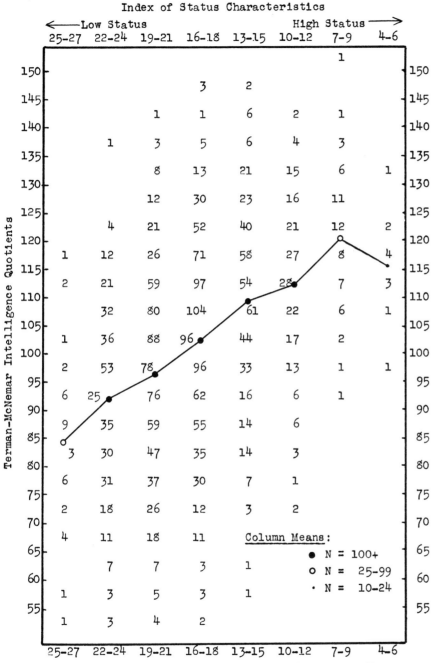

Fig. 8. — Scatter diagram showing relationship between Terman-McNemar I.Q.'s and social status for thirteen- and fourteen-year-old pupils (N = 2,454; r = .43).

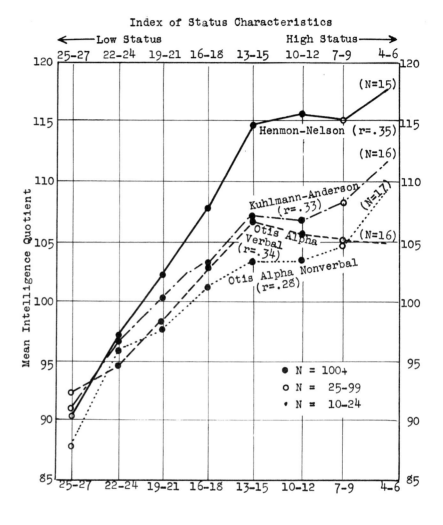

Fig. 9. — Mean I.Q.'s for nine- and ten-year-old pupils of varying social status.

the social-status scale.

It is clear from this figure that the Henmon-Nelson I.Q.'s run, on the average, considerably higher than do the I.Q.'s obtained from the other three tests. What is more striking, however, is that this differential is not uniform along the social-status scale. At the low-status levels all four tests yield substantially similar I.Q.'s. As the status level increases, however, high-status pupils receive increasingly higher I.Q.'s on all tests, but at a greater rate of increase for the Henmon-Nelson test. The lowest rate of increase is apparent in the Otis Alpha Nonverbal test, which, of course, merely confirms the evidence from the correlation coefficients. It is notable too that this Otis Alpha Nonverbal test, even though it shows the same leveling-off in the high-status ranges, does not contain the marked break characteristic of the other three tests.

Since these four tests were given to the same pupils, within the same week's time, it is apparent that the differences in performance must be due primarily to differences in the nature of the tests themselves. It seems reasonable to conclude, for example, that the Henmon-Nelson test has within it more material, or possibly a higher degree of motivation, of a type favorable to high-status children than do the other tests. Whether this is due to the Henmon-Nelson's tapping certain inherent abilities which are present in high-status children in greater amount than in low-status children, or whether it is due to the presence in the Henmon-Nelson test of material common to high-status culture and not to low-status culture — and thus discriminating unfairly in favor of high-status children — cannot be determined on the basis of the evidence thus far reported.

The meaning of the leveling-off of the relationship between I.Q.'s and I.S.C. in the higher status levels is likewise not easy to determine definitely. A number of possible interpretations may be suggested. Before discussing these, however, it will be helpful to examine the data resulting from a similar analysis of the tests given to the older pupils. These are reported in Figure 10. In interpreting Figure 10, care should be exercised in making any direct comparisons between the relative height or relative slopes of the different lines, since they are not all plotted in terms of the same kinds of units. The Otis Beta and Terman-McNemar lines represent mean I.Q.'s at the different social-status levels; the Thurstone Spatial and Thurstone Reasoning lines represent mean percentile ranks, based upon national norms; the California line represents mean percentile ranks based upon the local community where the test was given.

The lines of means for the Otis Beta and the Terman-McNemar tests indicate that for middle-status pupils (I.S.C. 10-18) the pupils' scores on the two tests are substantially identical but that at the low-status levels pupils do better on the Otis Beta than on the Terman-McNemar, while high-status pupils do better on the Terman-McNemar than on the Otis Beta. This merely points up again, of course, what has already been noted in connection with the correlation coefficients, that the Terman-McNemar I.Q.'s are somewhat more closely related to social status than are the Otis Beta ones. The difference in degree of relationship is not marked, however.

Another intertest comparison which can legitimately be made from the data in Figure 10 is that between the two Thurstone tests, since the scores from these two are in comparable form. On these two tests, Figure 10 indicates, as did the correlations reported earlier, that the Reasoning test is more closely related to social status than is the Spatial test. At

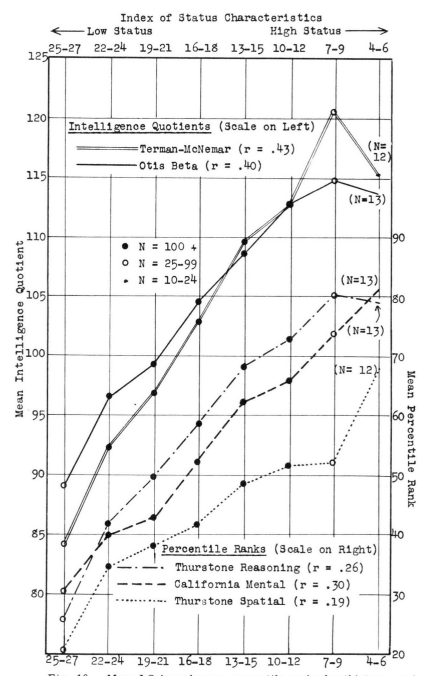

Fig. 10. — Mean I.Q.'s and mean percentile ranks for thirteen- and fourteen-year-old pupils of varying social status.

the extreme low-status end of the scale pupils do about equally well on the two tests, but the farther one goes up the social-status scale, the greater is the differential in favor of the scores on the Reasoning test.

For all five of the tests there is a steady progression upward of the mean I.Q. (or percentile rank) with advancing social status, at least up to the I.S.C. 7-9 level. The trend beyond that point cannot be determined clearly because of the very small number of cases available in the I.S.C. 4-6 group. On three of the tests the extreme high-status (I.S.C. 4-6) pupils show lower scores than those of the group just below them in the status scale, while on two of the tests the reverse is true. It seems probable that there is no real leveling-off of the I.S.C. -I.Q. relationship comparable to that which was noticeable for the younger pupils; at any rate, if there is such a leveling-off, it occurs at a point closer to the extreme upper end of the scale than was the case for the younger pupils.

Possible Significance of the Nonlinearity of the Relationship

This finding offers interesting possibilities for speculation as to the kinds of forces which may contribute to status differences in I.Q.'s. What might cause status differences which would behave in this rather unexpected manner? A number of suggestions are offered below, and the necessary assumptions underlying each one are indicated. After each of these possible explanations has been presented briefly, it will be pointed out that only one of them seems adequate to account both for the nonlinearity of the relationship for younger pupils and for the essential linearity of the relationship for older pupils.

First, it is entirely possible that the I.S.C. does not represent a linear scale with respect to social status. The amount of difference in social status represented by the difference between an I.S.C. of 10 and one of 11, for example, may be much smaller than that represented by a difference between an I.S.C. of 20 and 21. This kind of explanation hardly seems adequate to account for the data presented in Figure 9, however. If the true relationship between social status and I. Q. were linear, a condensing of the I.S.C. scale at the high-status end would result in a decelerating curve, but the change would be much more likely to occur as a gradual shifting of the slope of the curve than as a sharp break at a specific point. Nor could such an explanation account for the curve becoming completely flat, as is the case in Figure 9 — unless, indeed, the I.S.C. ceases to be a scale at all in its upper ranges. Furthermore, an explanation in these terms would lead one to expect the same kind of flattening-out of the curve at all age levels and with all tests, which is not what is actually found.

Second, it may be assumed that status differences in I.Q. are due primarily to genetic differences inherited from the parents and that the process of moving upward in the social-status scale in American society is such as to put a premium on parental intelligence through most of the status scale, but that in the upper-status ranges a point is reached at which other factors (family connections, "right" behavior, etc.) become all-important, and intelligence has little or no importance. On such a basis one might expect just the results reported in Figure 9. Parental intelligence would, in the lower and middle ranges of the status scale, be distributed roughly in accordance with social status but would be unrelated to social status in the upper range. Pupils' intelligence, by the inheritance hypothesis, would then show this same distribution. This kind of explanation would, however, lead one to expect the same kind of distribution of

I.Q.'s at all age levels; it is powerless to explain why the relationship is nonlinear for nine- and ten-year-olds but is apparently entirely linear at an older age level.

Third, it may be assumed that status differences in I.Q.'s are due primarily to differences in the stimulative quality of the environment which is provided for pupils at different social-status levels. According to this hypothesis, pupils at all status levels might start with equal inherited ability and still develop differently because some grow up in an atmosphere favorable to maximum mental growth, while others grow up in an atmosphere that is stunting and retarding. It could then be argued that the stimulative quality of the environment increases at each higher level of social status up to the upper-middle class but that beyond that level it does not. Such a hypothesis would be reasonable in terms of what is known about social-class characteristics. It is at about the upper-middle-class level that the home begins to become less child-centered and more social-activity-centered. Attending the "right" social functions and being seen with the "right" people becomes more important to the socially-ambitious upper-middle-class parent than providing rich and stimulating opportunities for his children. It is probable, however, that this shift from a child-centered middle-class home to a social-centered upper-class home is more marked at the top of the upper-middle-class group than at the bottom of that group. Many upper-middle-class families are strongly child-centered. Moreover, this explanation, like the preceding ones, would lead one to expect the same break in the nature of the relationship at both age levels.

A fourth explanation, somewhat similar to the preceding one, can be offered by assuming that the status differences in I.Q.'s are due primarily to differences in the motivation which pupils have for doing their best on school work in general and on intelligence tests in particular. It is well known that middle-class parents urge their children to do their best in school and to do the things that will please their teachers, whereas lower-class parents are more inclined to adopt a neutral, or even a negative, attitude toward the school and toward what seems to them its foolish book learning. It is entirely possible that this effect of parental motivation is felt in a fairly regular manner up through the lower-middle class but that above that level the parents become more interested in other things than the school welfare of their children. Not only do the social activities of the upper-middle-class and upper-class parents begin to interfere, but also their desires for their children are more in terms of seeing that they know the "right" people and that they learn the proper social graces than that they achieve high marks or outstanding records in school work. Again, however, this explanation will not explain the difference in the relationship at the two age levels.

Fifth, it may be assumed that status differences in I.Q.'s are due primarily to differences in the cultural opportunities which children from different status levels have for familiarity with the words, objects, concepts, and processes required for successful performance on intelligence-test items. It can then be argued that these cultural opportunities increase with advancing social status through most of the status range but that they do not do so at the top. It may well be, for example, that a pupil with an I.S.C. of 13 to 15 has a much richer cultural background, in terms of what is needed to answer the test items, than one with an I.S.C. of 19 to 21, but that a child with an I.S.C. of 4 to 6 does not have any correspondingly richer or broader cultural background than a child with an I.S.C. of

13 to 15. There may be an optimum point beyond which additional increments on the status scale indicate advancing "status" but do not carry with them additional cultural enrichment. Like the previous explanations, however, this one, at least in this particular form, seems to offer no explanation for the difference in relationship at the two age levels.

A slight modification of the explanation just presented, however, makes it possible to account for the age differences found. It may be assumed that status differences in I.Q.'s are due primarily to differences in the cultural opportunities which pupils from the different status levels have for familiarity with the words, objects, concepts, and processes necessary for successful performance on intelligence-test items. Thus far the assumption is the same as that underlying the explanation in the preceding paragraph. The lack of relationship at the upper-status levels may be assumed to be due, however, not to any lack in increased cultural opportunities characteristic of the high-status levels but instead to the fact that these increased cultural opportunities are simply not needed for satisfactory performance on the test. It may be that the tests for the younger pupils are pitched at a cultural level indicated by an I.S.C. of 13 to 15 points — that a cultural level this high is necessary for a child to have frequent access to the words, concepts, ideas, and procedures required for successful performance on the test. This would mean that any pupil having a lower cultural background than this would be handicapped on the test, but it would not necessarily mean that a pupil having a richer and more varied cultural background would have any extra advantage. If the test items are drawn primarily from a cultural experience represented by an I.S.C. of 13 to 15 points, pupils having that kind of cultural background, or better, could be expected to do equally well on the test, on the average, and differences would be of an individual nature only. Pupils with a more limited cultural background would, however, be expected to show systematically lower scores on the tests. These facts are exactly those found in the data represented by Figures 7 and 9. Since the tests for the older pupils, particularly the Terman-McNemar, Otis Beta, and parts of the California Mental Maturity tests, have a good deal more material of an obviously cultural nature in them, it would be reasonable to expect the leveling-off point either to be higher on the I.S.C. scale or to be nonexistent, which corresponds to the facts reported in Figures 8 and 10.

There is some definite evidence here, then, that the chief reason for the status differences in I.Q.'s may be the different opportunities which pupils from high- and low-status levels have for familiarity with the kinds of cultural materials and processes represented by the usual tests. In later chapters additional evidence will be presented which bears on this question of the probable reason for status differences. Status differences found on individual items will be analyzed in various ways in order to see whether the kinds of differences found are consistent with the kinds of hypotheses suggested in the preceding paragraphs.

For the sake of simplicity of presentation, the entire set of hypotheses will not be re-examined each time a new finding with respect to status differences is reported. Instead, in the chapters which follow, the status differences will be analyzed in various ways and factual findings reported without extensive interpretation. In chapter viii the major findings of the study are brought together and an attempt made to determine which of the various hypotheses just suggested in this section are reinforced and which

are refuted by each of the findings.[9]

Summary

The extent to which intelligence quotients as determined from nine different tests are related to socioeconomic status is examined by means of correlations based upon the total group of pupils at each age level. The correlations between I.Q.'s (or percentile ranks) and social status vary with the test used and the age level tested. They are moderate in size (.20 to .43), although definitely significant. The scatter diagrams indicate a great amount of overlapping, with many high-status pupils receiving low scores and many low-status pupils receiving high scores, even though high-status pupils tend, on the average, to receive the higher I.Q.'s. There is no clear evidence that the nature of the relationship between the I.Q.'s and social status is particularly different for Old Americans, for Scandinavians, or for ethnics, if allowance is made for the differences in range of status involved for these three groups.

The correlation is not a linear one for nine- and ten-year-old pupils. On all the tests given to these younger pupils social status is related to the I.Q. through the range from the lowest social status to approximately the lower end of the upper-middle class. In the upper reaches of the status level there is no tendency for the I.Q. to vary with social status. For the thirteen- and fourteen-year-old pupils the I.Q. continues to rise with increasing social status through almost the entire scale, although the evidence is not so clear at the very top, due to the small number of cases available.

9. For a further discussion of the possible implications of the lack of linearity, for example, see pp. 60-61.

CHAPTER XV

THE RELATION OF I.Q.'S TO SOCIAL STATUS: CONTRAST OF SPECIAL STATUS GROUPS

The preceding chapter presented data on the basis of which it was concluded that high-status characteristics tend to be associated with high I.Q.'s, and vice versa, but that the degree of relationship is far from high enough to enable one to predict an individual pupil's I.Q. on the basis of the status characteristics of an individual or family. Despite the relatively small correlations found, however, important and significant group differences in I.Q.'s may occur when the different status groups are taken as a whole. I.Q. differences for certain of these groups will be analyzed in this chapter.

Table 20 shows the distributions of I.Q.'s for two tests (those showing the greatest amounts of status differences in I.Q.'s for each age level) for the three special status groups which were established as described in chapter xi. It is clear from this table that there are marked differences in the distribution of I.Q.'s in some of the different status groups, although there is also considerable overlapping among them.[1] It will be noticed, for instance, that no low-status pupil secures an I.Q. of 140 or higher on these tests, although twenty-seven high-status pupils receive such high scores; no high-status pupil receive an I.Q. lower than 70 on these tests, although forty-nine low-status children do so. These status differences are also reflected in significant differences between the mean I.Q.'s for high-status and for low-status children at either age level. Table 20 indicates that the high-status children exceed the low-status children (either Old American or ethnic) by 17 to 18 points in the case of the nine- and ten-year-old children, and by 22 to 23 points in the case of the older children. These differences are from eleven to eighteen times their respective standard errors!

It is not possible to draw any conclusions as to the _meaning_ to be attached to these differences in the performance of high- and low-status pupils until the differences have been analyzed in terms of individual items in later chapters. It will be shown there, for instance, that verbal items and items involving knowledge of academic or bookish words show unusually large status differences. It is probable that the relatively large status difference reported here for the Terman-McNemar test is due in large part to the presence in that test of a substantial number of such items.

The differences between the mean I.Q.'s for low-status Old Americans and for low-status ethnics are very small; at neither age level is the difference even as large as its standard error. Such small differences as do exist are all in favor of the Old Americans at both age levels.

---

1. Possible implications of this overlapping for gaining insight into the nature of status differences in I.Q.'s are discussed in chapter viii (see pp. 59-60).

TABLE 20

DISTRIBUTION OF I.Q.'S OF PUPILS IN THREE STATUS GROUPS

| | Number of Pupils | | | | | |
| | Henmon-Nelson Test (Ages 9-10) | | | Terman-McNemar Test (Ages 13-14) | | |
Intelligence Quotients	High-Status Old American	Low-Status Old American	Low-Status Ethnic	High-Status Old American	Low-Status Old American	Low-Status Ethnic
150 and over	4	...	...	1	...	...
140-49	19	...	...	3	...	...
130-39	21	6	3	26	3	1
120-29	47	32	10	60	8	5
110-19	53	38	18	68	42	11
100-09	44	70	33	45	72	35
90-99	27	78	30	21	93	30
80-89	10	54	31	7	66	36
70-79	1	41	13	2	49	20
60-69	...	3	5	...	21	7
Below 60	...	...	...	...	7	6
Total	226	322	143	233	361	151
Mean I.Q.	115.8	98.4	97.1	114.9	93.0	91.6
Standard deviation	16.2	15.7	15.7	13.1	15.8	16.3

If the dispersion of the I.Q.'s is examined, by means of the standard deviations, it will be seen from Table 20 that there is virtually no difference in the degree of dispersion for the three status groups at the younger age level; for the older children, however, there is a statistically significant tendency (critical ratios, 3.1 and 2.7) for the high-status children to be more highly concentrated around their mean I.Q. than is the case for either of the two low-status groups.

The extent to which these relationships are confirmed by other tests given to these same pupils may be judged from Table 21, which reports the mean I.Q.'s for the different status groups on each of the tests. Column 3 of this table indicates that there is considerable lack of agreement as to a "typical" I.Q. for certain of the status groups. The typical I.Q. varies with the test used. The most striking example is the mean I.Q. for the nine- and ten-year-old high-status Old American group, which is 104 on the Otis Alpha Nonverbal test, 105 on the Otis Alpha Verbal test, 108 on the Kuhlmann-Anderson test, and 116 on the Henmon-Nelson test. For the low-status Old American groups at the younger age level, on the other hand, there is considerably more agreement, with the mean I.Q. varying from test to test within only a 2-point range. At the older age level the high-status Old Americans receive higher I.Q.'s on the Terman-McNemar test than they do on the Otis Beta test, while for the two low-status groups the situation is just reversed. On the basis of the data in column 3 it may be said that high-status groups have I.Q.'s averaging between 104 and 116, while low-status groups have I.Q.'s averaging between 92 and 98, with the exact positions varying according to the test.

Columns 4 and 5 of Table 21 indicate that there are very substantial differences between the mean I.Q.'s of the high-status pupils and of the low-status pupils (either ethnic or Old American), regardless of the test used. The I.Q. differences range from 8 points on the Otis Alpha Nonverbal test (younger pupils) to 22 points on the Terman-McNemar test (older pupils). The differences on three of the tests are necessarily expressed in percentile-rank terms and cannot, therefore, be directly compared with the differences expressed in I.Q. terms. On these three tests the differences in mean percentile rank for the high- and low-status pupils vary from 17 points on the Thurstone Spatial test to 33 points on the Thurstone Reasoning test. All these differences, whether in I.Q. or in percentile-rank form, are highly significant -- none of them being less than seven times its standard error. It is abundantly clear that whatever is measured by each of these tests is something which is found in measurably greater quantity in high-status pupils than in low-status pupils. This does not, of course, say anything as to the nature of what it is that the tests measure — merely that the data presented here establish beyond any doubt that there are genuine status differences in the traits measured, whatever the traits themselves may be.

In general, the tests used with the younger pupils show smaller I.Q. differences between high- and low-status pupils than do the two I.Q. tests used with the older pupils; but it should be noticed that the Henmon-Nelson test yields a status difference for the younger pupils somewhat larger than does the Otis Beta test for the older pupils. It is not possible, therefore, to say whether there is a genuine age difference in the status differential, or whether this is primarily a function of the kinds of test material included in the tests at the two age levels. Some evidence on this point will be presented in chapter xxi.

TABLE 21

STATUS DIFFERENCES IN MEAN I.Q.'S OF PUPILS IN THREE STATUS GROUPS

Test and Status Group* (1)	Number of Pupils (2)	Mean I.Q.'s and Percentile Ranks (3)	High-Status Old American vs. Low-Status Old American (4)		High-Status Old American vs. Low-Status Ethnic (5)		Low-Status Old American vs. Low-Status Ethnic (6)	
			Amount	Critical Ratio	Amount	Critical Ratio	Amount	Critical Ratio
Tests for Nine- and Ten-Year-Old Pupils (Scores in I.Q. Form)								
OAV { High-status Old American	223	105.4	8.9	10.0	11.6	10.6	2.7	2.6
Low-status Old American	326	96.5						
Low-status ethnic	145	93.8						
OAN { High-status Old American	223	104.4	8.1	8.7	9.4	7.8	1.3	1.2
Low-status Old American	316	96.3						
Low-status ethnic	114	95.0						
KA { High-status Old American	228	107.9	10.6	11.7	11.0	9.3	0.4	0.3
Low-status Old American	329	97.3						
Low-status ethnic	146	96.9						
HN { High-status Old American	226	115.8	17.4	12.6	18.7	11.0	1.2	0.8
Low-status Old American	322	98.4						
Low-status ethnic	143	97.1						

Table 21 – Continued

Tests for Thirteen- and Fourteen-Year-Old Pupils (Scores in I.Q. Form)

Test	Group	N	Mean						
OB	High-status Old American	235	113.2	15.9	17.3	17.5	14.2	1.5	1.2
	Low-status Old American	364	97.3						
	Low-status ethnic	155	95.8						
TMc	High-status Old American	233	114.9	21.9	18.3	23.4	14.8	1.4	0.9
	Low-status Old American	361	93.0						
	Low-status ethnic	151	91.6						

Tests for Thirteen- and Fourteen-Year-Old Pupils (Scores in Percentile-Rank Form)

Test	Group	N	Mean						
ThS	High-status Old American	235	52.7	16.6	6.9$^+$	21.2$^+$	7.2$^+$	4.7$^+$	1.7$^+$
	Low-status Old American	352	36.1						
	Low-status ethnic	154	31.4						
ThR	High-status Old American	232	74.0	28.4	12.9$^+$	33.3$^+$	12.1$^+$	5.0$^+$	1.8$^+$
	Low-status Old American	358	45.6						
	Low-status ethnic	154	40.6						
CMM	High-status Old American	235	68.6	27.4	12.4$^+$	30.7$^+$	11.8$^+$	3.3$^+$	1.3$^+$
	Low-status Old American	352	41.1						
	Low-status ethnic	151	37.8						

* Test abbreviations are as follows: OAV – Otis Alpha Verbal; OAN – Otis Alpha Nonverbal; KA – Kuhlmann-Anderson; HN – Henmon-Nelson; OB – Otis Beta; TMc – Terman-McNemar; ThS – Thurstone Spatial; ThR – Thurstone Reasoning; CMM – California Mental Maturity.

+ Attention is called to the fact that these critical ratios are derived from distributions of percentile ranks. For brief discussion of the effect of this and of the justification for this procedure see Note 7 in Appendix D.

Column 6 of Table 21 indicates that the I.Q. (or percentile-rank) differences between the low-status Old Americans and low-status ethnics are comparatively small and seldom statistically significant. The chance that there is a real difference between Old Americans and ethnics, when status is held constant, and that the obtained test differences are not merely sampling errors is increased, of course, by the fact that on all nine tests and at both age levels the differences, though small, are always in the same direction. On every test the Old American pupils do slightly better than the ethnic pupils, with the greatest I.Q. difference occurring on the Otis Alpha Verbal tests, and the least occurring on the Kuhlmann-Anderson test. On all the tests, however, the differences between these two groups are very small indeed when compared with the much larger differences between high- and low-status groups as indicated in columns 4 and 5 of Table 21.

To the extent that these I.Q. differences reflect differences in cultural background, the finding that Old American-ethnic differences (with social status held constant) are much smaller than the differences between status groups (with ethnicity held constant) is not surprising. Students of social-class phenomena have generally found that cultural differences between ethnic groups of the same social-class level are much smaller than cultural differences between social-class groups of the same ethnic background. Possible implications of this finding for gaining insight into the nature of status differences in I.Q.'s are discussed further in chapter viii.[2]

These same data, for the tests for the nine- and ten-year-old pupils only, are presented graphically in Figure 11. This chart shows dramatically the same relationships already pointed out in connection with Table 21 — the marked difference between the average I.Q. of the high-status pupils as compared to that for either of the low-status groups, the comparatively small superiority of the low-status Old Americans over the low-status ethnics, and the considerable variation in I.Q. level, especially for high-status pupils, depending upon the particular test used.

In Figure 12, the distribution of I.Q.'s on two of the tests is illustrated in a different graphic form. The two tests chosen for presentation in Figure 12 are those shown by the correlation coefficients previously reported to be the tests showing the highest and the lowest degree of relationship between social status and I.Q.'s. In computing the data for this chart, the entire range of I.Q. scores on these tests (more than 2,400 scores on each test) was divided into quarters, so that every individual's I.Q. could be described as being in the first, second, third, or fourth quarter with respect to the total group of pupils. The distribution of individuals in these different quarters within each of the special status groups is shown in Figure 12.

It will be seen at once that, for both tests, the composition of the high-status group is markedly different from the composition of the low-status groups. On the Terman-McNemar test, for example, 57 per cent of the high-status pupils have I.Q.'s high enough to place them in the top quarter of the total group of pupils, whereas less than 10 per cent of either of the low-status groups receive I.Q.'s in the top quarter of the total group. Similarly, less than 5 per cent of the high-status group is composed of individuals with I.Q.'s in the bottom quarter, while from 40 to 50 per cent of each of the low-status groups is composed of such individuals.

2. See pp. 61-62.

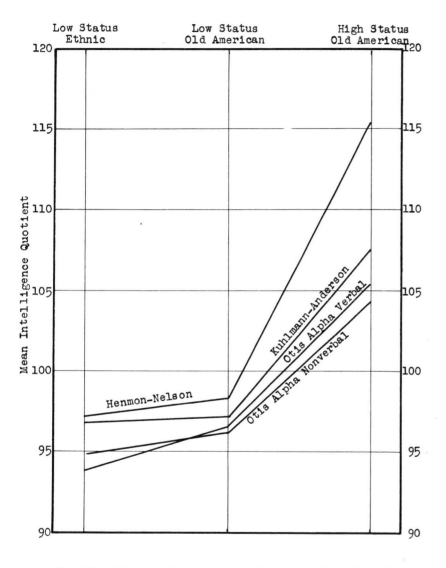

Fig. 11. — Mean I.Q.'s for nine- and ten-year-old pupils in three status groups. (Source: Data in Table 21.)

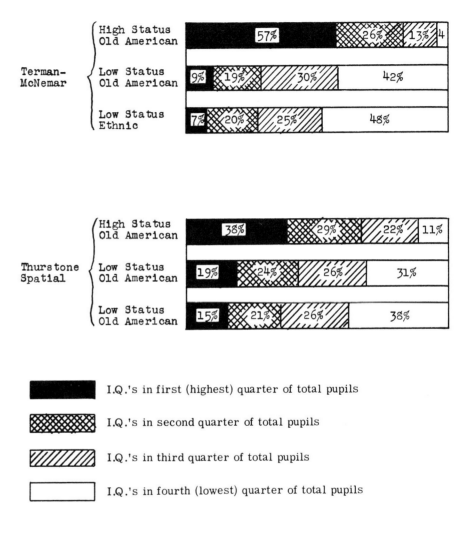

Fig. 12. — Distribution of thirteen- and fourteen-year-old pupils in three status groups, by I.Q.'s.

The Thurstone Spatial test shows precisely the same kind of relationships, although in much less extreme form. Even on this test, which shows less relationship between I.Q. and I.S.C. than any of the other tests used, twice as large a proportion of the high-status group is composed of individuals from the top quarter as is the case for the low-status pupils; three times as many low-status pupils are drawn from the lowest quarter in I.Q. scores as is the case for the high-status pupils. It is interesting to notice that on the Thurstone test all three status groups draw approximately 25 per cent of their population from each of the two middle quarters — close to the proportion which would be expected if there were no relationship between social status and I.Q. at all. The principal discrimination, it would seem, is at the high and low extremes of the I.Q. scale rather than in the middle ranges.

Summary

When the high- and low-status groups are contrasted, a considerable degree of overlapping of I.Q.'s is shown to exist, with many low-status pupils receiving higher scores than many of the high-status pupils. Despite this, however, there are substantial differences in the average I.Q.'s for the two status groups, always in favor of the high-status pupils. The I.Q. difference varies from 8 I.Q. points (Otis Alpha Nonverbal test for nine- and ten-year-old pupils) to 23 I.Q. points (Terman-McNemar test for thirteen- and fourteen-year-old pupils). Differences for the tests scored in percentile ranks vary from 17 to 33 percentile-rank points. The differences are all significant, the smallest being seven times its standard error.

Differences in I.Q.'s of the two low-status groups — one Old American and one ethnic — are small and not clearly significant, although every test shows the ethnic pupils slightly lower than the Old Americans.

CHAPTER XVI

MATERIALS AND METHODS USED IN THE ITEM ANALYSIS

It is interesting, perhaps, to know that high-status children secure higher scores, on the average, on all the intelligence tests than do low-status children. Evidence supporting this kind of conclusion is not new, however — nor is it, of itself, particularly revealing. The existence of such differences is a well-established fact, not only on the basis of the data in chapters xiv and xv, but also from a great many similar findings in other research studies referred to in chapter ii. What the differences mean, however, is far from clear.

Do these differences prove that the children of high-status families inherit superior genetic constitutions, including superior mental equipment? Do they mean that the children of high-status families have lived in more stimulating environments so that their "mental alertness" has been developed more fully than that of children of low-status families? Or do they mean that the tests are heavily laden with materials with which high-status pupils have more opportunity for familiarity than do low-status pupils? In short — are the differences evidence of important differences in the pupils being measured, or are they evidence of important shortcomings in the measuring instruments?

It is probably unnecessary to point out the great practical importance, for many educational procedures, of determining to what extent observed I.Q. differences between different social-status groups are a function of the tests themselves — their content, their manner of administration, etc. — and to what extent the differences are a function of important differences in the basic ability of the people in the various social-status groups. It is this problem, primarily, to which the present study is addressed. It is the special aim of the rest of the chapters in this report to throw further light on the extent to which the I.Q. differences reported in chapters xiv and xv may be due to the nature of the test items themselves.[1]

The findings will not be conclusive. The difficulty of identifying causal factors and the complexity of the interrelationships involved preclude any definitive answer on the basis of a single research study. But the accumulation of more analytical knowledge as to the specific nature of the differences observed in the I.Q.'s should yield greater insight into the meanings of those differences.

While much of this analysis will be presented in statistical terms, it should be pointed out that there are definite limits to the extent to which statistical analysis can provide any final answer to problems such as

---

1. Other studies, comprising parts of the larger research project on cultural factors in intelligence, described in the Preface, are designed to examine other aspects of this problem — such as the extent to which the observed differences may be due to social-status differentials with respect to test motivation, familiarity with test procedures, and other such general factors.

those involved in this area. Statistical manipulations can determine whether the social-status differences found when I.Q.'s are studied exist in connection with all individual test items, or whether there are certain items which show much greater social-status differences than do others. They can be used to compare the amount of social-status difference found for various types of items and may even occasionally suggest possible explanations for such differences. In the last analysis, however, statistical procedures can only (a) delimit the area within which the final explanation of any differences must be sought and (b) check the reasonableness of hypotheses by comparing empirical data with predicted or hypothecated data. They cannot determine the actual explanations themselves. The determination of most likely explanations must be done by means of judgment and insight and must, therefore, be subject to some subjective error. The statistical data provided should, however, narrow the area within which the subjective insight is required to operate and therefore reduce the likelihood of major errors being introduced.

Number of Items Available for Analysis

All the analysis in this and subsequent chapters will be in terms of the high-status and low-status pupil groups established as described in chapter xi. It will be recalled that these groups were as follows:

High Status - Old American
Low Status - Old American
Low Status - Ethnic

and that they were set up separately for two different age levels — nine- and ten-year-olds in one group, and thirteen- and fourteen-year-olds in another. The number of pupils in each of these groups and the number of tests available for each group have been reported in Table 7 on page 108.

Even though extra time was allowed for some of the tests, not all pupils were able to finish all the items. There were items at the end of many of the tests for which responses from only a portion of the pupils were available. This raised an important question with regard to the base which should be used in computing the percentage answering the item correctly. If the number of pupils answering the item correctly was divided by the total number of pupils who took the test, pupils who simply did not reach one of the later items and never attempted it would be counted as among the wrong responses and would reduce the percentage of right responses. If, on the other hand, the number of pupils answering the item correctly was divided by the total number of pupils who reached and attempted that item, a question could be raised as to whether the group then being analyzed was typical of the total status group which it was supposed to represent. The presumption might well be that those pupils who did not finish the test were a selected or biased sample from the total status group.

Examination of the item data indicated that the majority of the items (from 66 to 76 per cent of them, depending upon the status group studied) were reached and attempted by virtually all (95 per cent or more) the pupils in the group. From a third to a quarter of the items, however, were not attempted by all the pupils — some of them were reached by less than half of the pupils in one or more of the status groups. Since there were no data available as a basis for establishing clearly whether the pupils reaching items were representative of the total class group in cases where

they constituted substantially less than the total status group, it was decided to eliminate from the analysis any item which was not reached and attempted by at least 95 per cent of the pupils in each of the three status groups. In this way the representative nature of the pupil responses being studied was assured, and the problem of deciding which base to use for the percentages became unimportant. The loss in data resulting from eliminating these items is probably more than offset by the increase in quality and reliability of the data on the remaining items. The percentages were then computed for the remaining items on the basis of the total number of pupils taking the test. This included as wrong responses those few pupils (less than 5 per cent of any status group) who did not reach or attempt the item, but the error introduced in this way did not seem sufficiently large to justify the extra labor of computing the percentages on different bases for each item.

The preceding paragraph refers only to items omitted at the end of each pupil's test — items which it might be presumed the pupil did not reach and did not attempt. In some cases the pupils skipped certain items but did attempt items further on in the test. In such cases it was presumed that the pupil had skipped the items because they appeared difficult to him; he was accordingly credited with wrong responses on such items rather than as not having attempted them. This presumption was doubtless not justified in every instance, but it seemed the most reasonable one to make for most such cases.

The number of items remaining for study is indicated in Table 22. These data are reported separately for each of the three possible inter-status-group comparisons, since the number of items reached and attempted by 95 per cent of the pupils in the status group is not identical for the three groups.

The last three columns of Table 22 indicate that the item analysis of this study involves approximately 650 different test items, divided almost equally between the tests for the two age levels. These items comprise approximately two-thirds of the total items included in the entire set of tests used with each age group. The elimination of items because less than 95 per cent of the status groups being compared reached and attempted them resulted in the discarding of approximately one-third of the items, with the discards being most heavily concentrated in the Kuhlmann-Anderson, Terman-McNemar, and Thurstone Spatial tests. The larger proportion of such items in the Kuhlmann-Anderson and Terman-McNemar tests is due in part to the fact that these tests are composed of a number of subtests each of which is timed separately; in neither case was it possible to give the pupils any more time over that recommended by the authors. In the case of the Thurstone Spatial test, in which only about half of the pupils finished the test even in the extended time allowed, the reason is doubtless that the Thurstone test, being designed primarily as a speed test, contains many more items than pupils could normally be expected to finish. In any case, the items in this test are so similar in nature that the loss of a number of them should introduce no particular difficulty.

All item analysis reported in subsequent chapters is carried out on the basis of the items tabulated in the last three columns of this table. The particular items involved are listed in Appendix C.

TABLE 22

NUMBER OF ITEMS ANALYZED IN NINE INTELLIGENCE TESTS

Test	Total Number of Items in Test	Number of Items Included in Analysis		
		High-Status Old American vs. Low-Status Old American	High-Status Old American vs. Low-Status Ethnic	Low-Status Old American vs. Low-Status Ethnic
		Tests for Nine- and Ten-Year-Old Pupils		
Otis Alpha Nonverbal.......	90	90	90	90
Otis Alpha Verbal ...	90	90	90	90
Henmon-Nelson	90	60	48	48
Kuhlmann-Anderson ..	222*	94	97	89
Total	492	334	325	317
Per cent of total items.........	100.0%	67.9%	66.1%	64.4%
		Tests for Thirteen- and Fourteen-Year-Old Pupils		
Otis Beta	80	72	72	72
Terman-McNemar ...	162	102	111	101
California Mental Maturity	65+	54	60	56
Thurstone Spatial‡ ...	108	55	55	60
Thurstone Reasoning .	60	41	41	41
Total	475	324	339	330
Per cent of total items.........	100.0%	68.2%	71.4%	69.5%

* This number excludes subtests 14 and 24, which, because of their form, could not readily be analyzed in terms of performance on individual items.

+ This number excludes subtests 2 and 6, which were not administered to the pupils because of insufficient time in the scheduled class period.

‡ For a description of what was counted as an "item" on the Thurstone Spatial test see Note 8 in Appendix D.

For each item the number of pupils answering the item correctly in each status group was expressed as a percentage of the total number of pupils in the status group. The difference between these percentages for any two status groups was then used as a measure of the status difference in that item. An example will make the nature of this measure of status difference clear. The data for two sample items from one of the tests are given in Table 23.

TABLE 23

STATUS-DIFFERENCE DATA

FOR TWO SAMPLE TEST ITEMS

	Henmon-Nelson Item No. 7		Henmon-Nelson Item No. 8	
	High-Status Old American	Low-Status Old American	High-Status Old American	Low-Status Old American
Total number of pupils in status group	226	322	226	332
Number of pupils answering the item correctly .	204	212	205	252
Per cent of pupils answering the item correctly	90.3%	65.8%	90.7%	78.3%
Difference between percentages for two status groups ..	24.5%		12.4%	

The two percentage differences in the last line of this table are illustrative of the differences computed for all the items in all the tests and used as measures of differences in responses of the status groups. It is clear, for example, from the illustration in Table 23, that Henmon-Nelson Item No. 7 shows a larger status difference than does Item No. 8. An important modification of this status-difference measure was made (and will be discussed below),[2] but it is merely an adaptation of this basic computation of the difference between the percentages answering the item correctly in two status groups.

Consideration was given to the advisability of adjusting the various percentages for possible guessing and chance responses, but it was decided not to attempt to do so. The usual adjustment of item-response data, whether in scores or on individual items, is based upon the belief that to make

2. See pp. 168-72.

the adjustment results in a figure which indicates more closely the real knowledge of the pupil. Davis, in his recent monograph on item analysis, remarks, for example, that "it is clear that the definition of item difficulty in terms of the proportion of testees that actually <u>knows</u> the answer is a more fundamental definition than one merely in terms of the proportion of testees that marks the item correctly" (<u>55</u>, p. 4). This idea seems to assume that there is a fairly clear-cut line of demarcation between those who know the answer and those who do not —and that those who are in the "do not" category but still manage to mark the item correctly, presumably through chance, should not receive credit for doing so. Actually, it is probably true that, for most items, the knowledge of any sizable group of pupils will distribute itself along a continuum running from those who know the right answer unequivocally to those who have no idea whatever as to the right answer and who make a sheer guess, but with many in-between pupils — some who have an idea of the right answer but are not sure, some who really do not "know" the answer but have enough partial knowledge to make an intelligent "guess," etc. It may very well be true that there are few pupils who mark the answer to an item "out of the blue," so to speak, with no leads whatever as to the right answer — or with no misleads from wrong distractors. It is the assumption that all pupils who do not "know" the right answer mark the item in this "out-of-the-blue" fashion that underlies the usual formula for adjusting the percentage marking the item correctly.

There is a further difficulty about the usual formula for adjusting pupil responses for guessing. The formula assumes that the number of pupils who answer the item correctly by chance rather than by knowledge is equal to the number of pupils who answer all the incorrect responses, divided by the number of incorrect responses available. This is true only if the available responses are all equally attractive, or equally unattractive, to the pupil who does not "know" the correct response. This assumption is probably seldom fulfilled strictly in actual test items, and in many cases it may be seriously fallacious. In examining the wrong-response data for the test items included in the present study, it was very clear that there were a great many items for which the various available responses were not equally attractive to the pupils, even if the correct one is eliminated.

Because of doubt as to the psychological soundness of the clear-cut dichotomy between pupils who "know" and pupils who "guess" and because of the lack of any satisfactory manner of separating the two kinds of pupils anyway, it was decided not to attempt to adjust the percentages for possible random guessing. Pertinent to this decision also is the fact that, in this particular study, attention is being focused primarily, not upon some psychological reality in the pupils, to be revealed by the test item, but rather upon the item itself, in its role as a test item. If the nature of a particular item either invites or discourages guessing, that characteristic of the item should not be eliminated from consideration in the item analysis, since it is the actual "correct" responses of the pupils to the item, whether through guessing or through knowledge, which contributes to the pupils' scores. An exception to this statement should be noted in the case of the Thurstone Spatial test, since the right-minus-wrong method of scoring used for this test presumably eliminates most of the "correct" responses resulting from guessing.

Standard errors of the percentage status differences

The pupils tested in this program were regarded as samples drawn from a larger population of similar individuals, about whom it was desired to formulate generalizations. This "larger population" may be thought of as comprising all the children of these ages and social-status groups in all American cities with a social and cultural structure similar to that of the city in which the study was made. Since generalizations to a larger group of pupils were desired, it became important to know the size of the sampling errors involved. Some differences in pupil responses to individual test items might be expected to occur merely on a chance basis even if the two status groups of pupils were themselves not actually different with respect to the item — that is, even if they were, statistically speaking, drawn from the same universe.

When the status difference for an item is expressed as the difference between two percentages, estimation of the sampling error is comparatively simple. For this purpose the usual formulas for the standard error of a percentage and the standard error of the difference between two percentages were employed.[3] For every status comparison made, the standard error of the difference was computed. Critical ratios were then determined and levels of significance were established.

Wherever possible, in the reporting of data in later chapters, the levels of significance of item status differences will be indicated as being either 1 per cent, 5 per cent, or less than 5 per cent. Regardless of the test involved, or of the particular status groups being compared, any percentage difference of 14 points or more is significant at the 1 per cent level, and no percentage difference of 6 points or less is significant at the 1 per cent level. Differences between 6 and 14 points may or may not be significant, with the likelihood of their being significant increasing as the percentages approach 100 or 0, and decreasing as they approach 50. These statements apply to all item status differences when based on the total number of pupils in the status groups. They do not apply to the special wrong-answer analyses in chapter xxiii, where some of the percentages are based on only part of the pupils in each status group.

Measuring Status Differences in Items by Means of a Normalized Index

A major difficulty arises in attempting to use the difference between two percentages as a measure of status difference, in that a scale of percentages does not, usually, constitute a linear scale with respect to the trait being measured. It does so only if the trait being measured is distributed in the population rectilinearly. For this reason, the differences between two percentages may not mean the same thing at different points along the percentage scale. For example, the difference between 90 per cent of a group of pupils answering an item correctly and 80 per cent of another group answering the item correctly probably represents a considerably greater degree of difference in the difficulty of the item for these two groups than would percentages of 60 and 50 for the same two groups. If the trait is distributed "normally" or in any manner which is

3. The formulas are:
$$\sigma_P = \sqrt{\frac{PQ}{N}} \qquad \sigma_{P_1-P_2} = \sqrt{(\sigma_{P_1})^2 + (\sigma_{P_2})^2}$$
A modification of the traditional formula was introduced in the case of percentages over 90 or under 10. For explanation see Note 9 in Appendix D.

characterized by a concentration of a large number of cases in the middle ranges of difficulty and only a few at the extremes, then to pass from 50 per cent of the group to 60 per cent of the group will be done while traversing only a short distance on the difficulty scale, while passing from 80 per cent to 90 per cent of the people will involve a greater distance on the difficulty scale, since there are fewer people in these extreme ranges of difficulty and therefore greater "distance" between them.

Since a great many comparisons between the percentages of pupils passing a given item are to be made in this study, it becomes particularly important to eliminate this difficulty so far as it is possible to do so. This can be done completely satisfactorily only if the exact distribution of the trait or traits underlying the test items is known. There is no way of ascertaining the nature of this underlying distribution; in fact, it is quite likely that it varies somewhat from item to item. Nevertheless, in order to make any comparisons at all, it is necessary to make some assumption as to the most likely nature of the distribution of the factors being measured by the test items. The assumption that these factors are distributed according to the so-called "normal" curve is not capable of any satisfactory proof, but it seems reasonable to assume that the distribution probably more nearly approaches the "normal" one, with its bunching of cases in the middle and its tapering-off of cases at both ends, than it approaches a rectilinear distribution — which is the assumption necessarily underlying any comparison of item difficulty directly in terms of the percentage of pupils who answer the item correctly.

By making the assumption of normality in the distribution, it is relatively easy to establish a set of scaled values into which the percentage of pupils answering an item correctly can be converted, and which will be in such a form that equal differences between two such measures will represent equal differences in real difficulty no matter at what point along the scale they may be taken. This will be strictly true only to the extent that the trait or traits underlying the items are actually distributed normally. Any error introduced through variations from such normality will probably be much less, however, than that introduced by assuming rectilinearity of the distribution.

A number of different systems of scaled scores have been used by different authors to convert various sets of scores to normalized scales where equal distances would represent equal units of the variable being measured. Although they are expressed in different forms, they are usually based upon the use of the standard deviation of the distribution as a unit and a fitting of the scale to the normal curve. The particular system of such scores used in this study is that proposed recently by Davis, which he calls a "Difficulty Index" (55, pp. 7-8, 38). Davis' index is obtained by placing the 50 per cent point at the mean of a normal distribution and using 21.066 as the standard deviation of the distribution. This results in a set of index values ranging from 1 to 99, corresponding to percentages of 1 to 99, with an index value of 50 corresponding to 50 per cent, but with the other corresponding figures not on a unit-to-unit basis.

A slight modification of the Davis index was made in the interests of greater theoretical accuracy at the extreme ends of the scale. Davis computes his index by the formula as far as 1 per cent and 99 per cent, then arbitrarily assigns index values of 0 and 100 to 0 per cent and 100 per cent, respectively, so as to make his index range from a low of 0 to a high of 100. In the present case the index was extended by the formula to include a range three times the standard deviation each side of the mean,

and the index value for 100 per cent and for 0 per cent assigned to the mean plus and minus three standard deviations.[4] The effect of this modification is to spread out, more than does the Davis index, very small percentage differences at the extreme end of the scale; it has no effect unless more than 99 per cent of the pupils in one status group answer the item correctly. In any case, differences based upon extremely high percentages are relatively unreliable or unstable, as will be shown later in this chapter.

The nature of the variation between the percentage scale and the scale of normalized indexes into which the various percentage values were converted may be seen from Table 24, which gives sample equivalent values at various intervals along both scales. The importance of the difference in the distribution of the two sets of measures is very clear. In the left-hand portion of the table, for instance, it will be seen that the differences between a percentage of 100 and one of 90, on the one hand, and between one of 60 and one of 50, on the other, although the same size in terms of percentage points, are very different in terms of the index. The first is represented by 36 index points and the second by 5 index points. It is also clear that the difference between the two scales is most marked at the extremes. The distributions of percentages and equivalent indexes are not markedly different for the range from 20 to 80 per cent, for example. The

TABLE 24

SAMPLE PERCENTAGE VALUES AND THEIR

EQUIVALENT NORMALIZED INDEXES

Index Values Corresponding to Percentages Taken at Equal Intervals			Percentage Values Corresponding to Indexes Taken at Equal Intervals		
Per Cent	Equivalent Index	Difference between Adjacent Indexes	Index	Equivalent Per Cent	Difference between Adjacent Percentages
100%..	113}		100 ...	99%}	
		36			2%
90 ...	77}		90 ...	97}	
		9			5
80 ...	68}		80 ...	92}	
		7			9
70 ...	61}		70 ...	83}	
		6			15
60 ...	55}		60 ...	68}	
		5			18
50 ...	50}		50 ...	50}	
		5			18
40 ...	45}		40 ...	32}	
		6			15
30 ...	39}		30 ...	17}	
		7			9
20 ...	32}		20 ...	8}	
		9			5
10 ...	23}		10 ...	3}	
		36			2
0 ...	-13}		0 ...	1}	

4. The index equivalents for percentage values in these extreme ranges will be found in Note 10 in Appendix D.

differences are very marked, however, when the percentage rises above 90 or falls below 10.

The right-hand portion of Table 24 is, of course, the reverse side of the same relationship shown in the left-hand part of the table. Here it appears that a difference of 10 points on the index may represent a difference of anywhere from 2 to 18 points on the percentage scale, depending upon where along the scale of difficulty the difference occurs. The difference between these scales is an important one, and a clear understanding of the relationship between them is important for proper interpretation of the data which follow. Further examples of the variability which may occur in the difference between two indexes when the percentage difference remains constant and of the variability which may occur in the difference between two percentages when the index difference remains constant are given in Table 25.

In the first six lines of this table, illustrations are given in which the status difference is held constant when expressed in percentage terms,

TABLE 25

EXAMPLES ILLUSTRATING POSSIBLE VARIATIONS IN STATUS
DIFFERENCES WHEN EXPRESSED IN PERCENTAGE TERMS
AND WHEN EXPRESSED IN INDEX TERMS

Measure of Difficulty of Item for Two Different Status Groups				Measure of Status Difference	
Per Cent Answering Correctly		Equivalent Indexes		In Percentage Terms	In Index Terms
High Status	Low Status	High Status	Low Status		
Samples in Which Difference (in Percentage Terms) Held Constant					
98%	93%	93	81	5%	12
85	80	72	68	5	4
52.5	47.5	51	49	5	2
98	78	93	66	20	27
90	70	77	61	20	16
60	40	55	45	20	10
Samples in Which Difference (in Index Terms) Held Constant					
98.9%	97.9%	98	93	1%	5
88	83	75	70	5	5
54	44	52	47	10	5
98.9	90.9	98	78	8	20
92	68	80	60	24	20
68	31	60	40	37	20

first at 5 per cent and then at 20 per cent; it is shown that the status difference when expressed in index terms varies greatly. In the lower half of the table the status difference expressed in index differences is held constant; it is shown that such index differences may be translations of widely varying percentage differences. This table, and the one preceding it, merely illustrate that it is important which scale is used and that the interpretations to be drawn about the relative size of status differences for different items may vary substantially according to which scale is used. This is particularly true where a difference occurring near the center of the percentage scale is compared with a difference occurring near either of the extremes.

Throughout this study the status difference as measured by the difference between two indexes — not that measured by the difference between the percentages themselves — is used as the more valid measure whenever the size of status differences for different items is to be compared. This is done in the belief that it is more reasonable to suppose that the distributions of the traits being measured by these test items approximate a normal distribution than to suppose that they approximate a rectilinear one. Percentage differences are used in the present study only for the purpose of measuring the statistical significance of status differences, not as a measure of the size or amount of status differences.

Sampling errors of the index status differences

The estimation of the sampling error in a status difference when that difference is expressed in terms of the normalized index is much more difficult than when it is expressed in terms of percentages. No formula for the direct determination of the standard error of a normalized index is available. Considerable effort was devoted to an unsuccessful attempt to arrive at some satisfactory way of estimating how large an index difference would have to be in order to be statistically significant at any given level of confidence.

The statistical significance of an index difference is dependent upon three different factors: (a) the number of cases in each of the particular status groups being compared; (b) the point along the percentage scale where the difference occurs, as it affects the size of the standard error of the percentage; and (c) the point along the percentage scale where the difference occurs, as it affects the conversion of percentage units to index units. These last two factors are contradictory or offsetting ones, in that one tends to make differences at the center of the scale the most reliable ones, while the other tends to make these same differences the least reliable ones. The actual degree of statistical significance for any given difference is, therefore, a result of the balancing of three variables, and it is difficult to deal with all possible variations and intercombinations of them.

As a matter of fact, however, it is not really necessary to have any way of estimating the sampling error in an index difference directly, since the likelihood of any particular difference being or not being due to random sampling fluctuations cannot be affected by any change of the units in which the variable is expressed. While the amount of status difference varies according to the unit in which it is measured, the certainty with which that difference represents a true difference greater than zero does not change.

This may be put in a slightly different way by saying that no statistical manipulation of the original percentage figures can either increase or decrease the likelihood that the original difference was due only to chance sampling errors. This being the case, it is entirely proper (a) to make inferences as to the likelihood of the difference being due to chance fluctuation on the basis of the size of the difference, expressed in percentage form, as related to the standard error of that difference, and (b) to apply the inference to the difference as expressed in index terms. This is what was done in the present instance. An indication of the rather considerable overlapping between size of index differences and degree of statistical significance of those differences will be found in Table 26, which gives the results of a tabulation of the item differences (high-status Old American versus low-status Old American) on 658 items whose more complete analysis is reported in the next chapter.

Table 26 indicates that for these 658 items all index differences of 25 points or more are significant at the 1 per cent level and that no item with an index difference of less than 5 points is significant even at the 5 per cent level. Items with index differences between 5 and 25, however, are sometimes significant at the 1 per cent level, sometimes significant at the 5 per cent level, and sometimes not even significant at the 5 per cent level. This middle range of differences, whose statistical significance cannot be determined by simple inspection, includes more than 80 per cent of the 658 items reported in Table 26.

TABLE 26

DISTRIBUTION OF TEST ITEMS BY SIZE AND STATISTICAL SIGNIFICANCE OF STATUS DIFFERENCES

Size of Index Difference*	Difference Significant at 1 Per Cent Level	Difference Significant at 5 Per Cent Level	Difference Not Significant at 5 Per Cent Level	Total
35-39	1	. .	. . .	1
30-34	. . .	. .	. . .	. . .
25-29	8	. .	. . .	8
20-24	57	1	1	59
15-19	129	1	3	133
10-14	173	6	8	187
5-9	92	37	35	164
0-4	. . .	. .	87	87
(-1)-(-5)	. . .	. .	18	18
(-6)-(-10)	. . .	. .	1	1
Total	460	45	153	658

* Difference obtained by subtracting index value obtained from percentage of low-status Old American pupils answering the item correctly from index value obtained from percentage of high-status Old American pupils doing so.

Instability of the index differences at the extremes

Percentage differences which occur at the extremes of difficulty — items which are either very easy or very difficult for either group of pupils being compared — have smaller standard errors than do those which occur in the middle range of difficulty. The reverse is true, however, when the percentage differences are transformed into the normalized index described above. This occurs because the comparatively small standard errors (in percentage terms) at the extremes are "spread out" by the normalized index more markedly than the larger standard errors occurring near the middle of the difficulty scale.

This may be illustrated most easily by considering the standard errors of the percentage values and those of their equivalent index values — leaving until later the problem of the standard errors of the differences between two percentages, or between two index values. Sample standard errors, in both percentage and index terms, at various points on the scale of difficulty, are shown in Table 27.

Table 27 indicates that the standard error of 99 per cent, when based on a group of the size used in this table, is 0.7. The size of the standard error increases steadily as the percentage value decreases, until the standard error of 50 per cent is 3.3 percentage points. Since the index equivalent of the standard error is not symmetrical on both sides of the percentage value, it is more convenient to compare, not the size of the standard errors themselves, but the size of the range covered by plus-or-minus one standard error around each percentage value (or its equivalent index). If this is done, it will be seen that the standard-error range at the 99 per cent level of difficulty is very small (1.3 points) but that this is the equivalent, on the index scale of 12 points. On the other hand, the standard-error range at the 50 per cent level of difficulty is considerably greater in percentage terms (6.7 percentage points), but this larger range is the equivalent of only 4 points on the index scale.

It will be noticed from Table 27, however, that throughout most of the range of difficulty, the standard-error range, when expressed in index terms, is relatively constant. It is only clear at the extremes — when the index is in the high 80's or 90's that the standard-error range increases substantially.

This relative instability of the index with very high (or very low) percentages may also be illustrated by example. If 100 per cent of a group of 300 pupils answer a given item correctly, the shift of only 5 individuals from the right answer to a wrong one would move the index 18 points; if 99 per cent of the 300 pupils answer correctly, the shift of 5 individuals would move the index only 8 points. If 95 per cent of the 300 pupils answer correctly, the shift of 5 individuals would move the index only 3 points. If 90 per cent answer correctly, the shift would be only 2 points. Below 70 per cent, the shift of 5 individuals would move the index only 1 point.

The nature of this change in the stability of the index, and of the index differences, at different points on the difficulty scale was also examined empirically by a split-halves reliability analysis. The pupils available for each status group were split into two random groups (odd versus even pupils). For each of the items the percentage right for each status group was then computed for each of the random halves separately. These percentages were then converted into normalized indexes and the index differences computed. The 1,316 index values (one for high-status pupils and one for low-status pupils for each of 658 items) were then classified

TABLE 27

SAMPLE STANDARD ERRORS OF PERCENTAGES AND
OF EQUIVALENT INDEX VALUES

Percentage Values			Equivalent Index Values	
Per Cent	Standard Error*	Range ±1 Standard Error	Index	Range ±1 Standard Error+
100% . . .	0.0%	0.0%	113	0
99	0.7	1.3	99	12
98	0.9	1.9	93	8
97	1.1	2.3	90	7
96	1.3	2.6	87	7
95	1.5	2.9	85	6
94	1.6	3.2	83	6
93	1.7	3.4	81	5
92	1.8	3.6	80	5
91	1.9	3.8	78	5
90	2.0	4.0	77	5
80	2.7	5.4	68	4
70	3.1	6.1	61	4
60	3.3	6.6	55	3‡
50	3.3	6.7	50	4
40§ . . .	3.3	6.6	45	3

* Based on 223 pupils, the smallest number of pupils in either of the Old American status groups on any test. When based on 364 pupils, the largest number of pupils in any status group on any test, the standard-error ranges (in percentage form) are from 0.2 to 1.5 points lower than shown here; the index standard-error ranges are 1 or 2 points lower.

+ Obtained as indicated in following example: When the percentage is 99, the standard error is .67. The percentage value plus one standard error is 99.67, which has an index equivalent of 107; the percentage value minus one standard error is 98.33, which has an index equivalent of 95. The difference between the two index equivalents (107 and 95) is 12, as reported in the last column of the table.

‡ This apparent discrepancy occurs because the indexes have all been treated as whole numbers; if the indexes were computed to more decimal places, the discrepancy would disappear.

§ The computations for the lower half of the per cent scale are not shown, since they are exactly symmetrical with those reported for the upper half.

by the size of the index value. For each of the groups of index values the mean odd-even variation in the index was computed. By odd-even variation is meant the difference (without regard to algebraic sign) between the value of the index when computed from the odd-numbered pupils as compared with that obtained from the even-numbered pupils.

The results of this analysis are shown in Figure 13. While the odd-even variations reported in this chart serve to indicate the relative stability or instability of the index at various points on the scale, their absolute size has no readily interpretable meaning. They are variations based on split-halves; their size would be reduced if they could be based upon the total number of pupils. Furthermore, they should not be confused with the standard error of measurement, which is a measure of deviation between obtained scores and "true" scores, while these odd-even differences are deviations between two obtained scores.

It will be seen at once that the amount of instability in the index is by no means uniform at all points along the scale. Those index values which are high are obviously much less stable than those in the middle portion of the total index range. This confirms, of course, the results of the analysis of standard-error equivalences as reported in Table 27, on page 175. Figure 13 indicates further, however, that there is a critical point in the index scale at approximately 80. The odd-even differences tend to be markedly larger for those indexes above 80 than for those below that figure. The average odd-even variation for the 246 index values which are 80 or higher is 6.2, while the average odd-even variation for the 1,070 index values below 80 is 2.8.

The preceding paragraphs have dealt with the odd-even variations in the high-status and low-status indexes themselves. A similar analysis was made of the 658 index differences which result when the low-status index is subtracted from the high-status index for each item. It is these differences which constitute the basis for most of the item analysis to be reported in the rest of the volume. In studying the index differences, the odd-even variations (with respect to the differences) were tabulated according to the size of the index (whether for high-status or for low-status pupils) which was farthest from 50. The data resulting from this analysis are not reported in detail here, since they reveal relationships very similar to those already shown for the indexes, as depicted in Figure 13.[5] When both index values are between 20 and 80, the mean odd-even variation in the index difference fluctuates between 2 and 5 points, with no marked trend either upward or downward. The average odd-even variation for the 477 items in this range are 4.1 points. As the most extreme index rises above 80, however, the odd-even variation increases rapidly. The average odd-even variation for the 178 items with one or both indexes above 80 is 8.0 points.

On the basis of the data reported in Figure 13, and the similar analysis made for the index differences, it was concluded that the stability of the indexes, and of differences obtained from them, is relatively uniform so long as neither index value is above 80 or below 20 — but that the indexes and differences at the two extremes of the difficulty scale are much less reliable. Because of the higher reliability of the index data for the middle group of items, many of the comparisons in later chapters will be made on the basis of these middle items, with those based on extreme index

5. For a reference to a full report of this analysis, including the computation of reliability coefficients, see Note 1 in Appendix D.

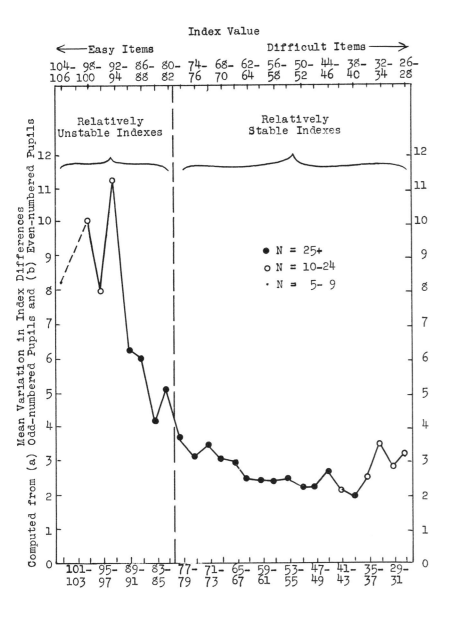

Index Value

←—Easy Items   Difficult Items —→

104- 98- 92- 86- 80- 74- 68- 62- 56- 50- 44- 38- 32- 26-
106 100 94 88 82 76 70 64 58 52 46 40 34 28

Relatively
Unstable Indexes

Relatively
Stable Indexes

● N = 25+
○ N = 10-24
· N = 5- 9

101- 95- 89- 83- 77- 71- 65- 59- 53- 47- 41- 35- 29-
103 97 91 85 79 73 67 61 55 49 43 37 31

Mean Variation in Index Differences
Computed from (a) Odd-numbered Pupils and (b) Even-numbered Pupils

Fig. 13. — Amount of split-half variation in indexes at different index levels (Old American pupils only).

values eliminated from the calculations. This means the elimination of items for which the percentage answering correctly was, for either group, either 92 per cent (index, 80) or higher or 8 per cent (index, 20) or lower. In a few cases, calculations will be reported on the basis of data from all items, including those with extreme indexes.[6]

General Logic of the Analysis Reported in Ensuing Chapters

Because a considerable body of detailed material is presented in the next seven chapters, there may be danger of not seeing clearly the general direction of the presentation. For this reason it seems wise to point out very briefly here the general logic which lies behind the particular order in which the material is presented. There are three essential steps in the analysis:

1. Determining the general size and statistical significance of the status differences which characterize the items in this study.

2. Determining the extent to which variation in the status differences from one item to another can be "explained" by discovering relationships to various more or less objective factors.

3. Examining individual items, largely on a subjective basis, as a means of identifying possible explanations for inter-item variation which still remains unexplained by the general factors identified in the preceding step.

In chapter xvii the general size of the status differences is examined. It is shown that these status differences vary from item to item, and some tentative hypotheses are suggested as to causes and factors which may be associated with this variation from one item to another.

In chapters xviii to xxi certain of these hypotheses which relate to factors which can be expressed relatively objectively are tested. The relations of status difference to position of the correct response, type of symbolism used in the item, type of question asked, difficulty of the item, and age of pupils are examined. The purpose of this analysis is to find, if possible, certain types of items which have typically large or typically small status differences, in order to see whether study of such types may not suggest explanations as to the reasons for the observed differences. Some definite relationships are established, while others are only tentatively determined.

In chapters xxii and xxiii detailed item-analysis data are presented for a number of individual items so chosen as to bring out possible explanations of the variation in status differences not accounted for by the more general factors whose relationship is studied in chapters xviii to xxi. Chapter xxii deals primarily with an analysis of status differences on the wrong responses to the item, while chapter xxiii deals primarily with status differences on the right responses.

Summary

In the nine tests which were used in the present study, there are

6. For a listing of the tables based on the items with "stable" differences only, and of those based on all items, regardless of difficulty, see Note 11 in Appendix D.

nearly a thousand items, approximately two-thirds of which are included in the analysis. The other third of the items are not included because they occur toward the end of their respective tests or subtests and were not reached by all pupils. They are eliminated so that there can be no question of the representative character of the pupils upon which the analysis is based.

The basic statistical measure used in determining the status differentials for these items is the difference between two percentages — the percentage of one status group answering the item correctly, and the percentage of another status group doing so. For most purposes, however, these percentages are converted into a normalized index so that they represent a linear relationship with respect to difficulty. This involves an assumption that the trait or traits underlying the items are distributed normally. When expressed in this index form, a difference of any given numerical size represents the same amount of difference in difficulty no matter at what point along the difficulty scale the difference occurs.

When sampling errors are considered, it is shown that, when differences are expressed in percentage terms, differences of 14 points or more are always to be considered significant at the 1 per cent level and differences of 6 points or less are never significant at the 1 per cent level. Differences between 6 and 14 may or may not be significant, with the likelihood of their significance increasing as the percentages approach 100 or 0, and decreasing as they approach 50. When the difference is expressed in terms of the normalized index, its standard error cannot be expressed accurately in any simple fashion. This is not particularly important, however, since conclusions as to the likelihood of any given difference being due to other than sampling errors may be drawn from the critical ratios based upon the differences in percentage form and applied directly to the differences expressed in index form.

It is shown that the index values are much less stable for very easy or for very difficult items than for those not at the extremes. For this reason, in much of the later analysis, items with index numbers over 80 or under 20 will be eliminated.

CHAPTER XVII

GENERAL SIZE AND STATISTICAL SIGNIFICANCE

OF STATUS DIFFERENCES FOR

INDIVIDUAL TEST ITEMS

This chapter reports the size and statistical significance of differences in the performance of pupils from different status groups on individual test items. In the first half of the chapter these differences will be considered in percentage terms; in the second half of the chapter they will be considered when expressed in terms of the normalized index described in the preceding chapter.

<u>Status Differences When Expressed in Percentage Terms</u>

The general level of difficulty of the items for the pupils in this study is shown in Table 28. The items were relatively easy for all three of the status groups, in the sense that the median difficulty of the items is considerably above 50 per cent for most of the groups. If the younger group of high-status Old Americans be examined, for instance, the median item difficulty for this group is seen to be 82 per cent, which means that half of the items were so easy for these pupils that they were answered correctly by 82 per cent or more of the pupils. The items were somewhat more difficult for the two low-status groups, but even for them half of the items were answered correctly by 70 per cent or more of the pupils. Comparable figures are shown for the older groups, where approximately the same relationships are found except that the items were relatively more difficult for the low-status pupils than was the case for the items given to the younger pupils.

The percentages in the bottom line of the table indicate that those items which were sufficiently easy to be answered correctly by 90 per cent or more of the pupils constitute from 21 to 41 per cent of the items in the tests for the younger pupils, depending upon which status group is used for the comparison. Such relatively easy items constitute a much smaller proportion of the tests for the older pupils, especially if difficulty be judged in terms of the low-status pupils; in the latter case only 3 or 4 per cent of the items were sufficiently easy that 90 per cent or more of the low-status pupils answered them correctly.

These same general relationships are indicated by the upper and lower quartiles reported in Table 28. In the tests for the younger pupils, for example, a quarter of the items were so easy that they were answered correctly by 81 per cent or more of the low-status and by 96 per cent or more of the high-status pupils; at the other end of the scale, the quarter of the items which were most difficult for the pupils include items which were answered correctly by 50 to 51 per cent of the low-status and by 70 per cent of the high-status pupils. It is clear that the tests — and particularly is this true of the tests for the younger pupils — are composed of many more "easy" items than of "difficult" items, if 50 per cent difficulty

TABLE 28

DISTRIBUTION OF TEST ITEMS BY DIFFICULTY OF THE ITEM FOR THREE STATUS GROUPS[*]

Per Cent of Group Answering Item Correctly	Number of Items from Tests for Nine- and Ten-Year-Old Pupils			Number of Items from Tests for Thirteen- and Fourteen-Year-Old Pupils		
	High-Status Old American	Low-Status Old American	Low-Status Ethnic	High Status Old American	Low-Status Old American	Low-Status Ethnic
100%	. . .	. . .	2	1	. . .	. . .
90-99	131	71	64	87	12	10
80-89	67	45	47	103	46	44
70-79	45	52	49	56	61	52
60-69	32	47	42	33	62	52
50-59	15	43	44	17	44	56
40-49	7	22	29	13	42	43
30-39	8	15	13	7	19	18
20-29	3	9	10	5	24	32
10-19	8	10	12	1	13	16
0- 9	1	3	5	. . .	. . .	. . .
Total[+]. . . .	317	317	317	323	323	323
Q_1	69.9	51.5	50.4	69.9	42.0	40.9
Median	81.6	70.0	69.7	80.8	60.5	52.7
Q_3	96.4	81.0	80.8	89.7	70.9	70.4
Proportion of items passed by 90 per cent or more of pupils	41.3%	22.4%	20.8%	27.2%	3.7%	3.1%

* For a statement as to the particular pupils and items on which the tables and charts in this chapter are based see Note 11 in Appendix D.
+ The total number of items indicated does not agree exactly with the totals in Table 22, on p. 165, since Table 28 includes only those items which were reached by 95 per cent or more of all three status groups, whereas Table 22 includes items reached by 95 per cent of any one of the three status groups. The figures reported in Table 28 are thus based on identical items for each of the three status groups.

be thought of as a dividing line between "easy" and "difficult."

The data in Table 28 indicate that many of the items do not present the same degree of difficulty for the different status groups. There are three possible intergroup comparisons to be made, as follows:

High-status Old American   versus   Low-status Old American
High-status Old American   versus   Low-status ethnic
Low-status Old American   versus   Low-status ethnic

The first two of these involve primarily differences in status, being comparisons between high- and low-status groups, although the second of them includes also the additional element of ethnicity. The third comparison is based entirely upon differences in ethnic background, since both groups are composed of low-status individuals. Because the first two differences are of quite a different order from the third, they will be considered separately.

Differences between high-status and low-status pupils

Data regarding the number of items showing varying degrees of difference for high-status and low-status pupils are given in Table 29. There is very wide variation among the items in the amount of status difference found. On a few items there is a difference of more than 45 points between the percentage of high-status pupils who answered the item correctly and the percentage of low-status pupils who did so. Most of the items with these large differences are found in the tests for the older pupils; in the tests for the younger pupils they are found in the comparison with low-status ethnics but not with low-status Old Americans. On the other hand, there are a considerable number of items, in the tests at both age levels, for which the status differences are very small. In the tests for the younger pupils from a fifth to a third of the items show differences of less than 5 percentage points between high- and low-status groups. There are even a few items which show small negative difference, that is, on which low-status pupils succeed in slightly larger proportions than do high-status pupils. In no case, however, are these negative differences large enough to be statistically significant.

Table 29 indicates not only the size of the status differences but also their statistical significance. The proportion of items showing differences which are statistically significant is also shown graphically in Figure 14. Approximately half of the items in the tests for younger pupils and about 85 per cent of the items in the tests for older pupils show differences which are significant at the 1 per cent level. If the 5 per cent level of significance is accepted as a standard, then more than 60 per cent of the items in the tests for younger pupils and about 90 per cent of those in the tests for older pupils show significant differences in favor of the high-status pupils. If there are items in these tests which do not show any real difference between the two status groups, they must probably be sought for among those items which do not show a difference significant even at the 5 per cent level. Such items constitute a little over a third of the items in the tests for younger pupils and about 10 per cent of the items in the tests for older pupils.

This question of possible zero differences on some test items is an important one. If there is some general quality termed "intelligence," and if all the items in these tests measure it even moderately well, the existence of items which show no differences between the status groups might

TABLE 29

DISTRIBUTION OF TEST ITEMS BY LEVEL OF SIGNIFICANCE
OF THE DIFFERENCES BETWEEN
HIGH-STATUS AND LOW-STATUS RESPONSES

Level of Statistical Significance, and Size, of Status Difference (in Percentage Form)*	Number of Items from Tests for Nine- and Ten-Year-Old Pupils		Number of Items from Tests for Thirteen- and Fourteen-Year-Old Pupils	
	High-Status Old American vs. Low-Status Old American	High-Status Old American vs. Low-Status Ethnic	High-Status Old American vs. Low-Status Old American	High-Status Old American vs. Low-Status Ethnic
Differences significant at 1 per cent level:				
45%-49% ...	...	1	2	1
40-44	...	1	4	12
35-39	...	4	11	25
30-34	6	9	25	32
25-29	19	16	50	47
20-24	42	48	50	48
15-19	47	39	56	56
10-14	49	47	67	49
5- 9	13	4	19	13
Differences significant at 5 per cent level:				
10%-14% ...	3	15	...	8
5- 9	31	16	11	9
Differences not significant at 5 per cent level:				
10.00%-14.99% .	...	1	...	...
5.00-9.99 ...	21	31	3	13
0.00-4.99 ...	84	70	23	21
(-0.01)-(-5.00) ..	19	21	3	4
(-5.01)-(-10.00) .	...	2	...	1
Total	334	325	324	339

* Difference obtained by subtracting percentage of low-status pupils answering item correctly from percentage of high-status pupils doing so.

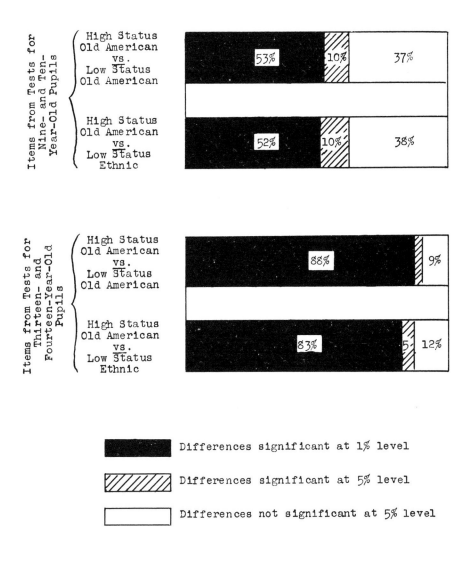

Fig. 14. — Distribution of test items by level of statistical significance of differences between performance of high-status and low-status groups. (Source: Data in Table 29.)

be taken as evidence that the differences found for such items are artificial, owing to the special nature of those items. Or, to put the matter in a different way, if different items are thought of as measuring different aspects of intelligence, then the existence of some items which show no status differences would demonstrate that there are at least some aspects of intelligence which are not characterized by status differences. In any case it is a matter of some importance to establish whether there are actually any substantial number of items in these tests which show no status differences or which show differences so small that they may readily be accounted for as chance variations.

Table 29, on page 183, indicates that there are, in all the tests at both age levels, either 153 or 164 (depending upon which low-status group is used for comparison) items which show differences between the high- and low-status groups that are not large enough to be significant at the 5 per cent level. This includes nearly a fourth of the total number of items analyzed.

Not all these items, however, should be thought of as having no status differences, in the sense implied by the preceding paragraphs. In the first place, although the 5 per cent level of significance may be accepted as indicating that differences are probably real ones and not due to sampling errors, it does not follow, of course, that all differences below that level are probably due to sampling errors only. In the second place, examination of the individual items showing these nonsignificant differences reveals that many of the small differences occur because the items are so easy that virtually all pupils in both status groups answer them correctly, while a few occur because the items are so difficult that the leveling effect of guessing may play a substantial part in the small differences found. In either of these cases, to regard the small differences as indicating items which do not show status difference would, while technically true, be misleading. Practically any item, no matter how obviously culturally biased it may be, can be made to show no status difference by giving it to pupils old enough that even the low-status pupils can answer it -- or by giving it to pupils so young that even the high-status pupils cannot do so.

The extent to which the 153 items whose status differences (for Old Americans) are not significant at the 5 per cent level may be regarded as indicating true no-difference test items is indicated by the data in Table 30. The first two columns of Table 30 show ninety-three items whose status differences are small enough that there is one out of four chances, or better, that the true status difference may be zero, and that the differences actually found may be due to sampling errors only. It is important to notice, however, that more than half of the ninety-three items are so easy that the average of the percentages passing them, for both status groups, is over 90. As pointed out earlier, this appearance of no-difference might be misleading if any attempt were made to generalize from this age group to a younger one, or from items of this level of difficulty to similar items at a more difficult level. Comparatively few of the items are so difficult that the leveling effect of chance guessing would seem to play an important part in the lack of status differences.

When the items defined in Table 30 as being either extremely easy or extremely difficult are eliminated from consideration, however, there remain twenty-seven items (the underlined entries in the table) whose status differences are small enough that there is one chance out of four that the true status difference, freed of sampling errors, would be zero

or negative. These twenty-seven items will be listed individually and discussed in chapter xxiii.[1] If the 10 per cent level of significance is used as a standard for selecting items with relatively insignificant status differences, Table 30 indicates that there are forty-nine items showing insignificant status differences even after elimination of the extremely easy and extremely difficult items.

This is not a large proportion of the total number of items, of course, but the existence of even forty-nine items showing status differences this small indicates that it may be possible to select intelligence-test items

TABLE 30

DISTRIBUTION OF TEST ITEMS BY LEVEL OF SIGNIFICANCE OF STATUS DIFFERENCE AND BY DIFFICULTY OF THE ITEM

Difficulty of Item*	Number of Items with Status Differences at Various Levels of Significance					
	P > .25		P = .10-.25		P = .05-.10	
	Age 9-10	Age 13-14	Age 9-10	Age 13-14	Age 9-10	Age 13-14
Extremely easy items:						
90%-99%	54	4	10	4	5	3
Items of moderate difficulty:						
80%-89%	7	1	5	2	4	2
70-79	5	..	3	1	3	1
60-69	5	2	3	..	3	..
50-59	3	1	4	1	1	..
40-49	..	2	2	..	..	..
30-39	1	..	1	..	..	..
Extremely difficult items:						
30%-39%	..	1	..	..	..	..
20-29	..	1	..	2	..	..
10-19	5	1	..	..	..	..
Total	80	13	28	10	16	6

* Difficulty measured by mid-point of percentage right for high-status Old American pupils and for low-status Old American pupils. "Extremely easy items" are defined as those for which mid-point difficulty is 90 per cent or higher. "Extremely difficult items" are defined as those for which the mid-point difficulty is 10 per cent or lower, or for which both percentages are within 10 points of the guessing expectancy for the particular item. "Items of moderate difficulty" include all other items.

1. See pp. 318-19, 324-28.

of the kind that are ordinarily regarded as acceptable test items but which show little or no status differences. If an entire test were to be made up of items such as these forty-nine, the amount of status difference in the resulting I.Q.'s would be far less than it is from the tests as now constituted. Possible implications of the existence of these small-difference items for gaining insight into the nature of status differences in I.Q.'s are discussed further in chapter viii.[2]

Differences between low-status Old American and low-status ethnic pupils

An entirely different situation is found with respect to the size and statistical significance of differences in item difficulty as between the two low-status groups. These differences are reported in Table 31. The overwhelming majority of the items do not show differences large enough to be significant at either the 1 per cent or the 5 per cent level. The difference between the percentage of low-status Old Americans answering the item correctly and the similar figure for low-status ethnics is less than 5 percentage points in the case of approximately 90 per cent of the items. Nor are the differences all in the same direction. The majority of the small differences that do occur are in favor of the Old American pupils, but on approximately a third of the items the differences are in favor of the ethnics.

Of the twelve items which do show statistically significant differences (at the 1 per cent level), three are found in the tests for the younger children and nine in the tests for the older children. Ten of them are items on which the Old American pupils do significantly better than the ethnics, while two of them are items on which the ethnics pupils do significantly better than the Old Americans. It should be noticed that at the 1 per cent level of significance six or seven items would be expected, in a group of items this large, to show "significant" differences merely as a result of sampling variations. The particular items which show these significant differences are listed and discussed briefly in chapter xxiii.[3]

The proportion of items showing ethnic differences at various levels of significance is shown graphically in Figure 15. The contrast between the distributions reported in Figure 15 and those reported in Figure 14, on page 184, is marked. It is clear that the differences between high- and low-status groups are of quite a different order from the comparatively small differences between ethnic and nonethnic pupils at the same status level. This is, of course, only to be expected, in view of the similar finding already reported for I.Q. differences for status and ethnic groups. Possible implications of this finding with regard to small ethnic differences for gaining insight into the nature of status differences in I.Q.'s are discussed further in chapter viii.[4]

There are two cautions to be observed in accepting the generalization that ethnic differences on intelligence-test items are not important if status is held constant. One is that other ethnic groups in other communities might yield different results — the degree of integration of ethnic groups into the total culture of the community probably varies widely from community to community. The other is that the comparatively small ethnic

2. See p. 64.
3. See pp. 348, 355-56.
4. See pp. 61-62.

TABLE 31

DISTRIBUTION OF TEST ITEMS BY LEVEL OF SIGNIFICANCE
OF THE DIFFERENCES BETWEEN LOW-STATUS OLD AMERICAN
AND LOW-STATUS ETHNIC RESPONSES

Level of Statistical Significance, and Size, of Ethnic Difference (in Percentage Form)*	Number of Items from Tests for Nine- and Ten-Year-Old Pupils	Number of Items from Tests for Thirteen- and Fourteen-Year-Old Pupils
Differences significant at 1 per cent level:		
15.00%-19.99%	1	2
10.00 -14.99	2	5
.		
.		
(-10.01) - (-15.00)	. . .	1
(-15.01) - (-20.00)	. . .	1
Differences significant at 5 per cent level:		
10.00%-14.99%	6	8
5.00 - 9.99	7	8
.		
.		
(-5.01) - (-10.00)	1	6
(-10.00) - (-15.00)	4	3
Differences not significant at 5 per cent level:		
5.00%- 9.99%	45	60
0.00 - 4.99	141	146
(-0.01) - (-5.00)	95	74
(-5.01) - (-10.00)	15	16
Total	317	330

* Ethnic difference obtained by subtracting percentage of low-status ethnic pupils answering the item correctly from percentage of low-status Old American pupils doing so.

Items from Tests for
Nine- and Ten-Year-Old
Pupils

6%   93%

Items from Tests for
Thirteen- and Fourteen-
Year-Old Pupils

7%   90%

▓▓▓▓▓   Differences significant at 1% level

▨▨▨▨▨   Differences significant at 5% level

☐   Differences not significant at 5% level

Fig. 15. — Distribution of test items by level of statistical significance of differences between performance of two low-status groups. (Source: Data in Table 31.)

differences may be due in part to dilution of the ethnic group by inclusion of some pupils who are not really ethnic in their cultural participation or background. The method of identifying ethnic pupils for this study was not an entirely satisfactory one.[5] Its limitations should be kept in mind in interpreting these findings.

Because of the very small number of items which show any significant difference between the responses of low-status Old Americans and low-status ethnics, it was decided to confine most of the remaining analysis to comparisons of the high- and low-status Old American groups and to eliminate the ethnic group from further consideration. This seemed justified because of the few items for which ethnicity seemed to have any clearly significant effect and because of the great saving in time and effort which could be made by confining later analysis to a single measure of status difference, rather than endeavoring to make all comparisons in terms of three different intergroup differences.

The rest of the analysis to be reported will, therefore, deal only with the two Old American groups — groups whose sole difference is one of socioeconomic status, without the additional factor of ethnicity. The term "status difference" will hereafter be understood always to refer to the comparison between the high-status Old American pupils and low-status Old American pupils, unless it is clearly indicated that it is used in some other way in a given context.[6]

Status Differences When Expressed in Terms of the Normalized Index

The preceding section, dealing with status differences expressed in percentage terms, has been included partly to give the reader some general idea of the size of differences as expressed in the original percentage units and also in order to indicate the number of items whose status difference is significantly greater than zero, so that it is reasonably certain that such differences are not due to chance sampling errors only.

As pointed out in chapter xvi, however, the use of the percentage scale for describing status differences is not very satisfactory, since the real amount of difference in difficulty represented by a percentage difference of any given size may vary considerably according to the portion of the percentage scale in which the difference occurs. Procedures were described in chapter xvi for translating the percentages into normalized index values and obtaining a new measure of status difference by subtracting the index for one status group from that for another. In this section the 658 items included in the analyzis of high- and low-status Old Americans will be re-examined in terms of this normalized index. This will be done only for the Old American pupils, since the data in the preceding section indicated that differences between the low-status Old American and low-status ethnic pupils are not usually significant.

The distribution of items by size of the index difference is indicated, for both age levels, in Table 32. In chapter xvi it was shown that index differences for items where one or both indexes were 80 or higher, or 20 or lower, were considerably less reliable than when the indexes were

<hr>

5. See pp. 99-101, 125-30.

6. For a list of the tables based on responses of Old American pupils only, and of those based on responses of both Old American and ethnic pupils, see Note 11 in Appendix D.

TABLE 32

DISTRIBUTION OF TEST ITEMS BY SIZE OF
STATUS DIFFERENCE WHEN EXPRESSED IN TERMS
OF THE NORMALIZED INDEX

Size of Index Difference*	Number of Items from Tests for Nine- and Ten-Year-Old Pupils		Number of Items from Tests for Thirteen- and Fourteen-Year-Old Pupils	
	All Items+	Stable Items+	All Items+	Stable Items+
35-39	. . .	. . .	1	. . .
30-34	. . .	. . .	. . .	. . .
25-29	1	. . .	7	4
20-24	19	3	40	23
15-19	42	34	91	72
10-14	75	58	112	94
5- 9	109	70	55	50
0- 4	71	47	16	15
(-1)-(-5)	16	5	2	2
(-6)-(-10)	1	. . .	. . .	. . .
Total	334	217	324	260
Mean index difference	8.8	8.9	13.6	12.9
Standard deviation	6.2	5.2	5.7	5.4

* Difference obtained by subtracting index value obtained from the percentage of low-status pupils answering the item correctly from the index value obtained from the percentage of high-status pupils doing so.
+ For a definition of the terms "All Items" and "Stable Items" see Note 11 in Appendix D.

not in those extremes of the difficulty range. For this reason, the distributions are shown in Table 32 both for the total number of items and also for the smaller number of more stable items both of whose indexes lie between 80 and 20. The means for the "stable" items are not significantly different from those for all the items (critical ratios, 0.2, 1.6); furthermore, the direction of the small differences between the means is reversed at the two age levels. The standard deviations are smaller when computed for the stable items than when determined from all the items, but only at the younger age level is the difference significant (critical ratios, 2.9, 0.8).

The tests for the older pupils show, on the whole, markedly more status differences than do the tests for the younger pupils; the mean index difference for the items from the tests for the older pupils is 13 or 14 points, while that for the items from the tests for younger pupils is less than 9 points. The difference between the means for the two age levels is eight to ten times its standard error. Whether this increase in status difference in the test items given to the older children represents an increased impact of differential cultural environment on the older children, or whether it represents a greater proportion of culturally biased material in the tests for older pupils, is not possible to determine from these data. This question will be discussed more fully, and additional data relative to it presented, in chapter xxi.

The standard deviation of the index differences for the older pupils is smaller than that for the younger pupils, when all the items are included, but this relationship is reversed when only the stable items are considered. In neither case is the difference large enough to be significant (critical ratios, 1.5, 0.8).

Means and standard deviations of the index differences, comparable to those just presented, are reported for each of the tests separately in Table 33. Since these data are expressed in terms of the normalized index, a difference of any given size signifies the same amount of difference in difficulty as between the two status groups no matter where it may occur along the difficulty scale. For this reason, direct comparisons of the amount of status difference shown by the items from the various tests are possible, despite some differences in the general level of difficulty of the different tests.

In Table 33 there are some variations in the means and standard deviations depending upon whether the "all items" or the "stable items" data are used, but the relative relationships from test to test are not, in most cases, changed. When the two sets of data yield different results, it is probable that the data based on the "stable" items are the more reliable. In most future tables only data based on these stable items will be reported.

Table 33 indicates that there is marked variation in the amount of status difference present in the items as among the different tests. On the Otis Alpha Nonverbal test, for instance, the average status difference is approximately 6 points, while on the Terman-McNemar test it is more than 16 points; the difference between these two means is fifteen to sixteen times its standard error. Even within a single age group there is considerable variation in the mean status differences. The items in the Otis Alpha Nonverbal test have an average status difference of approximately 6 points, while the Henmon-Nelson items have an average difference of 12 to 14 points; the difference is eight to ten times its standard error. Among the tests for older pupils the one showing the most status difference is the Terman-McNemar, with an average item difference of 16 or 17 points; while the one showing the least difference is the Thurstone Spatial (if based on all items) or the California Mental Maturity (if based on stable items only), with an average item difference of 9 to 10 points. The differences between the two extremes at this age level are from seven to eleven times their standard errors.

Examination of the standard deviations of the index differences indicates some interesting variations in the range of status differences within each of the tests. The test showing the least variability in status differences is the Thurstone Spatial, followed closely by the Thurstone Reasoning and the Otis Alpha Nonverbal tests. The ones showing the greatest variation in status differences are the Kuhlmann-Anderson and California Mental Maturity tests.

These differences in variability are not particularly surprising. The Thurstone Spatial test and the Thurstone Reasoning test — and to a somewhat less extent the Otis Alpha Nonverbal test — are composed of items which are quite homogeneous; it would seem reasonable to expect that whatever degree of status difference is characteristic of the type of item comprising each of these tests would be more or less constant for all the items in the test. Both the Kuhlmann-Anderson and the California Mental Maturity tests, on the other hand, consist of a number of subtests, each composed of a single type of item but with wide variation in type of item from subtest to subtest. The greater variability in status difference characteristic of the items in these tests is doubtless a reflection of this greater heterogeneity of the tests.

TABLE 33

MEANS AND STANDARD DEVIATIONS
OF STATUS DIFFERENCES, BY TESTS

Test	Number of Items		Mean Index Difference		Standard Deviation of Index Differences	
	All Items*	Stable Items*	All Items*	Stable Items*	All Items*	Stable Items*
Tests for Nine- and Ten-Year-Old Pupils						
Henmon-Nelson . . .	60	46	14.1	12.3	5.2	4.4
Kuhlmann-Anderson	94	59	10.2	9.7	6.7	5.7
Otis Alpha Verbal .	90	49	6.5	8.1	5.2	4.7
Otis Alpha Nonverbal	90	63	5.9	6.1	4.2	3.7
All items	334	217	8.8	8.9	6.2	5.2
Tests for Thirteen- and Fourteen-Year-Old Pupils						
Terman-McNemar .	102	92	16.7	16.3	4.8	4.3
Thurstone Reasoning	41	24	15.0	14.5	4.2	3.7
Otis Beta	72	51	14.1	13.0	5.6	4.7
Thurstone Spatial	55	49	9.8	9.4	3.1	2.9
California Mental Maturity	54	44	10.0	8.5	6.2	5.8
All items	324	260	13.6	12.9	5.7	5.4

* For a definition of the terms "All Items" and "Stable Items" see Note 11 in Appendix D.

The distribution of individual items in the various tests by size of status difference is presented graphically in Figure 16. For the purpose of this chart, the index differences are arbitrarily classified as "very large," "large," "medium," "small," and "very small," on the basis indicated in the key. The figure merely illustrates in a different form many of the same relationships pointed out in the preceding paragraphs. If the solid bars in the chart, representing index differences of 20 points or more, are examined, it will be seen that such large-difference items are very seldom found in any of the tests for the younger pupils and that they are not found in two of the five tests for older pupils.

If the solid and crosshatched bars, representing all items with status differences of 15 or more points, are examined together, it will be seen that more than a third of the Henmon-Nelson test is composed of such items, while only 3 per cent of the Otis Alpha Nonverbal items show status differences this large. If the white bars, representing relatively small status differences, are examined, it is seen that 9 per cent of the Henmon-Nelson items, but more than a third of the Otis Alpha Nonverbal items, are in this category. Figure 16 indicates that 84 per cent of the items in the Otis Alpha Nonverbal test are in the class defined as having either "small" or "very small" status differences, whereas only 26 per cent of the items in the Henmon-Nelson test show differences this small.

Much the same kind of relationships can be pointed out in connection with the tests for the older pupils. The Terman-McNemar test has the largest proportion (21 per cent) of items with "very large" status differences, followed by the Thurstone Reasoning and the Otis Beta tests. None of the items in the Thurstone Spatial and California Mental Maturity tests shows differences this great. Items defined as having either "very large" or "large" status differences comprise 62 per cent and 63 per cent, respectively, of the Terman-McNemar and Thurstone Reasoning tests, but only 21 per cent of the California Mental Maturity test and only 2 per cent of the Thurstone Spatial test.

The California Mental Maturity test is the only one of the tests for the older pupils which has any substantial number of items classified as having "very small" status differences. More than half of the items in that test yield status differences that are described as either "small" or "very small." Interestingly enough, however, the Thurstone Spatial test, which shows no items with "very large" differences and the smallest proportion of items with "large" differences, also has a comparatively small proportion of items showing "very small" differences. A larger proportion of this test (90 per cent) than of any other test consists of items with either "small" or "medium" status differences. The distribution of items for the Thurstone Reasoning test is similar to that for the Thurstone Spatial test in this respect, except that the general level of status differences is higher in the reasoning test. This comparative homogeneity of the two Thurstone tests has already been commented upon in connection with Table 33, on page 193.

If the tests for the two age groups are compared with each other, it is clear from Figure 16 that the proportion of items with "very large" and "large" status differences is considerably greater in the older tests, while the proportion of "small" and "very small" differences is considerably greater in the tests for the younger pupils. This is to be expected, of course, in view of the differences between the mean status differences at the two age levels, as reported in Table 33. It is still, however, impossible

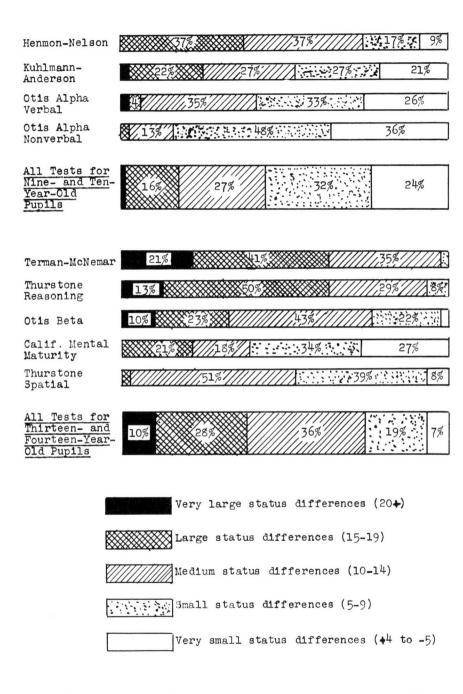

Fig. 16. — Distribution of items in nine tests by size of index status differences.

on the basis of these data to say that the greater status differences found for the older pupils necessarily indicate any real differences in the pupils at the older age level. It is entirely possible that the apparent age differences are due to differences in the type of test material by means of which the status differences are obtained. If, for instance, results from the Otis Alpha Nonverbal test are used as representing the younger pupils, and results on the Terman-McNemar test are used as representing the older pupils, one would conclude that there is a marked increase in status difference as the pupils grow older. On the other hand, if the younger pupils are represented by the Henmon-Nelson test, and the older pupils by the California Mental Maturity or Thurstone Spatial tests, one could as validly conclude that there is a marked decrease in status difference with advancing age. By proper selection of the tests it could be shown that there is no substantial change at all. It can be said that, on the whole, the tests for older pupils show significantly greater status difference than do the tests for younger pupils, but whether this is due to important differences in the pupils or primarily to differences in the test materials used at the two age levels it is impossible to say on the basis of the data thus far presented. Further evidence on the relation of age to the amount of status differential will be found in chapter xxi.

Tentative Hypotheses as to Causes and Associated Factors

Data reported in this chapter demonstrate the existence of substantial status differences with respect to many of the test items and the existence of some variability among the items in the amount of this difference. No attempt has been made thus far to determine possible reasons either for the existence of the differences or for the variation in their size. The remaining chapters of this report will be devoted to an attempt to analyze this interitem variation further. As a basis for the investigation to be reported next, the following tentative hypotheses are suggested:

1. The amount of status difference may be related to the position of the test response. (E.g., it may be that low-status pupils tend to check the first response-position more frequently than do high-status pupils.)

2. The amount of status difference may be related to the form of symbolism in which the test question is expressed. (E.g., it may be that verbal items tend to have characteristically larger or smaller status differences than do pictorial items.)

3. The amount of status difference may be related to the type of test question asked. (E.g., it may be that opposites characteristically show larger, or smaller, status differences than do analogies.)

4. The amount of status difference may be related to the difficulty of the item. This relationship might be direct (e.g., with the easiest items showing the least status difference) or inverse (with the easiest items showing the most status difference) or the relationship might be a more complex one.

5. The amount of status difference may vary with the chronological age of pupils.

6. The amount of status difference may be related to the opportunities

which pupils from different status groups have for familiarity
with the content of the item. (E.g., items dealing with objects with
which high-status pupils have special opportunities for familiarity
may show large status differences.)

7. The amount of status difference may vary with some other as yet
unidentified characteristics of the items.

The first five of these hypotheses are capable of relatively straightforward and objective investigation. An analysis of the status differences
in terms of these factors is reported in the next four chapters. The last
two hypotheses are more subjective in nature; investigation of the items
with respect to them will be deferred to chapters xxii and xxiii.

Summary

Differences between the proportion of pupils in three different status
groups answering each item correctly are examined in percentage form,
primarily to determine which differences are sufficiently large to be
clearly significant ones and which are not. It is shown that about half of
the items in the tests for nine- and ten-year-old pupils, and about 85 per
cent of the items in the tests for the thirteen- and fourteen-year-old pupils, show differences between high- and low-status groups large enough
to be significant at the 1 per cent level. On the other hand, more than a
third of the items from the tests for the younger pupils, and about a tenth
of those from the tests for the older pupils, show differences small enough
that they are not significant at even the 5 per cent level. A group of twenty-
seven items is identified which show small, statistically insignificant, differences even though the difficulty of the items is not at either extreme.

When the two low-status groups are compared — one Old American
and one ethnic — it is shown that on only 12 out of 647 items are the differences large enough to be significant at the 1 per cent level. For this
reason, it is decided to eliminate the separate consideration of ethnic
responses from the analysis reported in later chapters.

The differences between the high-status Old American and the low-
status Old American pupils are converted into the normalized index
described in chapter xvi, so that direct comparisons of the size of status
differences may be made validly. When this is done, it is found that the
average size of the status differential varies markedly from test to test
and from one age level to another.

At the close of the chapter some tentative hypotheses are put forth as
possible explanations of variation from item to item in the amount of status
difference. Some of these hypotheses are to be examined and tested in the
chapters which follow.

CHAPTER XVIII

STATUS DIFFERENCES IN RELATION TO POSITION
OF CORRECT RESPONSES

Preliminary tabulation of item data from one test suggested the possibility that low-status pupils might tend to mark the first response on
an item more frequently than other responses. It was thought that this
might represent a tendency on the part of low-status pupils to give up
without really trying and to mark the closest response without examining
all the possibilities. In order to test this hypothesis, status differences
were analyzed in several different ways.

Status Differences in Distribution of Wrong Responses

If it should be true that many of the low-status pupils tend to mark
the first response somewhat indiscriminately without looking adequately
at the rest of the possible responses, a piling-up of responses on the first
distractor would be expected. A tabulation of the responses, by position
of the response, was made for the items in two tests. The tests which
were analyzed with respect to this factor were the Henmon-Nelson test
(nine- and ten-year-old pupils) and the Otis Beta test (thirteen- and fourteen-year-old pupils). All the items in the Henmon-Nelson test and all
but twelve of those in the Otis Beta test are five-choice items. The twelve
four-choice items in the Otis Beta test were eliminated from the analysis
reported in this section.

Studying the distribution of pupil responses by the position of the
response is complicated by the necessity of making some allowance for
the correct response, since most of the large number of pupils checking
the correct response are presumably doing so for reasons largely unrelated to the position of the particular response among the five available
ones. Another difficulty arises from the fact that a number of pupils may
concentrate on a particular distractor, say, the first one, not because the
pupils have any predilection for that particular position per se, but because
in the particular item being studied that position happens to have an especially attractive distractor. In order to avoid the first difficulty, all correct responses are eliminated from this analysis, and only the distribution
of errors studied. The second difficulty was met at least in part by basing
judgments only on the averages of a number of different items, so that
variations due to the content of individual items might be expected to cancel
each other in large measure.

A summary of the distribution of wrong responses on the Henmon-
Nelson test is reported in Table 34. It should be emphasized that these
data are based only on those responses to these Henmon-Nelson items
which are incorrect ones. It cannot be stated positively that the results
reported here are representative of the test-marking habits of the total
number of pupils in either status group. To include the correct responses

TABLE 34

DISTRIBUTION OF WRONG RESPONSES ON HENMON-NELSON TEST
BY POSITION OF THE CORRECT RESPONSE IN THE TEST ITEM*

Position of Correct Response in Item	Number of Items	Status Group	Total Number of Wrong Responses+	Per Cent of Total Wrong Responses on Each Wrong-Answer Position					
				No. 1	No. 2	No. 3	No. 4	No. 5	Total
First	12	High status	542	..	29%	22%	30%	19%	100%
		Low status	1,512	..	28	26	25	21	100
Second	10	High status	367	40%	..	19	16	25	100
		Low status	1,138	28	..	24	20	28	100
Third	15	High status	880	33	39	..	12	15	100
		Low status	2,009	31	30	..	18	21	100
Fourth	12	High status	702	33	31	19	..	17	100
		Low status	1,744	27	32	22	..	20	100
Fifth	11	High status	431	37	20	24	19	..	100
		Low status	1,139	34	21	25	19	..	100
All wrong responses	60	High status	2,922	28%	28%	15%	14%	15%	100%
		Low status	7,542	24	24	18	16	19	100

* For a statement as to the particular pupils and items on which the tables in this chapter are based see Note 11 in Appendix D.

+ Excluding omitted items and items not reached by the pupil.

in this analysis would, however, appear to introduce an even greater likelihood of serious error.

If the pupils distributed their responses in a manner entirely unrelated to the position of the response, the percentages in this table would probably all be close to 25 per cent, since it seems unlikely that the intrinsic attractiveness of particular distractors has any special relationship to any particular position of the distractor.

In the first two lines of Table 34, representing the twelve items whose correct answer is in the first position, the distribution of errors is approximately a chance one, except that there is some tendency for pupils in both status groups to avoid the last position. In the second set of lines, representing the ten items whose correct answer is in the second position, it is notable that the high-status errors tend to concentrate fairly heavily on the first position, with a secondary focus on the last position. The low-status errors are distributed more equally over all the positions, with a slight concentration on the same first and last positions favored by the high-status pupils. The differences between these two distributions for the second position can be explained by assuming that a substantial proportion of the high-status errors are caused by pupils who mark the first response without even getting as far as the correct one in their examination of the item and that the low-status errors tend to be more the result of random guessing. There is a suggestion that those high-status pupils who get as far as the right answer are likely to answer the item correctly, since comparatively small proportions of the high-status errors are found on the third, fourth, and fifth responses.

If the fifteen items whose correct answer is in the third position are examined, the tentative suggestion offered above is reinforced, although in this case the tendency appears to operate for both status groups. Approximately two-thirds of the errors in both status groups are on the first two positions, as compared to about a third on the last two positions.

The twelve items whose correct answer is in the fourth position indicate a slightly different situation. Here it is noticed that for both status groups there are more errors on the first two positions than on the third and fifth positions. This suggests that there may be pupils who tend to check one of the first two positions, without really considering any of the later ones. To the extent that this explanation is a valid one, it appears to apply equally to both status groups; if anything, there is a slightly larger proportion of the high-status errors accounted for on these first two positions than is true of the low-status errors.

The data for the eleven items whose correct answers are on the last position again show the tendency for a slight piling-up of errors at the beginning of the sequence of distractors, but this time the concentration is on the first item alone rather than the first two.

As pointed out earlier, these data are somewhat uncertain because of the possibility that, with only ten or a dozen items being considered at a time, variations in the content of the particular distractors may play a part in influencing the results. This may well explain some of the lack of complete agreement in the data shown for each of these groups of items considered separately. In order to smooth out these differences as much as possible, the sixty items were thrown together into a single group, and the distribution of wrong responses computed in a manner exactly analogous to that shown for each of the subgroups separately.

At the bottom of Table 34, where the entire sixty items are considered together, there is a definite tendency for the errors in both status groups to be concentrated primarily on the first two positions, with no preference whatever between the first and second positions, and virtually none among the third, fourth, and fifth positions. Whatever status difference is involved in this concentration indicates that the errors of the high-status pupils tend to be thus concentrated on the first two positions even more frequently than do the errors of the low-status pupils, although the differences are not large. Because of the large number of cases upon which these percentages are based, however, all but one of the status differences (that on the fourth response) are significant at the 1 per cent level. The chi-square test, applied to the frequencies underlying the percentages in the last two lines of Table 34, likewise indicates a difference significant at the 1 per cent level.

Similar data with regard to the distribution of wrong responses for sixty items in the Otis Beta test for the older pupils are reported in Table 35. Most of the relationships observed in this table are similar to those already noted for the younger pupils but are more marked and definite. For each of the five subgroups of items, each of the first two responses (with a single exception) accounts for a larger proportion of the errors than is accounted for by any of the three later responses.

In the summary at the bottom of the table, based on all sixty items, the proportion of responses goes down steadily from the first position to the fourth, with a slight resurgence on the fifth response. More important, however, for the present study is the fact that precisely the same tendency is noticed for both status groups and that the distribution of errors is very similar for the two groups. None of the status differences on these responses is significant at the 1 per cent level, despite the large number of cases on which the percentages are based. This is true whether the status differences are tested for each response separately, by means of critical ratios, or for the distribution as a whole, by means of the chi-square test.

Status Differences in Omitting of Items

The distribution of wrong responses analyzed in the preceding section takes account of actual positive responses only and excludes items omitted rather than answered either correctly or incorrectly. Actually, of course, some pupils failed particular items through omitting them entirely rather than through marking them incorrectly. Since it was believed that low-status pupils work on test items less systematically and more haphazardly, it seemed reasonable to suppose that there might be a larger proportion of omitted items for the low-status pupils than for the high-status pupils. On the other hand, it might be that low-status pupils guess more frequently when they do not know the answer and that high-status pupils tend to omit the question in such cases.

In order to test these hypotheses, the distribution of omitted items was analyzed for the same two tests whose distribution of wrong responses is reported in the preceding section. The pertinent data resulting from this analysis are reported in Table 36. The first line of percentages in the lower half of this table indicates that the omitted items constitute a very small proportion of the total responses for either status group on either test. In each case, however, a larger proportion of omitted items is found for the low-status pupils than for the high-status pupils. While the status differences in this respect are very small (less than 2 percentage points on

TABLE 35

DISTRIBUTION OF WRONG RESPONSES ON OTIS BETA TEST
BY POSITION OF THE CORRECT RESPONSE IN THE TEST ITEM

Position of Correct Response in Item	Number of Items*	Status Group	Total Number of Wrong Responses+	Per Cent of Total Wrong Responses on Each Wrong-Answer Position					
				No. 1	No. 2	No. 3	No. 4	No. 5	Total
First	2	High status	68	...	72%	12%	9%	7%	100%
		Low status	246	...	55	15	12	18	100
Second	17	High status	655	39%	...	28	20	12	100
		Low status	2,190	37	...	26	19	18	100
Third	13	High status	520	41	30	...	14	15	100
		Low status	1,553	37	26	...	20	16	100
Fourth	21	High status	1,066	21	31	22	...	26	100
		Low status	2,822	23	32	22	...	23	100
Fifth	7	High status	547	32	32	15	21	...	100
		Low status	1,432	36	30	15	19	...	100
All wrong responses	60	High status	2,856	30%	25%	18%	12%	15%	100%
		Low status	8,243	31	23	17	13	16	100

* Excluding the twelve four-choice items in this test.
+ Excluding omitted items and items not reached by the pupil.

TABLE 36

STATUS DIFFERENCES IN PROPORTION OF OMITTED ITEMS IN TWO TESTS

Type of Response	Items from Henmon-Nelson Test (Ages 9-10)		Status Difference		Items from Otis Beta Test (Ages 13-14)		Status Difference	
	High Status (226 Pupils)	Low Status (322 Pupils)	Amount	Critical Ratio	High Status (235 Pupils)	Low Status (364 Pupils)	Amount	Critical Ratio
Number of Responses								
Right responses	10,303	10,828	. .	. .	13,383	15,897	. .	. .
Wrong responses	2,922	7,542	. .	. .	3,370	9,709	. .	. .
Omitted items*	299	756	. .	. .	126	411	. .	. .
Items not reached* . . .	36	194	. .	. .	41	191	. .	. .
Total	13,560	19,320	. .	. .	16,920	26,208	. .	. .
Percentages								
Number of omitted items as percentage of:								
Total responses	2.2%	3.9%	-1.7%	5.1%	0.7%	1.6%	0.8%	2.8
Total wrong and omitted items	9.3	9.1	-0.2	0.3	3.6	4.1	0.5	0.8
Number of wrong responses	10.2	10.0	-9.2	0.3	3.7	4.2	0.5	0.8

* "Omitted" items are defined as those which were apparently skipped by the pupil, since he did attempt items further on in the test; "not reached" designates items at the end of the test, following the last item marked by the pupil.

either test), they are nevertheless statistically significant differences in both instances.

The second line of percentages in the table indicates that, when the number of omitted items is expressed as a percentage of the total errors (wrong responses plus omissions), the status differences become much smaller; for neither test is the difference as large as its standard error. The third line of percentages expresses the number of omitted items as a percentage of the wrong responses. It indicates that on the Henmon-Nelson test there is one omission for every ten wrong responses, while on the Otis Beta there is one omission for every four wrong responses. In neither case, however, is there a significant difference between the status groups in this respect.

On the basis of these data it is concluded that, at both age levels, low-status pupils do omit items more frequently than do high-status pupils but that they do so only in about the same proportion that they also show an excess of wrong responses. Since the high-status pupils answer the items correctly more often than do the low-status pupils, as already shown in the preceding chapter, it is obvious that low-status pupils must exhibit a larger number of errors (either wrongs or omits) than high-status pupils. But the proportion of these errors which is accounted for by omission of the item is not significantly different for the two status groups.

Status Differences by Position of Correct Response

The possibility of status differences in the test-marking habits of pupils was studied also in another way. Status differences for items in which the correct response was in the first position among the distractors were compared with status differences for items in which the correct response was in the second position, etc. Unlike the preceding analysis, which was based on the items of two tests only, these comparisons were made for the items in all the tests (except for certain types of items listed in the second and third notes to Table 37). The results of this analysis are reported in Table 37.

No clear pattern of relationship between status difference and position of correct response is apparent in the data in Table 37. There are a few variations in the size of status difference shown, especially in cases involving only a few items, but the lack of any consistent pattern to these variations suggests that they are probably chance variations with no real significance. It is hardly surprising to find no appreciable relationship between the position of the correct response and the size of status difference, in view of the data in Tables 34 and 35 (pp. 199 and 202), which showed no important status differences in the manner in which pupils tended to distribute their responses.

One other analysis of the possible relation of status differences to position of responses was made. The Thurstone Spatial test items were omitted from the analysis reported in the preceding paragraphs because of the special nature of these items. The Thurstone Spatial test is composed of a series of "exercises" each of which consists of a geometrical figure at the beginning of a line, followed by six other figures which are either identical or similar in general appearance to the first one but turned at

TABLE 37

MEAN STATUS DIFFERENCES FOR ITEMS CLASSIFIED
BY POSITION OF CORRECT RESPONSE

Position of Correct Response in Relation to Other Possible Responses		Number of Items		Mean Index Difference	
Number of Choices in Item	Position of Correct Response	Age 9-10	Age 13-14	Age 9-10	Age 13-14
2*	Right....	. . .	5	. . .	8.0
	Left	. . .	6	. . .	7.0
3	First....	. . .	2	. . .	15.0
	Second..	. . .	3	. . .	15.0
	Third ...	. . .	6	. . .	11.0
4	First....	31	8	6.3	12.4
	Second..	26	15	7.5	9.7
	Third ...	23	15	6.7	8.3
	Fourth..	36	8	7.3	10.0
5	First....	8	13	12.8	15.5
	Second..	10	22	12.4	16.0
	Third ...	15	35	10.1	15.7
	Fourth..	15	30	13.3	14.1
	Fifth	12	26	11.4	16.1
6	First....	. . .	4	. . .	16.8
	Second..	. . .	2	. . .	12.5
	Third ...	. . .	3	. . .	19.0
	Fourth..	. . .	3	. . .	16.0
	Fifth	. . .	3	. . .	13.3
	Sixth	. . .	2	. . .	17.5
Not included in analysis[+]		41	49	. . .	. . .
All items		217	260	8.9	12.9

*   Excluding Thurstone Spatial test items, which are analyzed separately
    (see Table 38, p. 207). These eleven items are all California Mental
    Maturity picture items, calling for a right-left response.
[+] Construction items, completion items, Thurstone Spatial items (see
    note above), and items requiring the marking of more than one response
    -- none of which lends itself to this kind of analysis.

different angles from the first one.[1] The pupil is asked to mark those figures which are identical in shape to the first one. In each line of six responses either two or three are correct, to be marked by the pupil, but the pupil is not told how many correct ones he should find in any line.

One hypothesis suggested to explain the variation in status difference found for these items, since they have no apparent cultural content, was based on the supposition that the low-status pupils might have a greater tendency to give up after finding one correct response, without examining the rest of the figures in the line for possible further correct responses. Data for checking this hypothesis are reported in Table 38.

In the top half of Table 38 the forty-nine Thurstone Spatial items are classified according to whether they occupy the first, second, third, fourth, fifth, or sixth position in their respective exercises. There is apparently a slight tendency for pupils in both status groups to do somewhat better on the items in the last three positions than on those in the first three, although the differences are not large. For both the high-status pupils and the low-status pupils, however, the difference between the mean index value for the items occupying the third position and that for those occupying the sixth position is statistically significant.

The status differences, shown in the last column, are largest on the items in the fourth and fifth position and smallest on those at either end. The variation of the status difference from position to position is not great, however, and no two of the mean-difference values have a difference between them large enough to be significant even at the 5 per cent level. The lack of any consistent pattern to the variations adds to the likelihood that these variations are all random variations with no particular significance.

In the bottom half of Table 38 these same items are classified according to whether they are the first, second, or third correct item in their respective exercises. If, for example, in a given exercise, the first two figures are incorrect and the third one correct, this correct figure would have been classified under position No. 3 in the top of the table but as a "first correct item" in the bottom portion of the table. When the items are grouped in this fashion, there is a slight tendency, in both status groups, for the percentage of pupils answering correctly to be higher for the first two classes of items than for the third. It seems reasonable to suppose that this is a reflection of the fact that some pupils, having found two correct items in the exercise, give up without hunting as carefully for the third one as they did for the first two. This may be facilitated by the fact that eight of the twenty-one exercises contain only two correct items, while thirteen of them contain three correct items.

These variations in the proportion of pupils answering the first two correct items and those answering the third correct item are not large, however; for none of the figures in this portion of the table is the difference between any two means significant even at the 5 per cent level. That there is no important difference between the two status groups in this respect is indicated clearly in the last column, where it will be seen that the size of the index difference does not vary systematically with the

1. It will be recalled that a Thurstone Spatial test "item" is defined for
   the purposes of this study as each one of the correct responses in a
   line of figures; the entire line of figures, including several "items"
   as well as several incorrect figures, is referred to here as an "exercise." For further explanation see Note 8 in Appendix D.

TABLE 38

MEAN STATUS DIFFERENCES FOR THURSTONE SPATIAL TEST
ITEMS, BY POSITION OF THE ITEM IN TOTAL EXERCISE

Position of Correct Item in the Exercise	Number of Items	Mean Index for High-Status Pupils	Mean Index for Low-Status Pupils	Mean Index Difference
Position in Relation to Total Exercise				
First item ...	6	69.5	60.3*	9.2
Second item ..	9	71.4	62.6	8.9
Third item ...	10	69.0+	59.5‡	9.5
Fourth item ..	8	72.8	63.1	9.6
Fifth item ...	6	72.3	61.5	10.8
Sixth item....	10	74.7+	65.7*‡	9.0
All items .	49	7.7	62.3	9.4
Position in Relation to Other Correct Items in the Exercise				
First correct item	17	71.8	61.6	10.1
Second correct item	19	72.4	63.7	8.6
Third correct item	13	70.6	60.9	9.7
All items .	49	71.7	62.3	9.4

* The difference between these two means is significant at the 5 per cent level, using the t test for small samples.
+ The difference between these two means is significant at the 5 per cent level, using the t test for small samples.
‡ The difference between these two means is significant at the 1 per cent level, using the t test for small samples.

position of the correct item. The status difference is slightly larger for the first correct items in each exercise and smallest for the second ones, but this difference is not large enough to be significant even at the 5 per cent level. There is no evidence from these data to support the proposed hypothesis.

Summary

Pupils of both status groups tend to check the first two distractor positions, on five-choice multiple-choice items, more frequently than later ones, but no significant difference is found between the two status groups in this respect.

Low-status pupils omit individual items more frequently than do the high-status pupils, but only to the extent that they also mark more wrong answers than the high-status pupils; the proportion of errors which are accounted for by omissions is the same for both status groups. When status differences on the correct responses are examined in relation to the position of the correct response among the distractors, no consistent tendencies are discovered for either status group.

On the Thurstone Spatial test, a special examination indicates that the status differences do not vary systematically with the position of the item in relation to other items making up a single line or exercise on the test.

CHAPTER XIX

STATUS DIFFERENCES IN RELATION TO FORM OF
SYMBOLISM USED AND TYPE OF QUESTION ASKED

One of the aspects of culture which has long been recognized as an important factor in most paper-and-pencil test results is that involving the language or other form of symbolism in which the test items are expressed. While the use of language is a universal trait in all levels of American culture, the type of language, the particular vocabulary, and the form of syntax are known to vary widely among different status and other cultural groups.

In view of the wide differences known to be characteristic of high- and low-status homes with respect to reading opportunities, reading habits and customs, and type of spoken language, it seemed a reasonable hypothesis that status differences might be related to the question of whether items are expressed in terms of verbal material, pictures, meaningless numbers and letters, geometric designs, etc.

A second hypothesis to be examined in this chapter is that status differences may be related to the form of the test question — that the typical status differences for opposites, for example, may be larger, or smaller, than the typical status differences for analogies.

Symbolism in Which Item Is Expressed

As the items appear in the printed form of the test it is not difficult to classify them according to whether they are expressed mainly in terms of words, pictures, geometric designs, or other types of symbols. Allowance must be made, however, for the fact that no item in any of the tests in this study is entirely nonverbal. Some of the picture or geometric design items also include verbal instructions as to what to do with the picture or design; these instructions are usually printed in the test blank, but in two of the tests they are read aloud to the pupils. Even in the case of test items which themselves consist entirely of nonverbal material, there is the question of the pupil's understanding the instructions given him at the beginning of the test, so that he knows what it is that he is supposed to do with the test item.

Classification of the 658 items in terms of the kind of symbolism which the pupil has to work with in order to answer the item correctly resulted in the seventeen categories of items listed in Table 39. Approximately a third of the items in the tests for the younger pupils and almost three-fifths of those in the tests for the older pupils are of an exclusively verbal nature. There are also substantial numbers of pictorial and geometric design items, both with and without accompanying verbal material. For the older pupils there is a large block of items using meaningless letter combinations. The other categories of items included in Table 39 are represented by comparatively few items in each case.

A very definite relationship between amounts of status difference

TABLE 39

MEAN STATUS DIFFERENCES FOR ITEMS
CLASSIFIED BY FORM OF SYMBOLISM[*]

Form of Symbolism	Number of Items		Mean Index Difference[‡]	
	Age 9-10	Age 13-14	Age 9-10	Age 13-14
Verbal	73	154	12.5	14.9
Letters (meaningless):				
Without verbal[+]	2	24	} 13.2 {	14.5
With verbal oral	1	. . .		. . .
With verbal print	2	1		. . .
Numbers (meaningless):				
Without verbal	5	. . .	8.8	. . .
With verbal oral	3	. . .	. . .	. . .
With verbal print	9	4	8.6	. . .
Geometric designs (meaningless):				
Without verbal	28	49	7.0	9.4
With verbal oral	32	. . .	6.6	. . .
With verbal print	. . .	6	. . .	8.2
Stylized drawings:				
Without verbal	9	. . .	4.9	. . .
With verbal oral	9	. . .	6.8	. . .
Pictures of real objects:				
Without verbal	24	22	5.6	5.7
With verbal oral	17	. . .	7.7	. . .
Combinations of above categories	3	. . .	. . .	. . .
All items	217	260	8.9	12.9

* For a statement as to the particular pupils and items on which the tables and charts in this chapter are based see Note 11 in Appendix D.

+ "Without verbal" means with no oral or printed verbal material accompanying each individual item. In such cases there are, of course, verbal instructions, either oral or printed, at the beginning of the test in which the items appear.

‡ Not computed for less than five items.

and type of symbolism is revealed by the data in Table 39. Three relatively distinct "levels" of status difference may be identified. At both age levels, verbal items and those based on meaningless letter combinations show noticeably higher status differences than those using any other type of symbolism. The relatively few items dealing with meaningless number combinations show a somewhat smaller degree of status difference. The smallest status differences are found among the picture, geometric-design, and stylized-drawing items. At the older age level it is clear that the picture items yield smaller differences than the geometric-design items.

Certain of the comparisons just pointed out should be made with caution, however, because of the possibility that some of them may be related to the type of question asked rather than to the symbolism of the question. The forty-nine geometric-design-without-verbal items for the older pupils, for example, are drawn entirely from the Thurstone Spatial test, while the twenty-two pictures-without-verbal items for the older pupils are drawn entirely from the two subtests of the California Mental Maturity test. The twenty-four letters-without-verbal items for the older pupils are taken entirely from the Thurstone Reasoning test. In cases such as these it is possible that the relative size of the status differences may be more a function of the particular kind of question asked than of the form of symbolism in which it is expressed. This possibility will be examined further later in this chapter.

It should be noticed that in those cases, such as the geometric-design items, where there are several subdivisions, depending upon the presence or absence of supplementary verbal material accompanying a primarily nonverbal item, the differences between the subdivisions are usually very small and not always in the same direction. Apparently the presence of incidental oral or printed verbal material does not affect the size of the status difference to anything like the extent that occurs when the whole item is in verbal terms.

The major relationships which are apparent in Table 39 may be seen more clearly in Figure 17, which presents some of the data in graphic form. In this chart the order of status differences may be clearly seen, with letter-combination and verbal items showing the largest status differences, followed by number-combination items, and with geometric-design, picture, and stylized-drawing items showing the smallest amount of status difference.

The reader is again cautioned, however, against placing too great reliance upon these conclusions with respect to the effect of symbolism on status differential, particularly for the older pupils, since the form of test question is not held constant in the data presented in Table 39 and Figure 17. It is possible that the status difference found for some of these types of symbolism may be due, in part, to a preponderance of one or two question forms in certain symbolism categories. This possibility will be examined further after the method of classifying items by type of question has been explained.[1] Some possible implications of this variation of item status differences according to symbolism in the item are discussed further in chapter viii.[2]

The foregoing analysis of status differences for items with different forms of symbolism has dealt with mean differences and has assumed

1. See pp. 219-21.
2. See pp. 62-63.

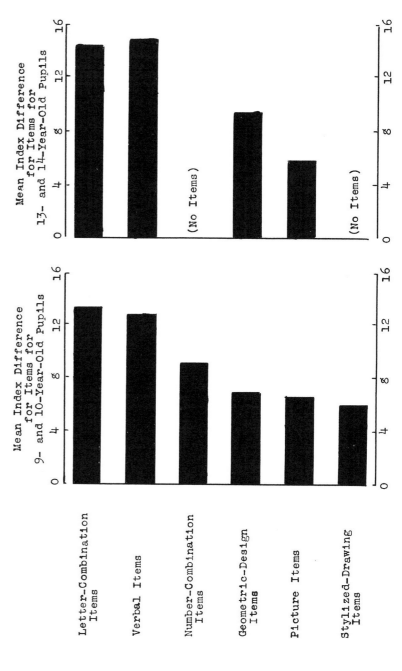

Fig. 17. — Mean status differences for items classified on the basis of symbolism used. (Source: Data in Table 39.)

that the means were sufficiently typical of their various categories to justify comparison of one mean with the other. There is likewise, however, considerable variation in the status differences shown by individual items within each symbolism group. The amount of this variation within each form of symbolism is indicated in Table 40, which reports standard deviations of the status differences for each of the major symbolism groups.

Table 40 indicates that the picture and the verbal items show greater spread of status difference than any of the other categories. This is, of course, entirely reasonable. The verbal and picture items necessarily have some cultural content, and variations in the extent to which this content is equally familiar to pupils from both status groups would be expected to produce variation in the status differences for the items. The other types of items shown in Table 40 have little apparent cultural content; it would seem that whatever status difference is found for one item should be substantially similar to that found for either items of the same general form; this would, of course, result in relatively small standard deviations. The lowest standard deviation in Table 40 is probably to be attributed to the fact that geometric-design items in the tests for the older pupils are found almost entirely (forty-nine out of fifty-five items) in the Thurstone Spatial test — and that these forty-nine items are very similar in form and apparent mental process tested.

Possible implications of these findings with respect to differences in the dispersion of item status differences within various symbolism groups

TABLE 40

STANDARD DEVIATIONS OF STATUS DIFFERENCES FOR ITEMS
CLASSIFIED BY MAJOR FORMS OF SYMBOLISM

Form of Symbolism	Number of Items		Standard Deviation of Index Differences*	
	Age 9-10	Age 13-14	Age 9-10	Age 13-14
Verbal	73	154	4.6	5.0
Pictures of real objects	41	22	4.7	3.8
Letters (meaningless)	5	25	. . .	3.7
Numbers (meaningless)	17	4	3.6	. . .
Geometric designs	60	55	4.3	3.0
Stylized drawings	18	. . .	3.3	. . .
Combinations of above categories	3	. . .	. . .	. . .
All items	217	260	5.2	5.4

* Not computed for less than ten items.

for gaining insight into the nature of status differences in I.Q.'s are discussed further in chapter viii.[3]

Type of Question Asked in Test Item

To test the hypothesis that high-status pupils and low-status pupils, coming from widely different cultural backgrounds, might have somewhat different methods of thinking, or different methods of attacking various types of problems, it seemed desirable to classify the items into categories based upon the type of mental process required of the pupil. Differential performance of the pupils in the two status groups on certain of the categories established on such a basis might then indicate types of mental processes in which one group or the other is superior.

Establishing of categories

To establish a system of categories on the basis of the mental process tested by the item is not easy, however — and the problem of assigning individual items to their proper position in any such system is a well-nigh insuperable one. It is frequently difficult to determine which of several possible mental processes is being tested by a given item; indeed, it is probable that many items test one aspect of one pupil and a quite different aspect of another pupil. Thus, the item in one test which reads:

Which word means the opposite of pride? — sorrow, proud, miserable, conceit, humility?

may be a test of the pupil's ability to read any one (or all) of the words in the item; it may be a test of the pupil's understanding of the meaning of any or all of the words; it may be a test of the pupil's familiarity with the concept of oppositeness; or it may be a test of some other unidentified aspect of the pupil's behavior. If the item is answered correctly, there is relatively clear evidence that the pupil has most of the qualities implied in the foregoing sentence (i.e., ability to read the item, understanding of the concept of oppositeness, and knowledge of at least the words "pride" and "humility"), although there is always the possibility that the pupil may have answered it correctly largely by luck or by elimination of responses which he knew to be incorrect. If, however, the pupil fails to answer the question correctly, it is impossible to tell which one or more of the various needed abilities was lacking. This means that one cannot tell just what such an item is testing and, consequently, that such an item cannot be accurately placed into a system of categories based upon the mental process tested.

Because of difficulties of this nature, no attempt was made to classify the items in terms of the actual mental process presumed to be tested. The items were, however, classified on another basis which, in many cases, may be closely allied to a possible classification in terms of the mental process tested. This set of categories will be described in the following paragraphs.

Examination of the test items reveals that there are many rather obvious "types" of intelligence-test questions. There are a whole group of items which ask the pupil to give the opposite of a given word; others ask the pupil to pick out the one of four words, or pictures, which does not "belong" with the other three; others ask the pupil to identify the characteristic or element which some stated object "always has"; etc. Clas-

3. See p. 63.

sification of the items on this basis -- that is, in terms of the type of question asked -- is considerably simpler and probably more reliable than attempting to classify them on the basis of the mental process tested.

Even this method of classification, however, presents some difficulties. It is sometimes difficult to decide whether a given item is sufficiently different from others of its same general type as to justify creation of a separate category or subcategory for it. Should, for example, items which give one word and ask the pupil to choose from a list of five words the one which is most nearly opposite to the given word be placed in the same category as items which list five or six words and ask the pupil to choose from the list two words which are opposites? As a general rule, whenever questions of this kind arose in setting up the categories, a separate category was created. It was thought that it would be desirable to have the items within each category as homogeneous as possible.

In all cases where the type-of-question-asked category included more than one variety of item as categorized on the basis of symbolism, the category was subdivided so that the final groupings of items would each be completely homogeneous with respect to both factors. When this was done, the 477 items with stable status differences were grouped into fifty-six categories.

The system of categories established, together with the number of items placed in each of the categories, is shown in Table 41. The arrangement of these various categories of items under the major subheadings shown in the table is a somewhat subjective one, and no claim is made that they could not be arranged equally well in other ways. "Selection of a synonym for a given word," for example, is placed as a subcategory under "meaning of words"; it could equally well be placed under "relationship between words or objects," as is done with "selection of the opposite of a given word. The definition or description of the individual categories is more objective, however, and with a few exceptions the placement of any individual item into its proper place in this system of categories is not difficult.

It will be noticed in Table 41 that there are some types of questions under which very substantial numbers of items are classified, while many of the types appear only a few times in all nine of the tests. In general, those types which involve large numbers of items are types of questions around which whole tests, or subtests, have been built. All the items of the Otis Alpha Nonverbal test, for example, are of the "Classification" type (C-1-a in Table 41); this accounts in large part for the large number of items found in this category.

A tabulation of the categories just described, according to the number of items contained in each, is reported in Table 42. While it would be desirable to limit the analysis of items by the type of question asked to those categories which comprise at least ten items each, Table 42 indicates that to do so would severely restrict the number of categories, and the number of items, which could be included. The analysis which is to be reported here includes, therefore, categories based on five or more cases. Mean status differences based on as few as five cases can certainly not be regarded as satisfactory, but if interpreted cautiously they may yield more information than if the items underlying them were not included in the analysis at all. In a few cases, closely related categories (e.g., C-1-a-v, vi, and vii in Table 41) were combined to secure a larger number of items.

TABLE 41

NUMBER OF ITEMS AVAILABLE FOR ANALYSIS, BY CATEGORIES BASED ON TYPE OF QUESTION ASKED AND ON FORM OF SYMBOLISM*

Type of Question Asked (and Form of Symbolism)*	Example+	Number of Items	
		Age 9-10	Age 13-14
A. Meaning of words (verbal only)			
1. Selection of a synonym for a given word	135	4	12
2. Selection of word best fitting a given definition or description	138	2	8
3. Selection of best definition	137	..	3
B. Meaning of sentences (verbal only)			
1. Selection of correct interpretation of a proverb	69, 70	..	7
2. Selection of best word to fill blank in a sentence	78, 118	4	..
3. Selection of correct conclusion to syllogism or other exercise in logical relationships	132	..	14
C. Relationship between words or objects			
1. Classification, with no category stated in test item			
a) Selection of one which does not belong in same category with others			
i) Verbal only	130	7	12
ii) Pictures only	139	24	..
iii) Geometric designs only	142	24	..
iv) Stylized drawings only	124	9	..
v) Letters only	145	2	7
vi) Numbers only	145	3	..
vii) Letters and numbers only	123	1	..
viii) Geometric designs and verbal print	122	..	6
b) Selection of three which do belong in same category (verbal only)		4	..
c) Selection of one which belongs in same category as three given objects			
i) Verbal only	131	..	4
ii) Pictures only	140	3	11
iii) Pictures plus verbal oral		..	..
2. Classification, with category stated in test item (verbal only)			
a) Selection of a category into which given word may be placed	92, 147	8	3
b) Selection of a field in which given word is used as a technical term	136	..	2
c) Selection of one which does not belong in same category with others, on basis of specific trait defined in test item	125	4	..

TABLE 41 – Continued

Type of Question Asked (and Form of Symbolism)*	Example+	Number of Items	
		Age 9-10	Age 13-14
3. Opposites (verbal only)			
a) Selection of the opposite of a given word	129	1	18
b) Selection of two words which are opposites	122	3	..
4. Analogies (verbal only)			
a) Selection of a fourth term of an analogy	93, 94	5	18
b) Selection of a third term of an analogy	116	..	3
5. Essential element: Selection of a trait or traits which are always characteristic of a given object, state, or process (verbal only)			
a) One trait	127	6	17
b) Two traits	134	5	..
6. Comparison			
a) Selection of the most important difference between two objects (verbal only)	62	2	..
b) Selection of the largest or smallest number (numbers plus verbal print)	124	3	..
7. Ordering (verbal only)			
a) Rearranging letters to make a word	75, 76	11	11
b) Rearranging words to make a sentence			
i) Selection of a specified letter in a specified word of a sentence obtained by rearranging a given set of words	79	2	3
ii) Identification of first and last words in a sentence obtained by rearranging a given set of words	122	2	..
c) Selection of the word which would come first or last in dictionary	122	1	2
d) Selection of the month of the year which bears some specified relation to another month or months	97	1	1
e) Selection of the middle one of five given words when rearranged according to some unspecified logical or time relationship	90, 108	..	2
D. Miscellaneous			
1. Manipulation of spatial images			
a) Determination of right- or left-handedness of an object pictured in various positions (pictures only)	141	..	11
b) Determination whether two figures or diagrams are similar in shape though one is turned in a different position from the other (geometric designs only)	144	..	49
c) Selection of two geometric figures which are component elements of a given geometric figure (geometric designs plus verbal oral)	147	5	..

(Continued on next page)

TABLE 41 – Continued

Type of Question Asked (and Form of Symbolism)*	Example+	Number of Items	
		Age 9-10	Age 13-14
2. Drawing geometric figures			
a) Copying a geometric drawing from a given model (geometric designs only)	..	4	..
b) Adding lines and special marks to geometric figures according to specific oral instructions (geometric designs plus verbal oral)	123	7	..
3. Analysis of series			
a) Selection of next element in an ordered series (letters only)	146	..	17
b) Errors in an ordered series			
i) Selection of a series of numbers which is incorrect (numbers plus verbal print)	108	..	1
ii) Indication of the error in an ordered series (numbers only)	..	2	..
iii) Correction of an error in an ordered series (numbers plus verbal print)	64, 65	..	2
c) Counting certain combinations of elements in a long unordered series (numbers plus verbal print)	..	6	1
4. Identification of pictures or drawings from specific oral descriptions			
a) Pictures plus verbal oral	122, 124	14	..
b) Geometric designs plus verbal oral	143	20	..
c) Stylized drawings plus verbal oral	..	9	..
d) Letters plus verbal oral	88	1	..
e) Numbers plus verbal oral	..	3	..
f) Pictures and geometric designs plus verbal oral	108	2	..
5. Solving arithmetical problems (verbal only)	133	..	14
6. Answering questions dealing with recall of facts in fields of history or science (verbal only)	..	..	10
7. Selection or naming of letters of the alphabet with specified positional relationship to other letters (letters plus verbal print)			
a) Selection	..	..	1
b) Naming	..	2	..
8. Selection of best reason for some social activity (verbal only)	73	1	1
Total	..	217	260

* The symbolism categories used here are those already defined in connection with Table 39.

+ The figures in this column refer to the numbers of tables in chapters xxii or xxiii, where sample items of most of the categories will be found.

TABLE 42

ANALYSIS OF TYPE-OF-QUESTION CATEGORIES*

Number of Items per Category	Number of Categories		Number of Items	
	Age 9-10	Age 13-14	Age 9-10	Age 13-14
20 or more	3	1	68	49
15-19	. . .	4	. . .	70
10-14	2	7	25	84
5- 9	10	4	67	28
1- 4	24	14	57	29
No. of items	17	26	. . .	. . .
Total	56	56	217	260

* Tabulated from data in Table 41.

Status differences by symbolism groups, with
type of test question held constant

Before examining the status differences which are characteristic of these different types of test questions, one further analysis of the relationship of status difference to symbolism will be presented. The question was raised in the preceding section of this chapter as to the extent to which variations in status differences apparently due to the form of symbolism might instead be really due to variations in the type of question asked, in cases where one or two types of questions comprise a symbolism group. Two of the types of test questions listed in Table 41 occur in several different forms of symbolism, so that it is possible to make some study of the variation of status difference with type of symbolism while holding the type of test question constant. The data for making this comparison are presented in Table 43.

The first category of items shown in Table 43 requires the pupil to select from four possible choices (pictures, drawings, sets of letter combinations, words, etc.) three which "belong together" and to mark the one of the four which does not belong with the other three. The items of this type include for the younger pupils all of the items of the Otis Alpha Nonverbal test, plus similar items, but in verbal form, from the Henmon-Nelson and the Kuhlmann-Anderson tests. For the older pupils these items include some letter-combination items from the Thurstone Reasoning test and some verbal and geometric-design items from the Otis Beta and Terman-McNemar tests.

The data in the first section of Table 43 show much the same kind of relationship already found for the entire set of items as reported in Table 39, on page 210. Those classification items which are in verbal form have the largest status differences, followed by classification items dealing with letter and number combinations. Geometric-design, picture, and stylized-drawing items all show smaller status differences, in that order.

This reinforces the interpretations drawn earlier from Table 39, except that here there is an indication that verbal items show larger status differences than letter-combination items when the type of question is held constant, whereas the earlier table indicated that both verbal and letter-combination items show about equally large status differences. The high mean difference reported in Table 39 for letter-combination items for the older pupils is probably due, in large part, to the fact that seventeen of the twenty-four items in that category involve completion of an ordered series, which it will be shown later is a kind of item characterized by larger status differences than other kinds of letter-combination items.[4]

The data in the first section of Table 43 also make it clear that the status differences in the verbal classification items cannot be due entirely

TABLE 43

MEAN STATUS DIFFERENCES FOR ITEMS CLASSIFIED BY
FORM OF SYMBOLISM,
WITH TYPE OF QUESTION HELD CONSTANT

Form of Symbolism	Number of Items		Mean Index Difference	
	Age 9-10	Age 13-14	Age 9-10	Age 13-14
	Selection of One Which Does Not Belong in Same Category with Others			
Verbal only	7	12	9.7	17.1
Letters only	2	7		10.7
Numbers only	3	. . .	8.8	. . .
Letters and numbers only	1	. . .		. . .
Geometric designs and verbal print . . .	. . .	6	. . .	8.2
Geometric designs only	24	. . .	6.2	. . .
Pictures only	24	. . .	5.6	. . .
Stylized drawings only	9	. . .	5.0	. . .
	Identification of Pictures or Drawings, etc., from Specific Oral Descriptions			
Pictures and verbal oral	14	. . .	8.5	. . .
Geometric designs and verbal oral . . .	20	. . .	8.2	. . .
Stylized drawings and verbal oral . . .	9	. . .	6.8	. . .

4. See Table 48, p. 227.

to differences in the ability of pupils to carry out the mental processes which make up the classification process, since the mental processes are presumably the same for the picture-classification items as for the verbal-classification ones.

The second category of items shown in Table 43 includes only items from the Otis Alpha Verbal test. For each of these items the examiner reads an oral instruction to the pupil, telling him, in a variety of ways, which one of the four pictures, designs, or drawings he is to mark. There are no verbal items of this type. The size of status difference characteristic of this type of item shows comparatively little variation according to the three types of symbolism reported here, although the few stylized-drawing items do show somewhat smaller differences than the geometric-figure and picture items. This is consistent with the data presented in Table 39, on page 210, where the only kinds of items presenting markedly different status differences involved either verbal symbolism or letter combinations. These two symbolism forms are not represented in the bottom half of Table 43.

Status differences for different types of test questions

In analyzing status differences in relation to the type of question asked by the item, it would be easy to arrive at erroneous conclusions by attributing to different types of questions status-difference characteristics which were really due to differences in the type of symbolism used, since the first part of this chapter has shown that the type of symbolism is definitely related to the amount of status difference to be expected. In order to avoid this possible error, status differences in relation to the type of question will be analyzed while holding the type of symbolism constant. Status differences for different types of questions presented in verbal form will be compared with each other, as will also status differences for different types of questions presented in pictorial or other nonverbal forms, but no comparisons will be made between types of questions involving different systems of symbols.

Data showing average status differences for different types of questions expressed in verbal symbols, for the younger pupils, are presented in Table 44. Great caution should be used in interpreting this table and other similar ones which follow. Many of the mean index differences are, of necessity, based upon comparatively few cases. None is based upon less than five cases, but even this lower limit leaves many of the means based upon too few cases to allow much confidence to be placed in them. When there are only five or six items, the mean index difference may be affected by idiosyncrasies of individual items — the cultural or noncultural nature of the content of some one or two items, for example -- in such a way that the averages shown in these tables may lead to erroneous interpretations. It is suggested that means based upon less than ten or fifteen items be regarded as suggesting possible tendencies rather than as indicating any close measure of the exact status difference for such items.

Some interesting relationships may be observed in Table 44. Only one of these categories of verbal items shows a mean index difference lower than the average for all items, and this one category, "Rearranging letters to make a word," is one which does not involve a very high level of language ability. Every category of verbal items which involves any understanding of the meaning of words yields status differences larger than the average status difference for all items at this age level. It is clear that the categories

TABLE 44

MEAN STATUS DIFFERENCES FOR VERBAL ITEMS CLASSIFIED BY TYPE OF QUESTION ASKED, FOR NINE- AND TEN-YEAR-OLD PUPILS

Type of Question Asked	Number of Items	Mean Index Difference
Selection of a category into which given word may be placed	8	15.5
Selection of fourth term to an analogy .	5	14.0
Selection of two traits which are always characteristic of a given object, state, or process	5	13.2
All verbal items	73	12.5
Selection of one trait which is always characteristic of a given object, state, or process	6	11.0
Selection of one which does not belong in same category with others	7	9.7
All items, both verbal and nonverbal	217	8.9
Rearranging letters to make a word . .	11	7.9

of nonverbal items, which will be discussed later, must, on the whole, show status differences below the average for all items.

The type of verbal item showing the largest status difference is that of "Selection of a category into which a given word may be placed," followed in second place by fourth-term analogies. Items involving the identification of one or two essential traits show close to the average status difference for all verbal items, with those requiring the identification of two traits showing slightly larger differences than those requiring one trait only. All these relationships must be regarded as somewhat tentative, however, since the number of items per category is small; in only one case does the number of items exceed ten.

Similar data for the verbal items from the tests for the older pupils are shown in Table 45. This table shows a larger number of categories for the older pupils, and a larger number of items in most of the categories than was the case in Table 44. This reflects the greater dependence of the tests for the older pupils on verbal material.

The type of item showing the largest status difference in Table 45 is one involving the selection of a category into which a given word may be placed — precisely the same type of item which showed the highest status difference for younger pupils. The second largest status differences are shown by proverb items, a type of item which does not appear in the tests for younger pupils. The third largest status differences are found for items requiring the selection of a word which does not belong in the same

TABLE 45

MEAN STATUS DIFFERENCES FOR VERBAL ITEMS CLASSIFIED BY TYPE OF QUESTION ASKED, FOR THIRTEEN- AND FOURTEEN-YEAR-OLD PUPILS

Type of Question Asked	Number of Items	Mean Index Difference
Classification, with category stated in test item:		
Selection of category into which given word may be placed	3 ⎫	18.2
Selection of a field in which given word is used as a technical term.	2 ⎭	
Selection of correct interpretation of a proverb	7	17.1
Selection of one which does not belong in same category with others	12	17.1
Selection of a trait which is always characteristic of a given object, state, or process	17	16.9
Selection of the opposite of a given word	18	16.3
Selection of synonym for a given word	12	15.8
All verbal items	154	14.9
Answering question dealing with recall of fact from field of history or science	10	14.9
Selection of fourth term of an analogy .	18	14.6
Selection of word best fitting given description or definition	8	14.2
All items, both verbal and nonverbal	260	12.9
Selection of correct conclusion to syllogism or to exercise in logical relationships	14	12.4
Solving arithmetical problems	14	11.4

category with other words in the item — a kind of item which yielded relatively small status differences for the younger pupils. Opposites, synonyms, and fourth-term analogies occupy positions not far from the average for all verbal items. Some possible reasons for the large status differences on proverb items will be suggested in chapter xxii.[5]

Only two kinds of verbal items yield smaller status differences for these pupils than are found for the average of all items. It should be noticed, also, that even in these extreme cases the status differences are still quite substantial — being, for example, nearly as large as the typical status difference for all verbal items for the younger pupils.

Similar data with respect to items expressed wholly or primarily in pictorial symbols are presented, for both age levels, in Table 46. The number of different categories which are expressed in pictorial form is too limited to make many comparisons possible, but the number of items per category is large enough to make more valid those comparisons which can be made.

The two categories of items listed for the younger pupils are both based on the picture items of the Otis Alpha test. The larger status differences are found when the test is administered as a "verbal" test, with a series of oral instructions to the pupils on each item; the smaller status

TABLE 46

MEAN STATUS DIFFERENCES FOR PICTORIAL ITEMS CLASSIFIED BY TYPE OF QUESTION ASKED

Type of Question Asked (and Form of Symbolism)	Number of Items	Mean Index Difference
Items from Tests for Nine- and Ten-Year-Old Pupils		
Identification of pictures from specific oral descriptions (pictures plus verbal oral)	14	8.5
Selection of one which does not belong in same category with others (pictures only)	24	5.6
Items from Tests for Thirteen- and Fourteen-Year-Old Pupils		
Determination of right- or left-handedness of objects pictured in various positions (pictures only)	11	7.5
Selection of one which belongs in same category as three given objects, but with category unstated (pictures only)	11	4.0

5. See pp. 268-73.

differences occur when the same picture items are administered as a "nonverbal" test, with only brief oral instructions at the beginning of the entire test. It seems likely that the relatively large verbal portion of the items when administered as "identification" items may help to explain their larger status difference. This conclusion must be a tentative one, however, since the nature of the mental process changes materially on some of the items according to which method of administration is used. For the older pupils, items requiring the identification of right- or left-handedness of pictures in various positions show considerably larger status difference than do the classification items in picture form. Both of these types of items are from the California Mental Maturity test.

Similar data with respect to items expressed primarily in geometric designs or stylized drawings are reported in Table 47. In this table there is little difference in the status differences for the types of questions available for the older pupils, but somewhat more variation for the younger pupils. In the latter case the two categories showing the largest status differences are items comparable to those also showing the largest status differences for the same pupils on pictorial items, as shown in Table 46. The one category which shows a markedly smaller status difference for the younger pupils is one which apparently involves mostly the ability to follow directions, together with certain motor skills; items of this type do not seem to require any marked degree of analytical thinking. It should be noticed that items accompanied by oral verbal material are found scattered throughout the list of categories; there is no apparent tendency for all such items to show high status differences.

Similar data with regard to items expressed in terms of meaningless letters, numbers, or combinations of both letters and numbers, are shown in Table 48. For the younger pupils there is little variation in relation to the type of question asked in items with this form of symbolism. For the older pupils, items requiring completion of an ordered letter series show larger status differences than are characteristic of items requiring the selection of a set of letters which does not belong with other sets of letters given. These two categories are the two subtests of the Thurstone Reasoning test.

Preceding tables have shown how status differences on test items vary with the form of symbolism used and with the type of question asked, but it is not easy to ascertain from these tables which combination of characteristics provides items with the largest — or the smallest — status differences. Table 49 lists the five types of items — considering both symbolism and type of question -- showing the largest status differences at each age level and the five types of items showing the smallest status differences at each age level.

The most dramatic relationship noticeable in Table 49 is the almost complete separation of verbal and nonverbal items. With a single exception, the five types of items showing the highest status differences at each age level are all verbal items; without exception, the types of items showing the smallest status differences at each age level are nonverbal items. Items involving some form of classification process are found in both the large-difference and the small-difference lists at both age levels. It is apparent once more that it is the type of symbolism which is important in these items rather than the type of question asked.

In this table, as in preceding ones dealing with these categories, it is necessary to draw conclusions on a tentative basis only, owing to the

TABLE 47

MEAN STATUS DIFFERENCES FOR GEOMETRIC-DESIGN
AND STYLIZED-DRAWING ITEMS CLASSIFIED
BY TYPE OF QUESTION ASKED

Type of Question Asked (and Form of Symbolism)	Number of Items	Mean Index Difference
Items from Tests for Nine- and Ten-Year-Old Pupils		
Identification of geometric figures from specific oral descriptions (geometric designs plus verbal oral)	20	8.2
Identification of stylized drawings from specific oral descriptions (stylized drawings plus verbal oral)	9	6.8
Selection of one which does not belong in same category with others (geometric designs only)	24	6.2
Selection of two geometric figures which are component elements of a given geometric figure (geometric designs plus verbal oral)	5	6.0
Selection of one which does not belong in same category with others (stylized drawings only)	9	5.0
Adding lines and special marks to geometric figures according to specific oral instructions (geometric figures plus verbal oral)	7	2.6
Items from Tests for Thirteen- and Fourteen-Year-Old Pupils		
Determining whether two figures or diagrams are similar in shape though one is turned differently from the other (geometric designs only) · · · · · · · · ·	49	9.4
Selection of one which does not belong in same category with others (geometric designs plus verbal print)	6	8.2

TABLE 48

MEAN STATUS DIFFERENCES FOR LETTER-COMBINATION
AND NUMBER-COMBINATION ITEMS CLASSIFIED
BY TYPE OF QUESTION ASKED

Type of Question Asked (and Form of Symbolism)	Number of Items	Mean Index Difference
Items from Tests for Nine- and Ten-Year-Old Pupils		
Counting certain combinations of elements in a long unordered series (numbers plus verbal print)	6	9.3
Selection of one which does not belong in same category with others:		
Letters only	2 ⎫	
Numbers only	3 ⎬	8.8
Letters and numbers only	1 ⎭	
Items from Tests for Thirteen- and Fourteen-Year-Old Pupils		
Selection of next element in an ordered series (letters only)	17	16.3
Selection of one set of letters which does not belong in same category with others (letters only)	7	10.7

relatively small number of items involved in some of the categories. When there are only five or six items, the mean index difference may be affected by individual idiosyncrasies in the individual items, the cultural or noncultural nature of the subject matter of the item, etc., in such a way that the averages shown in these tables may lead to erroneous interpretations.

In general, no very meaningful generalization appears to be possible regarding the types of questions showing large or small status differences, provided the form of symbolism is held constant.

Summary

The most definite and conclusive fact reported in this chapter is that the size of status difference in an item has a direct relation to the form of symbolism in which the item is expressed. Verbal items show the largest amounts of status difference. Items based on meaningless number combinations show smaller status differences, and picture, geometric-design, and stylized-drawing items show the least of all. Approximately the same relationships hold true for both age levels. The dispersion of status differences is greater for verbal and for picture items than it is

TABLE 49

MEAN STATUS DIFFERENCES FOR CATEGORIES OF ITEMS SHOWING
LARGEST AND SMALLEST STATUS DIFFERENCES AT EACH AGE LEVEL

Type of Question Asked (and Form of Symbolism)	Number of Items	Mean Index Difference
Items from Tests for Nine- and Ten-Year-Old Pupils		
Selection of a category into which given word may be placed (verbal only)	8	15.5
Selection of fourth term to an analogy (verbal only)	5	14.0
Selection of two traits which are always characteristic of a given object, state, or process (verbal only)	5	13.2
Selection of one trait which is always characteristic of a given object, state, or process (verbal only)	6	11.0
Selection of one which does not belong in same category with others (verbal only)	7	9.7
.	.	.
.	.	.
Selection of one which does not belong in same category with others (geometric designs only)	24	6.2
Selection of two geometric figures which are component elements of a given geometric figure (geometric designs plus verbal oral)	5	6.0
Selection of one which does not belong in same category with others (pictures only)	24	5.6
Selection of one which does not belong in same category with others (stylized drawings only)	9	5.0
Adding lines and special marks to geometric figures according to specific oral instructions (geometric designs plus verbal oral)	7	2.6
Items from Tests for Thirteen- and Fourteen-Year-Old Pupils		
Classification, with category stated in test item (verbal only):		
Selection of category into which given word may be placed	3 ⎫	
Selection of a field in which given word is used as a technical term	2 ⎭	18.2
Selection of correct interpretation of proverb (verbal only)	7	17.1
Selection of one which does not belong in same category with others (verbal only)	12	17.1
Selection of a trait which is always characteristic of a given object, state, or process (verbal only)	17	16.9
Selection of next element in an ordered letter series (letters only)	17	16.3
.	.	.
.	.	.
Selection of one set of letters which does not belong in same category with others (letters only)	7	10.7
Determining whether two figures or diagrams are similar in shape though one is turned differently from the other (geometric designs only)	49	9.4
Selection of one which does not belong in same category with others (geometric designs plus verbal print)	6	8.2
Determination of right- or left-handedness of objects pictured in various positions (pictures only)	11	7.5
Selection of one which belongs in same category as three given objects, but with category unstated (pictures only)	11	4.0

for geometric-design, stylized-drawing, number-combination, or letter-combination items, probably due to the larger cultural element in verbal and picture items.

A system of fifty-six categories is established on the basis of both form of symbolism and the type of test question asked, so that each category of item is homogeneous with respect to both of these factors. The categories of items showing the largest status differences are all ones composed of verbal items, while the types of items showing the smallest status differences are, in every case, nonverbal in symbolism. So long as symbolism is held constant, no broad generalization appears to be possible as to type of test questions which yield large status differences and those which yield relatively small status differences, although considerable variation in typical status differences for various types of test questions is found.

CHAPTER XX

STATUS DIFFERENCES IN RELATION TO DIFFICULTY
OF THE ITEM

It seemed important to determine whether the degree of status difference exhibited by test items varies in any consistent manner with the difficulty of the items. If the size of the status difference should be closely related to the difficulty of the item, that fact might aid in understanding the nature of the status difference. Furthermore, it is important to know to what extent the factor of difficulty of the items must be taken into account in comparing the status differences characteristic of different categories of items, as reported in the preceding chapter.

Gross Relationships

Two different measures of the difficulty of each item are available — the proportion of high-status pupils passing the item correctly and the proportion of low-status pupils doing so. An analysis of the relationship between size of status difference and these two measures of item difficulty, by means of correlation coefficients and correlation ratios, is reported in Table 50. The correlation coefficients indicate that the size of status difference is not markedly related to item difficulty, no matter which measure of item difficulty is used and no matter which age level of pupils is studied. The largest correlation is only .36. Two of the coefficients are so small that they may well be random variations due to sampling errors only.

The two correlations which do represent relationships that are clearly greater than that indicated by a zero correlation show, interestingly enough, quite different situations at the two age levels. In the case of the nine- and ten-year-old pupils the size of the status differential is somewhat related to the difficulty of the item for low-status pupils but not at all (for practical purposes) related to the difficulty of the item for high-status pupils. Furthermore, the negative sign means that the larger status differences are found on those items which are most difficult. For the older pupils the situation is precisely reversed, both as to the direction of the relationship with item difficulty and as to the measure of item difficulty which shows the significant relationship. Some explanation for this difference in the relationship at the two age levels will become apparent a little further on in this chapter.

The above comments have been based upon an assumption of linearity. The last column of Table 50, however, indicates that one of the four relationships is clearly not linear. The other three do not depart from linearity enough to make it very certain that the departures are not merely random sampling errors. In the case of the relationship between size of status differential and degree of difficulty for low-status pupils at the younger age level, however, the test for linearity shows that the difference between the correlation ratio and the correlation coefficient is almost certainly too large to be accounted for as a sampling error.

TABLE 50

RELATIONSHIP BETWEEN STATUS DIFFERENCE
AND ITEM DIFFICULTY[+]

Age Level and Status Group by Which Item Difficulty Measured	Number of Items	Correlation Coefficient	Unbiased Correlation Ratio‡	Linearity of Regression§
Nine- and ten-year-old pupils:				
High status	334	.07	.17	P > .05
Low status	334	-.29*	.46*	P̄ < .01
Thirteen- and fourteen-year-old pupils:				
High status	324	.36*	.38*	P > .05
Low status	324	-.06	.15	P̄ > .05

* Starred coefficients and ratios are large enough to be significantly greater than zero at the 1 per cent level of significance. Unstarred coefficients and ratios in the table are not large enough to be significantly greater than zero even at the 5 per cent level.

+ For a statement as to the particular pupils and items on which the tables and charts in this chapter are based see Note 11 in Appendix D.

‡ The correlation ratio used here is epsilon rather than eta, as explained on p. 143. The ratios given here have been corrected for broad grouping.

§ The P-values indicate the probability that the deviation from linearity would be as great as that found for these data by reason of sampling fluctuations only. In only one case is nonlinearity clearly indicated.

Analysis of the Relationship While Form of Symbolism Is Held Constant

Examination of the scatter diagrams underlying these correlations suggested that at least part of the curvilinearity might be due to the presence in the items analyzed of both verbal and nonverbal items. It was apparent that the relationship between status difference and item difficulty was probably quite different for verbal items than for nonverbal items. Correlations similar to those just reported were, therefore, computed for various subcategories of items for which it was possible to hold the form of symbolism constant. These correlations are shown in Table 51. The adjusted correlations in Table 51 are comparable to those reported in Table 50, except that in Table 51 the correlations are based upon items grouped so as to be homogeneous with respect to form of symbolism.

The unadjusted coefficients indicate that in five or six of the cases the relationship is definite enough to be almost certainly a real one, not due solely to sampling fluctuations. It is not entirely valid to compare the sizes of these unadjusted coefficients with each other, since the total range of difficulty characteristic of certain of the groups varies markedly, as indicated by the column of standard deviations. The correlations reported in the last column have been adjusted to allow for these differences of range.

TABLE 51

RELATIONSHIP BETWEEN STATUS DIFFERENCE AND ITEM DIFFICULTY, FOR DIFFERENT FORMS OF SYMBOLISM

Form of Symbolism	Status Group by Which Difficulty Measured	Number of Items	Correlation Coefficient	Standard Deviation of Index	Adjusted Coefficient+
				Adjustment of Coefficient to Common Range of Difficulty	
Nine- and Ten-Year-Old Pupils					
Verbal	High status. . . .	99	.62**	13.3	.72
	Low status. . . .	99	.28**‡	10.5	.44
Geometric design	High status. . . .	81	.04	16.7	.04
	Low status. . . .	81	-.23*	17.0	-.23
Picture	High status. . . .	95	-.07	16.6	-.07
	Low status. . . .	95	-.37**	17.6	-.37
Thirteen- and Fourteen-Year-Old Pupils					
Verbal	High status. . . .	190	.46**	14.2	.54
	Low status. . . .	190	.09	12.7	.13
Nonverbal	High status. . . .	134	.38**	12.4	.50
	Low status. . . .	134	-.06	11.4	-.09

* Starred coefficients are large enough to be significantly greater than zero at the 5 per cent level of significance. Double-starred coefficients are significant at the 1 per cent level. Unstarred coefficients are not large enough to be significantly greater than zero even at the 5 per cent level.

+ Coefficients adjusted to what they would be if the standard deviation of the index of difficulty in each case equaled 17.6, the largest standard deviation found for any of these ten distributions. The formula used is the one referred to in the first note to Table 18, p. 139.

‡ This correlation is somewhat misleading. Examination of the line in Figure 18, p. 234, which corresponds to this correlation, indicates that the correlation should be higher. For explanation of the reason for this relatively low correlation see Note 12 in Appendix D.

These correlations indicate some interesting, and rather puzzling, relationships, among which may be mentioned:

1. At both age levels the verbal items show a stronger relationship between status difference and difficulty of the item than nonverbal items show; this is especially marked for the younger pupils.

2. The verbal items show a stronger relationship for the younger pupils than they do for the older pupils.

3. For the younger pupils the direction of the relationship is reversed for verbal and for nonverbal items. The larger status differences are associated with the easier verbal items and with the more difficult picture and geometric-design items. For the older pupils the direction of the relationship is the same for both verbal and nonverbal items.

4. The verbal items show a stronger relationship of status difference to difficulty for the high-status pupils than to difficulty for the low-status pupils; this is also true for nonverbal items at the older age level, but the reverse is true for nonverbal items for the younger pupils.

The nature of these relationships may be seen more clearly in graphic form. The data for verbal items are presented graphically in Figure 18. The four lines in this chart represent the two different age levels and the two different measures of difficulty used. The bottom half of the chart makes it clear that, when item difficulty is measured in terms of difficulty for the high-status pupils, there is a definite and consistent relationship between status difference and item difficulty, with the size of the status difference increasing steadily as the items become easier. When item difficulty is measured in terms of the low-status pupils, as reported in the top half of Figure 18, the same relationship holds for the thirteen- and fourteen-year-old pupils but not for the nine- and ten-year-old pupils. For the latter pupils there seems to be some tendency for status difference to be related to item difficulty for relatively difficult items but not through most of the range of moderate and easy items.

These results are at variance with the early findings of Stern. Working in Germany in 1911, Stern found that status differences on Binet-Simon tests were larger for more difficult items than for the easier items (47, pp. 54-57).

Similar data for various types of nonverbal items are presented graphically in Figure 19. In this chart all the nonverbal items for the older pupils (picture, geometric-design, number-combination, and letter-combination) have been pooled, since there are too few to yield satisfactory means for the separate categories. None of the six lines in Figure 19 indicates any relationship between status difference and item difficulty even approaching that shown in Figure 18 as being characteristic of verbal items. In the case of the picture items, such slope as is present indicates a slight tendency for the status differences to <u>decrease</u> as the items become easier.

Analysis of the Relationship While
Type of Test Question Is Held Constant

One further analysis of these data will be presented. It is possible that the easier verbal items tend to be of one test-question form and the

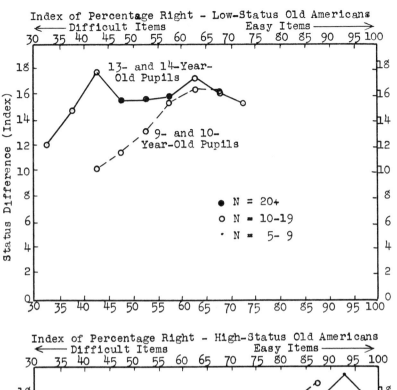

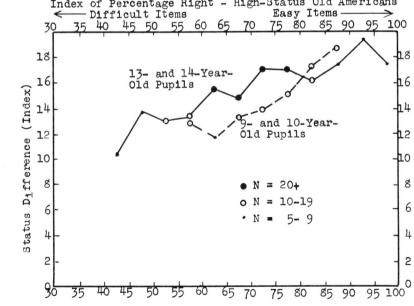

Fig. 18. — Mean status differences for items of varying degrees of difficulty for pupils in two status groups, for verbal items.

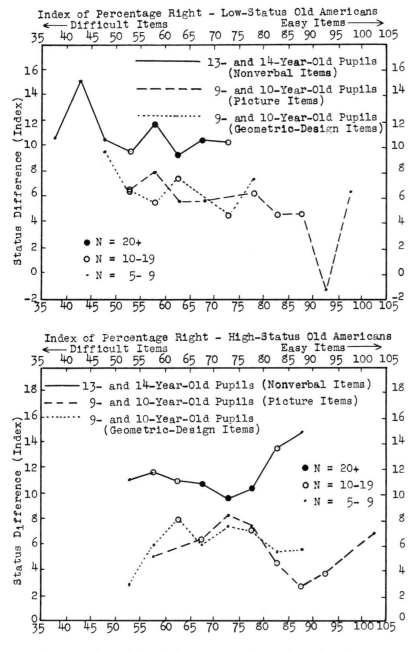

Fig. 19. — Mean status differences for items of varying degrees of difficulty for pupils in two status groups, for nonverbal items.

more difficult verbal items of a different test-question form. In that case the changes in status differences might be more a function of this change in form than of the change in difficulty itself. In order to study this question, the mean difficulty for each of the type-of-question categories (for verbal items only) was determined, and rank correlation coefficients were computed between mean difficulties and mean status differences. This measures the extent to which the typical difficulty of certain types of questions is correlated with the typical status differences for those types. The results are shown in Table 52. Since the rank correlations in Table 52 are based on only a few categories, their standard errors are large.

TABLE 52

RELATIONSHIP BETWEEN MEAN ITEM DIFFICULTY

AND MEAN ITEM STATUS DIFFERENCE,

FOR CATEGORIES OF VERBAL ITEMS

Age Level and Status Group by Which Item Difficulty Measured	Number of Categories of Items*	Rank Correlation Coefficient	Standard Error of Zero Coefficient	Critical Ratio
Nine- and ten-year-old pupils:				
High status	6	.77	.43	1.8
Low status	6	.54	.43	1.3
Thirteen- and fourteen-year-old pupils:				
High status	11	.66	.32	2.1
Low status	11	.03	.32	0.1

* Categories of items are those shown in Tables 44 and 45.

Despite the unreliability of these data, however, it is fairly certain that the ranking of verbal item categories by size of status difference, as was done in Tables 44 and 45 (pp. 222 and 223), is, in part, related to the order of difficulty for these categories; the easier the type of item, the larger the status difference is likely to be. This is particularly true for the tests for the younger pupils. For the items given to the older pupils it is true only for difficulty as measured by the high-status pupils.

These rank correlations indicate the extent to which the mean status difference from category to category tends to be related to the mean item difficulty for the same categories. In order to measure the extent to which status difference is related to item difficulty within the categories of verbal items, rank correlations were also computed for the individual items in each category separately. The resulting correlations were not very satisfactory, owing to the small number of items in each category and to the large number of ties in rank which occurred. For this reason they will not be reported in detail here.[1] In general, these data indicate that there

1. For a reference to a report of this analysis see Note 1 in Appendix D.

is probably, for verbal items, a positive degree of correlation between status difference and item difficulty as measured for high-status pupils, even within a single type of test question, and that the amount of such correlation is somewhere near .40 or .50. When the difficulty is measured for the low-status pupils, the amount of relationship is much smaller and may easily be due to chance errors alone.

So far as these data reveal, the nature of the relationship between status difference and item difficulty for verbal items cannot be simplified by saying that it is due either to the varying difficulty of different types of items or that it is entirely free of this factor. Status difference is related to item difficulty both within categories of the same question type and between categories of different question types.

It is not easy to assess the significance of the relationships reported in this chapter. They at first seem to be directly contrary to what might be expected in terms of the major hypothesis underlying this study — that is, that status differences are due, at least in part, to differences in opportunities for familiarity with the materials and processes necessary for answering the item correctly. It would seem reasonable to assume that, in terms of such an explanation, the larger status differences would be found on the more difficult items and the smaller status differences on the easier items. This is, however, the opposite of the relationship actually found, at least for verbal items. Possible implications of these findings for gaining insight into the nature of status differences in I.Q.'s are discussed further in chapter viii.[2]

Summary

The relationship of status differences to item difficulty is analyzed both by correlation procedures and also by categorizing the items on the basis of difficulty and computing the mean index difference for each group. This is done for the entire set of items at each age level, and also for items with the form of symbolism held constant.

In the case of verbal items, the size of the status difference varies markedly with the difficulty of the item, being largest for the easiest items and smallest for the hardest items. This is true throughout the range of difficulty, not merely at the ends where errors of measurement might influence the results substantially. The relationship is stronger when difficulty is determined for high-status pupils than when determined for low-status pupils, and it is stronger for the nine- and ten-year-old pupils than for the thirteen- and fourteen-year-old pupils. On the basis of somewhat unsatisfactory data it is tentatively concluded that the relationship between item difficulty and status differences, for verbal items, holds true both as between different types of test questions and also for individual items within the test-question categories.

In the case of nonverbal items, the relationship differs according to the age level. For the thirteen- and fourteen-year-old pupils, the relations are of the same general nature as for the verbal items, but smaller in magnitude. For the nine- and ten-year-old pupils, however, the relationship not only is less marked but tends to be negative, with the easier items showing the smaller status differences. In the latter case the relationship is strongest with the item difficulty determined for the low-status pupils —just the reverse of the relationship found for verbal items and for the nonverbal items at the older age level.

2. See pp. 64-65.

CHAPTER XXI

STATUS DIFFERENCES IN RELATION TO AGE OF PUPILS

All comparisons between status differentials for different groups of items made thus far have been made within one or the other of the two age groups — never across age lines. This has meant that the comparisons have always been based on the responses of pupils from different status backgrounds to the same items.

It has been apparent in some of the data presented, however, that the status differences on items given to the older pupils are, in general, somewhat larger than are those on items given to the younger pupils. It has not been entirely clear, however, whether this apparent age difference is due to differences in the types of items making up the tests or differences in the pupils themselves. Attention is called, for example, to the importance, for understanding age comparisons, of the finding that verbal items show larger status differences than do picture items and that this is true for both age groups. It so happens that nearly a third of the items for the younger pupils are picture items, while less than a tenth of the items for the older pupils are in picture form; conversely, about a third of the items for younger pupils are verbal items, whereas nearly three-fifths of the items for the older pupils are verbal items. It may well be that the larger status difference noticed for older pupils is explained largely by the greater concentration of verbal items in the tests for the older pupils and the greater concentration of picture items in the tests for the younger pupils.

Table 39, on page 210, has already presented some evidence which bears on this point. The most pertinent portions of that table are reproduced here as Table 53. These data indicate that for both verbal and geometric-design items the older pupils show significantly larger status differences than do the younger pupils, although the age differences are smaller than when the factor of symbolism is not held constant. Picture items, on the other hand, yield almost exactly the same degree of status difference at both age levels.

When the differences among the age differentials themselves (as listed in the next to the last column of Table 53) were tested for significance, it was found that all three of the symbolism-constant age differentials are probably significantly smaller than the age differential for all items (4.0) as reported in the last line of the table (critical ratios, 2.0, 1.7, and 3.3 for the symbolism groups in the order listed in the table). Furthermore, the age differential for picture items is probably, though not certainly (critical ratios 1.8 and 1.7), significantly smaller than the age differential for verbal and geometric-design items. Some of the increase in status differential for older pupils is apparently due solely to the fact that the tests used with this group are more heavily saturated with verbal items, while picture and geometric-design items constitute a larger proportion of the tests for younger pupils.

One further comparison of this sort can be made, holding both type of symbolism and form of test question constant while age differences

TABLE 53

MEAN STATUS DIFFERENCES FOR CERTAIN ITEMS GROUPED
ACCORDING TO FORM OF SYMBOLISM,
FOR TWO AGE LEVELS*

Form of Symbolism	Number of Items		Mean Index Difference		Difference between Mean Index Differences for Older and for Younger Pupils	
	Age 9-10	Age 13-14	Age 9-10	Age 13-14	Amount of Difference	Critical Ratio of Difference
Verbal items....	73	154	12.5	14.9	2.4	3.5
Geometric-design items, with no verbal material .	28	49	7.0	9.4	2.4	3.0
Picture items, with no verbal material	24	22	5.6	5.7	0.1	0.1
All items, regardless of form of symbolism .	217	260	8.9	12.9	4.0	8.2

* Data for this table selected from Table 39. For a statement as to the particular pupils and items on which all the tables in this chapter are based see Note 11 in Appendix D.

are studied. Out of the fifty-six categories of items listed in Table 41, on pages 216-18, there are three for which five or more items are found in the tests for the younger pupils and also five or more are found in the tests for the older pupils. There is one other case where closely similar categories are found at both age levels and where approximate age comparisons can probably be made, despite the slight variation in the type of items involved. The necessary data for making these four age comparisons are provided in Table 54.

Of the four age comparisons listed in the last column of Table 54, two show age differences with regard to the status differential that are smaller in size than that shown for all items, while two show age differences that are larger. It should be kept in mind that the comparisons in this table involve comparisons of items of the same type, with respect to symbolism and form of test question, but they do not involve identical items. It is possible that some of the age differences are due to variations in the cultural content of the actual words used in specific items. It may be, for example, that the rather large increases in status differential that are characteristic of the verbal classification items (first line of Table 54)

TABLE 54

MEAN STATUS DIFFERENCES FOR CERTAIN ITEMS GROUPED
ACCORDING TO TYPE OF QUESTION ASKED AND TO
FORM OF SYMBOLISM, FOR TWO AGE LEVELS*

Type of Question Asked (and Form of Symbolism)	Number of Items		Mean Index Difference		Difference between Mean Index Differences for Older and for Younger Pupils
	Age 9-10	Age 13-14	Age 9-10	Age 13-14	
Selection of one which does not belong in same category with others (verbal only)	7	12	9.7	17.1	7.4
Selection of a trait which is always characteristic of a given object, state, or process (verbal only)	6	17	11.0	16.9	5.9
All items in the tests .	217	260	8.9	12.9	4.0
Selection of one which does not belong in same category with others:					
Letters only	2 ⎫	...	8.8	... ⎫	
Numbers only	3 ⎬			⎬	
Letters and numbers only	1 ⎭			⎪	1.9
Selection of one which does not belong in same category with others (letters only)	...	7	...	10.7 ⎭	
Selection of the fourth term to an analogy (verbal only)	5	18	14.0	14.6	0.6

* Data selected from Tables 44, 45, and 48.

239

and the essential-trait items (second line of the table) are due to the presence in these items in the tests for the older pupils of words more culturally biased than those in the tests for the younger pupils.

In order to avoid the possibility of apparent age differences really being due to differences in the content of the items, a supplementary analysis was carried out by means of which certain age comparisons could be based upon identical items administered to younger and to older pupils. It was not possible to do this by means of the two age levels used in the rest of the analysis, since there were no items in common to the tests administered to the pupils at the two age levels. Instead, each of the age levels previously treated as a unit was split in half on the basis of chronological age. In this way, the test performance of nine-year-olds could be compared with that of ten-year-olds, on the same items. Similarly the test performance of thirteen-year-old pupils could be compared with that of fourteen-year-old pupils, on the same test items.

The average status differentials for items in three tests, treated in the manner just described, are reported in Table 55. The data indicate that there is no measurable difference in the size of the status differential

TABLE 55

AGE CHANGES IN MEAN STATUS DIFFERENCES FOR
IDENTICAL ITEMS IN THREE TESTS

Age Level	Mean Index Difference		
	Otis Alpha Nonverbal (58 Items)	Henmon-Nelson (44 Items)	Otis Beta (47 Items)
Ten-year-old pupils . . . . (10-1 to 11-0)	6.28	12.57	. . . .
Nine-year-old pupils . . . . . . (9-1 to 10-0)	5.72	12.36	. . . .
Fourteen-year-old pupils . . . (14-1 to 15-0)	. . . .	. . . .	12.89
Thirteen-year-old pupils . . . (13-1 to 14-0)	. . . .	. . . .	13.38
Increase in status difference for older pupils	0.55	0.20	-0.49
Standard error of the increase*	0.64	0.62	0.96
Critical ratio*	0.9	0.3	0.5

* Computed with allowance for the fact that index differences for the two groups are correlated. These standard errors and critical ratios are, of course, identical with those appearing in Table 56, p. 243, although in that table they are computed on a different basis.

for nine-year-olds as compared with that for ten-year-olds, or for thirteen-year-olds as compared with that for fourteen-year-olds, when the comparison is based upon the same items for both sets of pupils. The fifty-eight items in the Otis Alpha Nonverbal test show an average status difference of 5.72 points when given to nine-year-olds and an average difference of 6.28 points when given to ten-year-olds. The difference between these two averages is less than its standard error and so could easily be due to sampling errors only. The forty-four items in the Henmon-Nelson test show an even smaller change in the average status difference for nine-year-olds and ten-year-olds. The forty-seven Otis Beta items show a slightly smaller status difference for fourteen-year-olds than for thirteen-year-olds, but the difference is much too small to be significant.

These data do not prove that there is no change in the amount of status difference with changes in chronological age, but they do indicate that if there is any such change it is so slight that the amount which occurs in a single year's time cannot be measured by means of the items in these tests. With the year-to-year change in status differential as small as indicated in Table 55, and particularly with one of the pairs of years being compared showing a negative change, it is difficult to imagine that an increase of status difference of nearly four points from the nine- and ten-year-olds to the thirteen- and fourteen-year-olds (as shown in Table 53, on p. 239) would occur if the status difference were measured on the same test items. The only reasonable conclusion on the basis of these data is that it is much more likely that the larger status difference for the older pupils is due almost entirely to the nature of the test material by which it is measured rather than to differences in the pupils themselves.

This does not mean that there are not any items, or possibly even types of items, which do show substantial changes in their status differential within a year's time. That this is the case is indicated in Table 56, which shows the number of individual test items showing changes in status differential of various amounts. A number of the individual items do show increases in status differentials over a year's time amounting to more than 8 points. But offsetting these are a number of other items which show substantial decreases in status differential over the same time. When the changes in status differential of the 149 items reported in Table 56 were tested for statistical significance, one item showed a change significant at the 1 per cent level, and eight additional items showed changes significant at the 5 per cent level. This is equal to or less than the number of items one would expect to find showing "significant" differences from random sampling fluctuations alone. It is probable, therefore, that no significance should be attached to the particular items which show the "significant" status changes in Table 56.

The data presented here indicate that, when a fairly large number of items are taken as a whole, there is no evidence that the average status differential either increases or decreases with age — at least not in amounts which are measurable in one year's time. Possible implications of this finding for gaining insight into the nature of status differences in I.Q.'s are discussed further in chapter viii.[1]

Summary

The relationship of status differences to age level of the pupils is first examined by comparing the index differences for all items given to

1. See p. 66.

TABLE 56

DISTRIBUTION OF ITEMS IN THREE TESTS BY AMOUNT OF AGE CHANGE IN STATUS DIFFERENCE ON IDENTICAL ITEMS

Amount of Change in Index Differential in Year's Time*	Number of Items Showing Changes in Status Differential as Indicated		
	Changes from Nine-Year-Old to Ten-Year-Old Pupils		Changes from Thirteen-Year-Old to Fourteen-Year-Old Pupils
	Otis Alpha Nonverbal	Henmon-Nelson	Otis Beta
(+ 8)-(+10)	7	1	3
(+ 5)-(+ 7)	8	6	3
(+ 2)-(+ 4)	9	9	13
(+ 1)-(- 1)	10	13	4
(- 2)-(- 4)	16	8	15
(- 5)-(- 7)	7	5	6
(- 8)-(-10)	. . .	2	3
(-11)-(-13)	1	. . .	. . .
Total	58	44	47
Mean change	0.55	0.20	-0.49
Standard error of mean	0.64	0.62	0.96
Critical ratio	0.9	0.3	0.5

* Positive changes indicate increases in status difference with advancing age; negative changes indicate decreases in status difference with advancing age.

the nine- and ten-year-old pupils with those for all items given to the thirteen- and fourteen-year-old pupils, even though the items are not identical, or even entirely of the same time, at the two age levels. The comparison is then made in terms of a smaller number of items for which it is possible to hold constant the form of symbolism and type of test question while studying age differences. Finally, a special analysis is made of the status differences exhibited by nine-year-old pupils as compared to those shown by ten-year-old pupils and of the status differences for thirteen-year-old pupils as compared to those for fourteen-year-old pupils. In the latter analysis the age comparisons are based on identical items for both age groups being compared.

The data indicate that what at first appears to be a substantially larger status difference for older children as compared to that for younger children is reduced markedly when the form of symbolism is held constant in the comparison and disappears almost entirely when the comparison is based on identical items. It is concluded, therefore, that the greater status difference found for the tests for older pupils is probably due to differences in the nature of the test materials for the two age levels rather than to inherent differences in the status characteristics of the pupils at the two levels.

CHAPTER XXII

STATUS DIFFERENCES IN INCORRECT RESPONSES

FOR CERTAIN INDIVIDUAL TEST ITEMS

Previous chapters have shown (a) the existence of substantial status differences on many test items; (b) variation in the amount of this status difference among the different individual items; and (c) some explanation of part of this variability in terms of symbolism used in the item, type of question asked, difficulty of the item, and unreliability of the measurements. In order to arrive at some tentative hypotheses as to the kinds of factors which may explain the variability in status difference not accounted for by the above factors, it is necessary to examine the available data for a number of individual items.

In this chapter an analysis is made of wrong responses on a number of items to determine whether there are items which show distinctly different distribution of wrong responses for the two status levels and to use any such items as a basis for gaining further insight into the nature of status differences on test items. A similar analysis of the differences with respect to the correct response on certain items will be reported in the next chapter.

Nature of the Analysis of Wrong Responses

Even with the assistance of the I.B.M. test-scoring machine, the making of detailed wrong-answer analyses of a large number of items is a somewhat laborious task. In order to simplify the process as much as possible, the following kinds of items were excluded from the wrong-answer analysis, for the reasons given:

1. All items in the Thurstone Spatial test and in the first subtest of the California Mental Maturity test, since their two-choice form meant that an analysis of wrong answers would yield little information not already available from the right-answer data.

2. All items in the Thurstone Reasoning test, since the homogeneous and noncultural nature of the responses did not seem to offer much hope of providing useful interpretations of wrong-answer data.

3. Items in certain subtests of the Kuhlmann-Anderson test which did not lend themselves readily to simple wrong-answer tabulations, either because they are completion or construction items or because they require the correct choice of two or three words per item rather than one only.

4. Items for which neither status groups made as many as ten errors. Computation of percentages on the basis of smaller number of cases than ten would not be justified.

These exclusions reduced the number of items to be considered, at both age levels, from 658 to 471.

It was hoped that the wrong-answer analysis would yield valuable clues as to possible reasons for status differences on the items as a whole; it seemed reasonable, therefore, to concentrate the analysis most heavily on the items showing large status differences. Accordingly, wrong-answer analyses were made for all items (except those already excluded as explained above) which showed status differences, on the right answers, of 15 index points or more. For comparative purposes, such analyses were also made for all items having status differences of less than 5 index points. Wrong-answer analyses were also made for many but not all of the items having index differences between 5 and 14 points. In the case of two tests, one at each age level, the wrong-answer analysis was made for every item. The number of items for which wrong-answer data were thus obtained is 357, or 54 per cent of the total items being studied.

The selection of the most useful measure to use in analyzing the wrong-answer status differences presented some difficulty. The nature of this difficulty will be best indicated by an example. The number of right and wrong responses, by status groups, for a sample item, together with the same data converted into percentages on two different bases, is shown in Table 57.

When the number of responses on each distractor is computed as a percentage of the total number of pupils in the status group, as is done in the second portion of Table 57, certain relationships become apparent. It is clear that there is a highly significant status difference (critical ratio, 12.0) in the proportion of correct responses to this item. It is also clear that distractor No. 2, "drama," is the most potent distractor for both of the status groups. The critical ratios indicate that on all four of the distractors low-status children make proportionately more responses than high-status children and that these differences are all statistically significant ones.

It is not at all clear, however, how these status differences, computed in this fashion, should be interpreted. What is to be inferred from the fact that "drama" attracts 21 per cent of the low-status children and only 7 per cent of the high-status children? Does this mean specifically that a larger proportion of low-status children think that "sonata" is a term used in drama — or does it merely mean that a larger proportion of low-status pupils are not familiar with the term "sonata" at all?

The difficulty, of course, is that, whenever there is a substantial status difference on the right response, the low-status pupils must necessarily show higher percentages of pupils checking some or all of the wrong responses. It is impossible to determine with the data in this form how much of the low-status response to a given distractor is due to something unique in that particular distractor and how much it is merely a reflection of general inability to answer the item. Yet it is precisely this distinction which should be made, at least as closely as possible, in order to narrow the area in which explanation for the status difference should be sought.

When the numbers of wrong responses are computed as percentages of the total errors, however, rather than as percentages of the total number of pupils, the status differences observed are entirely different, as shown in the third section of Table 57. In this form it becomes clear that, despite the much larger number of errors in the low-status group, there is no particular tendency for any one of the distractors to attract a larger proportion of the errors of one status group than of the other. There may be some indication that a larger share of the low-status children who miss

TABLE 57

TWO KINDS OF WRONG-ANSWER DATA FOR A SAMPLE ITEM*

Status Group	Number of Pupils	Number of Wrong Responses	Distribution of Responses — Sonata is a term used in –						Total
			drawing	drama	music	poetry	phonetics	(omit)	
			Number of Responses						
High status	230	56	4	17	174	11	10	14	230
Low status	344	240	27	69	104	42	69	33	344
			Per Cent of Total Pupils						
High status	230	. . .	2%	7%	76%	5%	4%	6%	100%
Low status	344	. . .	8%	20%	30%	12%	20%	10%	100%
Difference	. . .	. . .	-6%	-13%	45%	-7%	-16%	-4%	. . .
Critical ratio	. . .	. . .	2.3	4.4	12.0	2.8	5.4	1.3	. . .
			Per Cent of Total Wrong Responses						
High status	56	. . .	7%	30%	. . .	20%	18%	25%	100%
Low status	240	. . .	11%	29%	. . .	18%	29%	14%	100%
Difference	. . .	. . .	-4%	2%	. . .	2%	-11%	11%	. . .
Critical ratio	. . .	. . .	0.9	0.2	. . .	0.4	1.8	1.8	. . .

* Based on Old American pupils only; ethnic pupils excluded. Also excludes three high-status and seventeen low-status pupils not reaching this item in the test.

the item do so by checking "drawing" or "phonetics" and that a larger proportion of the high-status pupils who miss the item do so by omitting it entirely. The status differences in these respects are not, however, highly significant. In general, it may be said that the pattern or distribution of wrong responses is about the same for both status groups.

It is true that the total number of wrong responses on this item is much greater for the low-status pupils than for the high-status pupils and that this is not ascertainable from the percentages reported in the third portion of Table 57. This does not seem to be a serious loss, however, since the greater incidence of total wrong responses for low-status pupils is a necessary corollary of the difference in right responses which is already known for the item. Knowing that the high-status pupils answer the item correctly more often than the low-status pupils do, one already knows that the low-status pupils must answer the item incorrectly more often; there is no need to establish this by elaborate analysis of individual distractors.

On items which show precisely the same distribution of errors for both status groups, but with a larger number of errors for the low-status group than for the high-status group, it seems reasonable to expect that the difference is probably related primarily to (a) the injunction, or general statement, of the item; (b) the correct answer; or (c) the general subject matter of the item as a whole. When, however, the distribution of wrong responses is different for the two status groups — not only in the total number of such errors but also in the pattern by which they are distributed over the available distractors — further insight may be gained by careful examination of the distractors for which significant differences are found.

A word of caution should be given with regard to one possible oversimplification in interpreting the data in this chapter. The pupil who looks at a test item does not, presumably, look at each possible distractor in isolation. He responds to the over-all impact of the total item upon him, an impact including all or most of the distractors and the various interrelationships among them. It is an oversimplification to speak of the status difference as being due entirely to characteristics of the correct answer or to the characteristics of some specific distractor. For purposes of analysis it is frequently necessary to isolate one part of the test item and to talk about the pupil's response to it, but the fact that such an interpretation is always an oversimplification should be kept constantly in mind. A number of items will be cited later in this chapter for which it seems fairly clear that status differences found for certain distractors are probably to be explained, not in terms of anything relating to that specific distractor, but rather in terms of the pupil's response to the test item in its totality.

For all the items analyzed by wrong responses the number of responses on each distractor was converted into a percentage of total errors in the status group, in a manner similar to that illustrated in the third section of Table 57. Whenever the total number of errors in the status group was less than ten, however, no percentages were computed, since such percentages would be very unstable. The statistical significance of the differences between the two percentages for the two status groups was then determined for each response on the item.

Of the 315 items for which status comparisons were possible, 43 per cent showed closely similar distributions of wrong responses or errors

248

for both status groups.[1] Seventy-five of the items, however, showed status differences with respect to one or more of the wrong-answer responses that were significant at the 1 per cent level. Sometimes the differences were in favor of the high-status group, sometimes in favor of the low-status group; sometimes there were two distractors on the same item, one of which accounted for a significantly larger proportion of the high-status errors while the other accounted for a significantly larger proportion of the low-status errors. These seventy-five items constitute the subject matter of this chapter.

Basis for Interpretation of Differences
in Wrong Responses

Since the analysis of this and the succeeding chapter is based largely upon a subjective process, it will be wise to state as clearly as possible the basis upon which the subjective judgments are made and the limitations which are inherent in them.

The chief purpose of the examination of items in these two chapters is to discover clues as to possible reasons for unusual degrees of status differences exhibited by certain items in the tests. Particular emphasis will be placed upon the possible relation between the subject matter, or content, of these items and the size of the status differences found for them. For this purpose it is necessary to have some conceptual framework within which to work. What kinds of content or subject matter might be expected to have some bearing on status differences in the items? This question obviously involves a second one: What are the differential experiences and opportunities characteristic of high-status and low-status living which might explain why the pupils in one status group do better than those in another on certain items?

A number of community studies have been carried out by Warner and associates working with him or following his general method of procedure. Fairly complete community analyses have been made of four communities -- one in New England, one in the South, and two in the Midwest. Partial studies of the same general nature have been carried out in several other cities in the Midwest and South.

After an examination of the published reports relating to a number of these studies, the present investigator prepared a statement summarizing certain of the characteristics which seem to distinguish the environments in which high-status children and low-status children are reared. This statement makes no attempt to catalogue all, or even the most important, of the characteristics which differentiate life in high-status culture from life in low-status culture. It is confined to a listing of those characteristics which may have some fairly obvious and direct bearing on the ability of children from different socioeconomic or status backgrounds to answer correctly the kinds of items found in the tests analyzed in this study.

In the interests of uniform terminology, the phrases "high status" and "low status" have been used throughout this statement. The community studies from which the data for this statement were drawn are social-class studies, however, and the characteristics listed are social-class ones. For the present purpose "high status" is taken as the equivalent of upper-middle class, and "low status" is taken as the equivalent of lower class and especially of lower-lower class. This is in accordance with the social-class equivalences established for the status groups as reported earlier.[2] The differences as stated apply to contrasts between high-status Old American groups only. In some of the characteristics listed there may be important ethnic differences; no attempt was made to identify these, however, since the examination of individual items deals entirely with status differences within the Old American group of pupils.

The statement of distinguishing characteristics is organized into three parts, the first dealing with differential school experiences which may give an advantage on intelligence test items to high-status pupils, the second dealing with differential nonschool experiences, and the third dealing with certain general factors which may affect differentially the motivation for school work of pupils from the two status groups.

It is impossible, of course, to generalize about the patterns of behavior and attitudes of large groups of people without greatly oversimplifying many of the relationships. It is believed, however, that the statement below describes general group characteristics fairly accurately, although it would certainly not apply to every family in either status group. For a more complete discussion of the differences listed here, and their origins and results, the reader is referred to the published reports (6, 7, 8, 12, 14, 16, 20) from which the following statement was prepared:

I. School experiences which high-status pupils may be expected to have more frequently than low-status pupils and which may give high-status pupils an advantage over low-status pupils on certain kinds of test items.

A. High-status pupils will be found predominantly in college-preparatory curriculums, while low-status pupils will be found predominantly in commercial and "general" courses. If test items are drawn from materials covered in the college-preparatory curriculums only (e.g., an item involving knowledge of abstract geometric terms), low-status pupils will be penalized.

B. Where pupils are divided into sections on the basis of "ability," the divisions will be at least in part based upon social-status lines. To the extent that curricular material for the different sections is differentiated and test items are drawn mostly from the material for the "high ability" group, low-status pupils will be penalized.

C. Low-status pupils tend to be retarded in school more frequently and more seriously than high-status pupils. At any given age level, low-status pupils will not, on the average, have had as advanced school work as high-status pupils.

D. School boards frequently spend more money for equipment and provide better educational facilities and better teachers for schools in predominantly high-status areas than for schools in predominantly low-status areas. Thus in actual practice the effective learning opportunities of the two groups may not be the same even though both have attended school the same length of time in the same school system.

---

1. "Closely similar" is defined as being such that for no one of the distractors for the item is the status difference large enough to be significant even at the 10 per cent level. For reference to a more detailed analysis of the different kinds of wrong-answer patterns found see Note 1 in Appendix D.

2. See p. 125.

E. The vocabulary and grammar taught in schools is "good" vocabulary and grammar from the high-status point of view; the school's efforts to inculcate it are, therefore, reinforced by the example and precepts of the child's parents and age mates. Since the school vocabulary and grammar are quite different from those typical of low-status homes, the school's effort are not reinforced by the culture in which the low-status child grows up.

II. Nonschool experiences which high-status pupils may be expected to have more frequently than low-status pupils and which may give high-status pupils an advantage over low-status pupils on certain kinds of test items.

A. High-status pupils live in larger, better-kept, and better-furnished homes than low-status pupils. A test item which requires familiarity with a fireplace, for example, would probably be easier for high-status pupils than for low-status pupils, although the relationship would vary with the region of the country and with its rural-urban nature.

B. High-status pupils are much more likely than low-status pupils to go on both short and long trips with their families. If test items deal with information that can be acquired from a zoo or museum in the city in which the pupil lives, for instance — or from travel in other parts of the country — high-status pupils will have an advantage.

C. High-status families are more active in churches, and their children in Sunday schools, than is true of the low-status families. If test items deal with materials which could be learned in Sunday school, low-status children will be at a disadvantage.

D. High-status families provide their children with a variety of toys and games. Low-status families have few or none. If a test item involves, for example, a process which may be learned through the playing of anagrams, high-status pupils will probably have an advantage.

E. High-status children are more likely than low-status children to be found in summer camps. If test questions deal with outdoor or camp life, urban low-status pupils may be at a disadvantage.

F. High-status children are more likely than low-status children to belong to such organizations as Boy and Girl Scouts.

G. High-status children are likely to have access to more, and to "better," books, magazines, and newspapers than low-status pupils. A test item involving geographical knowledge, for example, might give an advantage to high-status pupils, since magazines like the National Geographic Magazine are more likely to be found in high-status homes than in low-status homes.

H. High-status children will certainly have more access than low-status children to dramatic, operatic, and concert productions. A test item involving knowledge of a symphony orchestra instrument may for this reason be a culturally biased one.

I. High-status children are more likely than low-status children to have the desire, the encouragement, and the financial resources

251

to have one or more hobbies. A test item dealing with amateur photography, for example, may be a biased one on which high-status pupils would have an advantage.

J. Special educational facilities — dancing schools, art classes, music lessons, and the like — are more likely to be accessible to high-status pupils than to low-status pupils. A test question requiring knowledge of a musical instrument would probably give an advantage to the high-status pupils.

K. The parents of high-status children are mostly college educated, while the parents of low-status children are relatively poorly educated. This means that high-status children are exposed to "good" English in their homes and with their age mates (who are carefully selected by parents) and are rewarded by parental praise for speaking good English and reprimanded for speaking poor English. Low-status children hear "poor" English in their homes and from their age mates. For this reason, high-status pupils may be expected to have an advantage on test items requiring knowledge of vocabulary, since most items almost invariably are based on the kind of words more common in high-status usage rather than upon those more common in low-status usage.

L. The parents of high-status children spend more time in informal educational activities (teaching, reading, hiking, conversation, etc.) than do low-status parents.[3]

III. General factors which may affect the motivation and the effectiveness of the learning which high-status and low-status pupils derive from the school experiences which they do have.

A. High-status and low-status attitudes toward education and "self-improvement" are different.

1. High-status people place a high value on conformity of the individual to the "social" (i.e., middle-class) standards. Socialization of the child into middle-class society is important, and deviations from socially accepted patterns are not tolerated. The low-status code involves group loyalties, but they usually apply only to the gang and the family. Low-status behavior and ideology involve a disdain for the values of the middle class and a rebellion from any attempt to enforce or inculcate them. Greater importance is, therefore, attached by high-status families to the socializing influence of education. This function is of little importance in the eyes of the low-status families.

2. Both high- and low-status groups regard education as a means of social mobility through self-improvement. This is likely to be, however, a stronger drive for a larger proportion of

3. Davis, Gardner, and Gardner report, for instance, that "middle-class couples . . . spend many evenings at home alone, reading, sewing, conversing . . . . Lower-class parents do not attempt to entertain their children, nor are they entertained by them except as babies. Parents and children seldom converse together except to exchange particular information or when parents give commands" (7, pp. 102, 129).

252

the high-status families than of the low-status families.

3. High-status parents have relatively good educations themselves, and they expect their children to go through college; most of the low-status parents have had relatively little education, and their educational aspirations for their children are lower. The majority of low-status children do not expect to go to college.

4. There is more emphasis among low-status families upon the child holding an after-school job earlier than in the case of high-status families, and upon quitting school to go to work at an earlier age. This is partly economic, partly seeking for status satisfactions on the part of the low-status child, and partly a feeling that a person who is "too educated" is a misfit in the community.

B. High-status and low-status attitudes toward school authorities and school routine are different.

1. High-status families inculcate respect for the teacher and other school authorities, as part of a general respect for authorities and for law and order. Low-status families are not so acquiescent or submissive.[4]

2. High-status families watch the school progress of their child carefully, insist upon regular attendance, supervise homework, check report cards, and co-operate closely with the teachers and school authorities. Low-status parents take little interest in the daily progress of their children, permit more unsupervised roaming of the streets at night, and confine their contacts with the school to those insisted upon by the school authorities.

3. High-status families urge and encourage their children to work hard and to do their best on school work whether they are interested in it or not. They reward the child with praise, and sometimes with more tangible rewards, for working hard, and they punish laxness, thus reinforcing the school's own system of rewards and punishments. Low-status families take little interest in this.

4. The importance of getting high grades is regarded much more seriously by high-status families than by low-status families, and this attitude is inculcated into high-status children.

5. The greater degree of social and economic security which characterize high-status family life creates a more favorable psychological learning "climate" for high-status pupils than that which obtains for low-status pupils.

6. The greater stability and permanence of family relationships in high-status homes give the high-status pupil a greater sense of personal security and allow for a closer degree of parental supervision than is possible for the low-status child

who is frequently the center of bickering and antagonism between parent and step-parent.

7. Low-status children are frequently punished by means of whipping and other physical punishments which may lead to the development of aggressions which the low-status child takes out in resisting the authority of the school. This is not so likely to happen to high-status pupils because of differences in the kind and frequency of punishments inflicted by the parents.

C. High-status culture places a much greater emphasis upon language and upon its "correct" usage, than does low-status culture.[5]

1. The use of language in both spoken and written forms constitutes a more important part of the occupational activities of high-status persons than of low-status persons.

2. The use of "correct" language is regarded by high-status culture as a status symbol and is therefore heavily emphasized. For the low-status child the use of the form of language used by his age mates in the gang carries much more prestige value than does "correct" language.

D. Long-term goals for learning are more realistic and effective for high-status pupils than for low-status pupils.

1. High-status culture places great emphasis upon the child's working for long-term goals — professional education, career, marriage with economic security, etc. Low-status culture cannot emphasize long-term goals because for the most part they do not exist for the low-status pupils. When the school seeks to use long-term goals, low-status children recognize them as unrealistic.

2. The emphasis upon realistic long-term goals makes it possible for high-status parents to teach their children to work hard on school work for its own sake even if it seems of no momentary interest or importance. Low-status pupils see no reward for working hard at school unless it is an immediate one inherent in the interest of the material itself.

E. The school promises and encourages high-status values rather

---

4. "His /a lower-class boy's/ family and his gang teach him not to be afraid of a fight, not to be intimidated by the teacher and the police" (8, p. 26).

5. "In middleclass life, language is a serious business. The middleclass child learns very early that making a proper living depends on the right use of language. In many cases he learns that his father talks or writes for a living. In all cases he learns that his language is a mark of his station in life. 'Johnny, don't say that; nice boys don't talk like that,' says his mother over and over again . . . .

"For the lowerclass child, however, language does not count heavily in the task of earning a living. Unless he happens to be reared by parents who train him to 'climb the social ladder,' the lowerclass child is almost certain to stay far behind the middleclass child in the extent of his vocabulary, in the accuracy of his grammar, and in his interest in reading" (8, pp. 114-15).

than low-status values. Its efforts are thus reinforced at every turn by the interests and activities of the parents — in the case of the high-status child — but contradicted by the parents and age mates of the low-status child.

1. The school board, administrators, and teachers are all predominantly high status, and many of their actions consciously or unconsciously involve the imposition of high-status patterns of behavior on both high-status and low-status pupils.

2. In formulating judgments about pupils, high-status teachers usually apply high-status standards. The rewards of success thus go to the high-status children and to those low-status children who are socially mobile and who try therefore to be most like the high-status children.

It is the possible influence of factors such as those listed above which is sought for in the examination of individual items reported in this and in the next chapter. It will not be possible on the basis of the available data to arrive at final conclusions with regard to the reasons for status differences; it should, however, be possible to use these items as a basis for establishing some tentative hypotheses as a basis for further research.

After examination of the analytical data available for each item, the writer tried to use his own judgment and insight to find possible explanations for the status differences — explanations either in terms of known characteristics of high-status and low-status culture or in terms of reasonable hypotheses as to such characteristics. The subjective nature of this process should be frankly recognized. No claim is made that the explanations offered here are the only possible ones or that they are necessarily sufficient to account for all the status difference found for any given item. No claim is made that another analyst would necessarily make the same interpretations or agree with all those suggested by the present writer — or that he would not see in the data other possible interpretations not suggested here. The explanations suggested in the rest of this chapter represent the judgment and insight of one individual. The data upon which they are based are presented in full, so that the reader may make his own interpretations if he wishes to do so.

No attempt will be made to "explain" every significant difference found. To do so would be entirely beyond the power of the present investigator. It would involve an omniscience with regard to details of language, everyday happenings, and conceptual outlook in the life of high-status pupils as compared to those of low-status pupils which he does not possess. Furthermore, it would involve the entirely unwarranted assumption that there must exist some cultural explanation for all variations found. Where comparisons or possible explanations seem to the present writer to be significant, or to offer some promise of being so, they will be presented.

The mere fact that no explanation is suggested for an item in the pages which follow does not, of course, suggest in any way that there may not be an entirely legitimate explanation of the differences in these items, similar in nature to those suggested for other items. Indeed, the items included in this chapter are included because the status differences are large enough that it is unlikely that they could be chance sampling errors. It is to be expected, therefore, that some explanation exists for most of the differences -- even if the explanation is beyond the insight of the investigator.

There is danger, of course, in the procedure of looking for reasons

for differences which have already been shown to exist. There may be a tendency to rationalize these differences without sufficient checking. When a classification item, for example, exhibits an unusually large status difference, it would be easy to conclude that the status difference is characteristic of the classification process, without checking to see that other classification items show unusually small status differences. On some items which show virtually no status difference, it is possible to point out what seem to be perfectly reasonable explanations as to why a status difference on such items would be expected. A few examples of this sort will be found in this chapter. There can be no assurance that the writer has been entirely successful in his effort to avoid this fallacy. Checks are provided against more flagrant misinterpretations, however, by the statistical analysis of different types of items reported in chapters xvii to xxi and by contrasting the characteristics of large-difference items with those of small-difference items, which will be reported in chapter xxiii.

Two different methods of computing percentages of wrong responses were illustrated on pages 246 to 248, and the reason for selecting percentages based upon total errors rather than upon total pupils was explained. In interpreting the data for these seventy-five items which show significant differences, however, it was found that it was sometimes helpful to have the percentages computed both ways. For each of these items, therefore, percentage distributions will be given on both bases, but most of the interpretation will be derived from the percentages based on total errors. The two methods of computing percentages bring out somewhat different characteristics of the pupils' responses; having both of them in mind when the data are being interpreted is sometimes helpful. It is important, however, to keep the differences between the two sets of percentages clearly in mind when examining the item data in this chapter.

In examining the wrong-answer data computed as explained above, attention was directed in each item to four different kinds of status differences. These may be expressed in question form as follows:

1. Is the status difference with respect to the correct response large enough to be significant?

2. Is the most popular, or most attractive, distractor the same for both status groups, or does one status group concentrate most heavily on one distractor while the other concentrates most heavily on another?

3. On what distractors do the proportion of errors for the two status groups exhibit significant differences? In favor of which status group?

4. Is the degree of concentration of the high-status group on any wrong answer sufficient that the proportion of the total high-status group (not high-status errors only) checking the response is significantly greater than for the low-status group, contrary to normal expectations?

While all available data with respect to the item will be presented, primary interest will be centered, in this chapter, on the different patterns observed among the wrong responses. The interest in these items will be focused on trying to understand why more high-status pupils than low-status pupils checked a given response, not on merely explaining why both groups of pupils may have been more distracted by one response than by another. It is status differences that are to be analyzed.

For ease of discussion it will be convenient to classify these seventy-five items which show significant differences in the distribution of wrong responses according to the type of explanation which seems most reasonably to account for the kind of difference found.

Differential cultural familiarity with an object, process, or word

It has already been pointed out that there are many cultural objects or experiences which are found more frequently in the homes of one status level than in those of another. Grand pianos, evening dresses, and attendance at concerts or stage productions are undoubtedly more characteristic of high-status life than of low-status life. Work clothes, tenement-type housing and furniture, and attendance at a corner tavern are more characteristic of low-status life than of high-status life.

Several of the items which show significant wrong-answer distributions deal with some of these culturally biased objects or experiences -- in every case with objects or experiences which are probably more familiar in high-status than in low-status homes. In such cases it is certainly not surprising to find that a higher proportion of high-status pupils are able to answer the questions correctly. Several items of this type will be discussed here; additional ones will be found in the next chapter.

Objects. — The analytical data for the first item of this type are shown in Table 58. The form in which the data are presented in this table will be followed for all the items in this chapter. The first two lines of percentages show, for the high- and low-status groups, respectively, the percentage distribution of errors. For this item it will be seen that more high-status errors occur on the fourth response (the piano) than on any other, while more low-status errors occur on the first response (the harp) than on any other one. The double asterisks on two sets of these percentages indicate that the status difference with respect to each of these two distractors is large enough to be significant at the 1 per cent level. For later items a single asterisk on each of a pair of percentages will indicate a difference significant at the 5 per cent level. Unstarred pairs of percentages (for the error data) do not differ from each other by enough to be significant even at the 5 per cent level.

The second two lines of percentages show, for the two status groups, the percentage distribution of total responses, including both right and wrong responses. For this second set of percentages, the level of statistical significance is reported, by means of asterisk, only for (a) the correct response and (b) any wrong response for which the high-status pupils show a higher percentage than do the low-status pupils. When, as is usually the case, the data on the wrong responses show a higher proportion for the low-status pupils, the statistical significance is not reported.

It is important for proper interpretation of these data that the two different sets of bases be kept clearly in mind. Which set of percentages will be most useful in gaining insight into status differences will vary from item to item and according to the nature of the inference to be drawn with respect to the item. So long as the difference in the meaning of the two sets of percentages is kept clearly in mind, however, having both sets of data should give more insight into the nature of the responses than would either set of figures alone.

TABLE 58[+]

ITEM SHOWING STATUS DIFFERENCE IN WRONG RESPONSES

(Nine- and Ten-Year-Old Pupils)

Status Group	Base for Computing Percentages		Percentage Distribution of Responses				
	Number of Pupils	Number of Errors	Find the three things that are alike and draw a line through the one that is not like those three —				(omit)
High	...	77	25%**	....	...	60%**	9%
Low	...	170	51%**	....	...	36%**	6%
High	223	...	9%	2%	65%**	20%	3%
Low	319	...	27%	4%	46%**	19%	3%

[+] This is the first of a series of similar tables in this chapter, each of which presents data for an individual test item. An explanation of the asterisks in the table, and of the proper manner of interpreting the two sets of percentage figures, will be found in the text accompanying this first table. All the data reported for individual items in this chapter are based on Old American pupils only; ethnic pupils are excluded. The "omit" column includes only pupils who reached the point in the test where the particular item occurs. Pupils who did not reach the item (never more than 5 per cent of any status group) are not included in the table, although they were included in the original computations; for this reason the totals of the percentages will sometimes be slightly less than 100 per cent. All the items reproduced in this chapter are taken from copyrighted tests and are reproduced here by special arrangement with the owners of the copyrights. The items may not be reproduced in any manner without the prior permission of the test publishers.

In Table 58 it will be readily seen that the high-status errors tend to occur from checking the piano, while the low-status errors tend to occur from the checking the harp. Although the high-status errors are concentrated on the piano, there are not enough of them to cause the proportion of the total status group checking the piano to exceed by any substantial amount the proportion of the total low-status group checking it. Comparatively few pupils in either status group check the violin.

It is undoubtedly true that high-status pupils have more opportunity for firsthand familiarity with concert orchestras and also that they are more likely to have a piano in their own home. Is it possible that the high-status pupils who do not answer the item "correctly" think of the harp, drum, and violin as being orchestral instruments, while they think of the piano as a home recreational instrument? Would such a response be incorrect? On the other hand, is it possible that many low-status pupils, having little acquaintance with concert orchestras, do not recognize the harp as a musical instrument? If that should be the case, would it not be natural for them to see the other three objects as musical instruments and to guess that it must be the strange unknown object which is the different one? There is no way, on the basis of these data, to establish whether an explanation such as this is the correct one, but it seems reasonable, and it fits the data reported for the item.

A still further explanation may be suggested. The item presumably requires for its correct answering (a) an understanding of the distinction between stringed and nonstringed instruments and (b) knowledge that the piano, despite its outward appearance, is a stringed instrument. But is not this whole idea a fairly sophisticated notion for pupils nine and ten years old? Will not those pupils who by this age have had private musical instruction be far more likely to have the necessary musical knowledge? It may be safely assumed that the incidence of private musical instruction is much greater among high-status pupils than among low-status pupils. Certainly pupils who have pianos in their own homes will be more likely to know that the piano is a stringed instrument than will those pupils who have seen a piano only from afar.

The next item to be considered (Table 59) is very similar to the preceding one but is in verbal form and is taken from the tests for the older pupils. On this item the high-status errors tend to cluster on "guitar," while the low-status errors are heavily concentrated on "cello." Much of the same line of argument developed in connection with the preceding item will apply equally to this one. May it not be that some of the high-status pupils, with their presumed greater familiarity with concert orchestras, will classify the first four instruments in this item as orchestral, while a guitar is thought of as an instrument for personal recreational playing? As a matter of fact, could not such a classification be defended as correct, even though it does not conform to the idea intended by the test author? On the other hand, it seems entirely reasonable to guess that the low-status pupils who checked "cello" may in many cases have done so because they recognized the other four words as representing musical instruments but did not recognize the strange word "cello." One may even suspect that if they had seen a picture of a cello, or perhaps even have heard the word instead of seeing it in print, their responses might have been different. Certainly the ability to distinguish between a percussion instrument and a stringed instrument is related to the incidence of music instruction.

The fact that so few pupils of either status group check "harp" on

259

TABLE 59[+]

ITEM SHOWING STATUS DIFFERENCE IN WRONG RESPONSES

(Thirteen- and Fourteen-Year-Old Pupils)

Status Group	Base for Computing Percentages		Percentage Distribution of Responses					
	Number of Pupils	Number of Errors	Pick out the **ONE WORD** which does not belong with the others —					
			cello	harp	drum	violin	guitar	(omit)
High...	. . .	37	19%**	5%	. . . .	0%	76%**	0%
Low...	. . .	196	48%**	8%	. . . .	5%	37%**	2%
High...	233	. . .	3%	1%	84%**	0%	12%	0%
Low...	361	. . .	26%	4%	45%**	2%	20%	1%

[+] See note to Table 58, on p. 258, for explanation of method for reading this and all subsequent tables in this chapter.

this item, whereas a good many do so on the preceding pictorial item, may be due to (a) the presence in this item of an even less-well-known instrument, the cello; (b) the fact that the older children have had more opportunity through observing the school orchestra to learn what a harp is; or (c) the fact that some pupils may recognize the word "harp" as the name of a musical instrument, even though they may not know the appearance of a concert harp. Children's books frequently portray a celestial harp in a form which would scarcely aid a pupil in identifying a picutre of a concert harp!

A somewhat similar kind of explanation may be suggested for the item in Table 60. On this item the high-status pupils who do not select the correct "marbles" show a marked preference for "map" as the correct answer, to the extent that even on the basis of the total group of pupils, a slightly larger proportion of the high-status pupils than of low-status pupils check "map." The low-status pupils, on the other hand, tend to distribute their errors almost equally between "map" and "slate."

One possible explanation for this differenee occurs to the writer, although it must be admitted that the explanation is a highly conjectural one. It is possible that the high-status pupils see in "book," "marbles," "pencil," and "slate" four objects all of which are associated with school, while "map" may be a relatively unknown term to them. This presupposes (a) that maps have not yet played an important part in the school life of pupils of this age and (b) that the pupil does not make the same distinction between curricular and extra-curricular school experiences that the test-maker and the educator are prone to make! While it is doubtful that many of these pupils have ever had any firsthand experience with a slate, except possibly as a toy, they may recognize it as a school object from illustrations

260

TABLE 60

ITEM SHOWING STATUS DIFFERENCE IN WRONG RESPONSES

(Nine- and Ten-Year-Old Pupils)

Status Group	Base for Computing Percentages		Percentage Distribution of Responses					
	Number of Pupils	Number of Errors	Find the one that does not belong with the others in the list —					
			book	marbles	pencil	map	slate	(omit)
High...	...	84	8%	....	13%	61%**	17%**	1%
Low...	...	165	12%	....	6%	37%**	38%**	7%
High...	225	...	3%	63%**	5%	23%	6%	0%
Low...	327	...	6%	48%**	3%	19%	19%	3%

TABLE 61

ITEM SHOWING STATUS DIFFERENCE IN WRONG RESPONSES

(Nine- and Ten-Year-Old Pupils)

Status Group	Base for Computing Percentages		Percentage Distribution of Responses					
	Number of Pupils	Number of Errors	A fire always has --					
			wood	coal	gas	warmth	furnace	(omit)
High...	...	69	58%**	30%	4%	....	6%	1%
Low...	...	200	36%**	36%	11%	....	12%	6%
High...	226	...	18%	9%	1%	69%**	2%	0%
Low...	322	...	22%	22%	7%	38%**	7%	4%

in primers they have read. Low-status pupils, on the other hand, may check either "map" or "slate," the former following the same line of reasoning just suggested for high-status pupils, and the latter because a slate is to them an unknown object which they assume to be different from the others which they identify as school objects. The crux of this argument lies in the assumption that because of wider reading on the part of high-status pupils, and possibly because of having toy slates as well, the word "slate" might be more easily recognizable as a school object for high-status pupils than for low-status ones.

An alternative explanation may be that some pupils think of a book, marbles, a pencil, and a slate as objects which children themselves own, while a map is in a different category. It may be that the high-status pupils have a more highly developed property sense and so make this kind of classification more frequently than do the low-status pupils. Low-status pupils, for example, are not so likely to regard a book as a personal possession.

The next item (Table 61) is one dealing with subject matter which is probably culturally biased on the basis of home, rather than school, learning. This item requires the pupil to select an abstract quality, "warmth," which a fire always has, rather than some specific physical characteristic which many fires have. The rather substantial difference in the proportion of right responses for the two status groups may be due at least in part to greater facility of high-status children with abstract terms. It is probably true that abstraction as a thought-process and the use of abstract words are a more frequent part of high-status family conversation than they are of low-status family conversation.

Regardless of the difference on the right responses, however, there is an interesting contrast between the most popular distractors. Those high-status pupils who do miss the item check "wood" almost twice as often as "coal," while those low-status pupils who miss the item check

"wood" and "coal" approximately equally (with a slightly higher frequency for "coal"). It seems probable that many high-status children would think of "fire" as a fireplace fire, since the furnace is out of sight and is usually not the responsibility of the child in high-status homes. This being the case, the high-status pupils' preference for "wood" over "coal" is understandable. Low-status pupils, on the other hand, are not likely to have fireplaces in their homes and are probably much more likely to think of "fire" as signifying the stove which heats their house or rooms. This heating stove will be more in evidence in a low-status home than the furnace in a high-status home, and the low-status child frequently has some part in taking care of it. Since such stoves usually burn coal, the relatively greater incidence of low-status responses on "coal" is understandable.

Another item which may involve subject matter more likely to be familiar to one status group than to another is shown in Table 62. This item might well be expected to show a greater amount of status difference on various wrong responses than it actually does. It would not be surprising to find high-status pupils checking the fourth and fifth responses more frequently than the low-status pupils do, since it is probably true that "is gold" and "costs more" tend to be characteristic of the watches which high-status pupils see -- at least to a greater extent than would be true of the watches in a low-status household. The status difference on "ticks louder" may represent this kind of differentiation. The cheaper dollar and two-dollar watches do tick very loudly! While it is doubtful that very many tick more loudly than a clock, certainly an error of this kind for a low-status pupil would be easier to understand than for a high-status pupil who is familiar with his father's expensive gold watch! The fact that both status groups check "runs faster" more frequently than any other distractor seems completely beyond explanation. Could it be that some of these pupils are thinking of the second hand which they may have seen on a watch and not ordinarily on a clock?

TABLE 62

ITEM SHOWING STATUS DIFFERENCE IN WRONG RESPONSES

(Nine- and Ten-Year-Old Pupils)

Status Group	Base for Computing Percentages		Percentage Distribution of Responses					
	Number of Pupils	Number of Errors	The most important difference between a watch and a clock is that a watch —					
			runs faster	is smaller	ticks louder	is gold	costs more	(omit)
High...	...	36	33%	....	6%**	19%	33%	8%
Low...	...	128	27%	....	23%**	18%	23%	9%
High...	226	...	5%	84%**	1%	3%	5%	1%
Low...	322	...	11%	60%**	9%	7%	9%	4%

The item in Table 63 is interesting in that the status groups do almost equally well in selecting the correct answer (the status difference on the right response is not significant even at the 35 per cent level), but the distribution of wrong answers shows significant differences for the two groups. Both status groups check the kite more often than they do the balloon, but the high-status pupils show a more marked tendency in this direction, while the low-status pupils show a relatively greater tendency to check the balloon. The low-status concentration on the balloon is significant at the 1 per cent level; the high-status concentration on kite is significantly greater than the low-status one at the 5 per cent level.

Partial explanations for these differences are not difficult to see. If a pupil recognizes the third picture as that of an old-fashioned hot-air balloon (and almost certainly he can do so only from reading), he will probably see that three of the objects are flying objects while the truck is not. This is presumably the mental process which the author of the text expected, since the key calls for the marking of the truck as the right answer. If, however, a pupil did not recognize the hot-air balloon, because he had never had any opportunity for familiarity with hot-air balloons, he might well pick out the balloon itself as the correct response, on the ground that it is circular in shape whereas the other three are all angular. This ambiguity of the question makes it a bad test item in any case, but if, as seems probable, there is reason to believe that opportunity for the required familiarity with hot-air balloons is greater for one status group than for another, it is even worse.

The concentration of responses on the kite can likewise be accounted for on the basis that the kite may be regarded as having a recreational function, while the other three all have business functions, or that the kite is a child's toy and the other three are all adult equipment. It is not clear, however, why the kite should prove a more attractive response to high-status pupils than to low-status pupils. One possibility is that high-status

263

TABLE 63

ITEM SHOWING STATUS DIFFERENCE IN WRONG RESPONSES

(Nine- and Ten-Year-Old Pupils)

Status Group	Base for Computing Percentages		Percentage Distribution of Responses				
	Number of Pupils	Number of Errors	Find the three things that are alike and draw a line through the one that is not like those three —				
							(omit)
High....	...	84	...	0%	18%**	74%*	8%
Low....	...	133	...	2%	33%**	59%**	6%
High....	223	...	62%	0%	7%	28%	3%
Low....	319	...	58%	1%	14%	24%	3%

pupils tend to categorize more abstractly, in terms of function, while low-status pupils tend to categorize more concretely, in terms of physical shape.

Arithmetic processes. -- The five items which follow are all arithmetic problems or questions involving arithmetical processes. Even before examining the specific data for these items it may be remarked that arithmetic items would be expected, almost necessarily, to exhibit considerable status difference. It was pointed out at the beginning of this chapter that for various reasons low-status pupils are likely to be less well motivated for doing the most effective school work than are the high-status pupils. This being the case, items dealing with school-learned material are likely to show advantages for high-status pupils — advantages which may reflect the fact that those pupils have worked harder in the past, but which do not necessarily reflect differences in ability to solve problems. Furthermore, the fact that low-status children tend to be retarded in school grade as compared with high-status pupils means that at any given time when an intelligence test is given the low-status pupils have been exposed to less of the necessary school learning than have the high-status pupils..

On the other hand, it is known that low-status children actually have more opportunity than high-status children to use arithmetic processes in meaningful situations. The low-status children typically have more responsibility for helping with the family purchasing and for the actual handling of money, checking change, etc., than do high-status pupils. This may be expected to give them an advantage in dealing with arithmetic problems of a practical rather than of an academic type.

In the item in Table 64 the correct answer is "16" and the most potent distractor, for both status groups, is "12," but a larger proportion of the high-status group than of the low-status group is found to check "12," while the reverse is true for the distractor "3." The explanation for this seems to be a rather simple one. It is fairly clear that most of those pupils who check "12" instead of "16" do so because they have identified the error in the series but have overlooked, or did not understand, the direction which specified that they were not only to locate the error but to correct it. The pupils who checked "3," on the other hand, very likely did not understand the nature of a geometric series and merely noticed the first gap in a straightforward enumeration of digits. If this be the case, the first error can be regarded as a less serious one than the second, since the first indicates at least an understanding of what a series is — although accompanied by carelessness in reading or following the directions.

The item in Table 65 is similar to the one just discussed except that the kind of series involved is probably less likely to be covered by specific school teaching. The concentration of wrong responses for both status groups on "8" in this item apparently reflects the same kind of error noticed in connection with the preceding item, namely, the location of the error in the series but failure to observe the instruction to correct the error as well as to locate it. It will be noticed that the piling-up of high-status errors on this response is great enough to result in a slight reversal of the percentages when computed on the basis of the total number of pupils. It is not at all clear, however, why there is a significant secondary piling-up of low-status errors on the "4" response.

For the item in Table 66 it should be noticed that there is practically no status difference with respect to the correct responses. The item is so difficult for pupils in both status groups that only 12 per cent of the high-

TABLE 64

ITEM SHOWING STATUS DIFFERENCE IN WRONG RESPONSES

(Thirteen- and Fourteen-Year-Old Pupils)

Status Group	Base for Computing Percentages		Percentage Distribution of Responses					
	Number of Pupils	Number of Errors	One number is wrong in this series. 1 2 4 8 12 32 64 What should that number be? –					
			6	12	3	16	48	(omit)
High...	...	114	11%	54%**	13%**	....	12%	10%
Low...	...	266	19%	34%**	26%**	....	12%	9%
High...	235	....	6%	26%	6%	49%**	6%	5%
Low...	364	...	14%	25%	19%	23%**	9%	6%

TABLE 65

ITEM SHOWING STATUS DIFFERENCE IN WRONG RESPONSES

(Thirteen- and Fourteen-Year-Old Pupils)

Status Group	Base for Computing Percentages		Percentage Distribution of Responses					
	Number of Pupils	Number of Errors	One number is wrong in the following series. 1 7 2 7 3 7 4 7 5 7 6 7 8 7 What should that number be? –					
			6	7	8	4	5	(omit)
High...	...	85	5%	...	87%**	2%**	1%	5%
Low...	...	167	9%	...	63%**	15%**	5%	8%
High...	235	...	2%	64%*	31%	1%	0%	2%
Low...	364	...	4%	54%*	29%	7%	2%	4%

265

TABLE 66

ITEM SHOWING STATUS DIFFERENCE IN WRONG RESPONSES

(Thirteen- and Fourteen-Year-Old Pupils)

Status Group	Base for Computing Percentages		Percentage Distribution of Responses				
	Number of Pupils	Number of Errors	If a cubical block if (sic) ice 5 inches square weighs 6 $\frac{1}{4}$ pounds, how many pounds will a cubical block 10 inches square weigh? —				
			$12\frac{1}{2}$	$11\frac{1}{4}$	50	100	(omit)
High...	...	201	87%**	6%**	...	2%	5%
Low...	...	288	71%**	20%**	...	5%	5%
High...	235	...	74%**	6%	12%	2%	4%
Low...	352	...	58%**	16%	14%	4%	4%

TABLE 67

ITEM SHOWING STATUS DIFFERENCE IN WRONG RESPONSES

(Thirteen- and Fourteen-Year-Old Pupils)

Status Group	Base for Computing Percentages		Percentage Distribution of Responses					
	Number of Pupils	Number of Errors	At 4 cents each, how many pencils can be bought for 36 cents? —					
			40	32	36	9	144	(omit)
High...	...	18	11%	0%*	0%*	....	89%**	0%
Low...	...	67	9%	16%*	24%*	....	49%**	1%
High...	235	...	1%	0%	0%	92%**	7%	0%
Low...	364	...	2%	3%	4%	82%**	9%	0%

status pupils and 14 per cent of the low-status pupils get it right, despite the fact that 25 per cent of each group might be expected to hit the right answer if they merely closed their eyes and chose an answer at random. This is one of those items for which there is a very potent distractor which misleads the great majority of the pupils. Over half of the low-status and nearly three-fourths of the high-status pupils indicated "12 $\frac{1}{2}$" as the answer instead of the correct "50." This accounted for 87 per cent of the high-status errors and 71 per cent of the low-status errors. This error is an easily understandable one, of course, reflecting a lack of understanding of the nature of the volume of a cube. It is perhaps significant, however, that some 20 per cent of the low-status errors are of a different kind, involving the distractor "11 $\frac{1}{4}$" which was apparently arrived at by simply adding the "5 inches" and the " 6 $\frac{1}{4}$ pounds" mentioned in the injunction of the item. Very few of the high-status pupils made this gross error.

Even though the status difference on the right answer is practically zero for this item, due to its extreme difficulty for both status groups, there is evidence in the wrong-answer distribution to suggest that a number of the low-status pupils were even more seriously at fault in their analysis of the problem than were any sizable group of the high-status pupils. This status difference, like that for the number series just discussed, may well be due to differences in school learning brought about by differences in motivation, differences in retardation, and differences in proportion of pupils enrolled in formal mathematics courses.

The item in Table 67 was relatively easy for both status groups. Those errors which did occur tended to be made on "144" for both status groups. This was apparently the result of multiplying the two figures given in the injunction instead of dividing them. It might be argued that the substitution of multiplication for division in such a problem represents a less serious error than the substitution of addition or subtraction, which

presumably accounted for some 25 per cent of the low-status errors. If this is accepted, this item bears out the hypothesis developed earlier, namely, that the low-status pupils make more serious errors than the high-status pupils, even on items where the status difference on the right response is not large. This would be expected if the high-status pupils have the advantages mentioned earlier with respect to school motivation and grade acceleration. It is doubtful that the greater incidence of high-status pupils in more formal mathematics courses would give the high-status pupils any advantage on this particular item; as a matter of fact, this item is just the kind of material which frequently occupies a considerable proportion of the "general" mathematics courses in which the low-status pupils tend to be enrolled.

The last arithmetic item is the one reported in Table 68. This is a relatively difficult item for both status groups, but especially so for the low-status pupils. It is easy to understand how many of the pupils in both status groups arrive at "7" as the answer by adding up the number of boxes mentioned in the injunction and forgetting to allow for the implications of the "each." It is probable that those pupils who check "6" as the right answer do so as a result of adding the two 3's in the injunction, not only overlooking the implications of "each" but also forgetting to include the "large box." Here again the low-status errors show a heavier incidence on a response representing an even more serious error than the one which accounts for most of the high-status errors. This is not so specifically a type of arithmetic characteristic of the usual junior high school mathematics courses, but it is still probably true that a pupil used to handling numerical data and to thinking clearly with regard to it would have an advantage with respect to an item such as this one.

Proverbs. -- Four of the items which show significant status differences with respect to the wrong responses are items requiring familiarity with proverbs and the ability to interpret their meanings.

TABLE 68

ITEM SHOWING STATUS DIFFERENCE IN WRONG RESPONSES

(Thirteen- and Fourteen-Year-Old Pupils)

Status Group	Base for Computing Percentages		Percentage Distribution of Responses					
			If I have a large box with 3 small boxes in it and 3 very small boxes in each small box, how many boxes are there in all? —					
	Number of Pupils	Number of Errors	6	7	3	12	13	(omit)
High...	...	109	5%**	63%*	3%	28%	....	1%
Low...	...	265	18%**	50%*	5%	25%	....	2%
High...	235	...	2%	29%	1%	13%	51%**	1%
Low...	364	...	13%	37%	3%	18%	23%**	1%

The item in Table 69 consists of a proverb and four possible interpretations. The first and last responses are literal interpretations, using the same words as in the proverb; the middle two interpretations involve a figurative meaning to be read into the proverb. It will be seen that the high-status pupils distribute their relatively few errors over all three distractors, but with a slightly larger proportion going to the one distractor which does involve a figurative interpretation. This suggests that a good many of the high-status pupils who do not know the correct meaning of this proverb at least know that a proverb is to be given a figurative meaning. The low-status pupils, on the other hand, distributed their wrong responses much more heavily on the two literal interpretations and only rarely on the other figurative one. This suggests that many of the low-status pupils simply do not know that a proverb has a meaning other than the obvious one.

Since most of the well-known proverbs idealize the typical middle-class virtues, it may be suspected that their use by parents, and their inculcation into children by parents, is much more characteristic of middle- and high-status homes than of low-status homes. The fact that knowledge of proverbs would probably come mostly from reading may also be mentioned as a status factor.

The second proverb item (Table 70) reinforces the tentative conclusion advanced in connection with the previous item. Here again the high-status pupils who miss the item do so predominantly because of a distractor which presents another figurative interpretation. The low-status errors, on the other hand, are significantly more concentrated on the response which is most capable of a relatively literal interpretation.

The third proverb item (Table 71) presents a somewhat different pattern from those of the two items preceding it. On this item only one of the available responses is clearly a figurative one, while the others are all more or less literal interpretations. For this reason it is not possible

TABLE 69

ITEM SHOWING STATUS DIFFERENCE IN WRONG RESPONSES

(Thirteen- and Fourteen-Year-Old Pupils)

Status Group	Base for Computing Percentages		Percentage Distribution of Responses				
			The saying, "Idle brains are the devil's workhouse," means —				
	Number of Pupils	Number of Errors	The devil is lazy	People who are idle get into trouble	Many hands make light work	The devil works with his brains	(omit)
High...	...	33	36%	....	39%**	21%**	3%
Low...	...	133	37%	....	16%**	45%**	2%
High...	233	...	5%	85%**	6%	3%	0%
Low...	361	...	14%	63%**	6%	17%	1%

TABLE 70

ITEM SHOWING STATUS DIFFERENCE IN WRONG RESPONSES

(Thirteen- and Fourteen-Year-Old Pupils)

Status Group	Base for Computing Percentages		Percentage Distribution of Responses					
			There is a saying, "Don't ride a free horse to death." This means —					
	Number of Pupils	Number of Errors	Don't be cruel	Don't abuse a privilege	Don't accept gifts	Don't be reckless	Don't ride a horse	(omit)
High...	...	49	29%*	....	8%	61%**	0%	2%
Low...	...	153	48%*	....	10%	31%**	8%	4%
High...	235	...	6%	77%**	2%	13%	0%	0%
Low...	364	...	20%	53%**	4%	13%	3%	2%

TABLE 71

ITEM SHOWING STATUS DIFFERENCE IN WRONG RESPONSES

(Thirteen- and Fourteen-Year-Old Pupils)

Status Group	Base for Computing Percentages		Percentage Distribution of Responses				
			There is a saying, "A drowning man will grasp at straws." This means that —				
	Number of Pupils	Number of Errors	A man will sink more easily than a straw	Everyone should learn to swim	Desperate people cling to absurd hopes	Those who cannot swim should stay on land	(omit)
High...	...	13	6%**	33%	....	50%*	11%
Low...	...	132	42%**	27%	....	25%*	7%
High...	235	...	0%	3%	92%**	4%	1%
Low...	364	...	15%	10%	62%**	9%	2%

TABLE 72

ITEM SHOWING STATUS DIFFERENCE IN WRONG RESPONSES

(Thirteen- and Fourteen-Year-Old Pupils)

Status Group	Base for Computing Percentages		Percentage Distribution of Responses				
			The saying, "Little strokes fell great oaks," means —				
	Number of Pupils	Number of Errors	Continued efforts bring results	Oak trees are weak	Little strokes are best	Anyone can fell an oak	(omit)
High...	...	34	....	6%**	74%	18%	3%
Low...	...	186	....	23%**	58%	16%	3%
High...	233	...	85%**	1%	11%	3%	0%
Low...	361	...	48%**	12%	30%	8%	2%

to test directly the tentative hypothesis suggested for the first two proverbs. Some indirect evidence is available, however. In the first place, the size of status difference on right answers (even when measured in terms of the normalized index) is substantially larger than for the first two proverbs cited; furthermore, a relatively high percentage of the high-status pupils are able to answer this item correctly. This is precisely what would be expected if it is true that high-status pupils have an advantage over low-status ones in understanding that a proverb is to be interpreted figuratively. Since only one figurative answer is available, a high-status pupil might well be able to answer the item correctly by elimination, without necessarily really understanding the proverb at all. This would not be so true for the low-status pupils. There is no present proof that this explanation is a valid one, but the facts reported for this item are what one would expect them to be if the explanation were a valid one.

A second confirmation of the hypothesis may be obtained by noticing that for both of these items the distractor checked most frequently by low-status pupils is a very simple literal translation of the proverb; the distractor checked most frequently by the high-status pupils, while still mainly literal, is probably the least literal of the three incorrect ones available.

Of the three available incorrect responses on the fourth proverb item (Table 72), it will be seen that the least literal one is "Little strokes are best," which is the distractor which accounts for nearly three-fourths of the high-status errors and for more than half of the low-status errors. While the proportion of low-status pupils checking this response is three times as great as for high-status pupils (30 per cent against 11 per cent), the error accounts for a smaller proportion of low-status errors than of the high-status errors. The low-status pupils also check "Oak trees are weak" — a completely literal interpretation — very much more frequently than do the high-status pupils. This literal interpretation is checked by

12 per cent of the low-status pupils and accounts for nearly a fourth of the low-status errors. While the evidence supporting the earlier tentative hypothesis with regard to status differences in response to proverb items is not so unequivocal for this item as for the earlier ones, it still lends some support to the hypothesis.

There is one item (Table 73) where the only plausible explanation which occurs to the writer is to assume that a number of the students mistook the nature of the item. No very obvious explanation for the distribution of wrong responses is at first apparent. It is probably true that few of the children in either of the status groups have had very much first-hand contact with farms. Even those who may have at some time lived on a farm (mostly from the low-status group probably) presumably did so at an age when they were not likely to have acquired much understanding of the reason for crop rotation. The information which enables 91 per cent of the high-status and 73 per cent of the low-status pupils to answer the question correctly must have come for the most part from reading or from school learning. This may explain, at least in part, the difference on the correct response for the two status groups, but it does not of itself explain why a quarter of the errors of low-status pupils come from thinking that crop rotation provides the farmer a balanced diet, while not a single high-status pupil holds this notion.

This item is found on the same page of the test with a number of proverb items. If it should happen to be the case that some of the few high-status pupils who missed this item mistook the item for a proverb item, just such a distribution of wrong responses as found here might be expected. It will be recalled that on the earlier proverb items it was invariably true that the high-status pupils tended to avoid literal interpretations or those expressed too closely in the same terms as the proverb itself and selected instead a figurative interpretation even when it may have been an incorrect one. If they should have tried to do the same thing

TABLE 73

ITEM SHOWING STATUS DIFFERENCE IN WRONG RESPONSES

(Thirteen- and Fourteen-Year-Old Pupils)

Status Group	Base for Computing Percentages		Percentage Distribution of Responses				
			Farmers rotate crops because —				
	Number of Pupils	Number of Errors	Variety is the spice of life	It confuses the plant pests	It helps maintain soil fertility	It gives the farmer a balanced diet	(omit)
High...	...	21	71%**	24%	....	0%**	5%
Low...	...	96	41%**	35%	....	24%**	0%
High...	233	...	6%	2%	91%**	0%	0%
Low...	361	...	11%	9%	73%**	6%	0%

TABLE 74

ITEM SHOWING STATUS DIFFERENCE IN WRONG RESPONSES

(Thirteen- and Fourteen-Year-Old Pupils)

Status Group	Base for Computing Percentages		Percentage Distribution of Responses					
			A person who is sure he can accomplish a task is said to be —					
	Number of Pupils	Number of Errors	successful	confident	proud	fearless	brave	(omit)
High...	...	33	79%**	....	9%	3%	6%**	3%
Low...	...	174	47%**	....	20%	4%	29%**	1%
High...	235	...	11%	86%**	1%	0%	1%	0%
Low...	364	...	22%	52%**	9%	2%	14%	1%

here, they would doubtless have selected the first response — which accounts for nearly three-fourths of the errors made by high-status pupils. The low-status errors, on the other hand, are more nearly equally distributed over the three available distractors, suggesting a higher incidence of guessing.

Words. -- The explanation to be suggested for the one item in this section is closely related to the preceding ones but differs slightly in that it involves the possibility of different meanings or connotations being attached to the same word by pupils at different status levels, rather than differing degress of familiarity with an object or process itself.

That the proportion of the total high-status group answering the item reported in Table 74 correctly is much greater than the proportion of low-status pupils doing so is hardly surprising. A number of the words used in this item, including the two key ones, "accomplish" and "confident," are not the sort of words that are likely to occur very often in the everyday conversation of thirteen- and fourteen-year-old pupils. They are relatively academic or bookish words. The high-status pupils may occasionally hear these words used by their parents or friends; the low-status pupils are certainly not likely to do so. For the most part, however, children of this age are likely to have familiarity with such words as these primarily through the reading of books. This will, as pointed out earlier, give the high-status pupils a further advantage, since the availability of books and the incidence of book-reading is much higher among high-status families than among low-status ones.

Both status groups find "successful" the most potent distractor, although this response accounts for a much larger proportion of the high-status errors than it does of the low-status errors. A significant difference also occurs on "brave," which accounts for a larger proportion of low-status errors than of high-status errors. This item may have very interesting implications for a clearer understanding of differences in the outlook of pupils from different status levels. In a sense the main cultural center around which middle-class and high-status culture is focused is the business psychology and the business economy. If thirteen- and fourteen-year-old pupils may be assumed to reflect at all accurately the outlook of their parents, it is not surprising to find that high-status pupils think of "self-confident" and "successful" as closely related concepts and confuse one with the other.

On the other hand, one of the important characteristics of low-status life is its emphasis upon physical survival and upon the physical virtues which are important for that survival in a culture where physical aggressiveness is rated high. Where physical fighting is an accepted part of the culture, and carrying of weapons a part of the norm, is it surprising to find low-status pupils thinking of self-confidence and bravery as closely related concepts? It is notable that a very small proportion of the high-status pupils make this equivalence.

Different levels of effort on the part of the testee

Most of the items which show wrong-answer differences significant at the 1 per cent level, and which have not already been discussed in the previous section of this chapter, exhibit a fairly uniform pattern; a single type of explanation may be used to account for the status differences in many of them. An example of this type of item is shown in Table 75.

It is easy to see why the largest proportion of errors on this item falls on "blooms," since the letter-composition of "blooms" and of "blossom" is very similar. "Blooms" may be thought of as a near-right or next-best answer. It is not at first clear, however, why the high-status pupils should make this error so much more frequently (even as judged from the percentages based on total number of pupils) than the low-status pupils. Nor is it at once evident why the low-status pupils have a larger proportion of their errors on "observe" than is true for the high-status

TABLE 75

ITEM SHOWING STATUS DIFFERENCE IN WRONG RESPONSES

(Nine- and Ten-Year-Old Pupils)

Status Group	Base for Computing Percentages		Percentage Distribution of Responses					
	Number of Pupils	Number of Errors	If the letters s l o m o b s were arranged properly, they would spell —					
			molest	blooms	blossom	observe	lovable	(omit)
High...	...	109	4%	76%**	...	4%**	12%	5%
Low...	...	167	10%	46%**	...	17%**	17%	10%
High...	226	...	2%	37%**	51%	2%	6%	2%
Low...	322	...	5%	24%**	45%	9%	9%	5%

pupils. A great many items yielding data of this sort will be found. On the basis of them, the following hypothesis is suggested: High-status pupils tend to work harder on the test items, and relatively seldom do they guess; low-status pupils, on the other hand, give up more easily and are more inclined to more or less random guessing.

In terms of this hypothesis the data for the above item indicate precisely what would be expected. If the high-status pupils comparatively seldom indulge in guessing, then their answers will be distributed most heavily on those responses which are either close to correct or which for some other reason are definitely attractive; conversely their wrong responses will be comparatively light on such distractors as "molest" and "observe," where the words do not resemble the correct one so closely. The low-status pupils, on the other hand, if they indulge in more random guessing, will spread their responses out more nearly evenly. Some of the low-status pupils, of course, do not guess but are presumably misled in the same manner as the high-status pupils, resulting in a less marked piling-up of low-status responses on "blooms."

The status difference on "observe," in terms of this explanation, may be due, not to any special attractiveness of "observe" for the low-status pupils, but rather to its special unattractiveness for high-status pupils, most of whom are attracted to the more nearly correct "blooms." This illustrates the caution stated at the beginning of this chapter that a test item must frequently be considered as a whole and that its separate parts cannot always be considered completely in isolation from each other.

A number of items of this type will be presented in this section. They are all alike in that no convincing explanation of the status differences other than that just outlined occurs to the writer and that the distribution of their wrong-answer responses is such as to make the above hypothesis tenable. This means a distribution of high-status errors that involves a higher degree of concentration on some one or two responses than is the case for the low-status errors.

This hypothesis presupposes that some one, or possibly two, distractors are for some reason more attractive than the others, so that there will be a piling-up of wrong responses on that distractor if the high-status pupils do work harder at the item. In many of the items which follow, possible reasons for the special attractiveness of the most popular distractor can be seen at a glance. In some cases, however, no such explanation can be seen, although it is assumed that one exists. For ease of presentation, the items in this section will be grouped according to the kind of reason which seems to explain the concentration on the most popular distractor.

Next-best or near-correct response. — These are items similar to the one just used as an illustration, where the distractor which attracts the largest proportion of errors for both status groups can be considered the next-best answer after the correct one. Pupils who check it have presumably gone at the problem involved in the test item more or less correctly, but at some point have slipped and have arrived at the next-best rather than the best answer. In some cases this "next-best" answer can really be defended as a correct response, even though it is not so indicated in the scoring key.

The item reported in Table 76 is very similar to the one just discussed, and the suggested explanation for this item is precisely the same as that for the preceding one. It is clear that both "elucidate" and "dedicate," on which the high-status errors tend to be concentrated, are more easily confused with the right answer than are "elegance" and "elevate," on which the low-status pupils show a higher proportion of their errors than is true for the high-status pupils. If it is true that some of the low-status pupils are misled by "elucidate" and that the rest indulge in random guessing, the item results should be exactly what they are found to be here.

The over-all status difference in the next item (Table 77) may be at least in part accounted for by assuming that pupils who have had music

TABLE 76

ITEM SHOWING STATUS DIFFERENCE IN WRONG RESPONSES

(Nine- and Ten-Year-Old Pupils)

Status Group	Base for Computing Percentages		Percentage Distribution of Responses					
	Number of Pupils	Number of Errors	If the letters e l i c a d e t were arranged properly, they would spell —					
			eluci-date	dedi-cate	ele-gance	el-evate	del-icate	(omit)
High...	...	88	53%	19%	7%**	9%	....	11%
Low...	...	210	43%	15%	18%**	14%	....	10%
High...	226	...	21%	8%	3%	4%	61%**	4%
Low...	322	...	28%	10%	11%	9%	35%**	7%

TABLE 77

ITEM SHOWING STATUS DIFFERENCE IN WRONG RESPONSES

(Nine- and Ten-Year-Old Pupils)

Status Group	Base for Computing Percentages		Percentage Distribution of Responses					
			A sheet of music always has —					
	Number of Pupils	Number of Errors	rhythm	words	notes	covers	players	(omit)
High...	...	54	52%**	22%	....	11%	11%**	4%
Low...	...	162	30%**	29%	....	7%	27%**	7%
High...	226	...	12%	5%	76%**	3%	3%	1%
Low...	322	...	15%	15%	50%**	4%	14%	3%

lessons or pupils who have pianos or other instruments in their own homes may be expected to be more familiar with a sheet of music than would low-status pupils whose only contact with it might be through a store window or possibly in the schoolroom. The greater concentration of the high-status pupils on "rhythm" fits into the same general pattern already pointed out — a high-status concentration on a response which makes a certain amount of sense and which could be termed a near-correct answer. The low-status pupils, on the other hand, distribute their wrong responses more nearly uniformly over the four distractors.

In the item in Table 78 the distribution of wrong responses indicates that many of the high-status pupils who miss the item are at least working in the right direction and have a workable idea, while many of the low-status pupils are apparently completely unaware of the nature of what they are supposed to do or are completely unable to do it. Only a few high-status pupils miss this item, and nearly half of those who do so select a word which at least makes a perfectly grammatical sentence. As a matter of fact, it could be argued that placing "long" in the blank makes a technically acceptable sentence, although it obviously is not the one which the author intended. The largest proportion of low-status errors, on the other hand, is on "snow," apparently as a result of an uncritical association of snow with winter; this suggests that the low-status pupils either do not understand the item or that they are unable to proceed with it systematically. Not a single high-status pupil makes this error.

It will be noticed that the low-status errors on the item in Table 79 are fairly uniformly distributed over the entire range of possible responses, while the high-status errors tend to be much more heavily concentrated on the first response. It is possible that some of the pupils who checked the first response had in mind some sentence starting with "A father...," which might be taken as an indication that, even though they were unable to arrange all the words into a good sentence, they did get the idea of the

TABLE 78

ITEM SHOWING STATUS DIFFERENCE IN WRONG RESPONSES

(Nine- and Ten-Year-Old Pupils)

Status Group	Base for Computing Percentages		Percentage Distribution of Responses					
			The days are long in summer and .... in winter. Which word should be in the blank? —					
	Number of Pupils	Number of Errors	very	short	long	almost	snow	(omit)
High...	...	14	29%	....	43%	7%	0%**	21%
Low...	...	91	19%	....	26%	12%	36%**	7%
High...	226	...	2%	94%**	3%	0%	0%	1%
Low...	322	...	5%	72%**	7%	3%	10%	2%

TABLE 79

ITEM SHOWING STATUS DIFFERENCE IN WRONG RESPONSES

(Thirteen- and Fourteen-Year-Old Pupils)

Status Group	Base for Computing Percentages		Percentage Distribution of Responses					
			If the following words were rearranged to make a good sentence, the second word of the sentence would begin with what letter? — always, father, A, younger, his, than, boy, is —					
	Number of Pupils	Number of Errors	f	a	t	b	y	(omit)
High...	...	47	66%**	15%*	6%*	....	13%	0%
Low...	...	189	25%**	29%*	20%*	....	16%	10%
High...	235	...	13%	3%	1%	80%**	3%	0%
Low...	364	...	13%	15%	10%	47%**	9%	5%

277

problem and made a start on it. The greater scatter of the low-status responses suggests there may have been a considerable element of guessing or rather hit-and-miss trying by these pupils.

A slightly different, but similar, explanation is suggested by the wrong-answer data for the item in Table 80. It is virtually certain that at least five out of the six key words in this item (all except "hide") are ones for which high-status pupils will have considerable advantage over low-status pupils. They are academic or bookish in character. They are not words likely to occur very frequently, if at all, in the everyday conversation of pupils of these ages from either status level. The high-status pupils may hear such words used ocassionally by their parents; the low-status pupils are very unlikely to do so. In addition to occasionally hearing these words used by adults, pupils may acquire a familiarity with them through formal vocabulary study in school or through relatively widespread reading of a moderately advanced nature. In either case the high-status pupils will have greater opportunities for familiarity with such words than will low-status pupils.

This kind of explanation may account for a good deal of the status difference with respect to the proportion of pupils answering the item correctly. It does not, however, explain the particular variations in wrong responses observed for this item. It is noticeable that nearly half of the high-status pupils who do not answer this question correctly are misled by the distractor "hide," while only a quarter of the low-status pupils are thus misled. On the other hand, nearly a third of the low-status errors are found on "invade," while only about a tenth of the high-status errors are found on this distractor. Both of these differences are significant at the 1 per cent level.

The word "hide" may be used in a manner closely synonymous with "evade" -- indeed, it might even be argued that "hide" is as good a synonym for "evade" as is "shun," which the author keys as the correct answer. In any case the error involved is not a very serious one. The error involved in checking "invade," on the other hand, seems to suggest a total disregard of what a synonym is. One may suspect that these pupils were misled by the similar sound of "evade" and "invade" and either forgot or neglected to bother about the meaning of the words at all. If this is true, then the "hide" error made by the high-status pupils represents a mistake in fine discernment, but a fundamental understanding of what synonyms are and of approximately what "evade" means; while the "invade" error suggests a serious lack in one or probably both of these.

A number of other items exhibiting this same tendency will be listed with very brief comments, since the explanations suggested for each are very similar to those given for the previous items.

The item in Table 81 is a very difficult one; less than a quarter of the pupils in either status group are able to answer it correctly. The concentration of errors from both status groups on "a shoe" apparently represents a classification based upon a somewhat elastic concept of personal apparel. There is also a secondary low-status concentration on "a laundry," probably due to its association with respect to the three named articles. As in other items in this section, the concentration of wrong responses is greatest for the high-status pupils, with the low-status errors being spread out more widely.

The reason for the concentration of errors on the "19" response in the item in Table 82 is obvious and indicates that three-fourths of the high-status pupils and something over half of the low-status pupils who do not answer the question correctly are at least trying to do the problem. It seems reasonable to assume that most of the pupils who check "1" or "11" are either completely unable to handle simple arithmetical problems or are uninterested in trying! Such responses are more prevalent among the low-status pupils than among the high-status pupils.

It is probable that many of the pupils who check "orange" in the item in Table 83 are thinking of the word as representing a fruit rather than

TABLE 80

ITEM SHOWING STATUS DIFFERENCE IN WRONG RESPONSES

(Thirteen- and Fourteen-Year-Old Pupils)

Status Group	Base for Computing Percentages		Percentage Distribution of Responses					
	Number of Pupils	Number of Errors	Mark . . . the word which has the SAME or most nearly the same meaning as the beginning word of each line: evade —					
			vacate	invade	shun	hide	desist	(omit)
High...	. . .	112	23%	11%**	. . . .	42%**	14%	10%
Low...	. . .	268	20%	32%**	. . . .	25%**	12%	12%
High...	233	. . .	11%	5%	52%**	20%	7%	5%
Low...	361	. . .	15%	24%	25%**	18%	9%	9%

TABLE 81

ITEM SHOWING STATUS DIFFERENCE IN WRONG RESPONSES

(Thirteen- and Fourteen-Year-Old Pupils)

Status Group	Base for Computing Percentages		Percentage Distribution of Responses					
	Number of Pupils	Number of Errors	Which one of the five things below is most like these three: a towel, a shirt and a handkerchief? —					
			a laundry	a store	a bath	a sail	a shoe	(omit)
High...	. . .	180	19%**	1%	0%**	. . .	78%**	1%
Low...	. . .	308	31%**	6%	7%**	. . .	54%**	2%
High...	235	. . .	15%	1%	0%	23%*	60%**	1%
Low...	364	. . .	26%	5%	6%	15%*	45%**	2%

TABLE 82

ITEM SHOWING STATUS DIFFERENCE IN WRONG RESPONSES

(Thirteen- and Fourteen-Year-Old Pupils)

Status Group	Base for Computing Percentages		Percentage Distribution of Responses					
	Number of Pupils	Number of Errors	If you had 20 words in spelling and were marked 90%, how many words did you spell correctly? —					
			1	11	18	19	(omit)	
High...	...	42	14%	5%**	....	74%*	7%	
Low...	...	157	22%	20%**	....	56%*	2%	
High...	235	...	3%	1%	82%**	13%	1%	
Low...	352	...	10%	9%	55%**	25%	1%	

ITEM SHOWING STATUS DIFFERENCE IN WRONG RESPONSES

(Nine- and Ten-Year-Old Pupils)

Status Group	Base for Computing Percentages		Percentage Distribution of Responses					
	Number of Pupils	Number of Errors	Which word does not belong with the others? —					
			orange	red	green	circle	black	(omit)
High...	...	37	78%**	3%*	3%	....	0%	16%
Low...	...	90	50%**	19%*	12%	....	9%	10%
High...	226	...	13%	0%	0%	84%**	0%	3%
Low...	322	...	14%	5%	3%	72%**	2%	3%

a color. While this is by no means a correct response, since it can take no account of "circle," its checking does indicate that the pupil has tried the problem and that he has understood at least something of the classification process which the item requires. That is probably not true of those pupils, mostly low-status, who checked "red," "green," and "black." Random guessing seems to be the most likely explanation for these responses.

In the item in Table 84 it is assumed that "nephew" is the distractor which would most easily confuse those pupils who were really trying and not guessing. "Nephew" seems to be more closely related to the correct "cousin" than any other of the distractors.

TABLE 84

ITEM SHOWING STATUS DIFFERENCE IN WRONG RESPONSES

(Nine- and Ten-Year-Old Pupils)

Status Group	Base for Computing Percentages		Percentage Distribution of Responses					
	Number of Pupils	Number of Errors	The son of my father's brother is my —					
			aunt	nephew	cousin	brother	son	(omit)
High...	...	65	5%	74%**	....	14%	6%*	2%
Low...	...	170	11%	49%**	....	17%	18%*	5%
High...	226	...	1%	21%	71%**	4%	2%	0%
Low...	322	...	6%	26%	45%**	9%	10%	2%

For the item in Table 85 it is assumed that "taller than" represents a higher level of problem-solving — in the sense of exhibiting greater ability — than "just as tall as" because it involves a somewhat more complicated and less obvious comparison. It is clear that the unusual "(cannot say which)" response attracts no high-status pupils; the low-status responses on this distractor may well be mostly chance ones.

The five available responses to the item in Table 86 include three concrete terms and two abstract ones, with the correct answer being one of the two abstract ones. It is notable that not only do the high-status pupils answer the question correctly more frequently than do the low-status pupils but also that the few errors which they do make are predominantly on the other abstract term. The low-status pupils, on the other hand, make nearly half of their errors on a concrete term, "moon." It is true that, when the whole group of low-status pupils is considered, much the largest proportion check the correct "hours," indicating that it is not at all impossible for these pupils to think in abstract terms. There is, however, some indication that those low-status pupils who do not answer the item correctly prefer a concrete object to another abstract quality, even though "stillness" could probably be considered a more nearly correct response than "moon."

282

TABLE 85

ITEM SHOWING STATUS DIFFERENCE IN WRONG RESPONSES

(Thirteen- and Fourteen-Year-Old Pupils)

Status Group	Base for Computing Percentages		Percentage Distribution of Responses				
			If Paul is taller than Herbert and Herbert is just as tall as Robert, then Robert is (?) Paul —				
	Number of Pupils	Number of Errors	taller than	shorter than	just as tall as	(cannot say which)	(omit)
High...	...	34	76%**	....	21%	0%**	3%
Low...	...	116	45%**	....	35%	19%**	1%
High...	235	...	11%	86%**	3%	0%	0%
Low...	364	...	14%	68%**	11%	6%	0%

TABLE 86

ITEM SHOWING STATUS DIFFERENCE IN WRONG RESPONSES

(Thirteen- and Fourteen-Year-Old Pupils)

Status Group	Base for Computing Percentages		Percentage Distribution of Responses					
			Night always has —					
	Number of Pupils	Number of Errors	stillness	moon	clouds	ghosts	hours	(omit)
High...	...	21	67%**	24%*	10%	0%	....	0%
Low...	...	105	34%**	46%*	14%	3%	....	3%
High...	233	...	6%	2%	1%	0%	91%**	0%
Low...	361	...	10%	13%	4%	1%	71%**	1%

It is probably true that the daily conversation and vocabulary characteristic of low-status homes is much more heavily weighted with concrete terms than is the case in high-status homes. Davis and Havighurst, for example, have pointed out that "the middle-class handles chiefly symbols for a living, while the lower-class handles chiefly things" (8, p. 115). Since low-status pupils are less likely to hear and be familiar with abstract words and less likely to be accustomed to thinking in abstract terms, the results found for this item are not surprising.

In the next two items (Tables 87 and 88) the responses are such that two out of the four possible choices are much more likely to be selected than the other two. Since one of these two is in each case the correct one, the other automatically becomes the most popular distractor. As in the preceding items, it seems reasonable to suppose that the higher incidence of high-status errors on this most popular distractor represents a greater effort on the part of the high-status pupils, while the greater spread of low-status responses represents a higher incidence of guessing. The reason for the concentration of errors on the most popular distractor in each of these items is obvious.

A majority of the very few high-status pupils who missed the item in Table 89 check "boat," while nearly half of the low-status errors are found on "bicycle" and only a quarter of them on "boat." As in other items in this section, the concentration of errors on a single response is more marked for high-status pupils than it is for low-status pupils. A plausible explanation can be put forth for either of these two distractors. It can be argued with merit that a boat is associated with water and that the other four are all associated with land. This classification would probably not be so generally acceptable to many as the rather sophisticated distinction between transportation and communication which the author apparently intended. Should it, however, be counted as incorrect?

On the other hand, it seems reasonable for a thirteen- or fourteen-year-old pupil, of either status group, to think of telegraph, train, automobile, and boat as all being commercial objects which belong to someone else, while a bicycle is a personal belonging used largely for recreation. To an adult this may seem a somewhat unusual process of thinking, but is it "unintelligent" for a bicycle-owner to think of it in this way? The writer sees no reason, however, why the high-status pupils should be most misled by "boat" as a distractor, while the most effective distractor for the low-status pupils is "bicycle."

It seems likely that many of the pupils who check "December" as the correct answer to the item in Table 90 do so by selecting the middle one of the five words as given, without understanding, or heeding, the instruction that the months are to be rearranged in order. Or perhaps some of the pupils arranged the months alphabetically rather than chronologically. Should this be considered incorrect?

It is possible to explain the concentration of high-status errors on "knife," in the item in Table 91, by suggesting that many of these pupils probably consider the knife as a pocket instrument of their own, as opposed to thinking of it as a kitchen implement. Even if the percentages based on the total group of pupils are considered, a larger proportion of high-status pupils check "knife." This may reflect a greater incidence of pocket-knife ownership among high-status boys of this age. It may be that at an older age level this relationship would be reversed, with a larger proportion of low-status boys thinking of a knife as a weapon rather than as an eating implement.

TABLE 87

ITEM SHOWING STATUS DIFFERENCE IN WRONG RESPONSES

(Nine- and Ten-Year-Old Pupils)

Status Group	Base for Computing Percentages — Number of Pupils	Base for Computing Percentages — Number of Errors	Percentage Distribution of Responses — Mark the one of the two middle drawings that does not have a circle in the center — (drawing 1)	(drawing 2)	(drawing 3)	(drawing 4)	(omit)
High	...	30	13%	...	63%*	23%	0%**
Low	...	93	16%	...	41%*	22%	22%**
High	223	...	2%	87%***	9%	3%	0%
Low	326	...	5%	71%***	12%	6%	6%

TABLE 88

ITEM SHOWING STATUS DIFFERENCE IN WRONG RESPONSES

(Nine- and Ten-Year-Old Pupils)

Status Group	Base for Computing Percentages — Number of Pupils	Base for Computing Percentages — Number of Errors	Percentage Distribution of Responses — Mark the group of three letters that have the most loops — BTB	DWD	FMF	HFL	(omit)
High	...	40	...	72%**	20%	0%	8%
Low	...	134	...	51%**	34%	7%	7%
High	223	...	82%**	13%	4%	0%	1%
Low	326	...	59%**	21%	14%	3%	3%

TABLE 89

ITEM SHOWING STATUS DIFFERENCE IN WRONG RESPONSES

(Thirteen- and Fourteen-Year-Old Pupils)

Status Group	Base for Computing Percentages		Percentage Distribution of Responses					
	Number of Pupils	Number of Errors	Pick out the ONE WORD which does not belong with the others —					
			telegraph	train	automobile	bicycle	boat	(omit)
High...	...	10	....	0%	30%	10%**	60%*	0%
Low...	...	63	....	14%	17%	44%**	24%*	0%
High...	233	...	96%**	0%	1%	0%	3%	0%
Low...	361	...	83%**	2%	3%	8%	4%	0%

TABLE 90

ITEM SHOWING STATUS DIFFERENCE IN WRONG RESPONSES

(Thirteen- and Fourteen-Year-Old Pupils)

Status Group	Base for Computing Percentages		Percentage Distribution of Responses					
	Number of Pupils	Number of Errors	If the following words were arranged in order, which word would be in the middle? —					
			October	June	December	August	April	(omit)
High...	...	30	13%	17%**	60%**	....	7%	3%
Low...	...	131	15%	37%**	26%**	....	12%	9%
High...	235	...	2%	2%	8%	87%**	1%	0%
Low...	364	...	5%	13%	9%	64%**	4%	3%

TABLE 91

ITEM SHOWING STATUS DIFFERENCE IN WRONG RESPONSES

(Nine- and Ten-Year-Old Pupils)

Status Group	Base for Computing Percentages		Percentage Distribution of Responses					
	Number of Pupils	Number of Errors	Which word does not belong with the others? —					
			cup	tea-spoon	knife	fork	table-spoon	(omit)
High...	...	58	....	10%*	50%**	3%*	31%	5%
Low...	...	136	....	22%*	24%**	15%*	32%	7%
High...	226	...	74%**	3%	13%	1%	8%	1%
Low...	322	...	58%**	9%	10%	7%	14%	3%

The low-status pupils have more errors on "tablespoon" than on any other distractor, and high-status pupils have a secondary concentration on this response. This may result from thinking of the tablespoon as a serving instrument and of the other four as eating instruments. Such a classification could certainly be defended.

The item in Table 92 is an ambiguous test question in any case, since it can easily be argued that both "meat" and "food" are perfectly correct answers for the question as stated. It will be noticed that practically all the high-status pupils check one of these three correct or near-correct responses. The "meat" and "food" distractors also account for two-thirds of the low-status errors. Unlike the high-status pupils, however, quite a number of the low-status group check "swim," one of the two responses which cannot be justified as correct on any basis. This is apparently a case of marking a word which is associated with the given word instead of marking the one bearing the specified relationship. If the two most popular distractors are examined, it will be seen that "meat" accounts for a larger proportion of the high-status errors than any other distractor, while "food" is the most attractive one to low-status pupils. The greater reluctance of the low-status pupils to classify salmon as meat may be due to the greater incidence of Catholics in the low-status group in the community where this study was carried out.

Distractors with associational value. — The eight items in this section are similar to those in the preceding section in that there is a higher concentration of errors on some one distractor for the high-status pupils and a greater spreading of the errors over all the distractors for the low-status pupils. These items are different from the preceding ones, however, in that the explanation for the piling-up of high-status responses on the most popular distractor is apparently to be found, not in the substitution of a near-correct or next-best answer for the correct one, but in the sub-

TABLE 92

ITEM SHOWING STATUS DIFFERENCE IN WRONG RESPONSES

(Nine- and Ten-Year-Old Pupils)

Status Group	Base for Computing Percentages		Percentage Distribution of Responses					
	Number of Pupils	Number of Errors	Find the word in the last of the list which tells what kind of a thing the first word in the list is: salmon —					
			meat	water	swim	fish	food	(omit)
High...	...	56	46%*	0%	5%**	....	39%	9%
Low...	...	166	30%*	7%	19%**	....	34%	11%
High...	225	...	12%	0%	1%	75%**	10%	2%
Low...	321	...	15%	3%	10%	47%**	17%	6%

TABLE 93

ITEM SHOWING STATUS DIFFERENCE IN WRONG RESPONSES

(Nine- and Ten-Year-Old Pupils)

Status Group	Base for Computing Percentages		Percentage Distribution of Responses					
	Number of Pupils	Number of Errors	Artist is to picture as author is to —					
			brush	in-ventor	building	book	shop	(omit)
High...	...	53	23%	51%	8%**	....	8%*	11%
Low...	...	164	13%	37%	21%**	....	19%*	9%
High...	226	...	5%	12%	2%	77%**	2%	3%
Low...	322	...	7%	19%	11%	49%**	10%	5%

stitution for the correct word of one having associational value only.

In Table 93, for example, "inventor" accounts for the largest proportion of errors for both status groups, more than a third of the low-status errors and more than half of the high-status errors being found on this response. Many of the pupils who deliberately choose this response probably do so because of the association of "artist," "author," and "inventor" — all words designating classes of people. There is a secondary concentration of high-status errors on "brush." Three-fourths of the high-status pupils who make errors do so on words which may be said to have definite associations with the words in the analogy, even though not the ones required by the terms of the analogy. On the other hand, very few high-status pupils check either "building" or "shop" — words which apparently have little if any relation to any of the words in the analogy.

The low-status pupils are not, however, so discriminating. The low-status errors do, it is true, tend to concentrate somewhat on "inventor," but not so markedly as for the high-status pupils. Furthermore, the low-status pupils make a substantial number of responses on "building" and on "shop" — although it is hard to see any possible reason, other than random guessing, for these choices.

A similar kind of explanation is suggested by the data for the next item of this group, which are reported in Table 94. The heavy concentration of errors for both status groups is on a word which is closely associated with the third term of the analogy, but which does not bear to it the specific relationship required by the first two terms. It should be pointed out that on this item the amount of guessing to be accounted for in terms of the hypothesis of this section is not large, even for the low-status group. The data of this item do lend additional support to the hypothesis, however.

While the words in the item in Table 95 are not such as pupils are likely to use in their everyday converstaion, all except possibly "increase" are ones which they will presumably have heard, and used, a great many

TABLE 94

ITEM SHOWING STATUS DIFFERENCE IN WRONG RESPONSES

(Thirteen- and Fourteen-Year-Old Pupils)

Status Group	Base for Computing Percentages		Percentage Distribution of Responses					
	Number of Pupils	Number of Errors	Tree is to forest as person is to —					
			women	couple	human	crowd	men	(omit)
High...	...	104	3%	4%	90%**	....	0%	3%
Low...	...	249	3%	10%	80%**	....	6%	1%
High...	233	...	1%	2%	40%	55%**	0%	1%
Low...	361	...	2%	7%	55%	27%**	4%	1%

TABLE 95

ITEM SHOWING STATUS DIFFERENCE IN WRONG RESPONSES

(Thirteen- and Fourteen-Year-Old Pupils)

Status Group	Base for Computing Percentages		Percentage Distribution of Responses					
			Add is to subtract as multiply is to —					
	Number of Pupils	Number of Errors	arith-metic	in-crease	frac-tion	add	divide	(omit)
High. . .	. . .	31	10%	84%**	0%	6%	. . . .	0%
Low . . .	. . .	153	20%	63%**	11%	7%	. . . .	0%
High. . .	233	. . .	1%	11%	0%	1%	87%**	0%
Low . . .	361	. . .	8%	27%	5%	3%	58%**	0%

times in connection with school work by the time they have reached the age of thirteen or fourteen. It must be presumed that the pupils in both groups have had equal opportunity for familiarity with these words, except in so far as the greater school motivation of high-status pupils may have resulted in their making more effective use of those opportunities.

The least definitely school-oriented of these words is probably "increase," which may account for the larger number of pupils in both status groups who check it — possibly because it is unfamiliar. It seems more likely, however, that the checking of "increase" may frequently have represented a simple association of the idea of "multiply" with "increase," without the pupil's understanding clearly the structure of the analogy or the concept of analogy itself.

In the item reported in Table 96 the association of "March" and "April" for any pupil who has learned to recite the months in order is obvious. Precisely the same association is apparently involved in the item in Table 97. A somewhat similar explanation would account for the differences reported for the item in Table 98.

The item in Table 99 obviously depends at least in part upon definite school learning. While differences in learning opportunities of the two status groups may account for the status difference with respect to the right answers, they can hardly account for the variations in the wrong-answer distributions. It may well be that the slight concentration of both groups on "chromium" represents a familiarity with the shiny chromium on automobiles and an association of this with "silver." The 21 per cent of the low-status errors that are found on "lead" may well represent nothing more than a guessing factor; the reason for the very low high-status response to "lead," however, is not clear.

The last item of this group is reported in Table 100. Eagles, giraffes, and lizards are not part of the common culture of urban children — familiar-ity with them will probably come only through formal study, through visits

TABLE 96

ITEM SHOWING STATUS DIFFERENCE IN WRONG RESPONSES

(Nine- and Ten-Year-Old Pupils)

Status Group	Base for Computing Percentages		Percentage Distribution of Responses					
			Tuesday is to week as March is to —					
	Number of Pupils	Number of Errors	April	year	week	winter	night	(omit)
High. . .	. . .	75	65%**	. . . .	11%*	8%	7%	9%
Low . . .	. . .	175	46%**	. . . .	22%*	11%	14%	7%
High. . .	226	. . .	22%	66%**	4%	3%	2%	3%
Low . . .	322	. . .	25%	43%**	12%	6%	7%	4%

TABLE 97

ITEM SHOWING STATUS DIFFERENCE IN WRONG RESPONSES

(Nine- and Ten-Year-Old Pupils)

Status Group	Base for Computing Percentages		Percentage Distribution of Responses					
			Which month comes just before March? —					
	Number of Pupils	Number of Errors	April	Sep-tember	May	Feb-ruary	August	(omit)
High. . .	. . .	35	77%**	3%	6%*	. . . .	3%	11%
Low . . .	. . .	123	39%**	13%	20%*	. . . .	18%	11%
High. . .	226	. . .	12%	0%	1%	85%**	0%	2%
Low . . .	322	. . .	15%	5%	7%	62%**	7%	4%

TABLE 100

TABLE 98

ITEM SHOWING STATUS DIFFERENCE IN WRONG RESPONSES

(Thirteen- and Fourteen-Year-Old Pupils)

Status Group	Base for Computing Percentages		Percentage Distribution of Responses					
	Number of Pupils	Number of Errors	An heir always has —					
			money	lawyer	heir-looms	prop-erty	pred-ecessor	(omit)
High...	. . .	109	17%**	16%	39%	22%	. . . .	6%
Low...	. . .	252	30%**	18%	32%	17%	. . . .	3%
High...	233	. . .	8%	7%	18%	10%	51%**	3%
Low...	361	. . .	21%	12%	22%	13%	25%**	2%

TABLE 99

ITEM SHOWING STATUS DIFFERENCE IN WRONG RESPONSES

(Thirteen- and Fourteen-Year-Old Pupils)

Status Group	Base for Computing Percentages		Percentage Distribution of Responses					
	Number of Pupils	Number of Errors	Quicksilver is another name for —					
			chro-mium	tin	mer-cury	alu-minum	lead	(omit)
High...	. . .	35	37%	11%	. . . .	31%	3%**	17%
Low...	. . .	153	34%	12%	. . . .	28%	21%**	5%
High...	233	. . .	6%	2%	85%**	5%	0%	3%
Low...	361	. . .	14%	5%	57%**	12%	9%	2%

TABLE 100

ITEM SHOWING STATUS DIFFERENCE IN WRONG RESPONSES

(Thirteen- and Fourteen-Year-Old Pupils)

Status Group	Base for Computing Percentages		Percentage Distribution of Responses					
	Number of Pupils	Number of Errors	Which one of the five things below is most like these three: an eagle, a giraffe, and a lizard? —					
			a wing	a neck	a stone	a mouse	a tree	(omit)
High...	. . .	22	14%	64%**	14%	. . . .	0%*	9%
Low...	. . .	119	27%	34%**	11%	. . . .	15%*	13%
High...	235	. . .	1%	6%	1%	91%**	0%	1%
Low...	364	. . .	9%	11%	4%	67%**	5%	4%

to a zoo or exhibit, or through reading -- all activities in which high-status children will have the advantage. So far as the distribution of wrong responses is concerned, however, there is the same tendency exhibited on other items in this section for the high-status pupils who do make an error to do so by making the obvious association of "neck" with "giraffe." Some of the low-status pupils apparently make the same error, but their errors are also distributed more widely, probably as a result of more widespread guessing.

Distractors which are distinctly unfamiliar. — There are a few items whose wrong-answer data conform to the same general patterns as those presented in preceding sections but for whom the explanation for the most popular distractor seems to be in terms of its relative unfamiliarity. On these items there is some one distractor which is apparently relatively unfamiliar to pupils of both status groups. The errors of both status groups are concentrated on it, but the low-status errors are not concentrated so heavily, lending further support to the hypothesis that their responses involve a larger proportion of guessing.

On the item in Table 101 the errors for both groups are heavily concentrated on "hamlet" — even more markedly for the high-status pupils than for the low-status ones. Even on the basis of the total number of pupils, 79 per cent of the high-status pupils and 67 per cent of the low-status pupils are misled by this distractor. It seems perfectly clear that much of this concentration on "hamlet" is due to the unfamiliarity of the word to pupils at this age level. On this same item Bruce found that both white and Negro children checked "hamlet" significantly more frequently than other distractors. She thought this was probably due to the complete unfamiliarity of the word and concluded that "the inclusion of this word seems unfair since this is a test of concept formation, rather than vocabulary" (59, p. 71).

The item in Table 102 includes four short simple words and one

TABLE 101

ITEM SHOWING STATUS DIFFERENCE IN WRONG RESPONSES

(Nine- and Ten-Year-Old Pupils)

Status Group	Base for Computing Percentages		Percentage Distribution of Responses					
	Number of Pupils	Number of Errors	Find the one that does not belong with the others in the list —					
			town	house	village	hamlet	city	(omit)
High...	...	187	0%	...	0%	95%**	5%	1%
Low...	...	271	4%	...	3%	81%**	9%	3%
High...	225	...	0%	16%	0%	79%**	4%	0%
Low...	327	...	3%	13%	2%	67%**	8%	2%

TABLE 102

ITEM SHOWING STATUS DIFFERENCE IN WRONG RESPONSES

(Thirteen- and Fourteen-Year-Old Pupils)

Status Group	Base for Computing Percentages		Percentage Distribution of Responses					
	Number of Pupils	Number of Errors	A boy who often tells stories he knows are not true is said to --					
			brag	cheat	joke	lie	exaggerate	(omit)
High...	...	39	3%	5%	5%**	....	82%**	5%
Low...	...	116	12%	5%	29%**	....	53%**	0%
High...	235	...	0%	1%	1%	83%**	14%	1%
Low...	364	...	4%	2%	9%	68%**	17%	0%

which is long and presumably less familiar. The long, less familiar, word accounts for a substantial proportion of the errors of both status groups. The low-status pupils' answers are somewhat more widely distributed, indicating once more the likelihood of more guessing on the part of low-status pupils.

All the words in the item in Table 103 involve probable cultural bias in the sense that they are probably more familiar to high-status pupils than to low-status pupils, since they would be met mostly in reading. The distribution of wrong answers suggests, however, that "tabernacle" is probably the most unfamiliar of them all to pupils in both status groups and that there is more tendency for the low-status pupils to guess on this item.

TABLE 103

ITEM SHOWING STATUS DIFFERENCE IN WRONG RESPONSES

(Thirteen- and Fourteen-Year-Old Pupils)

Status Group	Base for Computing Percentages		Percentage Distribution of Responses					
	Number of Pupils	Number of Errors	Pick out the ONE WORD which does not belong with the others —					
			chapel	temple	tabernacle	cathedral	casino	(omit)
High...	...	32	3%	0%*	97%**	0%	....	0%
Low...	...	125	6%	14%*	68%**	7%	....	5%
High...	233	...	0%	0%	13%	0%	86%**	0%
Low...	361	...	2%	5%	24%	2%	65%**	2%

The item shown in Table 104 involves subject matter which is definitely part of school learning. All the factors of status differential with respect to school motivation, retardation, and curriculums, have applicability here. In addition, it is reasonable to suppose that children from high-status homes are more likely to have access to nature books and are more likely to belong to the Boy and Girl Scout organizations — and thus to have more opportunities for learning bird names. It is notable that the distractor attracting the greatest proportion of both groups is "grosbeak," which is undoubtedly the one of the four birds which would be least likely to be known. The fact that the high-status pupils show very few errors on the other three birds, while the low-status pupils show a fairly substantial number, suggests that the low-status pupils may have indulged in a larger measure of guessing.

The final item in this section is one about which some interesting speculations can be made. This item (Table 105) shows the second largest status difference of any item in the tests given to the older pupils — the largest status difference of all if only the "stable" items, as defined on page 370, are included.

TABLE 104

ITEM SHOWING STATUS DIFFERENCE IN WRONG RESPONSES

(Thirteen- and Fourteen-Year-Old Pupils)

Status Group	Base for Computing Percentages		Percentage Distribution of Responses					
	Number of Pupils	Number of Errors	Pick out the ONE WORD which does not belong with the others —					
			grosbeak	swallow	oriole	lark	gazelle	(omit)
High...	...	34	74%**	3%*	6%*	6%	....	12%
Low...	...	127	50%**	15%*	21%*	9%	....	4%
High...	233	...	11%	0%	1%	1%	85%**	2%
Low...	361	...	18%	5%	7%	3%	64%**	1%

TABLE 105

ITEM SHOWING STATUS DIFFERENCE IN WRONG RESPONSES

(Thirteen- and Fourteen-Year-Old Pupils)

Status Group	Base for Computing Percentages		Percentage Distribution of Responses					
	Number of Pupils	Number of Errors	Pick out the ONE WORD which does not belong with the others —					
			priest	organist	minister	rabbi	bishop	(omit)
High...	...	23	0%	....	0%	96%**	4%	0%
Low...	...	173	5%	....	8%	76%**	11%	0%
High...	233	...	0%	89%**	0%	9%	0%	0%
Low...	361	...	2%	48%**	4%	36%	5%	0%

It will be noticed that "rabbi" accounts for the great majority of the errors in both status groups. Of the five responses offered, it is doubtless true that "rabbi" would be the one most likely to be unfamiliar to pupils in both status groups. It is also possible that some of these children think of a rabbi primarily as a leader of a racial or cultural minority group, while they regard the other four as religious figures. The somewhat smaller concentration of low-status errors on this response can be explained in terms of greater guessing.

This item is a particularly striking example of an item which is very poor as an intelligence-test item because its meaning, and perhaps even its correct answer, may shift entirely depending upon the cultural group to which the person who is taking the test belongs. Is it to be regarded as wrong, for example, for a Catholic to say that "priest" does not belong with the other four because for him a priest receives his authority from a divine source while the other four are regarded as of a quite different order? Is it wrong for a Methodist to check "bishop" on the grounds that the other four terms all designate church leaders at the lowest level of authority, while the bishop is, in the Methodist church, a higher administrative official? Is it wrong for any pupil to check "rabbi" on the grounds that the other four choices are all figures in a Christian church — or on the grounds that a rabbi is a racial leader? The data for this item indicate, however, that only "rabbi" makes any serious trouble for pupils in either status group.

The general status difference on the item as a whole may also be explained in terms of the greater incidence of church and Sunday-school attendance among high-status pupils.

Distractors which look or sound like the given words. — There are two items (Tables 106 and 107) for which the apparent reason for the concentration of wrong responses is the similarity in sound or appearance between the distractor and the word given in the injunction of the item. For both items there is a heavier concentration of errors for high-status pupils than for low-status pupils.

Unknown reason for concentration. — There are thirteen items which exhibit the same general type of wrong-answer pattern as shown for the items in the preceding sections of this chapter, but for which no explanation of the concentration is apparent to the present writer. These items are listed in Table 108.[6] For each of these items there is a concentration of high-status errors on some one distractor which is more marked than any concentration of low-status errors. These items thus add confirmation to the hypothesis that low-status pupils indulge in more random guessing than do the high-status pupils. Although no obvious reason for the high-status concentration on one distractor is seen, it is presumed that there is some explanation, since in some of the items the degree of concentration is very marked and can hardly be accounted for in terms of chance.

No explanation

In preceding sections of this chapter possible explanations — and partial explanations — for status differences in the distribution of wrong responses have been suggested for sixty-three of the seventy-five items

6. For a reference to detailed wrong-answer data for these items, in form comparable to those reported for the items in earlier portions of this chapter, see Note 1 in Appendix D.

TABLE 106

ITEM SHOWING STATUS DIFFERENCE IN WRONG RESPONSES

(Thirteen- and Fourteen-Year-Old Pupils)

Status Group	Base for Computing Percentages		Percentage Distribution of Responses — Mark . . . the word which has the same or most nearly the same meaning as the beginning word of each line: opposed —					
	Number of Pupils	Number of Errors	censored	adverse	involved	oppressed	morose	(omit)
High...	...	133	22%	....	5%**	53%**	8%	13%
Low...	...	303	25%	....	21%**	39%**	10%	6%
High...	233	...	12%	43%**	3%	30%	5%	7%
Low...	361	...	21%	15%**	17%	32%	8%	5%

TABLE 107

ITEM SHOWING STATUS DIFFERENCE IN WRONG RESPONSES

(Thirteen- and Fourteen-Year-Old Pupils)

Status Group	Base for Computing Percentages		Percentage Distribution of Responses — Mark . . . the word which is OPPOSITE, or most nearly opposite, in meaning to the beginning word of each line: alert —					
	Number of Pupils	Number of Errors	illiterate	pert	sluggish	disabled	easy	(omit)
High...	...	79	52%**	15%	....	24%	5%*	4%
Low...	...	245	27%**	23%	....	31%	14%*	4%
High...	233	...	18%	5%	66%**	8%	2%	1%
Low...	361	...	19%	16%	32%**	21%	9%	3%

TABLE 108

THIRTEEN ITEMS SHOWING HIGHER CONCENTRATION OF WRONG RESPONSES FOR HIGH-STATUS PUPILS THAN FOR LOW-STATUS PUPILS BUT WITHOUT APPARENT EXPLANATION FOR THE CONCENTRATION

Item Number	Age Level	Item and Responses*
1	9-10	Bird is to feathers as fish is to — scales, tails,* song, beak, mouth.
2	9-10	Put a dot under the one in the last of this row that belongs with the first three —
		(Greatest high-status concentration of errors on the log)
3	9-10	Mark the drawing with black and white squares which is nearest the pitcher —
		(Greatest high-status concentration of errors on the first drawing)
4	13-14	Mark . . . the word which is OPPOSITE, or most nearly opposite, in meaning to the beginning word of each line: genuine — stolen, counterfeit, sincere, original, unworthy.
5	13-14	Mark . . . the word which is OPPOSITE, or most nearly opposite, in meaning to the beginning word of each line: disperse — approve, remove, gather, spare, whisper.

TABLE 108 – Continued

Item Number	Age Level	Item and Responses*
6	13-14	An uncle is to an aunt as a son is to a (?) – brother, father, sister, daughter, girl.
7	13-14	An electric light is to a candle as a motorcycle is to – a bicycle, an automobile, wheels, speed, police.
8	13-14	A ship always has – engine, guns, hull, passengers, freight.
9	13-14	An object or institution that will not perish or cease is said to be – stationary, stable, permanent, solid, sound.
10	13-14	Contentment always involves – devotion, position, satisfaction, elation, recognition.
11	13-14	Which of these series contains a wrong number? – 3-6-9-12-15, 1-4-7-10-13, 2-5-8-11-15, 2-4-6-8-10, 1-3-5-7-9.
12	13-14	If the following words were arranged in order, which would be in the middle? – plaster, frame, wallpaper, lath, foundation.
13	13-14	The first three objects in each row are alike in some way. Find another object in the same row that belongs with them – (Greatest high-status concentration of errors on the ladder)

* Response showing highest concentration of high-status errors is underlined.

for which such differences were found to be significant at the 1 per cent level. For the remaining twelve items no convincing explanation is apparent to the writer.[7] These twelve "no explanation" items differ from those in Table 108 in that these twelve items show a higher concentration of responses on some one distractor for the low-status pupils than they do for the high-status pupils. They do not, therefore, support the hypothesis suggested on page 275.

Conclusions

The various explanations suggested by the seventy-five items discussed in this chapter may be summarized in the three generalizations which follow. While none of the explanations offered, or the generalizations based upon them, should be regarded as completely established on a scientific basis, they can at least be regarded as promising hypotheses to be subjected to further investigation.

1. When items refer to objects, processes, or words, with which children from high-status and those from low-status homes have different opportunities for being familiar, status differences in the distribution of responses may result — differences which seem to conform to the hypothecated differences in opportunity. (Statement based on analysis of 17 items.)

   Specifically, such differential familiarity may be seen in the case of:

   a) Objects
   b) Arithmetic processes
   c) Proverbs
   d) Words

2. On items which include some distractor which for some reason is particularly attractive, high-status pupils are more likely to be attracted to that distractor, while low-status pupils tend to distribute their responses more nearly evenly over all available distractors. (Statement based on analysis of 46 items.) This may be evidence of a higher level of effort on the part of high-status pupils and of a greater tendency to guess somewhat indiscriminately on the part of low-status pupils.

   The "particularly attractive" distractor upon which the high-status responses tend to be concentrated may be any one of several types:

   a) Next-best or near-correct responses
   b) Distractors with associational value
   c) Distractors which are distinctly unfamiliar
   d) Distractors which look or sound like the given word
   e) Unknown reason for concentration

3. There are a number of items for which no ready explanation as to the status difference in wrong responses is apparent. (Statement based on 12 items.)

7. For a reference to a listing of these twelve items, with the wrong-answer data comparable to those reported for items in earlier portions of this chapter, see Note 1 in Appendix D.

Possible implications of these findings for gaining insight into the nature of status differences in I.Q.'s are discussed in chapter viii.[8]

Summary

The pattern of wrong responses on 315 items is compared for the two status groups. For 136 of the items the pattern is closely similar for both status groups; for 75 items, however, there are clearly significant status differences. These 75 items are examined subjectively for clues as to possible explanations or reasons for the significant status differences. As a basis for this subjective examination, a statement of ways in which the cultural experiences and motivations of high-status children may be expected to differ from those of low-status children is formulated. The statement is based upon research studies of social-class characteristics in a number of communities. The individual items are then examined to see whether status differences in the wrong-answer patterns may be explained in terms of differences in the cultural backgrounds. This is found to be the case for a large number of the items. At the same time an effort is made to gain insight into any other possible factors which might help to explain the observed differences.

---

8. See pp. 64, 66-67.

CHAPTER XXIII

STATUS DIFFERENCES IN CORRECT RESPONSES FOR CERTAIN INDIVIDUAL TEST ITEMS

In the preceding chapter a rather large number of items showing significant status differences with respect to wrong responses were examined and a number of tentative hypotheses put forth with respect to them. In the present chapter some additional individual items will be subjected to essentially the same kind of analysis, though more briefly, in an endeavor to determine whether additional hypotheses will be suggested on the basis of additional items or whether the same kinds of explanations put forth in the preceding chapter will serve to explain these items.

Items Showing Unusually Large Status Differences

For the purposes of this section, "unusually large status differences" are defined as status differences that lie at least 1.8 standard deviations above the mean status difference at each age level, with both the means and the standard deviations taken on the basis of the stable items only. This particular criterion of largeness is, of course, entirely arbitrary. It was decided upon primarily on the basis that this would provide a list (after certain eliminations described below) of approximately twenty-five items to be examined. This standard is met by items from the tests for the younger pupils which have index differences of 19 points or more and by items from the tests for the older pupils which have differences of 23 points or more.

Owing to errors of measurement, it is not possible to be sure that the "true" status difference characteristic of any given item is exactly as reported on the basis of this particular test administration. It is, however, virtually certain that the true differences for the items listed in this section are at least larger than the average difference for all the items at each age level.[1] In order to be even more certain that no item should be included in this consideration of large-difference items purely as a result of measurement errors, any item whose most extreme index value was 80 or higher (or 20 or lower) was excluded. These dividing points were selected because it was shown in chapter xvi that differences based upon indexes over 80 or under 20 are considerably less reliable than those bases upon indexes between 80 and 20.[2] An exception was made in the

---

1. For a reference to evidence supporting this statement, based upon somewhat unsatisfactory approximations to reliability coefficients and standard errors of measurement for the indexes and index differences, see Note 1 in Appendix D. Index differences which are 1.8 standard deviations above the mean are more than 3 standard errors of measurement above the mean.

2. See pp. 174-78.

case of a few items for which one index was above 80 but whose index difference was so large that even if the high index should fluctuate down to 80 the difference would still be as large as that required for inclusion in this section.

There are twenty-five items which meet the criterion just described. All of them have differences which are significantly greater than zero at the 1 per cent level of significance.

While all available data will be utilized in trying to understand possible reasons for observed status differences, the primary emphasis in this section will be on the status differences with respect to right answers rather than on differences within the distribution of the wrong answers, as was the case in the preceding chapter. Both right-answer and wrong-answer data will be given for all these items for which it is available; the wrong-answer data will be confined, however, to percentage distributions of the errors in each status group.

As in the previous chapter, this analysis is primarily subjective in nature. The qualifications and cautions stated in the preceding chapter apply equally well to this one.[3] No attempt will be made to suggest explanations for all the status differences. The items for which no plausible explanations occur to the writer will be listed at the end of this section so that the reader may endeavor to find explanations of his own if he desires to do so.

Differential familiarity with objects

Two of the items which show large status differences deal with materials which are obviously more likely to be familiar to pupils from high-status backgrounds than to those from low-status backgrounds. Item-analysis data for the first of these items are shown in Table 109. The manner of presentation of the data on the items in this section is somewhat similar to that used in the preceding chapter. Double asterisks are used to indicate status differences (on either the right answers or any wrong responses) which are significant at the 1 per cent level. Single asterisks will be used on later items to indicate status differences significant at the 5 per cent level. Any unstarred pair of percentages has a status difference too small to be significant even at the 5 per cent level.

The item in Table 109 has already been discussed in some detail in chapter xxii.[4] It will be recalled that the suggested explanation for the large status difference was in terms of the greater opportunities of high-status children for familiarity with concert orchestras, greater incidence of private music lessons for high-status pupils, and probable greater interest of high-status pupils in music opportunities within the school.

Much the same kind of explanation seems to apply to the second item (Table 110). It may be also that the greater prevalence of phonographs and of records, especially of a classical type, may operate to give the high-status pupils more opportunity for being familiar with the word "sonata."

Proverbs

Two of the large-difference items (Tables 111 and 112) are items which quote a proverb and ask the pupil to select the best interpretation

---

3. See pp. 248, 255-56.
4. See pp. 259-60.

TABLE 109[+]

ITEM SHOWING UNUSUALLY LARGE STATUS DIFFERENCE

(Thirteen- and Fourteen-Year-Old Pupils)

Status Group	Rights as Per Cent of All Pupils	Number of Errors	Percentage Distribution of Errors					
			Pick out the ONE WORD which does not belong with the others —					
			cello	harp	drum	violin	guitar	(omit)
High...	85%**	37	19%**	5%	.....	0%	76%**	0%
Low...	45%**	196	48%**	8%	.....	5%	37%**	2%

Status difference on right responses = 39% (23 index points).

[+] This is the first of a series of tables in this chapter, each of which presents data for an individual item. An explanation of the asterisks in the table, and of the proper manner of reading the table, will be found in the text accompanying this first table.

All the data reported for individual items in this chapter are based on Old American pupils only (except for the data in Table 147, on p. 356).

All the items reproduced in this chapter are taken from copyrighted tests and are reproduced by special arrangement with the owners of the copyrights. The items may not be reproduced in any manner without the prior permission of the test publishers.

TABLE 110

ITEM SHOWING UNUSUALLY LARGE STATUS DIFFERENCE

(Thirteen- and Fourteen-Year-Old Pupils)

Status Group	Rights as Per Cent of All Pupils	Number of Errors	Percentage Distribution of Errors					
			Sonata is a term used in —					
			drawing	drama	music	poetry	phonetics	(omit)
High...	74%**	56	7%	30%	.....	20%	18%	25%
Low...	29%**	240	11%	29%	.....	18%	29%	14%

Status difference on right responses = 46% (26 index points).

TABLE 111

ITEM SHOWING UNUSUALLY LARGE STATUS DIFFERENCE

(Thirteen- and Fourteen-Year-Old Pupils)

Status Group	Rights as Per Cent of All Pupils	Number of Errors	Percentage Distribution of Errors				
			There is a saying, "A drowning man will grasp at straws." This means that —				
			A man will sink more easily than a straw	Everyone should learn to swim	Desperate people cling to absurd hopes	Those who cannot swim should stay on land	(omit)
High . . .	92%**	18	6%**	33%	. . . .	50%*	11%
Low . . .	62%**	132	42%**	27%	. . . .	25%*	7%

Status difference on right responses = 30% (24 index points).

TABLE 112

ITEM SHOWING UNUSUALLY LARGE STATUS DIFFERENCE

(Thirteen- and Fourteen-Year-Old Pupils)

Status Group	Rights as Per Cent of All Pupils	Number of Errors	Percentage Distribution of Errors				
			The saying, "Little strokes fell great oaks," means —				
			Continued effort brings results	Oak trees are weak	Little strokes are best	Anyone can fell an oak	(omit)
High . . .	85%**	34	. . . .	6%**	74%	18%	3%
Low . . .	48%**	186	. . . .	23%**	58%	16%	3%

Status difference on right responses = 37% (23 index points).

of its meaning. Both of the items have been discussed in the previous chapter.[5] It will be recalled that the explanation given there was in terms of an apparent tendency for high-status pupils to check a figurative interpretation of a proverb and for low-status pupils to check a more literal interpretation. This was explained in cultural terms by reference to the fact that most proverbs deal with virtues prized especially by the middle class and are probably, therefore, emphasized much more in middle-class homes than in lower-class homes.

Formalized or bookish vocabulary

The seven items in this section are ones which show large status differences and which deal with a kind of abstract, unfamiliar, bookish vocabulary. An example is shown in Table 113. It should be noticed that on this item the number of low-status pupils answering the item correctly (24 per cent) is only slightly above the chance expectation on a five-choice item.

TABLE 113

ITEM SHOWING UNUSUALLY LARGE STATUS DIFFERENCE

(Thirteen- and Fourteen-Year-Old Pupils)

Status Group	Rights as Per Cent of All Pupils	Number of Errors	Percentage Distribution of Errors					
			Mark . . . the word which has the SAME or most nearly the same meaning as the beginning word of each line: introductory —					
			social	advisory	transitory	preliminary	internal	(omit)
High . . .	66%**	80	19%	28%	26%	. . .	11%	16%
Low . . .	24%**	273	23%	31%	21%	. . .	16%	10%

Status difference on right responses = 42% (23 index points).

It seems quite clear that this item involves six words most of which are rather difficult, all of which are abstract, and none of which will occur frequently in normal conversation for thirteen- and fourteen-year-old children of either status group. As a matter of fact, words such as these will not occur frequently even in adult conversation in most homes. The few homes in which such words might be generally familiar would undoubtedly be high-status homes.

Familiarity with these words will probably come for most children only from reading (and not comic books!) or from fairly formal vocabulary study in school. In both such activities the high-status pupils have considerably more opportunity than do the low-status pupils. This statement might be questioned with regard to the vocabulary study in school, since it can be argued that all children attend the same school. Only in a superficial sense is this true, however. By the time these pupils have reached

5. See pp. 269-72.

the junior high school grades, considerable differentiation of English work has occurred in the typical school program; the low-status pupils will, on the whole, tend to be found much less frequently in the "academic" English courses, or sections, where formal vocabulary drill is likely to be stressed, and much more frequently in "general" courses, "low-ability" sections, etc., where the emphasis is different.[6] Moreover, the problem of differential status-group motivation may become important in connection with the study of such words as the above, which involve little intrinsic motivation and which depend almost entirely upon school and family pressures to do well in school even with uninteresting and seemingly meaningless materials. In this case, the high-status pupil may be benefited by the continual pressures from parents who expect their child to make a commendable school record regardless of the interest of the material for him.

There are six other items (Tables 114 to 119) for which the large status differences may very well be due to the general nature of the vocabulary involved. These six items do not require any special comment. The status difference on the item in Table 119 seems somewhat surprising, in view of the widespread use of the terms "amateur" and "professional" in sports. One would rather expect that the low-status boys, at least, would exhibit no particular handicap on this item.

TABLE 114

ITEM SHOWING UNUSUALLY LARGE STATUS DIFFERENCE

(Thirteen- and Fourteen-Year-Old Pupils)

Status Group	Rights as Per Cent of All Pupils	Number of Errors	Percentage Distribution of Errors					
			Mark . . . the word which is OPPOSITE, or most nearly opposite, in meaning to the beginning word of each line: abundance —					
			lib-erality	frugal-ity	lux-ury	hun-ger	scar-city	(omit)
High . . .	91%**	22	23%	45%	14%*	14%	. . .	5%
Low . . .	60%**	140	16%	29%	34%*	16%	. . .	4%

Status difference on right responses = 30% (23 index points).

TABLE 115

ITEM SHOWING UNUSUALLY LARGE STATUS DIFFERENCE

(Thirteen- and Fourteen-Year-Old Pupils)

Status Group	Rights as Per Cent of All Pupils	Number of Errors	Percentage Distribution of Errors					
			Mark . . . the word which is OPPOSITE, or most nearly opposite, in meaning to the beginning word of each line: waste —					
			refuse	con-serve	devas-tate	dole	gen-erate	(omit)
High . . .	92%**	19	11%	. . .	37%	16%	32%	5%
Low . . .	60%**	142	26%	. . .	40%	13%	13%	8%

Status difference on right responses = 32% (24 index points).

TABLE 116

ITEM SHOWING UNUSUALLY LARGE STATUS DIFFERENCE

(Thirteen- and Fourteen-Year-Old Pupils)

Status Group	Rights as Per Cent of All Pupils	Number of Errors	Percentage Distribution of Errors					
			Order is to confusion as (?) is to war —					
			guns	peace	powder	thunder	army	(omit)
High . . .	88%**	28	57%	. . .	4%	7%	32%	0%
Low . . .	52%**	176	52%	. . .	7%	6%	32%	2%

Status difference on right responses = 36% (23 index points).

6. In the Rockford public elementary schools, English is not formally sectioned on an ability basis, but in all schools where a grade comprises more than one section the divisions are made on the basis of chronological age — which amounts to roughly the same thing, since the older pupils in any given grade will tend to be those with the lower I.Q.'s. In at least one of the suburban elementary schools the English work is sectioned in all grades on the basis of an achievement test score. In the junior high schools, English sections are established on the basis of intelligence tests and elementary-school records.

TABLE 117

ITEM SHOWING UNUSUALLY LARGE STATUS DIFFERENCE
(Thirteen- and Fourteen-Year-Old Pupils)

Status Group	Rights as Per Cent of All Pupils	Number of Errors	Percentage Distribution of Errors					
			Which word means the opposite of pride? --					
			sorrow	proud	miserable	conceit	humility	(omit)
High...	69%**	72	29%	7%	26%	36%*	...	1%
Low ...	29%**	253	37%	16%	21%	22%*	...	5%

Status difference on right responses = 40% (23 index points).

TABLE 118

ITEM SHOWING UNUSUALLY LARGE STATUS DIFFERENCE
(Nine- and Ten-Year-Old Pupils)

Status Group	Rights as Per Cent of All Pupils	Number of Errors	Percentage Distribution of Errors					
			When he awoke he was ... to find his dog gone. A word for the blank is —					
			noticed	sincere	portly	before	surprised	(omit)
High...	94%**	14	36%	7%	21%	14%	...	21%
Low ...	68%**	103	33%	21%	19%	17%	...	9%

Status difference on right responses = 26% (22 index points).

TABLE 119

ITEM SHOWING UNUSUALLY LARGE STATUS DIFFERENCE
(Thirteen- and Fourteen-Year-Old Pupils)

Status Group	Rights as Per Cent of All Pupils	Number of Errors	Percentage Distribution of Errors					
			Mark ... the word which is OPPOSITE, or most nearly opposite, in meaning to the beginning word of each line: amateur —					
			novitiate	musical	professional	inventor	experience	(omit)
High...	87%**	31	19%	26%	...	16%	26%	13%
Low ...	50%**	177	24%	28%	...	20%	18%	11%

Status difference on right responses = 37% (24 index points).

Abstract versus concrete words

In chapter xxii one item was reported which seemed to suggest the possibility that high-status pupils are more at home with abstract terms while low-status pupils tend to prefer concrete ones where there is a choice. This seemed a reasonable hypothesis, in light of the known characteristics of typical vocabulary usage at the two status levels. The large status difference for the item shown in Table 120 may be explained on this basis.

This item shows the third largest status difference (second largest, if only the "stable" items, as defined on p. 370, are considered) of all the items for the older pupils. The reliability of this large difference is

TABLE 120

ITEM SHOWING UNUSUALLY LARGE STATUS DIFFERENCE
(Thirteen- and Fourteen-Year-Old Pupils)

Status Group	Rights as Per Cent of All Pupils	Number of Errors	Percentage Distribution of Errors					
			A wheel always has —					
			circumference	spokes	tire	wood	metal	(omit)
High...	89%**	25	...	84%*	8%	4%	0%*	4%
Low ...	48%**	186	...	67%*	17%	1%	15%*	0%

Status difference on right responses = 41% (27 index points).

brought into some doubt, however, by the fact that the low-status ethnic pupils do substantially better (66 per cent right) on this item than do the low-status Old Americans. If the status difference is computed on the basis of the ethnics, the difference falls from 27 to 17 index points, and the item would no longer be included in the present list of large-difference items. On most items, differences between the two low-status groups are small, which tends to lend confidence to the stability of the low-status data. The reverse is true for this particular item.

Answering this question correctly depends upon the pupil's ability to select a general abstract trait rather than one of the more specific concrete ones which are frequently but not always characteristic of a wheel. If it is true that low-status pupils are at a disadvantage when dealing with abstract terms, that might contribute substantially to the very large status difference found on this item.

There is, however, a futher explanation to be suggested in connection with this item. Since the particular trait to be selected by the pupil, "circumference," is one which forms an important part of geometry and mathematics study, it is reasonable to expect that high-status pupils will have an advantage with respect to it, for reasons outlined in more detail earlier.

Words with different connotations at different status levels

There is one item (Table 121) whose large status difference may be due in part to difference in the meanings of certain words for pupils from different status backgrounds. This item yields the fourth largest status difference (third largest, if only the stable items are considered) of all the items for the older pupils.

High-status children are probably mostly enrolled in academic college-preparatory curriculums, whereas low-status children will be found in more substantial numbers in vocational and other nonacademic curriculums. This being the case, the low-status children will probably be much less familiar than high-status children with the subject of trigonometry — not because of any lack of intelligence itself but because they have had no

TABLE 121

ITEM SHOWING UNUSUALLY LARGE STATUS DIFFERENCE

(Thirteen- and Fourteen-Year-Old Pupils)

Status Group	Rights as Per Cent of All Pupils	Number of Errors	Percentage Distribution of Errors					
			Pick out the **ONE WORD** which does not belong with the others —					
			arithmetic	geometry	history	trigonometry	algebra	(omit)
High . . .	82%**	41	17%	7%	. . .	68%	5%	2%
Low . . .	37%**	226	7%	9%	. . .	75%	9%	0%

Status difference on right responses = 46% (27 index points).

occasion to be exposed to the term in any way that held meaning for them. That this latter explanation, perhaps coupled with the length of the unfamiliar word, may have contributed substantially to the large number of low-status pupils failing to answer this question correctly is indicated by the fact that 170 low-status pupils (47 per cent of the total group) checked "trigonometry" as the correct answer. This error accounted for three-fourths of all the errors made by low-status pupils. It is true, of course, that "trigonometry" was also the most attractive distractor for high-status pupils. In the latter case, however, it attracted only 28 out of the total group of pupils, although this accounted for 68 per cent of the relatively few errors made by the high-status pupils.

There is a further objection to this item — at least a theoretical one. The correct answer is stated by the authors to be "history," presumably on the grounds that the other four school subjects are all in the field of mathematics. There seems to be no real reason, however, for ruling out "arithmetic" as the correct answer on the grounds that the other four are high-school or college subjects, while arithmetic is normally an elementary-school subject.

This ambiguity in the question is itself a serious fault, but it becomes especially objectionable when it places an additional handicap on those pupils (predominantly low-status) who are retarded in school. In the present study, for example, thirteen- and fourteen-year-old pupils who are seriously retarded (mostly low-status) are found in the elementary schools rather than in the junior high schools. It would not have been surprising to find that these pupils tended to check "arithmetic" as being in a different category from the other subjects listed. It would be difficult to argue that such a response, for these pupils, would be incorrect — or unintelligent. The data shown above for this item indicate, however, that this was apparently not a serious factor in this item, since the "arithmetic" distractor accounted for only a small proportion of the low-status errors.

No apparent explanation of large status differences

There are twelve items which have unusually large status differences, as defined for the purposes of this section, but for which the present writer sees no obvious explanation in cultural terms. These twelve items are listed in Table 122.[7] All but one of these twelve items are verbal in form, but the vocabulary involved does not seem to be sufficiently difficult or culturally biased as to impose a serious status difference of the type described on pages 308 to 312. This is purely a subjective judgment, of course, and it may be that on some of these items more careful investigation, perhaps based upon an experimental approach, would reveal that a number of these words are likewise ones which are more familiar to high-status pupils because of differences in reading opportunites, reading habits, type of adult conversation heard in the home, etc.

Only two of the items in Table 122 appear to call for special comment. It seems rather surprising to find among a list of items showing unusually large status differences an item like No. 6, since it involves the knowledge that "rich" and "poor" are opposite terms. It would be reasonable to suppose that this particular set of opposites is one of which low-status children might be especially acutely aware. Possibly the results would be

7. For a reference to more detailed wrong-answer data for these items see Note 1 in Appendix D.

different at an older age level. On the one nonverbal item (No. 4) in Table 122, an examining of the distribution of wrong answers indicates that both status groups show some tendency for the second picture to be the most attractive distractor. This suggests that there may be some difficulty in understanding either the word or the idea of "opposite" in the accompanying oral instructions. There is some tendency for this to be more markedly true for low-status pupils than for high-status pupils, but the difference is not large enough to be significant even at the 5 per cent level and may well be a chance variation. It will be noted that there are three other items listed in Table 122 which involve understanding of the word or the idea of "opposite."

Items Showing Unusually Small Status Differences

The preceding section has presented twenty-five items showing relatively large status differences and has attempted to suggest possible explanations for some of the large differences. In order to have a contrasting group of items for comparative purposes, this section will present some items showing relatively small status differences. This can be done rather briefly, since there is no need to suggest lengthy explanations for status differences which do not exist! Three different lists of small-difference items will be presented.

The first will consist of items chosen on a basis comparable to that used for selecting the large-difference items in the previous section. The index differences for these items are all 1.8 standard deviations or more below the mean index difference for the two age levels. This standard means that these small-difference items from the tests for younger pupils have differences of -1 point, or smaller, and that those from the tests for older pupils have differences of 6 points, or less. For this purpose the scale of differences is thought of as one continuum, without regard to the zero point. A difference of -4 index points, for example, is thought of as being smaller than one of -1 point. As a matter of fact, there are only nineteen items which show negative status differences; fourteen of these are excluded from this section under the first, third, or fourth exclusions listed below.

It is almost certain that the "true" difference for these items, if it could be known, would be at least smaller than the average status differences for all items.[8] In addition, the following types of items were excluded from the list presented in this section:

1. Items for which either one of the two indexes is 80 or higher or 20 or lower.

2. Items for which the status difference is large enough to be significant at the 5 per cent level.

3. Items for which the percentage of each status group answering the item correctly is 90 or higher.

---

8. For a reference to evidence supporting this statement, based upon somewhat unsatisfactory approximations to reliability coefficients and standard errors of measurement for the index differences, see Note 1 in Appendix D. Index differences which are 1.8 standard deviations below the mean are more than 3 standard errors of measurement below the mean.

TABLE 122

ITEMS SHOWING UNUSUALLY LARGE STATUS DIFFERENCES FOR WHICH NO PARTICULAR EXPLANATION IS APPARENT

Item Number	Age Level	Item	High Status	Low Status	Differ- ence	Index Differ- ence
1	13-14	Pick out the ONE WORD which does not belong with the others — priest, organist, minister, rabbi, bishop	89%	48%	41%	28
2	9-10	Find the three things which are alike in each list — store, banana, basket, apple, seed, plum	96	70	26	27
3	9-10	There was no ...of a storm. A word for the blank is — sign, school, house, after, sea	94	69	26	23
4	9-10	Mark the picture at the opposite end of the row from the boy using the towel	87	56	31	21
5	9-10	Find the two things that the first thing is never without: cat — hair, owner, mouse, claws, milk	91	64	27	21
6	9-10	Find the two opposites in each list — old, rich, wide, poor, green, full	93	69	24	21

(Per Cent Right: High Status, Low Status, Difference)

TABLE 122 - Continued

Item Number	Age Level	Item	Per Cent Right			Index Difference
			High Status	Low Status	Difference	
7	9-10	Which of these words comes first in the dictionary? — apple, long, winter, snow, peach	94%	70%	24%	21
8	9-10	Find the two opposites in each list — soon, above, when, even, below, back	89	62	27	20
9	9-10	Think how the words would read if they made the best sentence you can get out of the words, then draw a line under what would be the first word and a line under what would be the last word in the sentence. Your sentence must make a statement, not ask a question — apples, trees, on, grow	93	70	23	20
10	9-10	Bird is to feathers as fish is to — scales, tails, song, beak, mouth	80	48	32	19
11	9-10	Find the three things which are alike in each list — sea, rock, mountain, lake, storm, river	88	62	26	19
12	9-10	Find the two opposites in each list — laugh, now, wait, whistle, study, cry	90	65	24	19

4. Items for which the percentage of each status group answering the item correctly is within 10 percentage points of the chance or guessing expectation for the particular item.

The first exclusion is comparable to one already explained in connection with the preceding section.[9] The second was adopted in order to restrict the list of small-difference items to those where there is a reasonable possibility that the real difference is zero. The third exclusion represents items which are so easy that virtually all pupils of both status groups are able to answer them correctly. In such cases the status differences necessarily tend to become very small. To study the content of such items would serve no particularly useful purpose. Such items not only do not exhibit any status differential but also do not exhibit any intelligence differential in the sense that — for pupils of this age — they have little power to discriminate between pupils of high and of low intelligence. The fourth exclusion represents items which are so difficult that the number of correct answers for both status groups can be largely accounted for on a guessing hypothesis. In such cases the substantial equivalence of right answers for both status groups does not necessarily mean any inherent lack of status difference in the content of the item.

When the above exclusions are made, twelve items remain to be considered. Of these items it can be said that it is almost certain that the "true" status difference of each is at least below the average for items of the appropriate age level and that for most of them it is well below the average. For each of them it is at least possible (5 per cent possibility, or more) that the status difference in the larger universe from which the present samples are drawn is really zero.

These twelve items are listed, with their pertinent data, in Table 123. Probably the first thing that will be noticed about the small-difference items in this table is that only two of the twelve items are primarily verbal in nature; most of them deal with pictures or geometric designs. The two items which are verbal in nature (Nos. 6 and 9) have a very simple vocabulary; in neither of them does the testing of vocabulary knowledge appear to be an important part of the item's function. Five of the items have as their main content meaningless geometric designs or drawings, usually of a very simple sort. It is apparent that most of these items are such that pupils from any status level would have no previous contact with this kind of material. The ideal of equal familiarity is thus at least approached by having the content unfamiliar to all.

The five pictorial items deal primarily with fairly simple everyday objects that most children would probably be familiar with at either status level. Three items (Nos. 7, 8, and 12) deal with a boy boiling water over a campfire, a diamond, a tennis racket, fancy gloves, skis, a surfboard, and a sailboat — all objects which might reasonably be expected to have some status bias. The data indicate, however, that low-status pupils are able to do practically as well on these items as do the high-status pupils.

The particular list of small-difference items reported in Table 123 was selected primarily on the basis of their status differences being almost certainly smaller than the average status difference for items at the two age levels. In chapter xvii a group of twenty-seven items were identified whose status differences were sufficiently close to zero that it was entirely possible that the true difference might be zero.[10] Ten of

9. See pp. 304-5.
10. See pp. 182-87.

these twenty-seven items are included in the list already reported in Table 123, but the other seventeen are different items. The twenty-seven items meeting the criteria set out in chapter xvii are listed, with their pertinent data, in Table 124.

Of the twenty-seven items in Table 124, eleven deal with geometric figures, eleven with pictorial materials, four with entirely verbal material, and one with letters or numbers in meaningless combinations. The few verbal items in this table are all simple in vocabulary and do not appear to test, primarily, the pupil's understanding of the words used in the items. Of the eleven geometric-figure items, almost all are comparatively simple designs, although they are by no means all easy for either status group. This is likewise true of many of the picture items. In at least five of the picture items, however, there are objects which might well be expected to introduce status differences. On Items Nos. 4, 9, 10, 16, and 26, for instance, it seems reasonable to presume that high-status pupils might have more opportunity than low-status pupils for familiarity with camping tents, bird cages, campfire cookery, diamonds, tennis rackets, kid gloves, fireplaces, and hot-air balloons. On none of these items, however, did the presence of these pictures discriminate heavily against the low-status pupils. On some items (e.g., No. 16) this may be due to the fact that only a superficial acquaintance with the object pictured is required. It does not require a very penetrating knowledge of fireplaces to know that they are sources of heat! On the other hand, in such items as Nos. 9, 10, and 26, it seems surprising that the low-status pupils can do as well as the high-status pupils despite what is presumably a lesser opportunity for the required knowledge.

The fact that so few verbal items occur in either of these lists of items showing unusually small status differences is itself a significant fact. For some purposes, however, it will be useful to examine the _verbal_ items which do show relatively small status differences; their characteristics may then be contrasted more directly with those of the large-difference items listed in the earlier part of this chapter. In preparing a list of small-difference verbal items, it was not possible to impose the same rigid conditions used in selecting the list of small-difference items presented in the two preceding tables.

Table 125 lists the ten verbal items which showed the smallest status differences, for nine- and ten-year-old pupils, after excluding extremely difficult and extremely easy items and those based on relatively unstable indexes. (Exclusions Nos. 1, 3, and 4, as listed on pp. 315-18.) It should be noticed that, in order to secure ten verbal items, it was necessary to include some with differences large enough to be significant at the 1 per cent level. Verbal items typically show status differences of such a size that there simply are not ten such items which exhibit differences that are not large enough to be significant, after eliminating the unstable and extremely easy and extremely difficult items.

Six of the ten items in Table 125 require the rearrangement of letters to form a word; in five of these six items the words to be formed are very simple ones with which all children this age would presumably be familiar; in the other item of this type (No. 2) the words are given in the test item so the pupil can solve the problem correctly even if he has never heard of the word itself. Two of the remaining four items require the pupil to identify a letter which is common to three words but missing from the fourth; the words involved in these items are quite simple, and in any

TABLE 123

ITEMS SHOWING UNUSUALLY SMALL STATUS DIFFERENCES (FIRST CRITERION)

Item Number	Age Level	Item	Per Cent Right			Index Difference
			High Status	Low Status	Difference	
1	9-10	Put a dot under the one in the last of this row that belongs with the first three—	71%	74%	-3%	-3
2	9-10	Draw a line from the biggest square to the smallest circle—	86	89	-3	-3
3	9-10	Mark the square in this row that you think is closest to the large F in the upper corner of the page—	60	63	-3	-2

TABLE 123 – Continued

Item Number	Age Level	Item	Per Cent Right			Index Difference
			High Status	Low Status	Difference	
4	9-10	Make a dot in the biggest square and a cross in the first circle — (Drawing for this item is the same as for Item No. 2 above)	83%	85%	-2%	-2
5	13-14	The objects . . . are either rights or lefts. Mark on the answer sheet under the R for rights, and under the L for lefts — R L	67	68	-1	-1
6	13-14	W is between X and Y. X is between Y and Z. Therefore — W is not between Y and Z, W is between X and Z, W is nearer to X than to Z	51	50	1	1
7	13-14	The first three objects in each row are alike in some way. Find another object in the same row that belongs with them	43	41	2	1

(Continued on next page)

TABLE 123 – Continued

Item Number	Age Level	Item	Per Cent Right			Index Difference
			High Status	Low Status	Difference	
8	13-14	The first three objects in each row are alike in some way. Find another object in the same row that belongs with them	46%	43%	3%	1
9	13-14	If a freight train travels at the rate of 20 miles an hour, how many miles will it travel in 4 hours? — 5, 24, 80, 60	86	84	2	2
10	13-14	Three of the four designs at the right are alike. Which one is not like the other three? —	78	74	4	2
11*	13-14	In each row mark every card that is like the first card in the row —	69	65	4	3

TABLE 123 - Continued

Item Number	Age Level	Item	Per Cent Right			Index Difference
			High Status	Low Status	Difference	
12	13-14	The first three objects in each row are alike in some way. Find another object in the same row that belongs with them —	54%	49%	5%	3

* The particular diagram which constitutes the "item" to which the data refer is marked in the answer space under the diagram.

TABLE 124

ITEMS SHOWING UNUSUALLY SMALL STATUS DIFFERENCES (SECOND CRITERION)

Item Number	Age Level	Item	Per Cent Right			Index Difference
			High Status	Low Status	Difference	
1	9-10	Find the three things that are alike and draw a line through the one that is not like those three —	81%	80%	1%	0
2	9-10	Mark the square with the little piece beside it that is partly curved outward and partly curved inward —	56	55	1	0
3	9-10	Find the three things that are alike and draw a line through the one that is not like those three —	61	60	1	1

TABLE 124 - Continued

Item Number	Age Level	Item	High Status	Low Status	Difference	Index Difference
4	9-10	Find the three things that are alike and draw a line through the one that is not like those three —	59%	58%	1%	1
5	9-10	Find the three things that are alike and draw a line through the one that is not like those three —	52	49	3	1
6	9-10	Mark the pair of curved drawings that are widest at the bottom —	76	75	1	1
7	13-14	(For text and picture for this item, see Table 123, Item No. 5)	67	68	-1	-1
8	13-14	(For text of this item, see Table 123, Item No. 6)	51	50	1	1
9	13-14	(For text and pictures for this item, see Table 123, Item No. 7)	43	41	2	1

(Continued on next page)

TABLE 124 - Continued

Item Number	Age Level	Item	Per Cent Right			Index Difference
			High Status	Low Status	Difference	
10	13-14	(For text and pictures for this item, see Table 123, Item No. 8)	46%	44%	3%	1
11	13-14	Mark the third string —	90	89	1	2
12	9-10	Find the three things that are alike and draw a line through the one that is not like those three —	68	66	2	2
13	9-10	Mark the person who needs a piece of paper half as big as the one that person has —	80	78	2	2
14	9-10	(For text and drawings for this item, see Table 123, Item No. 4)	83	85	-2	-2
15	13-14	(For text of this item, see Table 123, Item No. 9)	86	84	2	2

TABLE 124 - Continued

Item Number	Age Level	Item	High Status	Low Status	Difference	Index Difference
16	9-10	Find the three things that are alike and draw a line through the one that is not like those three —	77%	74%	3%	2
17	9-10	(For text and diagrams for this item, see Table 123, Item No. 3)	60	63	-3	-2
18	9-10	Which one of these numbers is the largest? — 42316, 17989, 26895, 37897, 55755	73	70	3	2
19	9-10	After each one of these . . . sets of letters, finish writing the word you can make out of them by changing the letters around. Notice that you are given the first letter in each word: U-E-O-H-S . . . . H	38	35	4	2
20	9-10	Find the three things that are alike and draw a line through the one that is not like those three—	67	63	5	2
21	9-10	Find the three things that are alike and draw a line through the one that is not like those three — 4 T F M	84	81	3	3

(Continued on next page)

TABLE 124 - Continued

Item Number	Age Level	Item	Per Cent Right			Index Difference
			High Status	Low Status	Difference	
22	9-10	(For text and pictures for this item, see Table 123, Item No. 1)	71%	74%	-3%	-3
23	9-10	(For text and drawings for this item, see Table 123, Item No. 2)	86	89	-3	-3
24	13-14	(For text and diagrams for this item, see Table 123, Item No. 11)	69	65	4	3
25	9-10	Find the three things that are alike and draw a line through the one that is not like those three —	86	83	3	3
26	9-10	Find the three things that are alike and draw a line through the one that is not like those three —	62	58	4	3
27	9-10	Find the three things that are alike and draw a line through the one that is not like those three —	91	87	3	4

TABLE 125

TEN VERBAL ITEMS SHOWING SMALLEST STATUS DIFFERENCES FOR NINE- AND TEN-YEAR-OLD PUPILS

Item Number	Item	Per Cent Right			Index Difference	Significance Level*
		High Status	Low Status	Difference		
1	After each one of these . . . sets of letters, finish writing the word you can make out of them by changing the letters around. Notice that you are given the first letter in each word: U-E-O-H-S. . . .H	38%	35%	4%	2	NS
2	If the letters s l o m o b s were arranged properly, they would spell — molest, blossom, observe, lovable . .	51	45	6	2	NS
3	A vertebrate always has — legs, toes, arms, teeth, backbone . .	37	32	5	3	NS
4	Find a letter which is in three of the words and then draw a line under the word which does not have that letter — truth, happy, people, riches	69	63	6	4	NS
5	After each one of these . . . sets of letters, finish writing the word you can make out of them by changing the letters around. Notice that you are given the first letter in each word: O-C-A-T. . . .C	80	75	6	4	NS
6	Find the two things that the first thing is never without: house — sidewalk, window, bed, furnace, door	81	73	8	6	5%
7	Find a letter which is in three of the words and then draw a line under the word which does not have that letter — are, bat, out, tell	51	38	13	6	1
8	After each one of these . . . sets of letters, finish writing the word you can make out of them by changing the letters around. Notice that you are given the first letter in each word: H-T-E-M. . . .T	54	42	12	6	1
9	After each set of letters, write the word you can make out of them by changing the letters around: N-M-A	86	78	8	7	5
10	After each set of letters, write the word which you can make out of them by changing the letters around: L-A-B-L	63	50	13	7	1

* "1%" and "5%" indicate differences significant at the 1 per cent and at the 5 per cent levels, respectively. "NS" indicates differences not significant even at the 5 per cent level.

case the pupil can solve the problem correctly without any knowledge of the meaning of the words.

Among the ten items in Table 125, only two (Nos. 3 and 6) require the pupil to make any distinctions as to the meaning of the words with which he is dealing. There are a great many items in the tests for younger pupils which do require the pupil to make distinctions based upon the meaning of words, but these items do not occur among these relatively small-difference items.

Table 126 lists the ten verbal items which showed the smallest status differences for the thirteen- and fourteen-year-old pupils, after making exclusions comparable to those described for Table 125. The items in this table exhibit some of the same characteristics as those for the younger pupils as listed in Table 125. In general, the items in Table 126 exhibit a fairly simple vocabulary. It is notable that not a single synonym and only one opposite (kinds of items dependent upon knowledge of exact meanings of words) appear in this list. There are some relatively difficult words in some of the items, but they occur in those items which, despite their inclusion in this list of small-difference items, show status differences significant at the 1 per cent level. Of the four items in the list whose status difference is not large enough to be significant at the 1 per cent level, every one involves relatively simple words.

Items Showing Contrasting Status Differences
Despite Similarity of Form

In order to gain further insight into possible reasons for status differences in these items, it seemed desirable to compare items which were similar in type of symbolism and in form of test question asked, but which had markedly different degrees of status difference. For this purpose the categories of items as already reported in Table 41, on pages 216 to 218, were used. From each of these categories of items — homogeneous with respect to symbolism and type of test question — items with unusually large status differences and items with unusually small status differences were selected. The minimum differences between large-difference and small-difference items in any category in this section are 13 points for the items for the younger pupils and 12 points for the items for the older pupils. Owing to errors of measurement, it cannot be said with confidence that in every case the true difference between the contrasting items is as great as that indicated by the data given, but it is unlikely that the true difference is ever really zero.[11]

In the selection of contrasting items for presentation in this section, the following types of items were excluded from consideration:

1. Items whose index difference is based upon an index value of 80 or higher, or 20 or smaller, except in the case of large-difference

11. The minima were selected so that, in each case, the status difference for a large-difference item would exceed that for a small-difference item by an amount equal to at least three times the standard error of measurement. The data are not reported here, since the method of arriving at standard errors of measurement for the index differences was somewhat unsatisfactory. For a reference to a more complete discussion of the means used for estimating reliability coefficients and standard errors of measurement for the index differences see Note 1 in Appendix D.

items whose index difference would maintain the requisite size even if the extreme index should fluctuate to either 80 or 20 as the case might be.

2. Items whose small difference is apparently due to the extreme percentage of correct responses for both status groups being either above 90 per cent or within 10 percentage points of the chance or guessing expectation for the item.

These exclusions are similar to the ones described in more detail in the preceding section.[12]

After making the above exclusions there are twenty categories of items in which there are found two or more items with contrasting status differences as just defined. Each of these sets of contrasting items will be considered briefly below.

Contrasting verbal items for which a cultural explanation is suggested

The first set of items to be presented in this section are items from the tests for the younger pupils which require the pupil to choose an essential trait of some given object. The pertinent data for two items of this type which show markedly different status differences are reported in Table 127. The two items analyzed in this table are typical of the other sets of contrasting items to be presented in this section. Both items use verbal symbols, and both involve the same form of test question. The status difference on the first one is much larger (17 index points) than that on the second one (3 index points).

It will be recalled that the first item in Table 127 has already been discussed from the wrong-answer point of view in the preceding chapter.[13] The explanation there, however, was aimed at explaining why high-status errors tended to concentrate on "wood" and low-status errors on "coal." That explanation seems to offer no reason to expect the large status difference in right responses on this item. It is more likely that the large status difference on this item arises from the fact that the correct answer is in abstract terms, as contrasted with the four distractors all of which are concrete terms. In an earlier section it was indicated that high-status pupils may be more familiar with the use of abstract terms, while low-status pupils may either be unfamiliar with them or shy away from them. The second item in Table 127, it will be noticed, involves terms all of which are concrete, so that this problem does not arise. It is, however, somewhat surprising to find this second item showing such a small status difference, since it involves knowledge that is definitely school-learned.

Data for similar items taken from the tests given to the older pupils are shown in Table 128. It will be seen at once that there is wide variation in the amount of status difference shown by this second set of essential-trait items. When the subject of the item is a wheel, the status difference is 27 index points; when the subject of the item is an orchestra, the status difference is only 8 points. Superficial consideration of these two extreme items would suggest that certainly a wheel is much less likely to be characterized by cultural bias than an orchestra. Probably the explanation for this seeming discrepancy is to be found in the fact that the "wheel" item

---

12. See pp. 315-18.
13. See pp. 261-62.

TABLE 126

TEN VERBAL ITEMS SHOWING SMALLEST STATUS DIFFERENCES
FOR THIRTEEN- AND FOURTEEN-YEAR-OLD PUPILS

Item Number	Item	Per Cent Right			Index Difference	Significance Level*
		High Status	Low Status	Difference		
1	W is between X and Y. X is between Y and Z. Therefore — W is not between Y and Z, W is between X and Z, W is nearer to X than to Z	51%	50%	1%	1	NS
2	If a freight train travels at the rate of 20 miles an hour, how many miles will it travel in 4 hours? — 5, 24, 80, 60	86	84	2	2	NS
3	Which tells best just what a lamb is? — an animal with wool, a creature with four legs and a tail, a young sheep, a lively small animal, a young animal that eats grass	77	70	8	5	5%
4	If the claim is unjust, refusal to permit its discussion before the Student Council is unwise. If the claim is just, refusal is inexcusable. But, the claim is either unjust or it is just. Therefore — The refusal is justified, The refusal is being discussed freely, The refusal is either unwise or inexcusable	60	48	12	7	1
5	Which one of the five things below is most like these three: a cup, a plate, and a saucer? — a fork, a table, a napkin, a bowl, a spoon	90	83	7	7	5
6	If the following words were arranged in order, which word would be in the middle? — plaster, frame, wallpaper, lath, foundation	65	51	14	7	1

TABLE 126 – Continued

Item Number	Item	Per Cent Right			Index Difference	Significance Level*
		High Status	Low Status	Difference		
7	An orchestra always has – violinists, piano, musicians, saxophone, singers	77%	65%	12%	8	1%
8	Which statement tells best just what a watch is? – It ticks, something to tell time, a small round object with a chain, a vest-pocket-sized timekeeping instrument, something with a face and hands	58	43	15	8	1
9	If he remains with his friend he will suffer loss, and if he leaves his friend he will suffer loss; but he must remain with his friend or leave him. Therefore – He should remain with his friend, It takes courage to leave a friend, He will suffer loss	71	56	14	8	1
10	Mark . . . the word which is OPPOSITE, or most nearly opposite, in meaning to the beginning word of each line: expel – remain, propel, exile, retain, contract	31	19	12	8	1

* "1%" and "5%" indicate differences significant at the 1 per cent and at the 5 per cent level. "NS" indicates differences not significant even at the 5 per cent level.

333

TABLE 127

ESSENTIAL-ELEMENT ITEMS SHOWING CONTRASTING STATUS DIFFERENCES

(Nine- and Ten-Year-Old Pupils)

Item	Per Cent Right		Index Difference	Significance Level*
	High Status	Low Status		
A fire always has – wood, coal, gas, warmth, furnace	69%	38%	17	1%
. . .			.	.
A vertebrate always has – legs, toes, arms, teeth, backbone	37%	32%	3	NS

* In all the tables in this section (Tables 127 to 146), "1%" and "5%" indicate differences significant at the 1 per cent and at the 5 per cent level, respectively. "NS" indicates a difference not significant even at the 5 per cent level.

TABLE 128

ESSENTIAL-ELEMENT ITEMS SHOWING CONTRASTING STATUS DIFFERENCES

(Thirteen- and Fourteen-Year-Old Pupils)

Item	Per Cent Right		Index Difference	Significance Level
	High Status	Low Status		
A wheel always has – circumference, spokes, tire, wood, metal	89%	48%	27	1%
A message always involves – telepathy, messenger, speech, communication, writing	81%	42%	22	1%
.			.	
.			.	
An orchestra always has – violinists, piano, musicians, saxophone, singers	77%	65%	8	1%

334

involves the selection of an abstract term, whereas the "orchestra" item involves only a selection from several concrete terms. This explanation will also account for the relatively large difference on the "message" item.

Similar data for items requiring the selection of opposites are reported in Table 129. All these items exhibit a rather substantial status difference. Even the ones with the smallest differences still show differences which are statistically significant. This is probably to be expected, since these items are frankly vocabulary items, involving discrimination in word meaning. Practically all of them deal with the kind of words with which pupils will have contact only through formal school study, rather advanced home reading, or possibly the conversation of relatively well-educated parents.

TABLE 129

OPPOSITE ITEMS SHOWING CONTRASTING STATUS DIFFERENCES

(Thirteen- and Fourteen-Year-Old Pupils)

Item	Per Cent Right		Index Dif-fer-ence	Sig-nifi-cance Level
	High Status	Low Status		
Mark . . . the word which is OPPOSITE, or most nearly opposite, in meaning to the beginning word of each line:*				
amateur — novitiate, musical, professional, inventor, experience	87%	50%	24	1%
waste — refuse, conserve, devastate, dole, generate	92%	60%	24	1%
pride — sorrow, proud, miserable, conceit, humility	69%	29%	23	1%
abundance — liberality, frugality, luxury, hunger, scarcity	91%	60%	23	1%
wax — pale, waive, shine, age, wane	39%	20%	11	1%
eccentric — particular, stupid, egocentric, ordinary, virtuous	40%	23%	10	1%
expel — remain, propel, exile, retain, contract	31%	19%	8	1%

* The injunction given at the head of the list of items is that used for all the items except the third one. The latter reads: "Which word means the opposite of pride? — sorrow, proud, miserable, conceit, humility."

The three items in the bottom half of the table, showing less than average status difference for this kind of item, are items which are quite difficult for both groups. On many of them the percentage of low-status pupils answering the question correctly is close to the chance level, with the percentage for the high-status pupils being not far above the chance level. The items showing the largest status differences, on the other hand, tend to be items which are relatively easy, at least for the high-status pupils.

There are several different types of classification items in these tests. Data for items showing contrasting status differences in one of the classification categories are shown in Table 130. The three large-difference items in Table 130 have all been discussed in previous sections, and explanations suggested for the large status differences on two of them -- explanations in terms of differences in opportunity for familiarity with either the objects or the words involved in the items.[14] The two small-difference items involve fairly simple everyday words and relatively familiar objects. Even on these words the high-status pupils do significantly better than the low-status pupils, but their superiority is not nearly so marked as on the first three items in the list. The high-status pupils, for example, do about equally well on the first and fourth items in Table 130, while the low-status pupils do very much better on the fourth item than they do on the first.

Data for items showing contrasting status differences in another kind of classification item are reported in Table 131. These two contrasting

TABLE 130

VERBAL CLASSIFICATION ITEMS (TYPE C-1-a-i)*
SHOWING CONTRASTING STATUS DIFFERENCES

(Thirteen- and Fourteen-Year-Old Pupils)

Item	Per Cent Right		Index Dif-fer-ence	Sig-nifi-cance Level
	High Status	Low Status		
In each line below, four of the words belong together. Pick out the ONE WORD which does not belong with the others —				
priest, organist, minister, rabbi, bishop . . .	89%	48%	28	1%
arithmetic, geometry, history, trigonometry, algebra	82%	37%	27	1%
cello, harp, drum, violin, guitar	85%	45%	23	1%
oats, rye, wheat, clover, barley	92%	81%	11	1%
nail, brad, awl, staple, tack	60%	43%	9	1%

* As defined in Table 41.

14. See pp. 259-60, 296-98, 313-14.

TABLE 131

VERBAL CLASSIFICATION ITEMS (TYPE C-1-c-i)*
SHOWING CONTRASTING STATUS DIFFERENCES
(Thirteen- and Fourteen-Year-Old Pupils)

Item	Per Cent Right		Index Difference	Significance Level
	High Status	Low Status		
Which one of the five things below is most like these three: an eagle, a giraffe, and a lizard? -- a wing, a neck, a stone, a mouse, a tree	91%	67%	19	1%
Which one of the five things below is most like these three: a cup, a plate, and a saucer? – a fork, a table, a napkin, a bowl, a spoon	90%	83%	7	5%

* As defined in Table 41.

items are a rather obvious example of the importance of the cultural content of some test items. The first deals with three animals which pupils in an urban environment will have opportunity for knowing about only through reading or visits to a zoo (or possibly occasionally through the movies). Clearly the high-status children can be expected to have more opportunity for acquiring this knowledge than the low-status children. The second item, on the other hand, deals with simple everyday objects familiar to any child from any status background. The high-status pupils do equally well on both of these items, but the low-status pupils do much better on the second than on the first. In fact, on the second item the status difference is not large enough to be significant at the 1 per cent level. This seems clear evidence that a large proportion of the difficulty which low-status pupils have with these classification items is due to their unfamiliarity with the words or objects to be classified rather than to any inherent inability to handle the classification process itself.

That the size of the status difference varies widely among items requiring the handling of logical relationships is illustrated in Table 132. It may be that high-status pupils find school work in geometry of some assistance to them in thinking clearly about the first item in this list. It has already been pointed out that a higher proportion of high-status pupils take geometry than is the case for low-status pupils -- both because of the larger incidence of college-preparatory students in the high-status group and because of the greater grade retardation of the low-status pupils.

The last item in Table 132, having virtually no status difference, obviously involves a much simpler vocabulary than either of the other

TABLE 132

LOGICAL-EXERCISE ITEMS SHOWING CONTRASTING
STATUS DIFFERENCES
(Thirteen- and Fourteen-Year-Old Pupils)

Item	Per Cent Right		Index Difference	Significance Level
	High Status	Low Status		
All squares have four equal sides. This figure does not have four equal sides. Therefore – It is a circle, It is not a square, It is either a triangle or a rectangle	83%	51%	19	1%
If the claim is unjust, refusal to permit its discussion before the Student Council is unwise. If the claim is just, refusal is inexcusable. But, the claim is either unjust or it is just. Therefore – The refusal is justified, The refusal is being discussed freely, The refusal is either unwise or inexcusable	60%	48%	7	1%
W is between X and Y. X is between Y and Z. Therefore – W is not between Y and Z, W is between X and Z, W is nearer to X than to Z	51%	50%	1	NS

items, although its unreal, symbolic method of expression might well have been expected to make special trouble for low-status pupils who have not had so much effective contact with formal algebra and geometry. The second item on the list, which shows a fairly small status difference despite a relatively academic vocabulary, is difficult to understand. It is true that the subject matter with which it deals might be familiar to both status groups, but it seems surprising that the involved syntax and difficult vocabulary does not introduce a larger status difference than is found for this item.

Variation in the status difference characteristic of items involving the solution of arithmetic problems is illustrated in Table 133. The propriety of including arithmetic problems in an intelligence test may be questioned. The authors of the test which includes most of the arithmetic items would probably defend them on the ground that the amount of arithmetic knowledge required for these problems is so slight that it may be assumed that pupils of the age for whom the test is designed may be assumed to have had equal opportunity to learn it and that the items really measure, not arithmetical knowledge, but clarity of the thinking process.

TABLE 133

ARITHMETIC-PROBLEM ITEMS SHOWING CONTRASTING
STATUS DIFFERENCES

(Thirteen- and Fourteen-Year-Old Pupils)

Item	Per Cent Right		Index Dif-fer-ence	Sig-nifi-cance Level
	High Status	Low Status		
On a road map each one-half inch represents 20 miles. How many miles are represented by 5 inches? -- 10, 20, 100, 200	68%	38%	17	1%
1 is to 3 as 9 is to — 18, 27, 36, 45, 81	74%	44%	17	1%
If I have a large box with 3 small boxes in it and 3 very small boxes in each small box, how many boxes are there in all? -- 6, 7, 3, 12, 13	51%	23%	17	1%
If you had 20 words in spelling and were marked 90%, how many words did you spell correctly? -- 1, 11, 18, 19	82%	55%	17	1%
Large envelopes that sell for 3 cents each can be had for 30 cents a dozen. How much is saved when bought by the dozen? -- 10¢, 6¢, 2 1/2¢, 9¢	89%	67%	17	1%
How many one-inch cubes can be placed in a box 5 inches long, 4 inches wide, and 3 inches high? -- 12, 23, 60, 100	76%	51%	15	1%
2 1/2 times what number equals 40? -- 16, 8, 15, 17	74%	47%	14	1%
If a man has walked west from his home 9 blocks and then walked east 4 blocks, how many blocks is he from home? — 13, 9, 12, 4, 5	67%	40%	14	1%
.			.	
.			.	
.			.	
If a freight train travels at the rate of 20 miles an hour, how many miles will it travel in 4 hours? -- 5, 24, 80, 60	86%	84%	2	NS

If the group of arithmetic items showing relatively large status differences is contrasted with the single small-difference item, it will be noticed that the small-difference item deals with a very common ordinary object that would doubtless be familiar to any child regardless of status or socioeconomic position. Some of the items with large status differences, however, likewise deal with objects probably thoroughly familiar to all thirteen- and fourteen-year-old children -- spelling tests, sheets of paper, etc. — so this explanation is not entirely inadequate. A number of the items showing large differences are, however, based on subject matter which may involve cultural bias. Road maps, boxes-that-fit-within-boxes, large envelopes bought by the dozen -- are all subjects that may well be more familiar to high-status pupils simply because of the kind of opportunities open to them in their homes and not because of any real superiority in intellectual ability on their part.

Contrasting verbal items for which
no clear cultural explanation is seen

In this section several sets of items showing contrasting status differences for which no clear cultural explanation is apparent will be presented. In some cases some possible explanations will be suggested, but in no case are they ones which seem to the present writer to be adequate to account for the substantial contrast of status difference characteristic of these sets of items.

On the two items in Table 134 it may be noted that the high-status pupils find the "cat" item easier than the "house" one, while for the low-status pupils the reverse is true. It is difficult to understand why the high-status pupils should find the "cat" item easy (91 per cent correct), while the low-status group finds the same item relatively difficult (64 per cent correct). Its subject matter is probably about equally familiar to both

TABLE 134

ESSENTIAL-ELEMENT ITEMS SHOWING CONTRASTING
STATUS DIFFERENCES

(Nine- and Ten-Year-Old Pupils)

Item	Per Cent Right		Index Dif-fer-ence	Sig-nifi-cance Level
	High Status	Low Status		
In each list, find the two things that the first thing is never without:				
cat -- hair, owner, mouse, claws, milk	91%	64%	21	1%
.			.	
.			.	
house -- sidewalk, window, bed, furnace, door	81%	73%	6	5%

status groups. It can hardly be argued that the thinking process involved in the question is one which is somehow related to social status, since precisely the same mental process is involved in the second item, which shows a relatively small status differences.

It occurred to the writer that the high-status group might have had relatively more difficulty with the "house" item because the houses with which they are most familiar do almost always have both sidewalks and furnaces. These two distractors might have been more potent for high-status pupils than for low-status pupils, since the latter would be more likely to be familiar with houses without these accoutrements. Bruce found this item easier for the rural children she studied than the test norms would indicate and suggested that it might "be due to the fact that the non-essential elements in these items are less prevalent in poor rural sections than among urban populations" (59, p. 75).

A special tabulation was made of the wrong answers on this item, although items involving the selection of two different words had been eliminated from the main wrong-answer analysis reported in chapter xxii. This analysis yielded some support for the hypothesis with respect to "furnace" but not with respect to "sidewalk." The high-status errors on "furnace" were more frequent than those on the other two wrong answers combined; the low-status errors were distributed relatively evenly over all three possible errors. The fact that the high-status pupils checked "sidewalk" the least frequently of all five choices may reflect the fact that they did not consider the sidewalk as part of the house.

There are several striking contrasts apparent in the set of items reported in Table 135, although no satisfactory explanation is seen for them. Why, for instance, should the "introductory" item and the "writhe" item present exactly the same degree of difficulty for high-status pupils, while the proportion of low-status pupils answering the "writhe" item is nearly double that answering the "introductory" item? Or why should the "introductory" item and the "counsel" item exhibit exactly the same degree of difficulty for low-status pupils, although the high-status pupils do much better on "introductory" than they do on "counsel"? The fact that items of this type, involving formalized, bookish vocabulary may be expected to have substantial status differences has already been discussed. It is not clear, however, why one of these items should show a status difference so much larger than that shown by the others.

A marked contrast in status difference is found for the two items in Table 136. Possible reasons for the relatively large status difference on the "sonata" item have already been discussed.[15] It is difficult to see any very convincing explanation why an item dealing with "chinchilla" should have a substantially smaller status difference than an item dealing with "sonata." Certainly the kind of argument which explains the status difference on "sonata" in terms of greater high-status opportunities for familiarity with a sonata as a musical form applies with at least as great force to superior high-status opportunities for familiarity with chinchilla fur. It will be noticed that the "sonata" item and the "chinchilla" item present approximately the same degree of difficulty to high-status pupils (74 per cent and 71 per cent) but that the "sonata" item is almost twice as difficult (29 per cent against 50 per cent) as the "chinchilla" item for low-status pupils.

On both of the items in Table 137 there is a strong piling-up of errors for both status groups on a "next-best" answer ("something to hold

15. See pp. 305-6.

341

TABLE 135

SYNONYM ITEMS SHOWING CONTRASTING STATUS DIFFERENCES

(Thirteen- and Fourteen-Year-Old Pupils)

Item	Per Cent Right		Index Difference	Significance Level
	High Status	Low Status		
Mark . . . the word which has the SAME or most nearly the same meaning as the beginning word of each line:				
introductory — social, advisory, transitory, preliminary, internal..............	66%	24%	23	1%
.			.	
.			.	
writhe — squeal, twist, split, hurt, crawl . . .	66%	45%	11	1%
counsel -- quarrel, yield, advise, assemble, represent	41%	24%	10	1%

TABLE 136

VERBAL CLASSIFICATION ITEMS (TYPE C-2-a, b)*
SHOWING CONTRASTING STATUS DIFFERENCES

(Thirteen- and Fourteen-Year-Old Pupils)

Item	Per Cent Right		Index Difference	Significance Level
	High Status	Low Status		
Sonata is a term used in — drawing, drama, music, poetry, phonetics	74%	29%	26	1%
.			.	
.			.	
Chinchilla is a kind of — fur, seasoning, chemical, malady, furniture	71%	50%	12	1%

* As defined in Table 41.

TABLE 137

DEFINITION ITEMS (TYPE A-3)* SHOWING CONTRASTING
STATUS DIFFERENCES

(Thirteen- and Fourteen-Year-Old Pupils)

| Item | Per Cent Right | | Index Dif-fer-ence | Sig-nifi-cance Level |
	High Status	Low Status		
Which tells best just what a pitcher is? — a vessel from which to pour liquid, something to hold milk, It has a handle, It goes on the table, It is easily broken	95%	73%	21	1%
Which tells best just what a lamb is? — an animal with wool, a creature with four legs and a tail, a young sheep, a lively small animal, a young animal that eats grass	77%	70%	5	5%

* As defined in Table 41.

milk" and "an animal with wool"). This seems to indicate that most of
the errors are due to inadequate thinking rather than to unfamiliarity with
at least the general content of the items. The concentration of errors on
these next-best responses is, however, characteristic of both status groups
and seems to offer no particular clue as to why the amount of status difference on the "pitcher" item should be so much greater than that on the
"lamb" item. As a matter of fact, it would be easy to explain why the
"lamb" item should show a larger status difference than the "pitcher"
item, since pitchers are presumably common to most households, while
familiarity with a lamb is likely to be acquired in most urban homes only
through reading.

The fact that some of the status difference on the first item in Table
138 may be accounted for by different connotations for the word "confident"
in the environments of the two different status groups has already been
pointed out.[16] That many of the words in the items in this list are academic or bookish may explain, at least in part, why the high-status pupils do better on the items than the low-status pupils do, but it is not clear
why the status difference is so much greater on the first two items than
on the last three. Why, for example, should the high-status pupils do only
slightly better on the last item than they do on the first, while the low-
status pupils find the last item much easier than the first? Or why do the

16. See pp. 273-74.

TABLE 138

DEFINITION ITEMS (TYPE A-2)* SHOWING CONTRASTING
STATUS DIFFERENCES

(Thirteen- and Fourteen-Year-Old Pupils)

| Item | Per Cent Right | | Index Dif-fer-ence | Sig-nifi-cance Level |
	High Status	Low Status		
A person who is sure he can accomplish a task is said to be -- successful, confident, proud, fearless, brave	86%	52%	22	1%
A man who acquires the property of others by deceit is called a -- traitor, swindler, burglar, prisoner, lawyer	67%	49%	10	1%
A boy who often tells stories he knows are not true is said to -- brag, cheat, joke, lie, exaggerate	83%	68%	10	1%
When a new kind of machine is thought of, it is usually called — a discovery, an adoption, a creation, a novelty, an invention	91%	82%	9	1%

* As defined in Table 41.

high-status pupils find the first item so much easier than the second, although the low-status pupils do about equally well on the two items? No
answer to these questions is seen by the present writer.

Contrasting picture items for which
no clear cultural explanation is seen

Three contrasting sets of picture items are presented in Tables 139,
140, and 141. For none of them does a convincing explanation for the observed contrasts occur to the writer. In some of them differences which
might reasonably have been expected are not actually found.

The high-status pupils find the first item in Table 139 easier than the
second, while the low-status pupils find the second easier than the first.
This results in a sizable status difference, significant at the 1 per cent
level, on the first item, and a zero status difference on the second item.
No satisfactory explanation of these contrasting items is apparent. It
would seem that the objects pictured in both of these items would be familiar to pupils from both status backgrounds. If there were any differential in familiarity, it would be reasonable to expect it to occur with
respect to the second item rather than the first — but this is contrary to
the facts obtained from the pupil responses.

It is equally difficult to see any satisfactory explanation for the wide

TABLE 139

PICTURE CLASSIFICATION ITEMS SHOWING CONTRASTING STATUS DIFFERENCES

(Nine- and Ten-Year-Old Pupils)

Item	Per Cent Right		Index Difference	Significance Level
	High Status	Low Status		
In each row you are to find the three things that are alike and draw a line through the one that is _not_ like those three —	89%	73%	13	1%
	81%	80%	0	NS

TABLE 140

PICTURE CLASSIFICATION ITEMS SHOWING CONTRASTING STATUS DIFFERENCES

(Thirteen- and Fourteen-Year-Old Pupils)

Item	Per Cent Right		Index Difference	Significance Level
	High Status	Low Status		
The first three objects in each row are alike in some way. Find another object in the same row that belongs with them —	59%	36%	13	1%
	46%	43%	1	NS
	43%	41%	1	NS

TABLE 141

PICTURE-MANIPULATION ITEMS SHOWING CONTRASTING STATUS DIFFERENCES

(Thirteen- and Fourteen-Year-Old Pupils)

Item	Per Cent Right		Index Difference	Significance Level
	High Status	Low Status		
The objects . . . are either rights or lefts. Mark on the answer sheet under the R for rights, and under the L for lefts —				
(For picture for this item, see No. 2 at bottom of table)	93%	81%	13	1%
(For picture for this item, see No. 3 at bottom of table)	95%	84%	13	1%
(For picture for this item, see No. 5 at bottom of table)	95%	84%	13	1%
(For picture for this item, see No. 1 at bottom of table)	94%	83%	13	1%
(For picture for this item, see No. 15 at bottom of table)	89%	76%	11	1%
(For picture for this item, see No. 7 at bottom of table)	67%	68%	-1	NS

variation in status differences shown in Table 140. It may be that low-status children are less likely to see thermometers in their homes and may for this reason have some difficulty in recognizing this object from the somewhat crude drawing. It is difficult to believe, however, that such a handicap would be more important than that which would seem to characterize the two small-difference items.

Answering the second item in Table 140 correctly depends upon making the distinction between organic and inorganic origins of materials, while the third item involves the recognition of four forms of water. Both of these are definitely school-learned matters; it would certainly not be surprising to find the low-status pupils penalized with regard to them. So far as the specific objects in these two items are concerned, one would expect the high-status pupils to have more familiarity with the diamond and possibly the watch; the low-status pupils might have the advantage with respect to the anvil and probably with respect to the recognition of the boy carrying a block of ice. The proportions of correct responses from the two status groups on these items indicate, however, that there is little if any status difference with respect to either of the items.

In the list of items in Table 141 there is only one that stands out as having a status difference contrasting with the others. There seems to be no obvious reason why Item No. 7 should show a slightly negative status difference, while other items, apparently very similar in their requirements, should show substantial status differences. It is possible, of course, that the data given for Item No. 7 represent an unusual case of substantial sampling or measurement error and that a readministration of this item would yield a status difference more in line with those of the majority of these apparently similar items.

Contrasting "noncultural" items for which
no cultural explanation is seen

There are three categories of geometric-design items and two of letter-combination items which include items showing contrasting status differences as defined for this section. For none of these five sets of items does the writer see any plausible explanation. There appears to be nothing in the content or mental process of the items themselves which would explain either the presence of status difference at all or the marked variation in its size from item to item. It may be that differences in motivation as applied to apparently meaningless material may be part of the explanation for the existence of status difference in these apparently culture-free items, but the motivation factor can hardly be used to account for wide variations in status difference from item to item.

The items and their pertinent data are presented in Tables 142 to 146, without further comment, so that the reader may endeavor to account for the differences if he wishes to do so.

Items Showing Significant Old American-Ethnic Differences

One further list of items remains to be presented. In chapter xvii it was shown that for the great majority of the test items there was not a significant difference between the responses of low-status Old Americans and low-status ethnics.[17] In fact, out of 647 items examined, only 12 showed a difference between these two low-status groups that was

17. See pp. 187-90.

TABLE 142

GEOMETRIC-DESIGN CLASSIFICATION ITEMS SHOWING CONTRASTING STATUS DIFFERENCES

(Nine- and Ten-Year-Old Pupils)

Item	Per Cent Right		Index Difference	Significance Level
	High Status	Low Status		
In each row you are to find the three things that are alike and draw a line through the one that is <u>not</u> like those three —	89%	69%	16 2	1%
	68%	66%		NS
	52%	49%	1	NS

TABLE 143

GEOMETRIC-DESIGN IDENTIFICATION ITEMS SHOWING CONTRASTING STATUS DIFFERENCES

(Nine- and Ten-Year-Old Pupils)

Item	Per Cent Right		Index Difference	Significance Level
	High Status	Low Status		
Mark the square to the left of the one that has five crosses in it —	68%	39%	16	1%
Mark the larger circle with the smaller circles in what we might call the lower left-hand corner —	74%	52%	13	1%

TABLE 143 – Continued

Item	Per Cent Right		Index Difference	Significance Level
	High Status	Low Status		
Mark the next drawing after the one that has six circles —	84%	65%	13	1%
Mark the square with the little piece beside it that is partly curved outward and partly curved inward —	56%	55%	0	NS
Mark the square in this row that you think is closest to the large F in the upper corner of the page —	60%	63%	-2	NS

351

TABLE 144

SPATIAL-MANIPULATION ITEMS SHOWING CONTRASTING STATUS DIFFERENCES

(Thirteen- and Fourteen-Year-Old Pupils)

Item*	Per Cent Right		Index Difference	Significance Level
	High Status	Low Status		
In each row put a mark under every figure which is like the first figure in the row.+	88%	66%	16	1%
	85%	81%	4	NS

352

TABLE 144 – Continued

Item*	Per Cent Right		Index Difference	Significance Level
	High Status	Low Status		
(diagram)	89%	85%	4	NS
(diagram)	92%	89%	4	NS
(diagram)	69%	65%	3	NS

* The particular diagram in each line which constitutes the "item" to which the data refer is marked in the answer space under the diagram.

+ The injunction given here is for the first, third, and fourth items in the table. The second and fifth items are introduced by: "In each row mark every card that is like the first card in the row."

353

TABLE 145

LETTER- AND NUMBER-COMBINATION CLASSIFICATION ITEMS SHOWING CONTRASTING
STATUS DIFFERENCES

(Nine- and Ten-Year-Old Pupils)

Item	Per Cent Right		Index Difference	Significance Level
	High Status	Low Status		
In each row you are to find the three things that are alike and draw a line through the one that is not like those three — RARARARRA MCMCMCMC DLDLDLDL EEEEGGGG	90%	70%	16	1%
4 T F M	84%	81%	3	NS

354

TABLE 146

LETTER-SERIES ITEMS SHOWING CONTRASTING STATUS DIFFERENCES

(Thirteen- and Fourteen-Year-Old Pupils)

Item	Per Cent Right		Index Difference	Significance Level
	High Status	Low Status		
In each series of letters decide what the next letter should be —				
a b b b c d d d e f f f g h h — g, h, i, j, k, l ...	66%	27%	22	1%
.				
.				
a b b c c c d d d d e e e — d, e, f, g, h, i ...	52%	33%	10	1%

significant at the 1 per cent level. Of these 12 items, 10 showed differences in favor of the Old Americans and 2 showed differences in favor of the ethnics. These 12 items are listed in Table 147.

Careful examination of the items in Table 147 does not suggest any explanation as to possible reasons for these differences. A number of the items deal with words and objects which are probably more familiar to high-status children than to low-status children, but that of itself is not sufficient to account for ethnic differences within the low-status group. A comparison of the size of the ethnic differences on these items with the size of the differences between high-status and low-status Old Americans on the same items (data not shown in the table) reveals that the ethnic differences are not, for the most part, as large as the status differences on these items. In only one case (No. 10) does the difference between the two low-status groups exceed that between the two Old American groups.

Attention was called in chapter xvii to the fact that, even though each of these ethnic differences is large enough to be significant at the 1 per cent level, one would still expect six or seven items to have differences as large as this from random sampling errors alone. That may account, at least in part, for the fact that there seem to be no reasonable explanations for the ethnic differences on these items.

Summary

A large number of items showing unusual status differences with respect to the right answers are examined with a view to determining possible explanations for the variation in size of status differences from

TABLE 147

ITEMS SHOWING DIFFERENCES SIGNIFICANT AT THE 1 PER CENT LEVEL BETWEEN LOW-STATUS OLD AMERICAN AND LOW-STATUS ETHNIC PUPILS

Item Number	Age Level	Item	Per Cent Right		Index Difference
			Old American	Ethnic	
1	13-14	Herring is a kind of — wig, flower, pattern, jewel, fish	94%	82%	14
2	9-10	A fire always has — wood, coal, gas, warmth, furnace	38	21	11
3	13-14	Burlap is a kind of — lumber, stone, hood, fabric, comedy	61	44	9
4	9-10	Apple is to tree as currant is to — bush, thorn, juice, eat, peach ...	37	23	9
5	13-14	Mark ... the word which has the SAME or most nearly the same meaning as the beginning word of each line: hazardous — adventurous, hard, annoying, speedy, dangerous —	55	40	8
6	13-14	A box always has — contents, wood, lid, hinge, depth	63	48	8
7	13-14	Pick out the ONE WORD which does not belong with the others — pepper, cinnamon, nutmeg, pickle, mustard	62	48	8
8	13-14	A bottle always has — hollowness, label, cork, glass, transparency .	44	30	8
9	13-14	How many 1 1/2 cent stamps would you give in even exchange for 30 one-half cent stamps? — 10, 15, 20, 45	28	17	8
10	9-10	Find the two in the rest of the row which would make the first one —	67	54	7
11	13-14	The box contains either gold or silver or crystal. It does not contain silver. Therefore— It contains crystal, It contains either gold or crystal, The conclusion is uncertain	74	85	-9
12	13-14	A wheel always has — circumference, spokes, tire, wood, metal ...	48	66	-10

item to item.[18] The items which are examined in this manner are (a) items showing unusually large status differences, (b) items showing unusually small status differences, (c) sets of items showing contrasting amounts of status difference although similar with respect to form of symbolism and type of test question, and (d) items showing significant differences between the two low-status groups (Old American and ethnic). In each of the above cases certain specific criteria are established, and all the items fitting such criteria are quoted in the text, with accompanying analytical data.

The kinds of explanations suggested by the items in this chapter are, for the most part, similar to those formulated in chapter xxii. The importance of the nature of the vocabulary is stressed particularly. It is shown that, when the test item is expressed in terms of strange, academic, or bookish words, the status differences are much greater than when the item is expressed in simple everyday words.[19] Differential opportunity for familiarity with certain objects is also stressed for a number of items. In other items, status differences are related to formal school learning or to an assumed greater ability of high-status pupils to handle abstract as opposed to concrete terms.

Practically all the items which show unusually small differences either are nonverbal in symbolism or are expressed in relatively simple everyday vocabulary and deal with objects or concepts which are probably equally familiar, or equally unfamiliar, to pupils at both status levels.

None of the analysis of this chapter is objective in nature, and none of the tentative hypotheses derived from the items in the previous chapter should be regarded as definitely established on the basis of this analysis alone. Greater confidence is created in the soundness of the tentative hypotheses, however, by finding that some of those derived from the items in chapter xxii may be used to account for the sizable status differences in many of the items examined in the present chapter.

Another important finding of the analysis reported in this chapter is the rather substantial number of items showing large status differences for which no reasonable explanation can be seen. This may, of course, merely reflect lack of insight on the part of the writer. The presence of such a large proportion of unexplained differences should, however, lead to caution in accepting the idea that all status differences on test items can be readily accounted for in terms of the cultural bias of their content.

---

18. Possible implications of the wide variation in amount of status difference among different items, for gaining insight into the nature of status differences in I.Q.'s, are discussed in chap. viii (see p. 64).
19. Possible implications of this finding, with respect to vocabulary, for gaining insight into the nature of status differences in I.Q.'s, are discussed in chap. viii (see p. 66).

APPENDIXES

St. Edward's School (Sister Francis Gertrude, principal)
St. James School (Sister M. Leocadia, principal)
St. Mary's School (Sister M. Samuel, principal)
St. Patrick's School (Sister M. Leandre, principal)
St. Peter's School (Sister M. Ludavine, principal)
St. Stanislaus School (Sister M. Archangela, principal)
SS. Peter & Paul School (Sister M. Winifred, principal)

Private school

Keith School (Mr. John H. Cooper, headmaster)

APPENDIX A

LIST OF CO-OPERATING SCHOOLS AND PRINCIPALS

Rockford public high schools

East High School (Mr. Harry C. Muth, principal)
Lincoln Junior High School (Mr. James W. Welsh, principal)
Roosevelt Junior High School (Mr. David Schoonmaker, principal)
Washington Junior High School (Mr. Robert D. Campbell, principal)
West High School (Mr. James E. Blue, principal)

Catholic high schools

Bishop Muldoon High School (Sister Cyril Edwin, O.P., principal)
St. Thomas High School (Rev. John J. X. Glynn, O.S.A., principal)

Rockford public elementary schools

Barbour School (Miss Blanche Chapman, principal)
Church School (Miss Frances Fosse, principal)
Ellis School (Miss Frances Fosse, principal)
Franklin School (Miss Irene M. Larson, principal)
Freeman School (Mrs. Jessie Summers, assistant in charge of
    special education)
Garrison School (Miss Irene M. Larson, principal)
Hall School (Mr. Leslie Lofdahl, principal)
Hallstrom School (Mr. Charles Armour, principal)
Highland School (Miss Emma Lundgren, principal)
Jackson School (Mr. Leslie Lofdahl, principal)
Kishwaukee School (Mr. John R. Wise, principal)
Montague School (Miss Blanche Chapman, principal)
Nelson School (Miss Emma Lundgren, principal)
Peterson School (Miss Olive Barber, principal)
Turner School (Miss Olive Barber, principal)
Walker School (Miss Dorothy Mandeville, principal)
Welsh School (Miss Dorothy Mandeville, principal)
Wight School (Mr. Charles Armour, principal)

County public schools

Lincoln Park School (Mr. Frank Juneberg, principal)
Morris Kennedy School (Miss Mae Mortensen, principal)
Rock River School (Mrs. Marion Fletcher, principal)

Catholic elementary schools

St. Anthony's School (Sister M. Clarissa, principal)

QUESTIONNAIRE BY WHICH SOCIOECONOMIC INFORMATION
WAS SECURED FROM PARENTS

The University of Chicago
Research Project in Rockford Schools

January, 1946

To the Pupil:

Please have your parent, or guardian, fill in this form at once. Then return it to the person who gave it to you. If it is lost, be sure to ask for another.

This paper is very important. So ask your mother, or father, or guardian to fill it in at once. Bring it back just as soon as you can.

Pupil's name: _____
     (First)   (Middle)   (Last)

Pupil's date of birth _____ Pupil's school _____ Grade _____
    (Month)(Day)(Year)

Pupil's address: _____

Father's name: _____

What kind of work does the pupil's father, or guardian, do? _____

(If father, or guardian, works in a factory, or store, or office, tell what kinds of jobs he does there) _____

If he has a title, like watchman, foreman, clerk, manager, president, owner, etc., write it here _____

What other kind of work has the father ever done? _____

How often is the father paid? Check one: Every week___ Once every two weeks___ Once a month___ By the day___ In business for himself___ .

What kind of work does the pupil's mother do? _____

What other kind of work has she ever done? _____

What grade, or year of high school, had the pupil's father finished when he stopped school? _____

What grade, or year of high school, had the pupil's mother finished when she stopped school? _____

How many years of his life has the pupil lived on a farm? _____

How old was the pupil when he began to live on a farm? _____

How old was the pupil when he stopped living on a farm? _____

In what country was the father born? _____ Mother? _____

APPENDIX C

LIST OF ITEMS INCLUDED IN THE STUDY

Test	Item Numbers*			
	Items Included in All Analysis	Additional Items Included in Analysis of High-Status Old Americans vs. Low-Status Old Americans	Additional Items Included in Analysis of High-Status Old Americans vs. Low-Status Ethnics	Additional Items Included in Analysis of Low-Status Old Americans vs. Low-Status Ethnics
Otis Alpha Nonverbal	1–90			
Otis Alpha Verbal	1–90			
Henmon-Nelson	1–48	49–60		
Kuhlmann-Anderson	12(1–4) 13(1–6) 14(1–7) 16(1–8) 17(1–6) 18(1–5) 19(1–3) 20(1–5) 21(1–7) 22(1–5) 23(1–5) 25(1–6) 26(1–5) 27(1–3) 28(1–3) 29(1–6) 30(1–3) 31(1–2)	19(4) 19(5) 22(6) 22(7) 28(4)	14(8) 18(6) 20(6) 21(8) 21(9) 25(7) 27(4) 30(4)	
Otis Beta	1–72			

APPENDIX C – Continued

Test			
Terman-McNemar	1(1-14) 5(1-16) 2(1-13) 6(1-17) 3(1-17) 7(1-7) 4(1-17)	1(15)	2(14) 4(19) 2(15) 5(17) 3(18) 6(18) 3(19) 6(19) 4(18) 6(20)
California Mental Maturity	1-15 51-62 36-47 66-80		16-20 63 48 49
Thurstone Spatial	3(1a-11c) 4(1a-10c)		4-11a,b,c, 4-12a,b,c
Thurstone Reasoning	1(1-22) 2(1-19)		

* The item numbers are those appearing in the published forms of the test and are self-explanatory except as follows:

(a) Wherever one number is followed by a second one in parentheses, the first number indicates a subtest number and the second number indicates the item number within the subtest.

(b) In the Thurstone Reasoning test, the items of which are unnumbered in the published form, the subtest indicates the page of the test, "1" being "Letter Series" and "2" being "Letter Grouping"; the item numbers have been assigned on each page reading down the left-hand column first, then down the right-hand column.

(c) In the Thurstone Spatial test, the items of which are unnumbered in the published form, the subtest indicates the page of the test, "3" being "Figures," and "4" being "Cards"; the item numbers on this test have been assigned on each page reading down the left-hand column first, then down the right-hand column, with one number to each line; in addition, small letters "a," "b," and "c," were used to indicate which of the several responses on a given line was being considered as the "item." (See Note 8, on p. 369, for a fuller statement as to what is considered an item on the Thurstone Spatial test.)

APPENDIX D

SUPPLEMENTARY NOTES

NOTE 1. Part III of the present volume is an abridged form of chapters iv to xxi of an unpublished doctoral dissertation which is on file in the library of the University of Chicago (3). Microfilm copies of the dissertation, or of any particular portion of it, may be obtained by writing to the Department of Photographic Reproduction, University of Chicago Library, University of Chicago, Chicago 37, Illinois. At a number of places in the present volume reference is made to the more complete material available in this dissertation. These references, and the relevant sections of the dissertation, are indicated below:

Page at Which Reference Occurs in Present Volume	Topic	Pages of Dissertation to Which Reference Is Made
88	Procedures used in computation of I.Q.'s and other derived scores	597-601
96	Method of making house-type ratings	645-50
96	Method of making dwelling-area ratings	651-55
98	Determination of social-class placements and the relation of social-class placements to the I.S.C.	602-18
99	Location of lines separating high-status from low-status pupils	613-18
99	Classification of pupils on the basis of ethnicity	168-71, 619-24
122	Graph showing distribution of I.S.C.'s and a normal curve fitted to the distribution	158
122	Analysis of distributions, for three special status groups, of ratings on occupation, education, house type, and dwelling area	160-67
125	Basis for estimating social-class equivalence of high- and low-status groups	625-32
126	Classification of pupils on the basis of ethnicity	168-71, 619-24
130	Descriptions of four "composite" typical families at different social-status levels	656-63
143	Analysis of nonlinearity of relationship between I.Q.'s and I.S.C.'s, using one-point social-status intervals	193-94
176	The reliability of the normalized index and of index differences	264-78
236	Rank correlations between item status difference and item difficulty within categories of items	368-75

NOTE 2. Some evidence is available for estimating the degree of bias which may have been present in the elimination of the 116 pupils who were eliminated because no I.S.C. could be computed for them (see Table 6, p. 106). For most of these pupils, ratings were available on one or two of the status characteristics, though not on the three – or four – necessary for computation of the index. In such cases a rough estimate of the probable index was made by averaging, for each individual, whatever ratings were available and assuming that the missing ratings would be similar to the average of those available.

On this basis estimated I.S.C.'s were secured for thirty-one of the younger pupils and for seventy-eight of the older pupils. The mean I.S.C.'s for the two age groups, based on these estimates, were 17.7 and 17.8. Both of these averages show slightly lower status than for the pupils included in the study, as reported in Table 14, on page 121, but in neither case are the differences statistically significant ones. (The critical ratios are 0.3 for the nine- and ten-year-old pupils and 0.9 for the thirteen- and fourteen-year-old pupils.)

NOTE 3. It will be noticed that the frequencies in the distribution of the California Mental Maturity percentile ranks reported in Table 13, on page 118, are not all equal as would normally be expected. This is due in part to irregularities in the distribution. Most of the variation is due, however, to the fact that, because of the necessity of reporting scores for these pupils to the co-operating schools at as early a date as possible, the percentile ranks were determined before the final group of pupils to be included in this study had been determined. The percentile-rank equivalents were determined from 2,586 pupils rather than from the 2,443 which are tabulated in Table 13. The 143 missing pupils were eliminated, after computation of the percentile ranks, either because they were Negro, Oriental, or Indian or because no I.S.C. could be obtained from them. That the amount of selection was not serious is indicated by the very slight departure of the mean percentile rank reported in Table 13 from the expected value.

NOTE 4. The correlation of percentile-rank scores, involving a rectangular distribution, with the I.S.C., involving a substantially normal distribution, as reported in Table 17, on page 137, is an entirely proper procedure if, as in Table 17, the percentile ranks are being considered as scores in their own right, and the interpretation of the correlations is applied to the percentile ranks themselves rather than to any underlying psychological trait. As a matter of fact, however, Pearson has shown that if two sets of variables are normally distributed, and one is transmuted into rank form, the r calculated from the modified data should be multiplied by 1.0233 to obtain the r which would have been obtained from the original raw data before ranking (57, p. 194). On none of the correlations reported in this table would this adjustment, even if appropriate, be more than .01.

NOTE 5. All the reliability coefficients cited on page 138 are taken from the manuals accompanying the tests. All are for either a single year of age, a single school grade, or are averages of several such limited-range coefficients. The Henmon-Nelson figure is a split-half coefficient; all the others were obtained from parallel forms of the test. Where the authors report several different coefficients, those applying to the age or grade range closest to that of the pupils in the present study are reported here.

The authors of the Kuhlmann-Anderson tests do not report reliability coefficients. The reliability coefficients reported by Thurstone for his tests are spuriously high, since they are based on the split-half procedure and his tests are speed tests; they are not, therefore, used here. The reliability coefficients reported by the authors of the California Mental Maturity test are likewise not used; they would be inapplicable because they are based on the whole test, whereas two subtests were omitted in the present study.

NOTE 6. The use of the z test in Table 18, on page 139, is based on the assumption that it is legitimate to use Fisher's z transformation for correlation coefficients adjusted for a different range from that from which they were obtained. This is probably not strictly true, since Kelley has shown that the standard error of a correlation coefficient adjusted in this manner is somewhat larger than that of the unadjusted coefficient (57, p. 316). Application of Kelley's formula to the coefficients in Table 18, however, indicates that the ratio of the standard error for the adjusted coefficient to that for the unadjusted coefficient would be as follows: for both Old American r's, 1.0; for both ethnic r's, 1.1; for both Scandinavian r's, 1.3. The effect of this adjustment would be to increase the standard errors and therefore to decrease the critical ratios in the last column of Table 18. Only in the case of differences involving the Scandinavian pupils would the adjustment be substantial – and in these cases the critical ratios are already so small as to indicate insignificant differences.

NOTE 7. The critical ratios for the last three tests in Table 21, on page 157, are derived from distributions of percentile ranks. Since the standard deviation of percentile ranks is inflated relative to that of the original scores (constituting about a fourth of the total range instead of about a sixth), the standard errors computed from the percentile ranks are larger, relatively, than they would be if computed from the original data before percentiling. A difference between means obtained from the original scores would, therefore, be significant at a higher level of certainty than would a difference between the means of the equivalent percentiles. The justification for reporting the critical ratios used in Table 21 is that the subject of this analysis is the percentile ranks considered as scores in their own right, rather than merely as representing some underlying unit distributed differently from the percentiles.

NOTE 8. The Thurstone Spatial test consists of forty "exercises," most of which have two or three different responses to be marked correctly. Since these responses are scored independently and credit does not depend upon successful completion of all of them, each of the correct responses is treated as a separate right-wrong item in this analysis. Since the test is scored by means of a right-minus-wrong formula, it would have been entirely proper to consider the incorrect responses (as well as the correct ones) on each of the exercises as separate right-wrong items. To do so, however, would have necessitated considering a blank on the pupil's paper as the correct response. This, in turn, would have counted any pupil who really omitted the item as answering it correctly. It seemed wiser not to attempt to include these responses. The only Thurstone Spatial items analyzed are, therefore, those for which the correct response requires a positive mark; omitted items are thus counted as wrong responses, just as they are on items from the other tests.

NOTE 9. It is well known that the formula for the standard error of a percentage is not very satisfactory at the extreme ends of the percentage scale. Some authors simply recommend that the formula not be used when the percentage is above about 90 or below about 10, since the formula underestimates the true standard error in such cases. In the present instance there were a number of items answered correctly by more than 90 per cent of one, or sometimes both, status groups; it seemed important not simply to eliminate these items for lack of any estimate as to the sampling errors. In all cases where the percentage was above 90, the standard errors of the percentages were estimated by using 90 per cent in the regular standard error formula; in other words, the standard errors for percentages above 90 were figured as though the percentages were 90. A similar adjustment was made for the very few cases in which percentages were below 10.

Since the "true" standard error of a percentage decreases as the percentage moves farther away from 50, although not at so fast a rate beyond 90 per cent as indicated by the regular formula, this modification presumably overestimates the size of the standard error and thus results in a conservative judgment as to the statistical significance of any difference involving such a high percentage.

NOTE 10. The modification of the Davis Index for extreme percentages, referred to on pages 169-70, was as follows:

Per Cent	Davis Index	Modified Index
99.86%-100.00%	100	113
99.83 - 99.85	100	112
99.81 - 99.82	100	111
99.76 - 99.80	100	110
99.74 - 99.75	100	109
99.68 - 99.73	100	108
99.63 - 99.67	100	107
99.59 - 99.62	100	106
99.53 - 99.58	100	105
99.44 - 99.52	99-100	104
99.38 - 99.43	99	103
99.27 - 99.37	99	102
99.17 - 99.26	99	101
99.06 - 99.16	99	100
98.95 - 99.05	99	99

NOTE 11. Most of the tables and charts in chapters xvii to xxiii which report results of various phases of the item analysis are based on the responses of Old American pupils only, with the responses of ethnic pupils excluded. This was done in order to simplify the analysis; it seemed justified by the very small differences found between the responses of Old American and ethnic pupils, so long as status level was held constant for the two groups, as reported in chapter xvii.[1] A few of the tables, however, include data for the ethnic pupils. The particular groups of pupils on which each table is based are indicated in the listing below.

Most of these same tables and charts are based on items with so-called "stable" status differences – with all items showing unstable differences eliminated from the calculations. "Stable" status differences are defined as those based upon two indexes neither of which is higher than 80 or lower than 20. "Unstable" status differences are defined as those based upon at least one index higher than 80 or lower than 20. These particular dividing points were chosen for reasons explained in chapter xvi.[2]

Most of the tables and charts reporting item-analysis data in chapters xviii to xxi are based upon "stable" items only; a few, however, include data for all items, including those with relatively unstable item differences. The particular types of items on which each table is based are indicated in the listing on the next page.

1. See pp. 187-90.
2. See pp. 174-78.

Number of Table	Pupils Included		Items Included	
	Old Americans	Ethnics	All Items	Stable Items
28-29	X	X	X	. . .
30	X	. . .	X	. . .
31	X	X	X	. . .
32-33	X	. . .	X	X
34-36	X	. . .	X	. . .
37-40	X	. . .	. . .	X
41	. . .	. . .	. . .	X
43-49	X	. . .	. . .	X
50-51	X	. . .	X	. . .
52	X	. . .	. . .	X
55-56	X	. . .	. . .	X
58-146	X	. . .	. . .	. . .
147	X	X	. . .	. . .

Similar information for the charts reporting item-analysis data is given below:

Number of Figure	Pupils Included		Items Included	
	Old Americans	Ethnics	All Items	Stable Items
14-15	X	X	X	. . .
16-17	X	. . .	. . .	X
18-19	X	. . .	X	. . .

NOTE 12. The correlation referred to in the third footnote to Table 51, on page 232, is somewhat misleading, and is apparently in conflict with the data presented graphically in Figure 18, on page 234. In the graph there is little apparent difference between the slope of the two lines based on the younger pupils; yet one of these lines yields a correlation of .62, while the other yields one of only .28. It so happens that the scatter diagram underlying the .28 correlation has seven items with low-status indexes above 70 and with status differences averaging 12.1, and also six items with low-status indexes below 40 and with status differences averaging 12.0. A glance at Figure 18 indicates that these cases at the extreme ends of the difficulty scale are not in line with the general trend of the larger number of items in the middle ranges. They are not plotted in Figure 18 because there are fewer than five items at any one point. These few extreme items have, however, a comparatively marked effect on the correlation coefficient, resulting in the misleadingly low coefficient reported in Table 51.

BIBLIOGRAPHY

BIBLIOGRAPHY

Reports of Other Phases of the Chicago Study of Cultural Factors in Intelligence Tests

1. DAVIS, ALLISON. Social-Class Influences upon Learning. ("The Inglis Lecture," 1948.) Cambridge: Harvard University Press, 1948. Pp. 100.

2. DAVIS, W. ALLISON, and HAVIGHURST, ROBERT J. "The Measurement of Mental Systems (Can Intelligence Be Measured?)," Scientific Monthly, LXVI (1948), 301-16.
   Part of this article appears, in somewhat modified form, as chapters iv and v of the present volume; this material is reproduced by special permission of the American Association for the Advancement of Science.

3. EELLS, KENNETH WALTER. "Social-Status Factors in Intelligence-Test Items." Unpublished Ph.D. dissertation, Department of Education, University of Chicago, 1948. Pp. xxi + 686.

3a. HAGGARD, ERNEST A., and OTHERS. "Intelligence Tests: Some Effects of Practice, Motivation, and the Presentation of Test Items on the Performance of Upper-Class and Lower-Class Children," submitted to the Psychological Monographs in 1951 for publication.

4. MURRAY, WALTER. "The Intelligence-Test Performance of Negro Children of Different Social Classes." Unpublished Ph.D. dissertation, Department of Education, University of Chicago, 1947. Pp. v + 128.

4a. _____. "The I.Q. and Social Class in the Negro Caste," Southwestern Journal, IV (1949), 187-201.

4b. _____. "The Performance of Negro Children of Different Social-Class Status on Specific Intelligence-Test Items," ibid., V (1949-50), 48-57.

5. STONE, DAVID RAY. "Certain Verbal Factors in the Intelligence-Test Performance of High and Low Social Status Groups." Unpublished Ph.D. dissertation, Department of Education, University of Chicago, 1946. Pp. vi + 104.

Social-Class and Social-Status Characteristics and Their Measurement

6. DAVIS, ALLISON, and DOLLARD, JOHN. Children of Bondage: The Personality Development of Negro Youth in the Urban South. Prepared for the American Youth Commission. Washington: American Council on Education, 1940. Pp. xxviii + 299.

7. DAVIS, ALLISON; GARDNER, BURLEIGH B.; and GARDNER, MARY R. Deep South: A Social Anthropological Study of Caste and Class. Directed by W. Lloyd Warner. Chicago: University of Chicago Press, 1941. Pp. xx + 558.
   The quotation on page 252 of the present volume is reproduced by special permission of the University of Chicago Press.

8. DAVIS, W. ALLISON, and HAVIGHURST, ROBERT J. Father of the Man: How Your Child Gets His Personality. Boston: Houghton Mifflin Co., 1947. Pp. viii + 245.
   The quotations on pages 253 and 254 of the present volume are reproduced by special permission of the Houghton Mifflin Company.

9. DAVIS, ALLISON, and HAVIGHURST, ROBERT J. "Social Class and Color Differences in Child Rearing," American Sociological Review, XI (1946), 698-710.

10. HAVIGHURST, ROBERT J., and TABA, HILDA. Adolescent Character and Personality. New York: John Wiley & Sons, Inc., 1949. Pp. x + 315.

11. HOLLINGSHEAD, AUGUST B. Elmtown's Youth: The Impact of Social Classes on Adolescents. New York: John Wiley & Sons, Inc., 1949. Pp. xi + 480.

12. VOLBERDING, ELEANOR, "The Eleven-Year-Old." Unpublished Ph.D. dissertation, Department of Education, University of Chicago, 1945. Pp. iv + 112.

13. WARNER, W. LLOYD, and ASSOCIATES. Democracy in Jonesville: A Study in Quality and Inequality. New York: Harper & Bros., 1949. Pp. xviii + 313.

14. WARNER, W. LLOYD; HAVIGHURST, ROBERT J.; and LOEB, MARTIN B. Who Shall be Educated? – The Challenge of Unequal Opportunities. New York: Harper & Bros., 1944. Pp. xii + 190.

15. WARNER, W. LLOYD, and LOW, J. O. The Social System of the Modern Factory. ("Yankee City Series," Vol. IV.) New Haven: Yale University Press, 1947. Pp. xvi + 245.

16. WARNER, W. LLOYD, and LUNT, PAUL S. The Social Life of a Modern Community. ("Yankee City Series," Vol. I.) New Haven: Yale University Press, 1941. Pp. xx + 460.

17. _____. The Status System of a Modern Community. ("Yankee City Series," Vol. II.) New Haven: Yale University Press, 1942. Pp. xx + 246.

18. WARNER, W. LLOYD; MEEKER, MARCHIA; and EELLS, KENNETH. Social Class in America: A Manual of Procedure for the Measurement of Social Status. Chicago: Science Research Associates, Inc., 1949. Pp. xiii + 274.

19. WARNER, W. LLOYD, and SROLE, LEO. The Social Systems of American Ethnic Groups. ("Yankee City Series," Vol. III.) New Haven: Yale University Press, 1945. Pp. xii + 318.

20. WEST, JAMES. Plainville, U.S.A. New York: Columbia University Press, 1945. Pp. 238.

Summaries of Studies Dealing with the Relation of I.Q.'s and Cultural Status

21. BURKS, BARBARA STODDARD. "A Summary of Literature on the Determiners of the Intelligence Quotient and the Educational Quotient," chap. xvi of Nature and Nurture, Part II: Their Influence upon Achievement, pp. 248-350. Twenty-seventh Yearbook of the National Society for the Study of Education. Bloomington, Ill.: Public School Publishing Co., 1928.

22. JONES, HAROLD E. "Environmental Influences on Mental Development," chap. xi of Manual of Child Psychology, ed. LEONARD CARMICHAEL, pp. 582-632. New York: John Wiley & Sons, Inc., 1946.

23. LOEVINGER, JANE. "Intelligence as Related to Socio-economic Factors," chap. v of Intelligence: Its Nature and Nurture, Part I: Comparative and Critical Exposition, pp. 159-210. Thirty-ninth Yearbook of the National Society for the Study of Education. Bloomington, Ill.: Public School Publishing Co., 1940.

    The quotations on pages 13 and 77 of the present volume are reproduced by special permission of the National Society for the Study of Education.

24. LORIMER, FRANK, and OSBORN, FREDERICK. "Variations in Cultural Intellectual Development among Groups Classified by Occupation or Social Status," chap. viii of Dynamics of Population, pp. 157-76. New York: Macmillan Co., 1934.

25. MURPHY, GARDNER; MURPHY, LOIS BARCLAY; and NEWCOMB, THEODORE M. "Nature and Nurture in Relation to Social Differences," chap. ii of Experimental Social Psychology, pp. 27-75. New York: Harper & Bros., 1937.

26. NATIONAL SOCIETY FOR THE STUDY OF EDUCATION. Intelligence: Its Nature and Nurture, Part I: Comparative and Critical Exposition. Pp. xviii + 471. Part II: Original Studies and Experiments. Pp. xviii + 409. Thirty-ninth Yearbook of the National Society for the Study of Education. Bloomington, Ill.: Public School Publishing Co., 1940.

27. _____. Nature and Nurture, Part I: Their Influence Upon Intelligence. Pp. ix + 465. Part II: Their Influence upon Achievement. Pp. xv + 397. Twenty-seventh Yearbook of the National Society for the Study of Education. Bloomington, Ill.: Public School Publishing Co., 1928.

28. NEFF, WALTER S. "Socio-economic Status and Intelligence: A Critical Survey," Psychological Bulletin, XXXV (1938), 727-57.

29. REVIEW OF EDUCATIONAL RESEARCH. "Growth and Development," Review of Educational Research, Vols. XI (December, 1941), XIV (December, 1944), and XVII (December, 1947).

30. _____. "Mental and Physical Development," Review of Educational Research, Vols. III (April, 1933), VI (February, 1936), and IX (February, 1939).

31. SCHIEFFELIN, BARBARA, and SCHWESINGER, GLADYS C. "Heredity and Environment," Part II of Mental Tests and Heredity, pp. 19-58. New York: Galton Publishing Co., 1930.

32. SCHWESINGER, GLADYS C. "Studies on Environmental Influences as They Affect the Development of Intelligence," chap. iv of Heredity and Environment: Studies in the Genesis of Psychological Characteristics, pp. 165-351. New York: Macmillan Co., 1933.

33. SOROKIN, PITIRIM A.; ZIMMERMAN, CARLE C.; and GALPIN, CHARLES J. "Rural-Urban Intelligence, Mental Health, Psychological Processes, and Predominant Attitudes," chap. xx of A Systematic Source Book in Rural Sociology, III, 226-351. Minneapolis: University of Minnesota Press, 1932.

34. STODDARD, GEORGE D., and WELLMAN, BETH L. "Environment and the I.Q.," chap. xiv of Intelligence: Its Nature and Nurture, Part I: Comparative and Critical Exposition, pp. 405-42. Thirty-ninth Yearbook of the National Society for the Study of Education. Bloomington, Ill.: Public School Publishing Co., 1940.

Original Research Studies Dealing with the Relationship of I.Q.'s and Cultural Status[1]

(In addition to those listed in the first section of this bibliography)

35. BINET, ALFRED, and SIMON, TH. The Development of Intelligence in Children. Translated by ELIZABETH S. KITE. Baltimore: Williams & Wilkins Co., 1916. Pp. 336.

    Consists of translations of five articles published in L'Année psychologique, 1905-11. The quotations on pages 29-32 of the present volume are reproduced by special permission of Henry Goddard.

36. BRIDGES, JAMES W., and COLER, LILLIAN E. "The Relation of Intelligence to Social Status," Psychological Review, XXIV (1917), 1-31.

37. BURKS, BARBARA STODDARD. "The Relative Influence of Nature and Nurture upon Mental Development: A Comparative Study of Foster Parent – Foster Child Resemblance and True Parent – True Child Resemblance," chap. x of Nature and Nurture, Part I: Their Influence upon Intelligence, pp. 219-316. Twenty-seventh Yearbook of the National Society for the Study of Education. Bloomington, Ill.: Public School Publishing Co., 1928.

38. BURT, CYRIL. "Influence of Sex and Social Status," Mental and Scholastic Tests, pp. 190-99. London: P. S. King & Sons, 1922.

39. CUFF, NOEL B. "Relationship of Socio-economic Status to Intelligence and Achievement," Peabody Journal of Education, XI (1933), 106-10.

1. This includes only those studies actually cited in chap. ii of the present volume. For a relatively complete listing of all such studies in the period from 1912 to 1947 see the 123 titles listed in the Bibliography of the study by Eells (3, pp. 672-83).

40. _____. "The Vectors of Socio-economic Status," ibid., XII (1934), 114-17.

41. HAVIGHURST, ROBERT J., and BREESE, FAY H. "Relation between Ability and Social Status in a Midwestern Community. III. Primary Mental Abilities," Journal of Educational Psychology, XXXVIII (1947), 241-47.

42. HAVIGHURST, ROBERT J., and JANKE, LEOTA LONG. "Relations between Ability and Social Status in a Midwestern Community. I. Ten-Year-Old Children," Journal of Educational Psychology, XXXV (1944), 357-68.

43. JANKE, LEOTA LONG, and HAVIGHURST, ROBERT J. "Relations between Ability and Social Status in a Midwestern Community. II. Sixteen-Year-Old Boys and Girls," Journal of Educational Psychology, XXXVI (1945), 499-509.

44. LONG, HOWARD HALE. "Test Results of Third-Grade Negro Children Selected on the Basis of Socio-economic Status," Journal of Negro Education, IV (1935), 192-212, 523-52.

45. OSBORN, RICHARDS C. "How Is Intellectual Performance Related to Social and Economic Background," Journal of Educational Psychology, XXXIV (1943), 215-28.

46. SALTZMAN, SARA. "The Influence of Social and Economic Background on Stanford-Binet Performance," Journal of Social Psychology, XII (1940), 71-81.

47. STERN, WILLIAM. "Children of Different Social Strata," The Psychological Methods of Testing Intelligence, pp. 50-57. Translated by GUY MONTROSE WHIPPLE. Baltimore: Warwick & York, Inc., 1914.
   The quotations on pages 5-6 of the present volume are reproduced by special permission of Warwick & York, Inc.

48. STOKE, STUART M. Occupational Groups and Child Development. ("Harvard Monographs in Education," No. 8.) Cambridge: Harvard University Press, 1927. Pp. 92.

49. TERMAN, LEWIS M., and OTHERS. The Stanford Revision and Extension of the Binet-Simon Scale for Measuring Intelligence. Baltimore: Warwick & York, Inc., 1917. Pp. 179.
   A fuller account of data reported earlier in No. 50. The quotation on page 77 of the present volume is reproduced by special permission of Warwick & York, Inc.

50. _____. "The Stanford Revision of the Binet-Simon Scale and Some Results from Its Application to 1,000 Non-selected Children." Journal of Educational Psychology, VI (1915), 551-62.
   The same data are reported somewhat more fully in No. 49.

51. WEINTROB, JOSEPH and RALEIGH. "The Influence of Environment on Mental Ability as Shown by Binet-Simon Tests," Journal of Educational Psychology, III (1912), 577-83.

52. YERKES, ROBERT M., and ANDERSON, HELEN M. "The Importance of Social Status as Indicated by the Results of the Point-Scale Method of Measuring Mental Capacity," Journal of Educational Psychology, VI (1915), 137-50.
   Substantially the same material appears in No. 53.

53. YERKES, ROBERT M.; BRIDGES, JAMES W.; and HARDWICK, ROSE S. "The Significance of Sociological and Racial Status," chap. vi of A Point Scale for Measuring Mental Ability, pp. 75-88. Baltimore: Warwick & York, Inc., 1915.
   Substantially the same material appears in No. 52.

References on Statistical Methods

54. CROXTON, FREDERICK E., and COWDEN, DUDLEY J. Applied General Statistics. New York: Prentice-Hall, Inc., 1939. Pp. xviii + 944 + xiii.

55. DAVIS, FREDERICK B. Item-Analysis Data: Their Computation, Interpretation, and Use in Test Construction. ("Harvard Education Papers," No. 2.) Cambridge: Graduate School of Education, Harvard University, 1946. Pp. v + 42.
   The quotation on page 167 of the present volume is reproduced by special permission of the Graduate School of Education, Harvard University.

56. HOLZINGER, KARL J. Statistical Methods for Students in Education. Boston: Ginn & Co., 1928. Pp. viii + 372.

57. KELLEY, TRUMAN L. Statistical Method. New York: Macmillan Co., 1923. Pp. xi + 390.

58. PETERS, CHARLES C., and VAN VOORHIS, WALTER R. Statistical Procedures and Their Mathematical Bases. New York: McGraw-Hill Book Co., 1940. Pp. xiii + 516.

Other Sources Cited

59. BRUCE, MYRTLE. Factors Affecting Intelligence Test Performance of Whites and Negroes in the Rural South. ("Archives of Psychology," No. 252.) New York: Columbia University, 1940. Pp. 99.

60. CATTELL, RAYMOND B.; FEINGOLD, S. NORMAN; and SARASON, SEYMOUR B. "A Culture-Free Intelligence Test: II. Evaluation of Cultural Influence on Test Performance," Journal of Educational Psychology, XXXII (1941), 81-100.

61. CHAPMAN, J. CROSBY, and SIMS, V. M. "The Quantitative Measurement of Certain Aspects of Socio-economic Status," Journal of Educational Psychology, XVI (1925), 380-90.

62. DAVIS, ALLISON. "The Public Schools and Ethnic and Color Groups." Unpublished report to the General Education Board, 1944.

63. EDWARDS, ALBA M. Alphabetical Index of Occupations, by Industries and Social-economic Groups, 1937. Prepared for the Bureau of the Census. Washington: Government Printing Office, 1937. Pp. 542.

64. GOODENOUGH, FLORENCE L. "The Measurement of Mental Growth in Children," chap. ix of Manual of Child Psychology, ed. LEONARD

CARMICHAEL, pp. 450-75. New York: John Wiley & Sons, Inc., 1946.
   The quotation on page 24 of the present volume is reproduced by special permission of Leonard Carmichael and John Wiley & Sons, Inc.

65. GREENE, EDWARD B. Measurements of Human Behavior. New York: Odyssey Press, 1941. Pp. xxi + 777.
   The quotation on page 36 of the present volume is reproduced by special permission of the Odyssey Press.

66. HENMON, V. A. C., and NELSON, M. J. The Henmon-Nelson Tests of Mental Ability: Elementary School Examination for Grades 3 to 8, Forms A, B, and C: Teacher's Manual (Revised). Boston: Houghton Mifflin Co., 1944. Pp. 4.
   The quotation on page 34 of the present volume is reproduced by special permission of the Houghton Mifflin Company.

67. KLINEBERG, OTTO. Characteristics of the American Negro. New York: Harper & Bros., 1944. Pp. xii + 409.

68. KUHLMANN, F. Tests of Mental Development: A Complete Scale for Individual Examination. Minneapolis: Educational Test Bureau, 1939. Pp. xi + 314.
   The quotation on page 37 of the present volume is reproduced by special permission of the Educational Test Bureau.

69. KUHLMANN, F., and ANDERSON, ROSE G. Kuhlmann-Anderson Intelligence Tests: For Ages Six to Maturity: Instruction Manual (Fifth Edition). Minneapolis: Educational Test Bureau, 1942. Pp. viii + 131.

70. OTIS, ARTHUR S. Otis Quick-scoring Mental Ability Tests: Manual of Directions for Alpha Test. Yonkers-on-Hudson, N.Y.: World Book Co., 1939. Pp. 22.
   The quotations on pages 33-34 of the present volume are reproduced by special permission of the World Book Company.

71. SULLIVAN, ELIZABETH T.; CLARK, WILLIS W.; and TIEGS, ERNEST W. Manual of Directions, California Short-Form Test of Mental Maturity, Intermediate S-Form. Los Angeles: California Test Bureau, n.d. Pp. 8.

72. TERMAN, LEWIS M., and McNEMAR, QUINN. Terman-McNemar Test of Mental Ability: Manual of Directions. Yonkers-on-Hudson, N.Y.: World Book Co., 1942. Pp. 12.
   The quotations on pages 34-36 of the present volume are reproduced by special permission of the World Book Company.

73. TERMAN, LEWIS M., and MERRILL, MAUD A. Measuring Intelligence. Boston: Houghton Mifflin Co., 1937. Pp. xiv + 461.
   The quotation on page 33 of the present volume is reproduced by special permission of the Houghton Mifflin Company.

74. THURSTONE, L. L. Multiple-Factor Analysis. Chicago: University of Chicago Press, 1947. Pp. xix + 535.
   The quotation on page 24 of the present volume is reproduced by special permission of the University of Chicago Press.

75. TYLER, RALPH W. "Educability and the Schools," Elementary School Journal, XLIX (1948), 200-212.

   A substantial part of this article appears as chap. vi of the present volume; this material is reproduced by special permission of the University of Chicago Press.

INDEX